Economic Sociology

Economic Sociology

State, Market, and Society in Modern Capitalism

Carlo Trigilia

Blackwell Publishers

Editorial Offices:
108 Cowley Road, Oxford OX4 1JF, UK
  Tel: +44 (0)1865 791100
350 Main Street, Malden, Massachusetts 02148-5018, USA
  Tel: +1 781 388 8250

First published in Italian under the name *Sociologia Economica* by Il Mulino, 1998
This edition published 2002 by Blackwell Publishers Ltd, a Blackwell Publishing company
Translated by Nicola Owtram, 2002

Library of Congress Cataloging-in-Publication Data

Trigilia, C. (Carlo)
    [Sociologia economica. English]
    Economic sociology : state, market, and society in modern capitalism /
Carlo Trigilia ; [translated by Nicola Owtram].
        p. cm.
Translation of: Sociologia economica.
Includes bibliographical references and index.
    ISBN 0–631–22535–8 (hbk. : alk. paper) – ISBN 0–631–22536–6 (pbk. :
alk. paper)
    1. Economics–Sociological aspects.   I. Title.
    HM548 .T7513 2002
    306.3—dc21   2001005820

A catalogue record for this book is available from the British Library.

Typeset in 10 on 12 pt Meridien
by Ace Filmsetting Ltd, Frome, Somerset
Printed in Great Britain by TJ International, Padstow, Cornwall

For further information on
Blackwell Publishers, visit our website:
www.blackwellpublishers.co.uk

Contents

Preface

A study of the history of opinion is a necessary preliminary to the emancipation of the mind. I do not know which makes a man more conservative – to know nothing but the past, or nothing but the present.
John Maynard Keynes, *The End of Laissez-Faire*

The aim of this book is to reconstruct the origins and developments of the research tradition which underpins economic sociology. This is not an easy task. Over recent decades, interest in this discipline has increased, as profound and rapid transformations have affected both developed and less developed countries. The body of specialized literature has grown and new textbooks and readers have been published. What has been lacking, however, is a systematic and comprehensive reconstruction of the sociological approach to the study of the economy. Therefore, I have sought to pursue two main aims in writing this book. First, I have tried to identify and describe the elements of continuity between past and present, between the writings of the classic authors and contemporary developments in the discipline. Second, I have sought to present the methodology and research themes of economic sociology in a manner that is accessible both for students and for specialists from other disciplines who are interested in the contribution that this approach can make.

A historical presentation may help contribute to the institutionalization of economic sociology. In the field of social sciences, an analytical perspective can be strengthened if a shared and recognized body of knowledge can be transmitted and continuously updated, adapting it to the research problems which emerge as society changes. However, in order to communicate the essential elements of a particular approach more effectively to students, or other interested readers, it is important to show that a longstanding and coherent research tradition exists, in both methodological and substantive terms. This is why a historical introduction to the development of economic sociology may be particularly appropriate.

Moreover, there is a second important reason for this mode of presentation. The physical and natural sciences develop through a cumulative process: as research advances, new general theories emerge, replacing those that precede them. In these fields the distinction between the history of a discipline and contemporary theories is clear-cut. For these sciences Alfred Whitehead's warning, mentioned by Robert Merton, is pertinent: "A science which hesitates to forget its founders is lost." This is not, however, the case for social sciences. Indeed, to some extent the opposite is true, despite repeated positivistic attempts to treat the social sciences as analogous to the physical and natural sciences. In other words, the social sciences cannot aspire to producing general theories; instead, they can develop historically oriented models, with definite boundaries in time and space, largely based on comparative methods. Society is in a process of continual change as a consequence of interaction between human beings. Thus, relations between economy and society, which are the focus of this work, are subject too to perpetual change. This means that the tools needed to understand society must take account of its diversity in time and space. The distinction between history of thought and theory is therefore less clear-cut than in the physical and natural sciences, and the historical presentation of a social science can be useful both for teaching and for communication with scholars from other related fields.

In other words, reference to the classic authors – the "founding fathers" – may be useful for methodological reasons, because one may identify a continuity and coherence in the study of relations between economy and society, which is important in students' training. However, it is also appropriate for substantive reasons, because it shows the contributions that economic sociology has made to the understanding of the origins and nature of particular forms of economic organization. These include the origins of capitalism in the West; the characteristics of liberal capitalism; and those of the more highly regulated and organized capitalism which has come into being since the thirties.

In this perspective the rhetorical question posed by George Homans some time ago – "Who cares of what old Durkheim said?" would not seem to be justified. Certainly, Durkheim, like Weber or Polanyi, has less to tell us if we wish to analyze contemporary society; however, the contribution of these authors is still crucial to understanding the problems of the societies on which they worked. If one wishes, for example, to understand the origins of modern capitalism in the West – one of the classic themes of economic sociology – one cannot neglect reading Weber's works. Certainly, successive historical and sociological analyses have added new elements and have contributed to redefining his interpretation. It cannot, however, be said that it has been "superseded" in the sense that theories in physics or biology are superseded when new knowledge is discovered.

Naturally, this does not mean that an introduction to economic sociology should examine Weber's work and other classics of the discipline from a merely historical perspective. It is not a question of reconstructing the social and intellectual context in which their ideas matured or of following their development over time. The aim is rather to highlight how the classics contributed to developing a theory of economic action as socially oriented action, and how they used this theory to throw light on some of the crucial problems which emerged over the last two centuries in the relations between the economy and society. In this way they contributed to developing a set of hypotheses on the functioning of the market, on economic development, and on consumer behavior, all of which can be found in the tools used by contemporary economic sociology to analyze how culture and social and political institutions influence economic activities.

It follows that the understanding of economic sociology on which this book is based establishes very close links between sociology and historical analysis. It does not share the presupposition that society can be studied like a system, like a 'machine' with its own laws, which impose themselves on the will of human beings. Experience shows that all attempts to study society in the same way as nature have given rise to results which are both disappointing in terms of knowledge and politically problematic. This is because all attempts to find laws which are universal and necessary for society not only have not worked, but have usually been accompanied by the attempt to impose a certain political solution to the problem of social organization. As I shall show below, economic sociology was born with Weber, who took a position that is exactly the contrary of this totalizing conception of the social sciences. It is a view which takes actors and their motivations – that is, the people that live in society, and orientations which change in space and time and which influence the social order – seriously. A more modest view assigns to the social sciences not the task of singling out "what must be done" but of clarifying the problems and choices, and therefore of contributing to the reflexive construction of society.

The book is divided into two parts. In the first, the problem of the origins of economic sociology is initially tackled. Economics and economic sociology – the study of markets and institutions respectively – were closely connected in the work of the classical economists, and especially in the work of Adam Smith. This viewpoint took the problem of economic development as its focus. It was as a result of the growing success of neoclassical economics, at the end of the nineteenth century, that economics withdrew from investigation of institutions and development. This empty space was occupied, at the end of the century, by economic sociology. It was in Germany above all, with Sombart and Weber, that the foundations of this new discipline were laid. And it was Weber who outlined this new scientific program with vision and clarity. The methodological and substantial contribution of the classics is then presented. Naturally the choice of authors may always be questioned. All the same, the classics focused on the problems of origins and transformations of modern capitalism. In other words, economic sociology developed as a sociology of capitalism: from its liberal forms, where the market plays a an important role in economy and society to the "great transformation" which followed the crisis of the 1930s and led to the more socially and politically regulated forms which came into being after the Second World War.

The era of the classics can be said to come to a close with Polanyi's and Schumpeter's famous works on the transformations of capitalism, which were published in the 1940s. The second and wider part of the volume is dedicated to the subsequent phase, which takes us up to the very recent past. In the years following the Second World War, Keynesian economics prevailed and economic analysis regained its capacity to grasp economic reality and to influence economic policies. The problem of development in the more advanced and industrialized countries was now examined mainly by Keynesian economics. At the macro level, the original tradition of economic sociology continued to perpetuate itself, mainly in the sociology of the development of less developed areas and countries, with the theory of modernization and other approaches up to current comparative political economy. At the same time, at the micro level, the original tradition disintegrated, giving rise to an increasing disciplinary specialization with the sociology of organizations, of labor studies and of industrial relations. These branches became better established and were institutionalized, but at the same time moved away from the direct investigation of the relations with the economic organization and development.

On the whole, it can be said that there was a decline in the specific tradition of economic sociology – particularly in the study of more advanced countries – which lasted until the 1970s. It was at this point that there was a visible upsurge of interest in the field, made tangible in the increasing body of studies and research that are outlined in the final chapters of the book. This trend first became apparent at the macro level. The crisis of Keynesian welfare state, the spread of inflation, as well as stagnation and unemployment, all showed the shortcomings of the Keynesian model, and triggered new research on the role of social and political institutions in the economy. In addition, the difficulties of the Fordist–Taylorist forms of productive organization – the micro-level underpinnings of the golden age of post-war development – also spurred the search for new perspectives. The emergence of flexible production models drew attention to how institutional context influenced economic forms of organization and the capacity of these latter to adjust rapidly to increasingly unstable markets. These new research perspectives at the micro and macro levels led to studies of the institutional variety of contemporary capitalism and their relations with the phenomenon of globalization.

The two parts into which the book is divided are strictly related. However, in order to facilitate the use of the book by students, each part is organized and presented so that it may be read as a single unit, according to specific needs. Each section considers the relationship between economics and sociology. Indeed, from its origins to its most recent phase, the dialogue with economics has been crucial for economic sociology. In recent years this exchange has been even more frequent and, as is shown in the final chapters, has been shaped by a sort of "double movement." On the one hand, economists have increasingly come to recognize the importance of institutions, at both micro and macro levels. On the other hand, there has been a reaction by sociologists to the "imperialism" of economics, which has led not only to the development of non-economic explanations of institutions, but has also underlined – more clearly than in the past – the impact of social and political institutions on the organization and evolution of the economy. It is unlikely that these tendencies can lead to an integrated study of the economy, and perhaps this is not even desirable. It is instead to be hoped that the dialogue will continue and become more highly focused, and that the scholars of the two traditions will come to know each other better and take closer account of each others' work. Concrete reality is, of course, not divisible and it combines both economic and social factors. Therefore, when one moves from analytical models to empirical–historical studies it is necessary for both economists and sociologists to take into account the complexity of social phenomena, as the most careful scholars in both traditions have always done.

Acknowledgments

I could not have written this book without benefiting from the lively tradition of economic sociology that developed in Italy over the last three decades. This analytical perspective has found a fertile ground, and has brought together sociologists, political scientists and economists who did not hesitate to trespass across the traditional boundaries between disciplines. Research has burgeoned on issues such as flexible specialization and industrial districts, development of backward regions, neo-corporatism and concertation, the rise and decline of the Keynesian welfare state, and the economic and social consequences of the European Union. Therefore, to a certain extent, this book reflects a collective endeavor, although I take sole responsibility for it. I am grateful to the colleagues and friends with whom I have been able to work in *Stato e Mercato*. This journal, founded twenty years ago, has greatly contributed to research and debate on the new economic sociology. A number of colleagues made helpful comments on earlier versions of the work: Arnaldo Bagnasco, Marco Bellandi, Lorenzo Bordogna, Colin Crouch, Paolo Giovannini, Massimo Paci, Gianfranco Poggi, Francesco Ramella, Marino Regini, and Sidney Tarrow. I am also grateful to Massimo Baldini, Angela Perulli, Geny Piotti, and Silvia Nencioni for research assistance. I owe a special thanks to Colin Crouch, Henry Farrell, and Jonathan Zeitlin for their help in revising the English translation, and to Nicola Owtram who translated the book from Italian. My students in Palermo, Trento, Florence and Harvard helped me, with their questions and remarks, to clarify the many themes of the book.

Introduction: What is Economic Sociology?

In everyday life, one often hears opinions of various sorts about economic activity. For example, the claims that German industry is so successful because it has such high levels of technical competence and professional training; that Japan's economic development has benefited from its strong tradition of social values and structures, which have favored cooperation; or that the Italian economy is hampered by the inefficiency of public services. These opinions can also be more general. For example, the claims that the working classes are less important now than they used to be because of new technologies; that underdevelopment has led to large and sprawling cities where most of the population lives in dreadful conditions; that the economic prosperity of Western countries weakens the class conflict as well as the unions and left-wing parties.

These opinions may or may not be based on facts. They are of interest, though, in that they show very clearly how common sense suggests that economic and social phenomena are related. Some of these examples emphasize how the cultural and social characteristics of a country influence its economy. Others call attention to more general tendencies and to the reverse causal relationship: how economic phenomena can influence social and political life. Both kinds of example, however, may bring us closer to economic sociology's domain of research.

As a first approximation, we may say that economic sociology involves *a body of study and research aimed at establishing the links between economic and social phenomena.* The objective is to deal with questions such as those above through the scientific method – which is to say by applying greater rigor and control than one does in everyday language, and with the aim of identifying regularities in the relationships between the phenomena under examination. It should be pointed out, though, that this is a different sort of science than that found in the physical and natural sciences; it does not aim to formulate universal laws, as in the case of natural phenomena, nor can it provide sure remedies to resolve problems. The social sciences can only hope to increase the shared knowledge of the members of a society about the questions of collective life – namely, to help clarify collective choices.

We will return to this question later, but first we must more precisely define economic sociology's field of research.

1   Two Definitions of Economy

Economic phenomena can be defined in various ways. Clearly, these reflect different theoretical orientations, which will be described in greater detail in the following chapters. One may start with two fairly representative approaches, which have important implications for how one may look at the relationship between economy and society. They have been suggested by Karl Polanyi (1977, ch. 2), a social scientist whose work cannot be confined within traditional disciplinary boundaries.

In the first, the economy is presented as *a body of activities which are usually carried out by members of a society in order to produce, distribute, and exchange goods and services.* The economy here is conceived as an institutionalized process – it is guided by relatively stable rules – of interaction between men and nature in the satisfaction of a society's needs. These needs are not exclusively physical; they may also be cultural, scientific or military. However, to the extent that the production and distribution of goods and services is needed to satisfy them, the economy is involved.

Although it is apparently straightforward and easy to understand, this definition is not widely accepted. That is to say, not all economists subscribe to it and a second definition is more typically found in economics textbooks. In this formulation, the emphasis is on "economizing" as a synonym for economic phenomena, which is to say, on *activities which involve the rational allocation of scarce resources in order to obtain the most from the means available.* On this view, individuals carrying out economic activities are motivated by the rational pursuit of their interests, while the rules conditioning the interaction between them are set by the market as a result of the effect of demand and supply on prices. The ways in which goods and services are produced can therefore be explained through the "maximizing" choices of individuals in a market context. Thus, for example, one may suppose that individuals will be willing to buy more of a good if the price is low, because of the relationship between demand and supply, and vice versa if the price is high. For their part, if the price is high, the producers of the good will tend to supply more of it, and vice versa. So it becomes clear that the amount and price of goods produced will depend on the trade-off between the demand of both consumers and producers on the market. The same mechanism is true for the distribution of income among various economic actors. For example, payment for labor will depend on the relationship between demand and supply. If the supply of labor grows with respect to demand, wages will tend to decrease as a consequence.

The first definition of economy mentioned above is more general. It allows us to see how the satisfaction of needs and economic behavior can be handled in different ways, depending on how society is organized. For example, in primitive societies economic activities are not distinct, but take place in the context of family and kinship relations which regulate how goods are produced, distributed, and exchanged. In the great empires of antiquity, for example, the state played a very important role in the regulation of economic activity, while in capitalist societies –

based on the private ownership of the means of production – the economy has freed itself from these social and political controls. Thus the satisfaction of needs depends more on the functioning of "self-regulating" markets, where resource allocation and price setting are conditioned by relations of demand and supply. For example, neither traditional rules nor the political order determine reward for individual labor (as happened in the feudal system); this instead depends on the relationship between the demand and supply of labor on the market.

It is in this latter context that the definition which is more widely shared by economists finds its historical roots. Indeed, it comes as no surprise that economics as an autonomous scientific discipline has emerged as capitalist society has established itself, as we shall see later. This is because the assumptions about the maximizing behavior of individuals and its effects on demand and supply in the market reflect the increasing independence of the economy from social and political structures. Thus, in contexts in which self-regulating markets prevail, the satisfaction of needs and individual life chances are conditioned by the employment of available resources on the market.

These two definitions of economic phenomena should not be considered as mutually exclusive. Rather, they represent two theoretical perspectives on the economy that provide particular advantages and constraints which one should be aware of. For example, the definition used more widely by economists has given us a far better understanding of the self-regulating mechanisms of the market, i.e. of the influence of the movements of demand and supply on price setting and resource allocation. By using a few and simple assumptions about the utilitarian roots of behavior, and taking institutions as a given, economics has been able to develop theoretical models to a high level of generalization, with the application of mathematical tools. This has also provided instruments for formulating economic predictions and normative principles, that is, criteria to guide the choices of economic actors. On the more specifically theoretical plane, however, difficulties emerge when one needs to understand contexts in which the self-regulating market has a limited role, or simply does not exist. Take, for example, the precapitalist contexts mentioned above, or even capitalist societies when the different paths and growth rates of their economies are examined. The problems become even clearer when one asks, for example, why some countries industrialized before others, or why some economies coped better with the economic problems of the 1970s. In all these cases the institutional context must be considered to provide a convincing interpretation.

It is in precisely this set of issues that the advantages of the first definition emerge; it is more open to the study of the interaction between economy and society. It is also, for this reason, better suited to the perspective on the economy offered by economic sociology, as well as by anthropology and economic history; a perspective that seeks to understand the particular features of a certain period or territory. One must always be cautious in making generalizations, given the differences of approach between the various social sciences and even within them. This said, all these disciplines share a feature that differentiates them from economics in that they hold that *economic activity is an institutional process*. They do not start from the isolated individual with utilitarian motivations to reconstruct the aggregate effects of individual behaviors on the level of production and distribution of goods and services. They focus instead on the institutions which regulate economic activity.

One can define *institutions* as *a set of social norms which orient and regulate behavior and which are based on sanctions which seek to guarantee compliance on the part of individuals*. These sanctions can be either positive, in the sense that they encourage a certain kind of behavior through approval or material incentives, or they can be negative, tending to prevent a certain type of action. And again, they can be informal when they are based on the disapproval of others, or they can be formal, as when they are established by the law (in this case one can speak more specifically about legal rules). For example, in economic behavior, there may be ethical standards in business which are based only on social approval in a certain environment, or else there may be norms which are based on formal sanctions (those of civil and labor law) which regulate the market exchange of goods and capital, or of labor. Other kinds of norms – no less important – define the aims of the actors rather than the ways in which they are pursued, as illustrated in the previous examples. In other words, they can involve the way in which labor is conceived or, more generally, the commitment to economic activities as opposed to those in other areas of activity, e.g. military activity (in traditional societies) or leisure and consumption (in contemporary societies).

These distinctions will be discussed in greater detail further on; at this point it is simply useful to note that the concept of institution refers – in sociological language – to a set of phenomena which is usually wider than everyday usage would suggest. In common language, when one talks about institutions, one is usually referring to public institutions (parliament or government) or judicial or military institutions. The term institution may also sometimes be used to indicate the concrete collectivities that institutions regulate; for example firms, unions or business organizations. However, the sociological meaning of institution is wider because it includes the system of rules on which these collectivities are based and which make possible their functioning – for example, the norms which regulate the right to property and labor relations. It is therefore useful to keep the concept of institution distinct from that of *organization*, using the latter term to indicate the concrete collectivities which co-ordinate a set of human and material resources to achieve a certain end (examples of economic organizations are firms, unions, chambers of commerce, etc). While organizations may be actors, institutions cannot.

By examining institutions, one may create a bridge between economy and society. Economic phenomena are situated in a historical context – in a specific period of time and in a particular territory. Thus, one can evaluate how economic behavior and structures – that is, the set of stable relationships between a specified set of actors – are affected by the institutional context, and how they affect it in turn. This does not mean that individual choice does not count, but that it does not take place in a void, that it is socially oriented and may take place within wider or narrower margins depending on the type of society. Therefore, economic sociology does not study the economy in general, but instead analyses specific economic systems, for example, capitalist economies, feudal economies, the economies of primitive societies, and so on, together with the specific characteristics that these take on in particular cases. The concept of *economic system* is crucially important in this perspective; it tends to underline *the different ways, over space and time, in which institutions orient and regulate economic activities*.

2 Economic Sociology: Schumpeter and Weber

The difference of perspective between economics and the other social sciences – in particular economic sociology – also emerges in a famous definition by Joseph Schumpeter, an economist who was very sensitive to relations between economics and social analysis. Schumpeter (1954) attributed to economic sociology the task of explaining how people "came to behave as they do" (1954, p. 21) and he specified that actions must be related to the institutions which affect economic behavior, such as the state or private property and contracts. For its part, economics deals with the questions "how people behave at any time and what the economic effects are" (1954, p. 21).

This distinction is useful in clarifying the research perspectives of the two disciplines in the sense that has already been discussed. However, it requires further specification and qualification. First, it should not be used too rigidly. A sociologist or an economic historian who wishes to evaluate how a particular country has developed will tend to consider both economic variables – such as the availability of capital and labor – and non-economic variables – such as political and sociocultural structures – together. Moreover, it is clear that an economist who seeks to bring his analysis closer to empirical reality will have to consider the role of institutions – whether explicitly or implicitly – to improve his hypotheses. For example, it is difficult to study the labor market in contemporary capitalist societies without taking the role of unions into account. Schumpeter would of course have agreed, and his research, which was always open to institutional questions, confirms this. He felt that the theoretical economists should master economic sociology, just as they should master history and statistics.

Schumpeter's definition must however be integrated, in line with his historical and evolutionary conception of the economic process. In actuality, the economic sociologist should not simply limit his enquiry to the influence of the institutional context on the economy, as the previous definition might seem to suggest. As we have already noted, he/she would examine causal relations running in the opposite direction, taking an interest in the social, political, and cultural consequences of economic development. In studying capitalist societies, he/she would attempt to evaluate, for example, the extent to which economic structures increased social and political conflict, or led to changes in family structures or relations between town and country. In this way it becomes possible to formulate hypotheses for the interpretation of institutional change, in particular change in the organization of economic activities – one of the most difficult tasks for traditional economics with its ahistorical tools. To return to the above example, one could evaluate how capitalist economic structures have given rise to social and political conflicts which have in turn led to greater state intervention in the economy and the role of the unions and industrial relations in general. As a consequence, the previous institutional framework regulating economic activity was modified (sometimes a transformation of this kind is referred to as a transformation from liberal to organized capitalism). The bidirectionality of research – from society to economy and vice versa – should not be presented simply as an extension of the field of analysis, but as having its own intrinsic motivation: it allows one to focus on change in economic structure.

Max Weber, who made a crucial contribution to the scientific agenda of economic sociology, highlights the bi-directionality of sociological research on the economy very clearly. For him, a "social–economic science" was in substance a science of the relations of interdependence between economic and social phenomena. While economics above all involves the "technical–economic problems of prices formation and markets in the modern exchange economy," the main aim of economic sociology is to shed light on "economically relevant" and "economically conditioned" phenomena (Weber [1904] 1949, pp. 64–6). The former concern the influence of non-economic institutions, such as religious or political institutions, on the functioning of the economy; the latter illustrate how not only political orientations, but also aspects of social life which might seem very far removed from economic issues, such as aesthetic or religious phenomena, are in fact influenced by economic factors. In setting out his scientific agenda Weber explicitly contrasted his views with those of Marx. In his polemics against the more naïve and mechanistic variants of Marxism, he tried to show both that the influence of economic structures on the characteristics of a society could not be ignored, and that a crude materialistic interpretation had little scientific merit.

Another aspect of the Weberian approach also needs to be recalled. The study of issues which are "economically conditioned" or "economically relevant" leads – as in all sciences – to the search for regularities and causal links between the phenomena under investigation. Weber believed that this tendency in sociology should under no circumstances lead to a search for general laws that would establish causal links between economic and non-economic features of social life beyond a specific context. The formulation of generalizations – which Weber called "ideal types" – has specific spatial and temporal limitations and essentially aims to improve historical knowledge. As we will see, this position has not been unanimously accepted. For other scholars, such as Talcott Parsons in particular (1937), the limits that historical research imposed on theoretical generalizations was a barrier to the scientific development of sociology, that ought to be overcome. However, the efforts to move towards theoretical models with a high level of generalization have not culminated in very satisfying outcomes.

3   Sociology, Anthropology, and Economic History

In the previous discussion, we have drawn a distinction between economic sociology and economics. In so doing, we have argued that sociology's attention to institutional issues and historical and evolutionary phenomena has brought it closer to anthropology and economic history. We may now examine the ways in which the analytical perspectives of these three disciplines are different. Naturally, these differences are relative and are often – when dealing with actual topics – much less important. Similarities in research practices sometimes extend to economists themselves (especially those who are more distant from the mainstream). However, we may draw distinctions in three main areas: the object of investigation, the tools used, and the level of theoretical generalization.

There is an established research tradition within economic anthropology that studies the economic structures of primitive societies; among its most important instruments of research is the method based on "participant observation," given the difficulty of using other techniques in this type of context. In general, the characteristics of a society are reconstructed in their totality, although theoretical generalizations originating from research experience are elaborated explicitly and contribute to orienting the analysis. For example, there has been discussion of the term "reciprocity" as a general category suitable for interpreting the economic organization of primitive societies.

Economic history traditionally concentrates on the past, makes use of documentary analysis, and has a particularistic orientation that aims to reconstruct concrete phenomena, for example, the process of industrialization of a specific country or area. In contrast to anthropology and economic sociology, it uses explicit theoretical generalizations in a very limited way and often is suspicious of them. It should be remembered, however, that the economic historian must nonetheless use theoretical hypotheses about the causal linkages between the phenomena under study. In contrast to the anthropologist or the economic sociologist, though, these references usually remain implicit: they are not formalized, nor are they discussed independently of the object of inquiry. Of course, there are many exceptions to this – an increasing number of economic historians make use of the instruments and hypotheses of sociologists and economic anthropologists in their work.

In economic sociology, the main subject of research is contemporary society, even if there is an important tradition studying the process of modernization. The tools employed are documentary analysis and, above all in the study of contemporary societies, empirical research based on interviews or the direct collection of information, which can also be analyzed quantitatively. It tends to take a more generalizing approach than economic history; more precisely, it seeks to elaborate theoretical generalizations about the relationships between economic and non-economic phenomena, such as, for example, the cultural conditions that helped foster capitalist development, or the relationship between industrialization and social conflict, or the relationship between economic structure and urbanization, and so on. Despite some disagreement as to the level of generality that the discipline should aim at, in practice, research usually involves the formulation of theoretical models that are limited to particular contexts in space and time.

4   The Scientific Status of Economic Sociology

The previous discussion has cautiously situated economic sociology in an intermediate position between the generalizing approach of economics and the more particularistic perspective of history. What does this imply for the scientific status of the discipline? There is wide consensus that the search for "general laws" connecting phenomena is an essential objective of scientific activity. As we have seen however, Weber held that this aim was impracticable when he outlined the scientific agenda of the discipline. We may confront this question directly by examining the problems that a "monist" perspective on scientific activity faces when applied to social phenomena.

According to the monist viewpoint, there are no qualitative differences between the natural and social sciences. Four unifying points can be identified within this perspective: (a) there is only one scientific method, based on the formulation of hypotheses and empirical testing; (b) conceptual activity seeks to develop causal explanations of the phenomena, that is, to set out the conditions under which it is likely that a certain event will take place; (c) scientific activity is nomological: it tends, over time, and through the increase in knowledge, to formulate general laws; (d) the differences in the respective objects of the physical and natural sciences on the one hand, and the social sciences on the other, only involve particular technical problems. Thus, if it is easier or more common to identify regularities in natural than social phenomena, this implies only that observation is more difficult in the social sciences; certainly, it is more difficult to apply the experimental method. This explains why the social sciences lag behind the natural sciences, although it is possible to catch up over time through accumulating knowledge.

The more controversial points here are (c) and (d). Let us address them through examining Raymond Boudon's reasoning (1984), as elucidated in several examples that he lays out, which I have simplified for the purposes of exposition. The first comes from economic theory. It predicts that if the price of a product rises (A), the demand for that product will fall (B). As can be seen, this is a classic example of law in the sense of (c), i.e. it is a good example of a conditional law of the type "every time a certain phenomenon A occurs, another phenomenon B will follow." However, it is also easy to discern that the validity of this law is linked to certain conditions, K, when we limit ourselves to the same product. We must suppose that product P is substitutable with another, Q, with the same characteristics but less expensive than P, and that it is equally familiar to consumers. In a situation of this kind there is a high probability that the consumer will move his demand towards the less expensive product. The aggregate effect of individual decisions of this kind will in turn lead to an overall fall in the demand for P.

Individual choices are not always so easy nor are the aggregate effects always so clearly cut. In fact, the opposite is more often true. We can also hypothesize that product Q is not as well-known as P; that although it might be as well-known, it does not have the same characteristics; that Q does not exist and that P is therefore the only product available on the market. In each of these cases we successively increase the margins of uncertainty for individual choice. One must evaluate whether it is better to spend more on the old product, or whether one can save a bit of money but lose a little in terms of quality, or whether one may continue buying P. But this process of evaluation brings the criteria of choice – which are called preferences in economics and normative orientations in sociology – to center stage. They are independent of the situation of choice and are influenced by the effects of actors' experiences, which can vary widely in space and time. The aggregated effects of these choices are consequently far more difficult to define a priori, which in turn presents major obstacles for general predictive theory.

Let us turn to a second, more sociological example, also suggested by Boudon. Linking economic and social phenomena may lead one to formulate a law as follows: if economic conditions deteriorate (A), collective violence (revolts, unrest, strikes, etc.) will increase (B). Historical and empirical research does not in fact support this relationship, at least not on such a general level. This helps us to understand how difficult it is to formulate laws for society which are similar to those of the natural sciences. In other words, one can claim that a uniform deterioration in living conditions does *not* determine a parallel willingness to participate in forms of collective discontent. This choice is influenced by the resources available and the normative orientations of actors, which, in their turn, will condition the degree to which they are prepared to tolerate a worsening of living conditions, and the extent to which they perceive collective violence as legitimate. However, even supposing that these factors increase individual willingness, they do not necessarily lead to an immediate collective effect. For this to occur other conditions must be taken into account too – for example, the availability of leaders to organize the protest. For their part, the potential organizers will evaluate the chances of success and will consequently be influenced by the prevailing institutional arrangements (for example, whether there is a right to demonstrate, or, where there is not, the strength of the police, etc.). In sum, it is not possible to establish a general causal connection between a worsening of economic conditions and collective violence.

These simple examples demonstrate the difficulty of formulating laws of the type "if A, then B" in the study of social phenomena. Two points emerge in particular: the complexity of the conditions which influence action and the importance of actors' normative orientations. The latter may enormously complicate the set of factors which must be taken into consideration when formulating conditional laws because they introduce a strong degree of variability. They may in fact change in space and time according to the context in which they are formed. In such a situation it is still possible to formulate general laws but – as we have seen in the first example – these need to be based on restrictive conditions and this clearly limits their empirical applicability.

A path of this type is frequently followed by economics. The tendency of the discipline is to overlook the role of institutions and their influence on individual action, instead searching for ideal situations in which choice is objectively rational – in which, that is, any individual would be likely to react in the same way (in the above example this would be to cease consuming product P). This leads to a tendency to privilege analytical–deductive models in which it is possible to determine the behavior of the actor in advance. These models can be interesting from the theoretical point of view insofar as they allow for the application of sophisticated mathematical techniques. However, this does not mean that such situations are the most common on the historical–empirical level. In fact, the opposite is usually true.

For its part, economic sociology attaches more importance to the institutional forms of the economy in determining individual behavior. This gives rise to a more complex and variable picture of the actor, whose motivations can no longer be reducible to simple utilitarian orientations. The scope of generalization is more limited and confined to more strictly defined spatial and temporal boundaries. This has led to a more inductive approach in which causal connections – as well as being limited – are also more empirically grounded. Obviously, the differences between economics and sociology involve general tendencies rather than hard boundaries. Just as some economists work more on the empirical level, so some sociologists dedicate their time to developing theories.

Does this mean that to understand social phenomena one must oscillate between abstract theorizing and narrow empiricism? Not necessarily. The experience of real research shows us that the best work, that is to say, the most effective in terms of increasing knowledge, avoids extreme positions of this type. Thus it tends to avoid the nomological orientation of "positivist monism," but also the radically particularistic stance of "historicist dualism."-------- For this latter, only the natural sciences can establish general causal links since each social phenomenon is distinct, preventing one from making any sort of theoretical generalization.

The scientific status of economic sociology – and of the social sciences in general – is however based on a conception that is different from that of both monism and dualism. The application of the scientific method, based on the verification of hypotheses, does not necessarily require the formulation of general laws. Indeed, this is not the aim of the social sciences; they instead aspire to the formulation of models. While laws are expected to be generally applicable, models are ideal reconstructions of specific situations, defined by particular conditions limiting their validity in space and time. They are elaborated on the basis of a historical–empirical situation, but do not treat it exhaustively. Instead, they serve to interpret it. While Boudon called this approach to the social sciences "formal theory," recalling Simmel, it also comes close to Weber's ideal types. Weber proposed these last in a methodological debate where he sought to set out a scientific programme for economic sociology, envisaging a specific space for research that would break free of the limits of historicism and positivism.

This discussion should by now have made clear the most fundamental factor limiting the possibility for deriving general laws from social phenomena. It is necessary to take account of the normative orientations of actors, which may vary over time and space, in order to reconstruct their aggregate effects; these may take, for instance, the form of social conflict or entrepreneurship, supply of labor or consumption of goods, and so on. This view can be defined as "methodological individualism," insofar as it attempts to explain social phenomena from the starting point of individual motivations. However, one can understand these last in a different way. Thus, for example, sociology tends to emphasize the influence of social factors (i.e. values, norms, power relations, etc.) on individuals, while in economics a more atomistic conception of the actor prevails, which sets non-individual factors to one side. Thus, economics places greater emphasis on the rational pursuit of individual interests by isolated actors. It should however be noted that, despite these variants, methodological individualism can be contrasted as a whole with "collectivism," or better, with "methodological holism." The latter is more typical of those monistic approaches that seek their inspiration in positivism and argue that the social sciences must follow the methods of the natural sciences. These approaches do not specifically take individual motivations into account, but link them to the conditions which influence them. A simple, but common, example of this procedure can be seen in many of the analyses which try to establish correlations between aggregate variables – a method which is typical of the natural sciences. Thus one may study the influence of the general level of education on economic development or that of economic growth on political behavior, etc. Naturally, such work can lead to useful results, but it may be difficult to generalize, because it is ill-suited to taking account of actors' motivations, which may lead these actors to react differently to changes in the conditions under which they operate.

Methodological holism is not limited to behaviorism. As we will later see, it has a complex history and a variety of forms, from the positivist sociological tradition of Comte, through functionalism, to certain variants of Marxism. In general, what links these approaches – which are of course very different – is their search for the natural laws of society, and thus for clear principles on which one can link order and social change, whether they be values or economic structures, or the functional needs of the social system. In order to treat society like nature, however, actors need to be reduced to stylized enactors of the constraints imposed by the system.

5 Interpretative Pluralism: Science and Values

The dividing line between individualism and methodological holism runs through the history of the social sciences, and may also be seen in economic sociology, where it nourishes interpretative pluralism (that is, the coexistence of different interpretative models). However, this pluralism – which characterizes the study of society – may also be seen in the different variants of individualistic methodology. All of them share the aim of analyzing the interaction between the external conditions of action and the motivations of actors, so as to reconstruct the aggregate effects of this interaction, which determine a particular phenomenon. As we have seen, this is a difficult objective to achieve; different solutions have been offered to these difficulties. There are two main reasons for this pluralism.

The first has to do with the complexity of the object of investigation. The conditions which influence action are legion, and vary in space and time. It is difficult to isolate them from each other and understand them. The same is true for motivations. It is not easy to reconstruct the normative orientations of actors, the criteria of choice which guide them, and thus the meaning that actors attribute to their actions. And in fact, for precisely this reason, some scholars maintain that one should not investigate the motivations of individual actions. The result of these constraints is therefore to widen the margin of discretion of the individual scholar in his selection of conditions and motivations and in his description of the relationships between them. This is where the second reason comes in. In widening the margin of discretion, the values of the researcher become important; he is himself a member of the society being studied, and has his own values, preferences, and criteria of orientation, which will also guide him in his work.

It is important to remember therefore that the social sciences take societies that change over time as their objects of study, and that the people who study these societies also live in them and are influenced by them. Even if the values of the individual researcher are also important in the natural sciences, the difference lies in the greater space that the object studied leaves to these values in the social sciences, and thus in the greater degree of interpretative pluralism that results. Must we, however, be sceptical about the extent to which the study of social phenomena can be scientific?

The answer is no if, as I have tried to show, one does not assume that a study of this kind must have the same characteristics as the natural sciences. In other words, even if the researcher's values play an essential role in selecting problems and choosing a framework on which to build models and interpretations, the results need not be arbitrary, and may be subjected to rational criticism, particularly if these values are explicit, and the analytical models and the empirical evidence on which they are based, are presented clearly. This in fact allows the scientific community to subject the various models to rational examination, evaluating their appropriateness for the phenomena that they seek to explain.

From this perspective, interpretative pluralism is an unavoidable feature of social sciences (although it can be mitigated): it is intrinsically bound up with the historical character of the society itself. Despite this constraint, social sciences – including economic sociology – can make a significant contribution to a conscious reconstruction of society as long as they do not exaggerate their responsibility and claim to have a recipe-book for various social problems. There is, moreover, another important difference between this conception of social sciences and research aimed at discovering general laws, which concerns the practical implications of knowledge. The search for laws of nature in society, and for unambiguous principles governing their evolution can lead one to claim that one has found a scientific foundation for practical choices. If one believes that economic and social life must respond to certain general laws which it is pointless to try to change, there is nothing left to do other than to understand these laws and adapt to them. From this point of view there is not much difference between positivism, a certain kind of Marxism and functionalism. All these approaches tend to feed the recurring illusion of having found scientific solutions to practical problems and political choices. And just as they do not leave much space to interpretative pluralism at the theoretical level, so they also tend to have totalitarian consequences for politics.

Once more we can call on Weber to see how the problem of the relationship between theory and practice, between knowledge and political action, may be redefined once one abandons the illusion of general social laws. In defining the boundaries of economic sociology, Weber warned against seeking a scientific basis for value judgments. He distinguished between "relevance to values" and "value judgments" (Weber [1917] 1949, pp. 21–2). Relevance to values underlines that, as we have seen, in the selection of the topic of research and the discovery of causal connections between phenomena, the researcher is inevitably guided by his own values. This does not however invalidate the scientific value of the work if the hypotheses and the evidence are presented properly and can therefore be examined critically. Value judgments instead refer to the desirability of certain aims. They cannot be justified on a scientific basis. In his famous address, *Science as Vocation*, given in Munich in 1919, Weber took up Tolstoy's famous question, "As science does not, who is to answer the question: 'what shall we do?'" (Weber [1919] 1991, p. 152). He goes on to warn however that, "only a prophet or a savior can give the answers. If there is no such man . . . then you will certainly not compel him to appear on this earth by having thousands of professors, as privileged hirelings of the state, attempt as petty prophets in their lecture-rooms to take over his role" (Weber [1919] 1991, p. 153).

What is science then supposed to do? It should above all put itself at the service of clarity. Although neither value judgments nor the political choices over economic and social organization can be established scientifically, not all judgments should be dismissed from scientific discussion. It is true that ultimate values cannot be established through scientific methods. They can only be the result of a collective choice. However, the social sciences may help to make these choices by clarifying the conditions for their fulfillment, and the advantages and disadvantages that they may involve. On this view the task of economic sociology is not to demonstrate, in scientific terms, that – for instance – the economic organization of Japan is more efficient than that of the United States or Europe, or vice versa; it is instead to clarify the implications and consequences of a certain way of organizing the economy in society. By clarifying the origins of certain choices, one may help avoid the temptation for facile transplants and imitations. At the same time, evaluating the consequences of a particular economic form, its dynamism, and its implications in terms of the conditions of work, social life, and political power is important to help orient collective decisions.

Economic sociology – and the social sciences in general – can help clarify the implications and consequences of the ends pursued by the members of a society, and thus help modify these ends as appropriate. In other words, it can contribute to the conscious production of society. However, in order for this to take place, two closely connected conditions are necessary: freedom of research and scientific discussion has to be guaranteed and protected, which can take place only in an open and democratic society.

Part I

The Classics and the Sociology of Capitalism

Chapter 1

From Classical Economics to Economic Sociology

1 The Birth of Economics

It is impossible for any society to survive without some form of economic activity to sustain it. And yet it was only fairly recently – during the 1700s – that economic phenomena began to be studied in their own right; that is, that economics was born as a scientific discipline. Why is this? It cannot solely be attributed to the slow pace at which knowledge of society has developed. It also involves the "visibility" of economic activities and their autonomy *vis-à-vis* other social structures. Specifically, only when the production and distribution of goods and services began to be clearly separated from religious and political regulations and constraints did it become possible to study the "laws" of economics as such. The economy could now be analyzed as a phenomenon that was self-regulating according to its own principles. These principles were those of the market: production and distribution depended on the interplay between demand and supply on the market, a game in which actors were sought to maximize the likelihood of individual gain.

Karl Polanyi (1968, 1977) was one of a group of authors who insisted on the primal link between economic enquiry and the consolidation of the market. To substantiate this view, he referred to anthropological and historical work that studied primitive and archaic economies. In these contexts, economic activities were embedded into a system of non-economic institutions. This means that the production and exchange of goods tied to agriculture, breeding, fishing, and handicrafts, were organized on the basis of the principle of "reciprocity" or "redistribution," rather than "market trade."

In the case of *reciprocity*, goods and services were produced and distributed on the basis of shared solidaristic commitments to other members of the family group or tribe. Such duties were usually linked to the prescriptions of the prevailing religion, and forms of reciprocity, both within the family group and in larger groups, were foreseen. In this way, different types of products could be exchanged, and, in fact, the economies of these primitive societies were characterized by a continuous exchange of goods. It is clear then that individual economic behavior was not motivated by the incentive for individual gain in this context, and that the quantity of goods produced was not subject to the free play of market forces. If one wishes to understand the economies of these primitive societies, one must take account of the complex network of reciprocal social obligations that linked members and motivated their behavior.

Reciprocity in primitive societies often went together with *redistribution*. For example, prevailing social norms might prescribe that the head of a village or the tribe be given certain products. These would then be put away, conserved and periodically redistributed on special ceremonial occasions, according to variable rules that entailed different levels of inequality. Such forms of economic organization allowed a specialized division of labor across wider territories. For example, it was typical of the economies of the great bureaucratized empires, such as ancient Mesopotamia, Egypt, the Incas in Peru, and the Roman Empire. In these cases, wide scale redistribution went together with the introduction of differentiated political structures, of a "center" that established the rights and duties of people with regard to the economy. Over time, the level of economic activity increased, and money began to be used. Economic behavior began to be constrained not only by shared social duties, but also by specific formal rules that were given force by political power, although this was usually legitimized in religious terms. In this case too, therefore, one cannot separate the study of the economy from the study of the political structure in which economic activity was embedded.

According to Polanyi, one must take account of reciprocity and redistribution as mechanisms of regulation in order to understand European feudalism too, with its complex network of relations between the monarch and liege-lords, and between the latter and the inhabitants of their estates. However, it is interesting to note that, the medieval period saw – in Europe more than elsewhere – the constituting of a growing and autonomous space for the *market* as an instrument for organizing economic activity – increasingly at the expense of the other two "forms of integration," reciprocity, and redistribution.

To understand this process, one must not subsume all types of exchange under the rubric of "market trade." Exchange involves the relatively pacific acquisition of goods that are not immediately available through a bilateral relation. According to the type of relationship existing between the parties, three forms of exchange can be identified. First is "gift trade" which, as we have seen, was typical of a relationship of reciprocity regulated by shared norms (Polanyi 1977, p. 94). "Administrated trade" was instead characterized by transactions that were rigorously controlled by the political power, as seen in the archaic economies of the large empires of antiquity (Polanyi 1977, pp. 94–5). In both cases, the reason for exchanging commercialized goods was not located in the relationship between demand and supply, but in social or political norms; the demand and supply relationship was specific to market trade in the strictest sense. The importance of market exchange grew slowly but surely in the Western world until finally, during the 1800s, "self-regulating" markets (that is, markets which determine prices through demand and supply) became the primary instrument regulating the production and distribution of goods and services in the developed world. Thus, economic behavior was no longer conditioned by social or political duties but was driven instead by the seak of the gain or the fear of hunger. The political system limited itself to an external role, guaranteeing property right and the freedom of bargaining, while the life-chances of individuals came increasingly to depend on their sale of the resources at their disposal on the market. It was in this context that economic research, as an independent field of enquiry based on the laws of the market, was able to develop. It was only the emancipation and unbundling of economic activities from social and political constraints – as Polanyi emphasized – that enabled economics to emerge as a science.

2 The Foundation of Political Economy and Adam Smith's "Great Synthesis"

During the 1700s in particular, two important trends began to emerge. First, economic inquiry became increasingly detached from studies of religion and/or politics, where it had been confined to a relatively limited role until the market had begun to become more important. Second, the study of economic phenomena took on a more positivistic orientation. The prestige that the scientific method had acquired in the natural sciences had an ever greater influence on the investigation of social phenomena, lending greater importance to the verification of hypotheses and to a more precise distinction between interpretation and prescription, between explanation of phenomena and proposals for intervention. Just as the emancipation of the economy from society was slow, and reached its culmination in Europe, so too the creation of economics as an autonomous discipline was gradual and tied to events within Western culture.

Many "pieces" of economic analysis had accumulated over time, particularly towards the end of the sixteenth century. However, it was only during the second half of the seventeenth century – through the work of the physiocrats and Adam Smith – that the idea of the economic sphere as an autonomous system of interacting parts reached maturity. At the same time, the distinction between "scientific" analyses of the functioning of the economy and proposals made by political economy (that is to say, suggestions for how political authority might intervene through regulation) also became clearer. The creation of political economy was accompanied by an explicit and conscious reflection of the relationship between economy and society. Thus it can be seen that a type of economic sociology developed prior to the emergence of the field within the sociological tradition itself, and – in a certain sense – prepared the ground for such outcome. Only later, towards the end of the 1800s, with the advent of the neoclassical economists did the differences between economics and sociology become clearer.

One may find much earlier observations on the activity of production and distribution of goods than those discussed above. Amongst the most coherent and influential were the comments of Aristotle and the medieval Scholasticists, St. Thomas Aquinas in particular. The term *economics* comes from Greek and originally refers to householding (from *oikos* "household" and *nomia* "a set of norms or laws") and was used by Aristotle in the sense of "administration of domestic matters." Only in the seventeenth century did its use extend from the private sphere to the public one, with the work of the first *mercantilist* economists, where the term came to refer to the study of the features and economic problems of a national state. It was at this point that *political economy* began to be discussed (Montchrétien published his *Traité de l'économie politique* in 1615). This expression conjoined two points: the close ties of the economy with national states, that is to say, the limited extent to which economic activities were emancipated from political regulations at this time; and the lack of real distinction between analyses of economic phenomena and the discussion of economic policy. The term *political economy* would continue to be used when these factors had diminished in importance, and indeed was still present in Smith's *Wealth of Nations* (1776). Only later, towards the end of the eighteenth century, would the term *economics*, as opposed to *political economy*, come into use. This use, introduced into Britain and the United States through Alfred Marshall's textbook (*Principles of Economics*, 1890), tended to underline the autonomy of economics from politics and the distinction between scientific analysis and economic policy (Schumpeter 1954).

The terminology thus illustrates how economic activities were analyzed. In this regard, an essential precondition had been the diffusion, especially in the 1600s, of one particular branch of political economy which analyzed problems and characteristics of economic activity strictly in light of underpinning the nation-states which were then emerging. This set of heterogeneous investigations was grouped together under the name of *mercantilism*, to which authors such as Thomas Mun, William Petty, and John Law contributed. Their vision of economics was not systematic but very practical, nor did they worry about discovering or establishing "general laws." What they promoted was the collection of data on empirical phenomena such as commerce and taxation, so as to provide practical advice in terms of political economy. This approach may be categorized as both inductive and concrete, and contrasted with the more deductive and systematic approach of the French *physiocrats*.

This latter group – known as *les économistes* – developed its analyses around the middle of the 1700s. Among its better-known members were François Quesnay, the Marquis of Mirabeau, Pierre-Paul Mercier de la Rivière, and Pierre-Samuel Dupont de Némours. Physiocracy means "government of nature" and, indeed, the physiocrats started from the assumption that there were natural laws governing society similar to those that existed in the physical world. For these authors, there was a "natural social order" that might come to be understood through reason. The more that society organized itself in accordance with these laws, through the help of science, the more might both individual and collective well-being be increased. One essential feature of natural laws was the right to property. If this right was recognized and adequately guaranteed, and was not hindered by positive law, it could better foster the pursuit of individual interests. This, in turn, would help to create greater individual and collective wealth. It would thus be necessary to free agriculture from its remaining feudal constraints, to liberalize commerce in cereals, and to rationalize the fiscal system through a single tax. In other words, their main aim was to reinforce the role of the agricultural bourgeoisie. In his famous *Tableau économique*, first published in 1758, Quesnay proposed the idea of the economy as a "self-regulating machine," as a set of interacting phenomena, all affecting each other according to their own laws, that could be studied in isolation from other social relations. This was clearly an essential contribution to the foundation of economics as an autonomous science.

In Adam Smith's (1723–90) view, economy and society – market and institutions – were still closely related. While the stereotypical view of Smith sees him as the champion of *laissez-faire* (an expression which he does not use), he clearly believes that the pursuit of individual interest and the workings of the market will only conduct to the general good when they are constrained by precise institutional rules (sociocultural, legal, political-organizational). Smith therefore saw the study of these institutional constraints as an integral part of research into the "causes of the wealth of nations." Economics and economic sociology were, in consequence, closely linked in his work.

Smith taught moral philosophy at the University of Glasgow for more than ten years, and, in 1759, he published *The Theory of Moral Sentiments*. In this book he attempted to demonstrate that public benefits do not derive from private vices, as Mandeville's caustic formulation in *The Fable of the Bees* (1714) had it. He believed, instead, that they derive from the pursuit of individual interest in socially controlled forms. In what way might it be said that individual interest is socially disciplined? Using more modern terminology, it might be argued that this occurs through the process of socialization, a mechanism that Smith labelled "sympathy." This involves identifying with values shared with other members of society, who may approve or disapprove of our behavior. The law-based sanctions suffered by those who violate formal rules may reinforce these mechanisms. In this way, human action is shaped by society and its institutions (through formal and informal norms) and cannot be explained by a "natural" individual tendency to search for one's own interest. Smith in other words, was not an utilitarian.

Smith's appreciation of the influence of institutions can also be seen in his more specifically economic work, the famous *An Inquiry into the Nature and Causes of the Wealth of Nations*, published in 1776. This text was basic to the formation of economics as a scientific discipline, and has become well-known principally because Smith precisely and systematically presents "laws" on the functioning of the market in the production of goods and the distribution of incomes. In addition to examining static equilibrium, a substantial part of the book examines the "causes of the wealth of nations," which is to say dynamic equilibrium, or economic growth. In the section on static analysis, the role of institutions is viewed as a given; in contrast, in the dynamic part they are presented as a variable that can, depending on their characteristics, favor or discourage development.

Smith's work on static equilibrium presupposed that new wealth was not created, but rather that existing wealth was used to satisfy needs. In this context, capitalist institutions were taken as given. Taking for granted that land belonged to owners who lived on the proceeds, that capital accumulated in the hands of capitalists who lived on the profits, and that workers depended on the sale of their work for a wage, Smith asked how the production of goods and distribution of incomes took place. He supposed – as did the economists following him – that there were many sellers, that information circulated freely, and that the resources of capital and labor could be easily transferred from one use to another. In this institutional context, the quantity of goods produced will tend to correspond to the demand that exists for such goods. In the final analysis, consumer demand will determine what is produced, given the costs of production for each good. If the quantity of certain goods offered falls below demand, price will increase, as competition between buyers who wish to obtain the good drives them to pay more. However, precisely because of this, it would be more advantageous to use additional resources in the production of that good, moving them from other uses. The opposite, obviously, tended to happen if the amount offered was more than that demanded. As for the distribution of income, it was also assumed that there was a particular market price for wages, profits, and incomes. For example, wages tended to rise if the demand for labour was greater than supply, and vice versa. Smith thus described a situation in which members of society were not rewarded for their participation in economic activity through traditional means (reciprocity), or through legal regulation guaranteed by the power of the state (redistribution), as in the feudal system. Instead, remuneration depended on the market and its laws.

In contrast, in Smith's analysis of economic development, institutions were not a given but a variable. The wealth of nations was linked to the amount of capital invested in economic activities. As this increased, so did the market for the goods produced and exchanged, which enhanced the division of labor. According to Smith, this was important because this division favored the growth in productivity, that is, the amount of goods that could be produced by each single worker with a greater level of specialization. What did the amount of capital invested thus depend on? If one was to see genuine economic growth, it was necessary that the accumulation of capital be stimulated and regulated by the appropriate institutions. There were two important conditions for this: (a) the advantages of competitive capitalism over monopolistic capitalism, and (b) the ability of the state to produce collective goods, thereby favoring economic development.

The first condition requires that in every productive activity there be a high number of capitalists ready to invest money in competition between each other, without being able to manipulate either supply or prices. Smith believed that the right political choices had to be made if this was to be achieved. In other words, he thought that institutional obstacles to the mobility of capital and labor should be reduced. This was the root of his criticisms of protectionist politics and mercantilism, to which he devoted a great deal of space in *Wealth of Nations*.

Let us suppose – as Smith does in his detailed analysis of the British case – that there is a generalized situation of competitive capitalism. What determines the superiority of this structure to the monopolistic one? There are two answers to this question. The first, more traditional, involves the efficient allocation of a given set of resources (static equilibrium). From this point of view, monopoly is sub-optimal because it alters price and supply. In other words, it means that consumers must pay more for goods that they demand. However, there is also another possibility, which has to do with the dynamic effects of competition, although this has usually been overlooked (Rosenberg 1960, 1975). Thus Smith held that a low rate of profit would have beneficial consequences for the prosperity of society. In other words, more intense competition lowers the rate of profit for the individual capitalist, but stimulates entrepreneurship and innovation and thus leads to an increased division of labor and higher productivity. Clearly, for Smith, the mere pursuit of individual interest is not enough to guarantee development.

One may point to two other institutional conditions, besides the effect of low profits, that define the structure of competitive capitalism. The first involves the direct engagement of the capitalist, as an entrepreneur, in the management of his firm. Smith clearly opposed the shareholder model of company organization, in which managers administer money that is not their own, and, as a result, have less incentive than owner-entrepreneurs to behave efficiently. The second condition involves recompense for labor. It is not unreasonable to say that Smith supported a policy of high wages on the part of entrepreneurs to improve productivity. In other words, he believed that higher wages would lead to more active and harder working laborers, thereby encouraging the growth of productivity.

The other institutional variable influencing economic development involves the role of the state. This should, first of all, refrain from developing protectionist policies that obstruct the market, but should fulfill three basic functions. First, it should ensure national defense, second, it should guarantee security and the proper administration of justice, and, third, it should provide the necessary public services for economic activity and education. All three areas of state activity were extremely important for society, but they could not be adequately carried out by the private sector because they did not involve a sufficient rate of profits. Smith was strongly convinced that a skilled work force was essential not only to maintain the social and political balance of a country, but also for economic development itself. However, the market did not provide this resource, and indeed tended to impoverish it through the division of labor.

In conclusion, Smith believed that development would take place when institutions came to approach the model of competitive capitalism outlined above. When this was so, they would be able to reconcile economic efficiency and social consensus, in large part because they would foster development, thereby increasing the wellbeing of all social classes. In addition, the competitive market would reduce inequalities (leading to low profits and high wages), making them more dependent on individual commitment to labor. This image of capitalist development, in which the economy fosters a high level of social integration, would subsequently be subjected to vigorous challenges and would indeed be belied by later developments. The long march of capitalist development would be far more difficult, contested and riddled with tensions and conflicts than Smith could ever – from his standpoint at the onset of the whole process – have predicted. However, his model of the relations between economy and society in competitive capitalism constitutes an essential reference point not only – and this is usually recognized – for the construction of economics, but also for economic sociology. He showed that the study of institutions is particularly important if one wanted to analyze economic development. Economics and economic sociology were thus still very closely linked in Smith's thinking.

3 The "Dismal Science"

In the forty years between the publication of *Wealth of Nations* by Smith (1776) and *On the Principle of Political Economy and Taxation* by David Ricardo (1817) and *Principles of Political Economy* by Thomas Malthus (1820), a twofold change occurred in economic thought. On the one hand, the prospects for the growth of wealth and spread of prosperity came to be evaluated more pessimistically than in Smith's initial, optimistic assessment. On the other, economic analysis became more developed and established, especially in Britain, although it took what might be described as an "economistic" turn.

This more pessimistic orientation of economic analysis – which later prompted Thomas Carlyle to call it the "dismal science" – came to fruition in the Britain of the Industrial Revolution. The market had extended and consolidated its role as an instrument regulating economic activity, but with enormous and long-lasting social consequences. Social tensions and insecurity came about as a result of the abandonment of the countryside, growing urbanization, and the precarious and unforgiving conditions of life and labor for a growing number of men, women, and children. Economists saw the poverty in which the greater part of the population subsisted as a necessity that could not be alleviated by economic growth. Poverty was thus, in their eyes, not so much a social as a natural problem.

In his famous *An Essay on the Principles of Population* (1798), Thomas Malthus (1766–1834) underlined the constant tendency of all living beings to multiply more than the means of subsistence at their disposal would allow them to, so that there was a perpetual threat of overpopulation. Every rise in wages leads workers to multiply, leading to a greater supply of labor which, in turn, pushes wages to the subsistence level as a result of greater competition on the job market. In this fashion, hunger balances out the excesses of reproduction. In this perspective, the chances of increasing wealth were far more limited than they had appeared to Smith. The institutions of capitalist economy do not legitimate themselves through their capacity to increase riches, but rather are the lesser of two evils. This viewpoint was the source of opposition towards the measures taken to alleviate poverty (the *poor laws*), then under discussion. According to Malthus, this kind of intervention would only worsen matters, artificially supporting growth in a population for which there was insufficient means of support, thereby distorting the functioning of the labor market.

This pessimistic stance was also shared by David Ricardo (1772–1823). In his view, the most important question was how income was distributed among the three main social classes – landowners, capitalists, and laborers. Demographic pressure meant that new areas of land were constantly being farmed, leading to an increase in the income that the owners could make on the better areas. As a result, the agricultural profit rate went down and the prices of agricultural goods increased. This made the cost of living for laborers rise. Thus, wages would also rise, and the overall profit rate would fall, putting a brake on the accumulation of capital and the growth of wealth. Ricardo came to an important political conclusion as a result of this reasoning: It was important to remove any form of agricultural protectionism based on duties on imports (laws of this type – the famous *corn laws* – had been introduced in Britain 1815 as a result of pressure from landowners). The import of agricultural products at a lower cost would curb the drop in profits that was lowering incomes, and would therefore help to create wealth. Adopting this strictly liberal position, Ricardo disagreed with Malthus, who had supported landowners in their conflict of interest with capitalists. With a vision that would later find support in Keynes, Malthus reached the conclusion that there was a tendency towards overproduction in capitalist economies. In other words, there was a risk that not all goods produced would be sold given the lack of a corresponding demand by consumers – consumption by capitalists and workers not, in fact, being sufficient. Only through consumption by a wide range of landowners, as well as workers who did not produce directly (for example, those employed in services) was it possible to sustain demand for the goods produced. Through encouraging this it was thus theoretically possible to counter the fall in the rate of accumulation rate, and therefore the decrease in wealth.

Classic economists are usually grouped together as a result of their similar views of economic research. Indeed, the adjective *classic* underlines this commonality. However, the above discussion has already highlighted several important differences between the original approach adopted by Smith and those of Malthus and Ricardo. Certainly, these authors all held that economic analysis should study development, the mechanisms regulating the growth of wealth, and how to increase it over time. In pursuing these objectives, they all believed that the way in which income was distributed among the social classes was crucial for economic development. There are, however, some essential differences.

For Malthus and Ricardo, whose explanatory framework was simpler than Smith's, economic development depended in essence on the increase of profits, in the sense that a higher profit rate allowed more resources to be invested and also gave more incentives to do so. They disagreed, however, over the conditions under which a high rate of profit emerged. For Ricardo, agricultural rent needed to be limited through a strict liberal policy; for Malthus instead, agricultural rent (as well as non-productive labor) needed to be protected because it allowed the excess goods produced by capitalists to be consumed. Smith appears to have taken a different position. For him, low profit rates and high wages rates stimulated – as we have seen above – the entrepreneurship of capitalists and the commitment of laborers, and therefore the division of labor and growth in productivity. This, in his view, would create a higher overall level of profits and therefore greater wealth, which could be reinvested in new activities. For Smith, technical progress should thus be included in the explanation of economic development. It was this factor that led him to be more optimistic than Malthus and Ricardo.

One must emphasize a further important methodological implication differentiating Smith from his successors. For Smith, economic actors were subjects who *interpreted the situation* in which they worked and pursued their interests according to norms of behavior that were influenced by the social context in which they acted. This allowed, as a result, for a kind of variability in behavior that depended on institutions, that is, on non-economic factors. Thus, attention was drawn to the more or less competitive character of the economic organization, the ways in which firms were run (the kind of control imposed by managers or the entrepreneur/ owner), laborers' commitment to work, and the capacity of the state to produce collective goods.

Neither Malthus nor Ricardo accepted this position: they instead put forward an economistic point of view, which would develop as the discipline became established. Economic actors were not, in this case, viewed as subjects interpreting situations with relative autonomy. Rather, they were seen merely as *calculators* whose aim was to maximize according to their interests, which were in turn rigidly defined by their class situation (that of a waged worker, capitalist or landowner). It was thus possible to reconstruct behavior deductively, reducing the margins of variability and developing strong generalizations on change in the economy from the starting point of how income was distributed among the classes. At this point, it was no longer necessary to worry about the effects of institutions on economic phenomena. Economic research could concentrate on a more limited range of variables and thus radically disassociate itself from the institutional framework. In other words, economics and economic sociology could separate one from the other. While this allowed greater analytical precision and a greater degree of generalization for economics, it incurred the cost of losing adherence to historical–empirical reality, which led to the harsh criticisms discussed below.

4   The Critique of German Historicism

As capitalist development extended, over the 1800s, the relation between society and economy seemed to become more problematic. Growing tensions emerged as the Industrial Revolution got under way in Britain and began to have repercussions on the Continent. The old traditional and artisanal economies were threatened by competition from industrial production. Economic development and the spread of the market thus led to differences in the relative success of different territories that showed no signs of being resolved. At the same time, the transformation of the countryside and the growth of the working class went together with extremely difficult living and working conditions for a growing proportion of the population. The outlines of the "social question" began to emerge distinctly. In this context, classical economics, as it was then articulated, was accused of being unable to explain concrete phenomena or to provide valid guidelines for intervention. We may single out two types of criticism in particular. The first, made by German historicism, focused on territorial differences in economic development and how they might be overcome. The second, which would have a remarkable influence on successive historical events, was that of Marx, who questioned the interpretation of relations between social classes in capitalist development.

In the first few decades of the 1800s, Germany was highly politically fragmented (Germany was unified only after 1866). Economic development was also more limited than in Britain or France. This helps us understand why various authors from the German historical school of political economy began to explore the differences in economic development of different national states. They criticized the abstractions of the theoretical schema of classical economics as being unable to tackle this question, and believed that the answer would be found in research that would take better account of actual reality, and that would thus use the historical method rather than the analytical–deductive one. In this way, territorial differences in development were traced back to the determining influence of non-economic factors. This historical research would also have to clarify how cultural, social, and political factors interacted with economic variables to give rise to specific forms of economic organization. These authors' insistence on the variability of real-world economies and their develoïpment over time called the rigidly liberal orientation of classical economics into question once again, and legitimized more interventionist forms of political economy, particularly in terms of tariff protection.

German historians have generally proposed different classifications for the "stages of development" of the economy, which were viewed as resulting from a combination of economic and institutional factors. A first formulation of such stages can be found in the work of Friedrich List, who anticipated the historical school. However, various other approaches also emerged during the second half of the nineteenth century in the work of Wilhelm Roscher, Karl Knies, Bruno Hildebrand, and later, Gustav Schmoller and Karl Bücher. They counterposed the need for a complete description of "living reality" in its historical evolution to the theoretical pretensions of classical economics, which claimed that it could identify the laws by which the economy functioned.

This led to a certain amount of theoretical fuzziness, which Max Weber (1903–6) described in his famous critique, where he emphasized how this kind of work suffered from what can be called "encyclopaedic descriptivism," in which a multitude of variables are considered. In the end, different paths of economic development were explained through ambiguous interpretative instruments with no scientific control, such as the concept of *Volkgeist* (spirit of the people). These concepts expressed the assumption that economic development was fundamentally influenced by the overall culture of a particular population, an argument which remained theoretically weak. Historicism focused on the real limits of political economy and emphasized the role of institutions in economic analysis, but it did not manage to provide a satisfying response to the problem of the differences of economic development over space and time. However, as we will see later, the historicist critique of classical economics was to be very important in the emergence of an autonomous discipline of economic sociology.

5 Marx's Critique

While historicism focused on the national differences associated with economic development, Marx concentrated on social classes. Both approaches sought to move beyond the limits of classical economics by refusing to separate economic research from its institutional context, and by situating economic analysis in an historical context. The influence of the German intellectual tradition can be seen in these similarities. For German idealism, and for Hegel in particular, history was a continuous act in progress, which, as it went through different phases, led to a progressive realization of human reason – considered as a super-individual entity. Every historical moment was to be analyzed in its *totality*; cultural, political, and economic features were closely interconnected. However, while historicism remained bound to an idealistic vision of historical development, in which cultural development conditioned economic organization, Marx reversed the relationship between cultural and socioeconomic features, which he saw as the true driving forces behind historical development. Moreover, his aspirations were more theoretical than those of the historicists. He did not intend simply to demonstrate a generic connection between the different aspects of social reality. Rather, he wanted to formulate a general theory of historical development, within which he focused his attention on capitalist society and its transformations, on its "laws of movement," as he underlined in the Preface to the first edition of *Capital: A Critique of Political Economy* (1867).

Marx thus criticized the classical economists for their inability to adequately describe the conflict between capitalists and workers characteristic of capitalist economies. This inability had forestalled evaluation of the changes that the class struggle would, in his view, inevitably involve for the forms of economic organization typical of capitalism, finally giving rise to a socialist society. Marx shared the more pessimistic view of development which Malthus and Ricardo had first expressed. However, while these authors had highlighted the natural limits of economic growth, Marx chose to emphasize the existence of the social constraints intrinsic to the basic institutions of capitalist economies. In other words, he focused on private ownership of the means of production, and waged labor, as mechanisms regulating the production of goods and the distribution of incomes. As opposed to the vision of social harmony found in Smith, in which capitalist economies in a liberal regime would enhance the growth of wealth and cooperation between social classes, Marx set out a *dialectic* vision, influenced by German idealistic philosophy. Capitalism would generate a growing polarization between the social classes and this would lead to a progressive intensification of conflict, which in turn would lead to the overthrow of old forms of economic organization.

His pessimistic prognosis regarding the ability of capitalist economies to continue producing and distributing wealth results in large part from his emphasis on the exploitation of the working class as the driving force behind the economy through the creation of surplus value and profit. In *Capital* (1867–94), Marx developed the presuppositions lying behind his criticisms of political economy. He wanted to show that capitalist development created over time the economic conditions for the strengthening of the working class, the overthrow of capitalist economy, and the advent of socialism.

In a capitalist economy based on the private ownership of the means of production, goods cannot be produced if there is no profit for the holders of capital. But where does profit come from? When an individual worker is used in the productive process, he creates added value over what is necessary to pay his wages. This difference constitutes a surplus of labor that forms the source of surplus value, and thus of profit. However, in a competitive situation, the individual capitalist entrepreneurs have an interest in – indeed, they are forced to – introduce new machines, thereby increasing fixed capital at the expense of labor. In this way, they reduce the cost of labor and enjoy greater profits until other capitalists are also pushed into introducing the same innovations. This, however, has two main consequences: First, it leads to unemployment and worsens the living conditions of the working class; second, it leads to a tendency for the rate of profit to fall, reducing the stimulus to production. Profit, in Marx's view, depends only on the exploitation of labor, which is reduced through the use of more machines and less labor. In addition to this the working class becomes more organized over time and as a result of cyclical crises, thus lowering the margins for exploitation.

Marx's most important criticism, from the strictly economic point of view, concerns his belief that technical progress has no role in the creation of wealth. Thus, he overlooked that the introduction of new technologies would generally lead to an increase in the productivity of labor. If wages rise no higher than productivity, then this produces not a fall but a rise in profits. These can be used for new investments, and so a new demand for labor compensates that eliminated through mechanization. However, if Marx's overemphasis on labor exploitation in the analysis of the origins of profit and economic development led him to be pessimistic, it also showed how such a vision of the economy could also lead to an over-valuation of the class conflict and its effects.

Naturally, Marx was well aware that the making of a working class as a self-aware historical actor that aimed to change the structure of economy and society, did not only depend on economic factors. In his work – specifically, *The German Ideology*, (1845–6) and *Manifesto of the Communist Party* (1848) both written together with Engels – he frequently discussed, when referring to the working class, the sociocultural and political factors that led a group of individuals in competition between themselves to act collectively (the passage from a "class in itself" to a "class for itself"). These factors included the concentration of people in big factories and big industrial cities, ease of communication, homogenization of living and labor conditions, political and union organization, and the struggle against capitalists. All these features play an important role in the development of class consciousness and solidarity. In addition, in his works of historical analysis (*The Class Struggles in France* and *The XVIII Brumaire of Louis Napoleon*, published in 1850 and 1852 respectively), Marx also seemed aware of more complex differentiations in the class structure and the autonomous influence of culture and politics on the consciousness and action of the social classes. Despite this, he remained convinced that the economic dynamics of capitalist development would inevitably create a progressive polarization between the two basic social classes, capitalists and workers, a growth in the consciousness and organization of the working class, and an overwhelming tendency towards conflict. He also believed, after the fashion of the classical economists, that the mechanisms of the competitive market would inevitably lead to the spread of the capitalist mode of production, reducing differences between countries.

It is therefore possible to see how Marx overestimated the importance of class conflict. This was for two main reasons: First, Marx's pessimistic forecasts about the progress of the economy, which he thought could be established with the precision of the natural sciences, were not justified by subsequent events. Second, the influence of sociocultural and political factors – which Marx considered to be "superstructure" – proved more important than the supposedly deeper "structure" of economic factors. Capitalist economies' capacity to reproduce themselves, even if this involved continuous changes, their capacity to create and distribute wealth and to ensure social mobility did not, in fact, lead to the polarization envisaged by Marx. At the same time, the cultural and political–institutional specificities of different countries had a profound effect on the modalities of the class conflict and therefore on its effects on economic development.

If historicist criticism of political economy, in its efforts to take proper account of institutions, led to theoretical imprecision and historical description, Marxist criticism, for its part, despite its efforts to advance an institutional analysis of the economy, led to an overly rigid theory, where the role of non-economic institutions was greatly reduced. Marx wanted to substitute an economic sociology of capitalism for classical economics, but his philosophical training pushed him irremediably towards the formulation of laws of historical development that cannot be subjected to scientific control, even if he himself gave them the same value as natural laws. After Marx, the study of classes and conflict – in productive units and society – remained extremely important in the attempt to evaluate economic development and its differences across space. However, the next phase of economic sociology developed an orientation that was more sensitive to the interdependence between economic and social phenomena, and gave wider autonomy to cultural and political institutions in influencing class conflict and economic organization.

6   The "Marginalist Revolution"

For classical economists – and in particular for Smith – the analysis of the economy was scarcely differentiated from that of the institutions regulating its functioning. However, Malthus and Ricardo had already commenced what has here been described as the economistic turn. With this, economic analysis and the analysis of institutions became more clearly separated. Both Marx and the historicists reacted to this tendency, although in different ways. Their criticisms focused attention on the role of institutions and emphasized the need to locate economic investigation historically, which however led to serious analytical problems. Over the last few decades of the nineteenth century a different definition of the relations between the analysis of the economy and institutions began to take shape. It was through what has been called the "marginalist revolution" that neoclassical economics became more clearly and rigorously distinct from the study of institutions. In doing so, it cast off its explicit links with any specific historical context and took up a more general and ahistorical perspective. At the same time, the study of the relationship between institutions and economic activities itself became a more distinct and specialized field of enquiry. Indeed, it became the basis of an analytical and disciplinary perspective that was more precise and definite: that of economic sociology.

During the early 1870s, several important works on economic thought were published. The British economist Stanley Jevons (1871), the Austrian Carl Menger (1871) and the French Léon Walras (1874) are generally seen as having established the basis for the "marginalist revolution" and for neoclassical economics. Working independently of each other, these three authors all reached similar conclusions, calling several features of the classical approach to economics into question. While a detailed discussion of these points – especially their work on value theory – is beyond the scope of this book, it is interesting to note certain crucial implications of their arguments for the analysis of institutional factors, and the resulting process of differentiation between economics and economic sociology.

The fundamental question posed by neoclassical economists can be summed up in Jevons's formulation (quoted by Blaug 1968, p. 274) "Given, a certain population with various needs and powers of production, in possession of certain lands and other sources of material: required, the mode of employing their labour which will maximize the utility of the produce." As can be seen, this formulation was far removed from the investigation into the causes of the wealth of nations. The distancing of economics from its original classical perspective had three important consequences: (a) static analysis was preferred to dynamic analysis; (b) the prevalent approach was normative and deductive, rather than descriptive and interpretative; (c) institutional variables were excluded from the explanatory picture.

The first important implication is that economic development was replaced by the efficient allocation of given resources with respect to given ends, as the main preoccupation of economics. The analytical perspective now adopted thus became static. We know that the main problem considered by the classics was the growth of resources. The historicists and Marx criticized this perspective, reaching different conclusions, but only because they believed that the economists did not adequately situate their analysis within time and space. In abandoning the dynamic perspective, the neoclassicals left this kind of criticism behind. They no longer described or interpreted a particular form of historical organization, but wanted to explore the most efficient way of allocating resources, given certain conditions, *in general terms*.

This takes us on to the second consequence. Economics became a science of choice. In other words, as Lionel Robbins (1932, p. 15) puts it "Economics is the science which studies human behaviour as a relation between ends and scarce means which have alternative uses." Economizing – choice over the most efficient allocation of scarce resources – came to be the core assumption of economic research. This, however, implied, in turn, a deductive analytical orientation. Specific objectives on the part of actors (maximization of interest or utility) were postulated, as were conditions constraining action (the perfect competitive market), from which particular results were determined (economic equilibrium). These features were the consequence of the normative turn taken by economic discourse (Parsons 1934). Economics showed which allocation of resources would be most efficient if people were to behave in a certain way and acted according to certain rules of the game. Only to the extent that such conditions came close to those existing in historical–empirical situations could economic research explain an actual situation, and move beyond the merely normative analysis.

These implied a third consequence – economics no longer referred to institutional variables. The units of analysis were isolated individuals who developed their own aims independently of others and tried to maximize the resources available in conditions of perfect competition. This implied that:

(a)   The aims of single actors were given, in the form of a stable hierarchy of preferences over consumption and labor. Economics did not examine the origin of these preferences, seeing them as an exogenous input into the functioning of the economic machine;

(b)   The means, that is, the available resources (in terms of natural resources, technologies, capital, and labor) were also treated as given. Again, their specific location in space and time (the problem of economic development), and their distribution between different actors, were tied to institutional factors that were not taken into consideration by the economic perspective, which was now static;

(c)   Individual actors could maximize utility according to their preferences through exchanging resources in the different markets (of goods and factors). Their behavior was thus influenced exclusively by the rational individual calculation of means *vis-à-vis* ends, disregarding factors dependent on the institutional context.

Why were institutions excluded from the analytical picture? The reason for this was simple, and was clearly set out by Carl Menger (1882). If institutional variables had been brought into the picture, it would have been impossible a priori to maintain the degree of regularity and predictability in actors' behavior that neoclassical economics needed to formulate models describing the functioning of the market economy. In order to deal with these problems, one had to assume stable and uniform behavior on the part of actors, which in turn permitted deductive reasoning about the consequences of such behavior. In contrast, if one wished to evaluate the influence of social factors on the economic behavior of individual actors, one had to take an inductive view, starting from experience (how actors really behaved) in order to arrive at empirical generalizations and specified causal relations between the phenomena studied. Inevitably, however, this required one to accept a greater variety in behavior, which was not compatible with the analytical perspective of economics. Economic analysis and the study of institutions thus had to be separated from each other.

This break with the classics meant that economics retreated from the thickets of institutions, so as to conform to the canonical rules of theoretical generalization and analytical precision found in the more established – physical and natural – sciences, which increasingly fascinated economists. As a result, economics increasingly tended to involve the application of mathematical theory. This made it easier to quantify economic phenomena, even though it led to the exclusion of factors and problems which were less easy to formalize, and thus reinforced the analytical–deductive orientation of the discipline.

To what extent did neoclassical economists manage to approximate the standards of rigor of the more established sciences? They could only do so under very restrictive conditions. By supposing that competitive market conditions existed, they explicitly limited the theoretical model's applicability, so that it only applied to situations in which the production and distribution of goods took place exclusively through market exchange, without the influence of other institutional factors. However, we also know that on the historical level it is difficult to find situations that fully satisfy these conditions. As a result, there was a gap between the *analytical validity* and *empirical applicability* of the model, on which the criticism of neoclassical economy was traditionally centered. Neoclassical economists were aware of this, and they answered the criticism of abstractness in two ways. The first, clearly exemplified by the positions of Carl Menger (1882) and Vilfredo Pareto (1916), emphasized the analytical–abstract bent of economic investigation and delegated to other specific disciplines (sociology) the study of the influence of institutions on the economy. The second answer, presented in the influential work of the British economist Alfred Marshall (1890), rejected a restrictive conception of the boundaries of economics. His position was more in line with the classical tradition – with the arguments of Smith and John Stuart Mill – and he sought to defend the empirical validity of economic knowledge, and not only its analytical validity. To this end, he continued to refer to institutional factors within his analytic framework, and thus tended to include economic sociology within economics, renouncing the pretensions of neo-classical economics to a high level of generalization.

7   Why Economic Sociology Came into Being in Germany

The above discussion helps us clarify why neoclassical economics, by rejecting the analysis of institutions, left greater space to sociology. But in what context did this space begin to be filled? Where did economic sociology come into being as an autonomous reflection on the relations between economy and society? Up to this point, we have reconstructed the elements of this perspective insofar as they were located within *economic* thought. Between the end of the nineteenth century however, and the beginning of the new century, economic sociology began to free itself of the economics and to take on a specific profile within sociology. This happened mainly in Germany, in the work of Max Weber and Werner Sombart. The location of this new development was not accidental.

The German intellectual context was very different to those of Britain and France. In Britain, for example, there was a strong economic and evolutionist tradition in sociology influenced by the work of Herbert Spencer (1877–96). The French context was instead marked by the influence of Auguste Comte's (1830–42) positivism on the infant field of sociology. In both cases, sociology came into being as a separate science with a strong positivist underpinning. In other words, it sought to apply the methods of the natural sciences to the study of social phenomena, with the aim of discovering the laws governing the general functioning of society. The tendency towards general theory – towards a synthetic science of society – discouraged the affirmation of economic sociology as a specific and independent area of study.

The sociocultural context of Germany was, however, very different. It was strongly influenced by idealistic philosophy, which, on the one hand, oriented the economic tradition towards historicism, and, on the other, distanced sociology from British and French positivism, and thus from the search for the general laws of society. Above all, one must acknowledge the vital role played by Max Weber (1864–1920), in providing a methodological foundation to economic sociology as an independent discipline. At the beginning of the 1900s, he systematically engaged with two main interlocutors – economic historicism and the German idealistic philosophy – in numerous essays (1903–6; 1904).

Weber was very well aware of the necessity of developing a theoretical interpretation that would be more precise and rigorous than that of the historicists, but this did not lead him to seek the general laws of society in accordance with Comte and Spencer's positive sociology. On this point, he agreed with the German philosophical critique of sociology. According to this latter view, people, as conscious beings, forged social institutions and modified them continually through cultural development. It was thus not possible to construct generalizations that predicted the course of human action, because this did not have the regular or uniform features that characterized natural phenomena. However, neither did this mean that it was not possible to carry out the scientific study of social phenomena. For Weber, a scholar of society, like one of nature, should work with concepts, generalizations and abstractions, because this is indispensable to any knowledge. And the historian who seeks only to describe a particular empirical reality inevitably uses theoretical schemes of explanation, even if these are often only implicit,

unrigorous, or even questionable, as in economic historicism. There was, however, one particular aspect of the social sciences that Weber emphasized. He believed that their objective was not to formulate general laws, but to explain historical
phenomena. In other words, the validity of sociological generalizations and causal
explanations of sociology were inevitably limited in space and time. In this respect,
a crucial instrument is the construction of *ideal types*. These are conceptual tools
that bring together certain features of historical phenomena in an internally consistent picture, as in the case of the spirit of capitalism and Protestant ethic which
were analyzed in a famous study by Weber. They are based on empirical evidence,
but they are not a mere description of reality. They rather involve "the analytical
accentuation of certain elements of reality" for heuristic reasons. In other words,
the ideal types are useful for the construction of hypotheses on the causal relationships between social phenomena within specific spatial and temporal boundaries
(Weber [1904] 1949, p. 90).

So what, then, in Weber's view, was the relation between sociology and history? The first was oriented towards studying patterns of behavior and their causal
connections, while the second aimed to explain particular phenomena. This did
not mean, however, that the aim of sociology was, as the positivists thought, to
ascertain the general laws of society. Sociological knowledge has its own autonomy
and specificity, but it remains instrumental *vis-à-vis* historical knowledge, seeking
to make history intelligible and to avoid the risks of theoretical vagueness or the
use of ambiguous theoretical terms which had plagued the historicists. This meant
that sociology, to the extent that it studied behavior as being influenced by social
relations, could contribute to more effective knowledge when it examined specific
activities. For example, by means of ideal types, it could seek to evaluate how
economic activity was influenced by shared expectations of behavior that oriented
action, as in the Protestant ethic, or certain sorts of state organization; in other
words the formal or informal norms which constituted the institutions of a given
society.[1]

The twofold rejection of a general positivist sociology and of historicism opened
the way to the affirmation of economic sociology as an independent discipline.
The "social–economic science" or "sociology of economics"[2] took the reciprocal
interaction of economic and sociocultural phenomena as its object of study. It
analyzes phenomena that are "economically relevant" as well as "economically
conditioned" (see Introduction). In this sense, Weber learned from Marx, although
he emphasize the interdependence between economic and social phenomena as
opposed to Marx's economic determinism.

Both Weber and Sombart – who shared the latter's methodological position –
pointed out how economic sociology had taken a different – and in some senses
intermediate – path between historicism and neoclassical theoretical economics.
They took Menger's side in the methodological debate (*Methodenstreit*), where he
opposed the historicists. They believed that analytical economic theory had a legitimate right to exist, but that this should not be confused with its empirical validity. Weber emphasized that the propositions of classical and neo-economic theory
were "ideal types," analytical constructs that took as their starting point the presupposition that economic behavior was determined exclusively by the rational
pursuit of interests. They were useful – like all ideal-typical constructions – in

evaluating and comparing effective behavior. However, Weber repeated that only very rarely, and in a rather approximate fashion, was actual economic behavior actually influenced by such motivations. For this reason, neither Weber nor Sombart were interested in this type of consideration of economic phenomena. They believed that it was instead important to begin a theoretical study on the economy in its sociocultural context, one that could overcome the defects of historicism. This was the reason for their interest in Western capitalism, its origins, functioning, and prospects. Their economic sociology was intended as a theoretical contribution to historical knowledge and it developed as a sociology of modern capitalism. In pursuing this objective, they made a decisive contribution to defining the analytical space of economic sociology.

Chapter 2

The Origins and Developments of Capitalism: Simmel and Sombart

Sombart, Weber, and Simmel were trained in the German school of historicism. However, they were very aware, unlike their teachers, that this school's attention to the influence of institutional variables on the economy now had to be consolidated upon a stronger theoretical base. Unlike the authors of the historical school, the founders of economic sociology believed that it was possible to study relations between economy and society scientifically. This would not aim to formulate general laws of society, as did positivist and organicist sociology, but would be articulated through analytical models of historical phenomena such as capitalism. In other words, it would aim to create forms of generalization that would be limited in space and time, and would both be based on the results of historical research, and orient such research in turn. This is why economic sociology was interested in capitalism as a research problem. In this chapter and the following one, we shall examine the answers that it gave to questions about the origins, features, and development of capitalism. The first work to be analyzed is by Simmel, after which we shall move on to look at the more specific and detailed contributions of Sombart and (in the following chapter) of Weber. These latter were the most important in establishing economic sociology around the turn of the century.

1 Simmel's *Philosophy of Money*

1.1 Philosophy and economic sociology

The Philosophy of Money by Georg Simmel (1858–1918) is complex, written in his characteristically unsystematic style, but rich in sudden and brilliant comments and insights. It was published in 1900 and a new edition was printed in 1907. While the book cannot be called a work of economic sociology, it would equally be wrong to label it as a work of philosophy, as it has often been described. In fact, Simmel's objective was to clarify the genesis and features of modern society, and to evaluate the effects these had on people's lives.

To be sure, this was not sociology as a synthetic science of society, in the sense that the positivists conceived of it (Simmel 1908). For Simmel, society was not a system; nor was it an organism constituted of various parts linked through their functions. It was instead a set of institutions that came about through interactions between human beings and, in turn, conditioned their behavior once institutions had been consolidated. Simmel talks of this process in terms of emergence of "pure forms." The aim of sociology was thus to study the origins and characteristics of such forms – in other words, to analyze models of institutionalized behavior (Simmel 1907).

Money was one of these institutions. For Simmel, however, its crucial importance lay in the fact that it played a wide and profound role in the relations between people in modern society. In order to clarify the origins and consequences of the use of money, or of the money economy, it was essential to understand modern society. Weber notes that Simmel tended to identify the "money economy" too closely with "capitalism." However, one could say instead that capitalism, for Simmel, was a specific economic system for the production and distribution of goods that was consequent on the monetary economy, so that he took it for granted and paid attention to the instituional prerequisites of capitalism. Even so, the investigation of the non-economic causes of the money economy and its social consequences had much in common with the sociology of capitalism developed by Sombart and Weber. And it is in this sense that it is relevant for our purposes.

The similarities between the three German sociologists are particularly clear on the methodological level; a confrontation with the ideas of Marx permeates *The Philosophy of Money*, just as it does the work of Sombart and Weber. Four points of similarity may be emphasized:

(a)   They emphasized the cultural and institutional assumptions underlying the money economy and, therefore, capitalism;
(b)   Simmel and Sombart recognized the crucial role played by several groups of actors (foreigners, Jews) in the diffusion of the money economy as a result of their social marginalization. Weber focused more on the role of protestant entrepreneurs;
(c)   They agreed on the social consequences of the money economy, such as the increasing depersonalization and rationalization of social relations and life paths;
(d)   Finally, all of them saw socialism – contrary to Marx – as a further step towards a more pronounced economic and political bureaucratization.

Already in the *Preface* to the *Philosophy of Money* (1907), Simmel clarified his intention of integrating Marx's interpretation, using a formulation that was very similar to the one used a few years later by Weber, in sketching out a scientific program for economic sociology (see Introduction): "Every interpretation of an ideal structure by means of an economic structure must lead to the demand that the latter in turn be understood from more ideal depths, while for these depths themselves the general economic base has to be sought, and so on indefinitely" ([1907] 1978, p. 56). It should be noted that Simmel's position, like Weber's, recognized an autonomous analytical space for political economy. This space was not, however, exclusive, because every economic exchange could not only be analyzed through economic instruments, but could also be treated through an analysis that "examines its preconditions in non-economic concepts and facts and its consequences for non-economic values and relationships" ([1907] 1978, p. 55).

1.2   The non-economic conditions of money

Indeed, it was just such an analysis that Simmel carried out. What, then, were the "non-economic assumptions" of money and the money economy? Even if Simmel did not reason in a systematic fashion, we can say that he saw capitalism as an economic system that presupposed the private accumulation of capital. This, in turn, required that money be used in a more widespread way as an instrument of exchange, leading to a widening of the circle of actors involved in the money economy. However, in order for money to be a driving force for economic activities, one basic non-economic condition had to be present – a growing trust in the capacity of money to be converted at any time into concrete goods: "Without the general trust that people have in each other society in itself would disintegrate . . . In the same way, money transactions would collapse without trust" ([1907] 1978, pp. 178–9). The accumulation of capital thus presupposed an accumulation in trust and this cultural condition was, in its turn, supported by institutional factors: the legitimization and efficacy of political power and the guarantees provided by the legal order. In this sense, money became a "public institution" ([1907] 1978, p. 172).

However, it should be noted that a relationship of interdependence was established between the money economy, on the one hand, and the centralized state and judicial system on the other. The former grew thanks to the guarantees provided by the latter, but the latter were reinforced in their turn by the consequences of the diffusion of money as a means of exchange. As for this point, Simmel also underlined that the money economy was a powerful factor in the dissolution of the "natural economy" based on auto-consumption. In this way it promoted the formation of a centralized state, which would carry out the fundamental function of controlling money. The modern state could thus also grow through the developing of taxation, which allowed the bureaucracy and military to be maintained, subject to a central power. These instruments would contribute, in turn, to the weakening of the old feudal system and the strengthening of the money economy, guaranteeing the developing of exchanges.

These, then, were the institutional conditions favoring the money economy, and thus capitalism. But who were the protagonists of the diffusion of money and exchange? Here, Simmel presented a hypothesis that would be further developed by Sombart. He believed that the individuals and social groups who were excluded from fully enjoying the rights in force in a particular society would devote themselves more readily to the accumulation of money in order to attain social positions that they were unable to reach through traditional means. In addition, the social and legal sanctions that normally discouraged members of a traditional society based on a "natural economy" from using money did not hold for these actors (a typical example of this was the hostility of the Church towards usury). Some good examples of socially marginalized groups involved in commercial and financial activities were foreigners and Jews, although Simmel also mentioned the *Moriscos* in Spain, the pariahs in India, and the Quakers in Britain.

Foreigners and socially excluded groups introduced the phenomenon of money and the money economy into traditional society and were, therefore, the principal agents of change preparing the way for the development of capitalism. It should, however, be noted that Simmel did not deal with the specific problem of the origins of capitalist entrepreneurialism, unlike Sombart and Weber, who discussed this in detail. He seemed more interested in the conditions that permitted the pursuit of this activity, which is to say the accumulation of capital on the one hand, and the dissolution of the natural economy on the other.

1.3   The consequences of the money economy

Simmel's prevailing interest was to examine the consequences of the money economy for social relations and ways of life. He highlighted the ambivalence of these effects, discussing both their positive and negative aspects.

Thus, money favored the growth of individual liberty, because it made social relationships in the spheres of exchange and production interchangeable. In production, it was possible to choose among various suppliers, which depersonalized relations between buyers and sellers, and made both more independent. Moreover, there was not only greater freedom in the choice of economic partners, but also greater choice of objects, breaking the ritualism and fixity of traditional forms of consumption. As a result, there was an increased freedom with regard to objects too.

This change was also felt in the sphere of production, where the dependence of the vassal on his lord, or of the apprentice on his master in a medieval guild gave way to a specific and explicit labour contract. These depersonalized relationships and linked them to the pursuit of a limited objective, which did not include the world outside work, and most importantly made each party interchangeable (even if Simmel acknowledged that waged labor enjoyed rather less of this liberty). It was clear then that this might lead to worse remuneration and working life than in the medieval natural economy, in which lords were obliged to protect their serfs, but this might be considered to be the necessary price of freedom: "the worker pays the price, in the form of the instability of money wages, for the freedom made possible by the introduction of money wages" ([1907] 1978, p. 338).

In other words money increased individual liberty. However, it increasingly became transformed from a means to reach specific aims, into a goal in its own right. As the money economy began to condition individual behavior more and more, people lost ever more control over their goals, as money reshaped social organization. Thus, for example, even while economic development favored the growth of science and technology, these latter acquired value as ends, independently of the capacity of people to verify the effective quality of the needs that they were now able to satisfy. Thus, not only did means tend to turn into ends, but there was an attenuation of the quality of social relations in everyday life. In other words, individual freedom led to an increased depersonalizing of relationships. Rationalization and calculation became diffused into all areas of life, so that calculability became "the essence of modern times." The ways in which time and space were used were increasingly shaped to the needs of the money economy, which, like a powerful corrosive, dissolved age-old traditions of solidarity: qualitative values became quantitative ones. People acquired more individual liberty in this process, but also found themselves more isolated, and less capable of defining their collective goals. Later, in his descriptions of men living in the metropolis, the true prototype of modernity, Simmel wrote: "The individual has become a mere cog in an enormous organization of things and powers which tear from his hands all progress, spirituality and value . . ." (Simmel [1903] 1950, p. 422).

Simmel did not believe that socialism would remedy the consequences of the monetary economy, which had ever more come to permeate modern society. For him, socialism was, in large part a reaction to the loss of old collective traditional ties, and an attempt to construct a new collective solidarity. However, such a reaction, were it eventually to be successful, paradoxically seemed destined to tighten the stranglehold of rationalization and the calculability of social relations that had been imposed on human beings. Indeed, it would lead to the increased bureaucratization of "state socialism" – very far removed from the new solidarity that socialism aimed to create.

2 Sombart's *Modern Capitalism*

While Simmel's recourse to the sociology of economic life was a consequence of his wider philosophical interest in the condition of human beings in modern society, Sombart instead had the objective of consciously constructing an economic sociology. The first edition of *Modern Capitalism* was published in 1902. This was followed by a second edition in 1916, which was completely revised, and a third, and last, edition of the work, including a section on full capitalism, which came out in 1928. In the Preface to the second edition, Sombart underlined that his analytical perspective "is aimed at inserting economic life into the great context of human social existence " (Sombart [1916] 1922, p. xv). In order to do so, he believed that it was necessary to move beyond the debate between neoclassical political economy and historicism, that is, between the "abstract–theoretical" school and the "empirical–historical" school. The new "social science of economic life" thus had theoretical objectives, and sought to contribute to the scientific explanation of economic phenomena. However, it set out to do this within a historical framework, establishing well-defined spatial and temporal boundaries. Economic sociology was linked to history, because historical research served in the formulation of theoretical generalizations, which in its own turn could orient historical research and empirical verification. Thus it can be said that, for Sombart, there could be no history without theory (Sombart 1929). In order to understand how society influenced economic behavior through its institutions, it was necessary to use the appropriate analytical instruments. One had to have conceptual tools that allowed, for example, to distinguish the functioning of the capitalist economy from other kinds of economic organization, and more precisely to capture the differences between diverse economic systems.

Much of Sombart's work was dedicated to creating such tools, both in *Modern Capitalism* and his other essays.

2.1 Conceptual tools for economic sociology

For Sombart, economics was "the human activity aimed at researching means of subsistence" ([1916] 1922, p. 13). Like all other living creatures, human beings had to satisfy their needs through the products they obtained from nature through labor. Their needs varied over time, and new "cultural" needs came to be added to those tied up in physical survival. However, in any case, meeting these needs always involved the production of goods and services that could be distributed and consumed according to shared rules. This was what was meant by the economic activity that men have always carried out, even if "the forms of economic life differ deeply in time and space" ([1916] 1922, p. 13).

This conception of economics was different from that adopted by neoclassical economics, which identified it instead with economizing and which hypothesized the existence of actors rationally pursuing their interests in the context of the market. However, a framework of this kind was not necessary to the satisfaction of needs through the production and distribution of goods and services. It was difficult, for example, to explain primitive and precapitalist economies in this framework. Sombart's definition – which was actually typical of economic sociology[1] – allowed for a more wide-ranging of the differences that characterize economic behavior, and the organization of activities aimed at providing human subsistence, over space and time.

Here, we need to consider three features of economic systems:

(a) *economic mentality* or *economic spirit*, that is to say, the set of values and norms orienting the behavior of individuals participating in economic activity, i.e. economic actors;
(b) *economic organization*, which refers to the set of formal and informal norms regulating the exercise of economic activity by actors within a particular society;
(c) *technology*, lastly, involves the technical knowledge and procedures used by actors to produce goods and services and to satisfy their needs.

These three features vary over space and time. Together, they allow an *economic system* to be identified, or rather "a particular form of economy, i.e. a particular organization of economic life in which a particular economic mentality is prevailing and a particular technique is applied" ([1916] 1922, p. 22). The concept of economic system allows us to build a bridge between economy and society, by allowing us to evaluate how society has historically influenced economic organization through the motivation of actors, regulatory institutions, and institutions affecting the production and use of scientific knowledge and technology. In this way, Sombart commented, "in the concept of economic system is the historically conditioned nature of economic life " ([1916] 1922, p. 22).

Let us now examine how these conceptual instruments may be applied, by comparing, for example, the precapitalist and capitalist economies, using the three constitutive features of systems mentioned above. First, as regards economic spirit,

Sombart distinguished between an orientation to *subsistence* and an alternative *acquisitive* orientation. In the former, economic behavior was basically aimed at satisfying natural and cultural needs (these two phenomena being defined in a stable and rigid way for different social groups on the basis of tradition), and production was mainly aimed at consumption. The affirmation of the acquisitive principle instead implied that economic activity should be directed by the search for greater monetary gains,[2] and be aimed for the most part at the market. Another important difference lay in the contrast between the *traditionalist* spirit – based on passive obedience to received rules – and the *rationalist* spirit, which searched systematically for the most appropriate means to fulfill goals. As a result, it was more open to innovation in economic behavior and new techniques. Finally, economic mentality could be either *solidaristic* or, instead, more *individualistic* in its orientation.

As regards organization, Sombart considered various aspects, the most important being the contrast between, on the one hand, *binding economic activities*, which were tied to norms regulating their operation (a good example of this was the corporatist order of medieval society), and, on the other the existence of a wide sphere of *economic freedoms* which were legally recognized. Other important factors were *private* or *public ownership* of the means of production, the orientation of production towards either *consumption* or *market exchange*, and firm organization based on the *small family firm*, or on *large firms* with waged labor.

Technology also showed differentiated features: it could be based on *empirical* procedures, which were founded on received knowledge and accepted passively, or on *scientific* procedures, which allowed for the scientific explanation of phenomena and the rational application of knowledge.

Linking all the different dimensions together, capitalist economies can be defined and distinguished from the feudal–artisan economies that existed before them. The *capitalist economic system* was characterized by an acquisitive, rationalistic and individualistic mentality, which developed together with the free economic organization based on the private ownership of the means of production and on firms producing goods for the market using waged labor. Sombart distinguished between this system and two other types – the direct economy, in the dual form of the direct peasant economy and of the landowner, and the artisan economy.

Three periods were identified in each system: *rise, maturity*, and *decline*. This meant that, particularly at the beginning, one system coexisted with others in a transitional phase. An *economic age* was a historical period in which a particular economic system dominated. As for capitalism itself, Sombart considered the first phase, that of *first capitalism*, to have ended around the end of the eighteenth century, while the successive period of *full capitalism* predominated over the whole of the nineteenth century, concluding with the First World War. In the years following this, greater elements of *organization* began to emerge, and, according to Sombart, attentuated the original capitalist features of the economy.

2.2   The origins of capitalism

How does one economic system change to another? Sombart tried to answer this question clearly (particularly in chapter one of the third edition), and in doing so, he distanced himself from both historicism and Marxism. In line with his meth-odological views, he presented a historically delimited theoretical response. His argument did not, that is, refer to economic changes in general, but to the birth of the first form of capitalism, and how it developed towards full capitalism.

It was impossible, in Sombart's view, to analyze capitalist development using a general concept of a people's culture, as the historicists did, without taking ac-count of the motivations guiding economic actors, and especially entrepreneurs. For its part, Marxism had adopted an economistic approach that led it to discount the role of entrepreneurs *vis-à-vis* the weight assigned to the accumulation of capi-tal and technology in the area of productive forces. To put it more precisely, Sombart rejected methodological holism and instead sought to explain economic change in the framework of methodological individualism. He attempted, that is, to describe the process of change from the starting point of the specific motivations of actors and the consequences of their actions.

The "activating forces" of development were to be sought in those actors who introduced a new economic outlook (and thus changes in the way that productive factors were combined and the economy organized) into the old system. It was entrepreneurs who triggered economic change. Their behavior was certainly in-fluenced by the institutions operating in a certain society, such as the state, the legal system, religious persuasions, the prevailing culture, scientific and technical knowledge, etc. However, once a new economic spirit formed under the influence of these factors, entrepreneurs – who were the propagators of this spirit – intro-duced important innovations. Initially, these were limited, because only a few actors were involved and because their actions did not succeed in affecting the old economic system in any profound way. In time, however, the new economic men-tality would spread and led to a change in the institutions.

How did entrepreneurship come about? Sombart felt that two factors had to be analyzed in order to answer this question. First, the economic spirit of capitalism needed to be better defined; then, the social conditions favoring the diffusion of the kind of enterprise fueled by such spirit needed to be ascertained.

The capitalist spirit

For Sombart, the capitalist mentality involved two, quite distinct components. "We call capitalist spirit the feeling resulting from the fusion of the spirit of enterprise and the bourgeois spirit" ([1916] 1922, p. 329). The spirit of enterprise was, thus, an "aspiration to power" where this was understood as a desire for affirmation and social recognition that pushed men to break with tradition and search for new paths. As Sombart put it, This is "the spirit of Faust," deeply rooted in the soul of Western man. It is certainly true that its origins can be found in the spiritual his-tory of the West, and in Christianity. However, Sombart also emphasized how the progressive secularization of society, which could be seen in its "earthly and worldly" features, was manifested in Western man's autonomy from tradition and from the controlling power of religion in ever wider spheres of activity. This process first became manifest in the political sphere, where it was visible in the building of the modern state, and in the advance of scientific knowledge, with its technical appli-cations. Only later did the spirit of enterprise become extended to the economy in the sense that the quest for earnings was no longer limited, as in the past, to conquest, adventure, or the search for precious metals. Instead, it was carried forward systematically within economic life itself, in the organization of productive activities. It was at this stage that the first component began to emerge, which we may define as *political entrepreneurship*. The actors involved in this were those "who use the power deriving from the position of privilege within the state" ([1916] 1922, p. 839), and they included princes, state functionaries, and property owners. They were clearly typical of the mercantilist form of political organization, where enterprise was more dependent on political power.

However, before the spirit of enterprise could fully be extended to the economy, and give birth to the capitalist economy, it had to merge with the bourgeois spirit. Acquisitiveness, the search for gain in the economy, would have to be combined with rationalism, with an orientation towards the "orderly administration of capital," made of "diligence, moderation, parsimony, economy, and faith in contracts" ([1916] 1922, p. 329). Sombart found traces of this mentality existing already in the *Libri della famiglia*, written around 1450 by Leon Battista Alberti, an architect from a rich Florentine merchant family. It was expressed even more clearly in the eighteenth-century writings of Benjamin Franklin, to which Weber too referred.

The origins of these cultural features were, for Sombart, strictly related to the matrix of Christian religions (Jewish as well as Catholic and Protestant). They took form for the most part in European cities, and were closely tied to the events taking place in the communes and social groups that developed in such areas, that is, among merchants and artisans. It was in this setting that so-called *bourgeois entrepreneurship*, made up of "all those who come from below," first became wedded to an entrepreneurialism that stemmed from politics, and then went on to dominate the organization of economic life over the course of the nineteenth century, during the epoch of full capitalism.

The formation of entrepreneurship

One of the most important vehicles for the development of capitalist enterprise was thus bourgeois entrepreneurialism. However, Sombart held that the matrix of Christianity and the urban setting were insufficient conditions for its formation. He believed that one had to take account of more specific variables, allowing one to identify the particular groups that had nourished bourgeois enterprise. He paid special attention to three groups: heretics, foreigners, and Jews (the last two of which had already been discussed in Simmel's analysis). Why did the life conditions of these groups favor the creation of entrepreneurship?

By *heretics*, Sombart referred to those individuals who did not belong to the state religion. Along with the creation of the modern state and the Protestant Reformation, the political and social category of the heretic and the heterodox – that is, those who did not belong to the religion promulgated (either legally or *de facto*) by the state – came into being. The most significant of these groups was, of course, the Jews, who had settled all over Europe; there were also Protestants who lived in Catholic countries, Catholics living in Protestant countries, and Protestants who did not belong to the state Church. Those who did not belong to the prevailing religion were only semi-citizens, either formally or *de facto*. They found it difficult to attain public office, or other forms of public and social recognition, and indeed were sometimes explicitly precluded from these forms of status. This stimulated entrepreneurialism, because "heretics, which were excluded from the participation in public life, could express their own vital strength only in economic activities. Only these gave them the possibility to get the prominent status within the community, which the state denied them" ([1916] 1922, p. 878).

Heretics also stimulated entrepreneurialism in another way, that is, through migration, which led to the creation of another social category, that of *foreigners*. Of course, not all migrations had religious motivations, but in general migration had important consequences for entrepreneurialism, for three main reasons. First, because migration involved selection, in which those who chose to leave were the most enterprising, determined, and courageous. Second, these individuals, when they had become foreigners in another country than that where they had come from, were more likely to break with old customs and traditional social relations. Finally, because they had very limited possibilities of social mobility except through economic activity: "both for the migrants and the colonists there is no past, no present, there is *only the future* . . . it seems almost natural that profit is the only important thing left for them, the only means to build their future" ([1916] 1922, p. 886).

Finally, there were the Jews. According to Sombart, they were particularly important for the development of capitalism, especially through their entrepreneurialism in the spheres of commerce and credit. It was these activities, in particular, that explain why Jews remained foreigners in the different countries that they had spread to across the world. Their social marginalization was moreover reinforced by their tendency – deriving from their religious identity – to isolate themselves and to avoid identifying with any particular nation, maintaining international ties with the rest of the Jewish community. However, this factor favored, in turn, their entrepreneurial bent and success, because it nurtured relationships of trust that facilitated economic activity on the international market.

The model of capitalist development

Sombart therefore emphasized entrepreneurialism in his explanation of capitalist development. In his view this involved a certain economic mentality, nurtured by the Christian religion and the Western city, and stimulated in a particular direction by the social marginalization of certain social groups. However, the German sociologist's explanation of capitalist development was not exclusively cultural. The capitalist mentality became established in close interdependence with a set of institutional factors that contributed to its formation and were themselves conditioned by it. In this sense, it can be said that for Sombart, entrepreneurs were a catalytic element – they "light the fuse " of capitalist development ([1916] 1922, p. 867).

1   Sombart, like Simmel, believed that the contribution of the state was essential. The spirit of Western enterprise was expressed, above all, in the construction of the modern state. The state in its turn stimulated technological development, which was essential for military efficiency, and thus for its reinforcing. The policy of con-

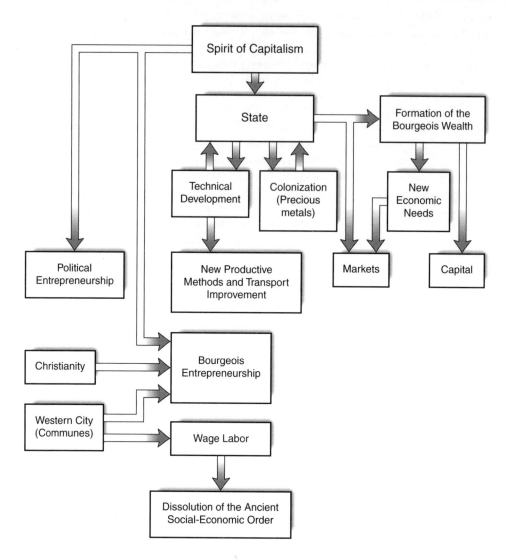

Figure 2.1   *Sombart's model of capitalist development*

quest and colonial enterprise, and the mercantilist approach more generally, were linked to the struggle for supremacy among the various states. The objective was to increase stocks of precious metals, since this would provide more resources for public finances and thus military power.

2   The interdependence that arose between state, technical development and the policy of acquiring precious metals, had both *direct* and *indirect* effects on capitalist development. The most important direct effects involved (a) the state's influence on a politically rooted entrepreneurialism through mercantilist policies (tariff protection, colonial policies, etc.). It also, however, affected entrepreneurialism from

below. In particular, it helped create the social situation of heretics – who had no part in the state religion – and through their migration fostered the entrepreneurialism of the foreigners. Moreover, through its military procurement, the state enlarged the nascent market for manufactured goods. (b) The new, rational technology, based on the advancing of scientific knowledge, was important for capitalist development above all because it favored the growth of industry and improved the transportability of goods. (c) The policies of colonization and conquest, which increased the availability of precious metals, favored the growth of consumption and the spread of the market.

The *indirect* influences of the construction of the state were above all seen in the formation of bourgeois wealth: (a) The interdependence between the state, technology and the influx of precious metals fed the formation of private capital, an essential requirement for development. According to Sombart, mercantilism favored the accumulation of capital. However, he emphasized too how this process had measurable consequences for the growth of land rents, which was sustained by landowners' more entrepreneurial orientation. (b) In addition, the formation of bourgeois wealth led to new needs, especially among the richer social strata. This led to the expansion of the market, because private demand for goods was added to that of the state.

3   However, the decisive factor that allowed capital, the market and new technologies of transport and production to be exploited was, in Sombart's opinion, entrepreneurship. The state contributed to this, as we have already seen, through mercantilism and political entrepreneurship, but the encounter between the spirit of enterprise and the bourgeois spirit, which manifested itself in a more specifically capitalistic entrepreneurialism from below, was decisive. The bourgeois spirit originated independent of the state. It formed under the cultural influence of Christian religion and the particular environment of the European city, as marked in the experience of the communes. The state entered into this process insofar as it contributed to creating the conditions to exclude certain groups from citizen rights, which in turn made heretics, foreigners, and Jews more sensitive than other groups to the capitalist mentality and to the bourgeois spirit in particular.

4   Once bourgeois enterprise had lit the fuse of capitalist development, it led to *the wide-scale dissolution of the ancient social order*. Sombart discussed the dissolution of traditional forms of agricultural economy, and of domestic work in the countryside and in craft activities: "The dissolution was the consequence of the penetration of modern rational economic principles into the legislation, the administration and economic management, and of the growing intensification of the economic activities, which is very important for agriculture" ([1916] 1922, p. 331). These economic and political changes resulted in the proletarianization of agricultural labor and a crisis in the organization of artisanal activities, freeing the work force for a nascent modern industrial sector. Peasants, in particular, were progressively deprived of the opportunity both to exploit common land (of their rights over common property), and to earn a supplementary income from rural and domestic industry. The circle thus closed and the new bourgeois capitalism could combine capital and labor with new technology to produce goods for an ever-expanding market.

5   Over time, capitalist development contributed to *changes in the legal and state-political order*. During the transition from the precapitalist economy to the first stage of capitalism, mercantilism and political regulation had played an important part. The next phase saw an increased push towards a liberal state orientation in economics, and the recognition of a wider sphere of economic liberty in which firms could operate, as capitalist entrepreneurialism became more established. Moreover, the security of the economic process grew, both through the enforcement action of the state, which underpinned the security of economic traffic, and through the introduction of a rational monetary system, which facilitated exchange. Thus, full capitalism became established in the nineteenth century.

2.3   Full capitalism

In the third edition of his work, Sombart described the changes that took place during the phase of full maturity of capitalism, which ended with the First World War. These were all linked to the growing rationalization of economic life, which manifested itself in the tendency to seek and apply the best-adapted means of pursuing the profit of the firm. This principle had an ever more decisive effect on the production, distribution, and consumption of goods. It is possible to evaluate the effects of rationalization by considering the various components of the economic system.

The capitalist spirit

First, Sombart highlighted the growth in intensity of the capitalist spirit, and its extension to wider social groups and new geographical areas. He believed that this was due both to internal change and external factors. The entrepreneurial mentality saw an ideological transformation that led to the *secularization of the capitalist spirit*. The religious motivations that had supported the behavior of entrepreneurs gave way to a more secular creed: "At this point faith has become only a matter of Sunday mornings," it is replaced by "a modern bourgeois-capitalist concept of duty"(1928, vol. III, p. 27) which affirmed work and productivity as the primary sources of economic well-being and social recognition. Thus, a "love for one's own activity" developed, narrowing entrepreneurs' range of activities outside work (for example, art, politics, friendships, etc.) and thus a more intense channeling of vital energies into economic activity than in the past. These energies were by the same token less restricted by the religious factors that had sustained them in the past.

The intensifying of commitment was also a result of external factors. Amongst these was the push towards *a greater specialization of the entrepreneurial function*, that involved the delegation of a series of tasks, that had originally been relatively undifferentiated, to employees, allowing the entrepreneur to concentrate his efforts on various strategic functions of direction. These last varied according to the sector of activity. For example, in the mechanical industry the *technician* prevailed, his success being tied to knowledge of the productive process; in the production of goods of mass consumption the *trader* was extremely important, given his knowledge of and ability to handle the markets; in big, highly capitalized industries, the skills of the *financier*, who knew how to move on the capital markets and how to combine finance and industry, were vital. Naturally, these different types often came in mixed forms, even if Sombart noted that they involved a historical evolution in the direction of the *progressive abstraction of entrepreneurial activities*. It is in the last figure – the financial expert – that this is most strikingly found.

In this way Sombart enabled us to see – even if only implicitly – the important changes involved in the formation of entrepreneurialism. So as to understand the origins of capitalism, he mainly highlighted its normative components, the values that had been important for the first entrepreneurs – that is, the bourgeois spirit, which had found sustenance in its religious surroundings, and had been stimulated by social marginalization. Cognitive components, such as productive and commercial knowledge, while they were important, had been secondary. In the new situation, the balance had tilted in the other direction – specialized cognitive components now fuelled entrepreneurialism, in a setting of unhindered and socially legitimized economic innovation. The result was what can be called a *democratization of entrepreneurialism*. Sombart noted that it was now easier for members of all groups to become entrepreneurs. What counted was having the right sort of knowledge. Credit institutions had played an important role in opening these new opportunities, as they provided the necessary capital to realize good ideas (a theme which Schumpeter treated in greater depth).

Other contextual factors besides secularization and specialization favored the intensification of the capitalist spirit. Some of them were, in fact, negative, and pushed towards greater effort in confronting the new obstacles that obstructed entrepreneurial action. These included the *greater severity of competition* on the goods market, and the *strengthening of the working -class movement*, which affected the labor market. Sombart had a different view of this last problem than the economists. He did not worry about the distortion of the labor market that the workers' movement might lead to, but rather underlined the positive contribution that it might make to economic development in dynamic terms. The trade-union and political claims of the working-class movement not only improved the social integration of workers (thanks also to the new legislation on labor), but pushed entrepreneurs to innovate continually in order to increase productivity and to compensate in this way for the higher costs of labor.

As well as these negative factors, there was a powerful positive stimulus that intensified and extended the capitalist spirit. This involved the effects of the evolution of technology. An ever-increasing rate of technological change continually generated opportunities to change the conditions of competition, because it allowed new goods to be produced or for production to take place at a lower cost. This required constant attention and a greater capacity on the part of entrepreneurs to use technology. It also led to a trend towards the rationalization of technological development, which revealed itself through a greater *institutionalization of applied research and training*, and a growing incorporation of these activities within the firm, and especially the larger firm in which the position of " the professional specialized inventor" was established (1928, vol. III, p. 91).

The organization of the economic system

The intensification of the capitalist spirit and its links to technology led to important changes in the economic system, which, Sombart saw as involving the way in which economic activity was regulated. The strengthening of capitalist enterprise led both indirectly (on the political level) and directly (on the economic level) to a greater rationalization of the mechanism of regulation, enhancing the opportunities for firms to make profits.

One of the first areas to be affected by rationalization was the legal order and state intervention in the economic field. This was already mentioned in the discussion of Sombart's account of the *transition from the mercantilist to the liberal phase,* which was supported by the growing entrepreneurial bourgeoisie. The firm's scope for free action was recognized in the separation between public and private law, the reinforcement of forms of legal protection for contracts, and the introduction of a rational monetary system. It was not only the legal system that was rationalized, however. Other fields, such as labor, consumption and the firm were also rationalized, mainly through the actions of the entrepreneurs themselves. Sombart examined all three aspects, pioneering areas of investigation that would later become important and independent fields in economic sociology.

We have seen that capitalist development created a growing labor supply that fed the industrial firms through migration and urbanization, while breaking up traditional forms of economic organization in the countryside and in craft activities. Sombart pointed out that it was not, in fact, only the lowering of incomes in the countryside and small commercial and artisanal towns that encouraged this exodus, but also the attractiveness of the individual liberty and urban life style offered by large cities. The urbanization of the large industrial cities, and of the metropolises (which had a well developed service and administrative sector as well as industry) ensured an adequate labor force for the new industries.

However, entrepreneurs were faced with a more complex problem. They found that they needed to adapt their workers in cultural and vocational (that is, in technical competencies) terms for factory work. Sombart believed that the Protestant religion helped considerably in this process of adaptation, and retained – in partial disagreement with Weber – that the Protestant creed was more important for workers than for entrepreneurs, because it made the "economic education" of the worker easier, and fostered his commitment to work and discipline. Of course, this was a particular and limited situation, involving a small range of workers in certain countries. Moreover, the influence of religious ideas lessened over time for both workers and entrepreneurs.

Entrepreneurs made recourse to harsh discipline and to economic incentives in their efforts to bring through cultural and vocational adaptation (using, for example, piece-work rates), but above all sought to intervene in the organization of labour and in recruitment. There was limited availability of qualified workers, which led to higher labour costs. "It was necessary to change the whole labor process radically by adapting most of the tasks to the abilities of the large mass " (1928, vol. III, p. 430). This led to the *decomposition of labor.* Complex tasks were broken down into a set of easier tasks that could be done by less skilled workers. Thus the importance of specialized workers was reduced and their role in the productive process changed, while the number of semi-skilled and unskilled workers increased. The apportioning of tasks changed the relationship between workers and machines, attenuating workers'autonomy and ability to influence how work was organized. It was the machine system, typical of the assembly line,[3] that instead conditioned the distribution of competencies through its working procedures. Like Marx, Sombart clearly perceived that the subordination of the worker to the machine was becoming established in large-scale modern industry.

However, all this had advantages for the capitalist firm. It allowed labor costs to be reduced, because the firm could draw on a larger supply of labour; it facilitated the adaptation and training of workers; and finally, it allowed the application of new methods of "scientific organization of labor" based on a more rigid planning of timing and procedures.[4] The "Taylorist" rationalization of labor, as this was called, was quite extensive and came to be extended to recruitment. This now involved more formal procedures aimed at checking the psychological and physical suitability of the worker for the duties he would be expected to do (tests, for example, came to be used on a widespread basis).

Rationalization began to involve not only labor, but also the firm as a whole, with the formulation of a series of prescriptions, involving general rules to which firms usually conformed, so as to enhance the profitability of their structures. The outcome of this process was the *depersonalization of the firm*. Increasingly, firms were organized like *bureaucracies*, with a clear hierarchy of roles and precise procedures governing relations between the different levels and various competencies within the firm. For example, the tasks of planning which were carried out by researchers and engineers were clearly separated from the duties of workers. Citing the automobile-manufacture industrialist, Henry Ford, Sombart noted that personal and "community" factors now had to be limited as much as possible, precisely so as make it easier to plan and predict behavior, and thus allow a greater interchange of individuals between the different roles required in the machine-firm.

Another aspect of internal rationalization involved the *condensation of the firm*. By this, Sombart meant the intensive exploitation of economies of space, materials, and time. What this meant, in practice, was the growing concentration of machines and men within the firm so as to increase the capacity of production. Thus, more capital was invested in machines, but there was a correspondingly greater exploitation of these instruments of production in order to improve yields. Sombart emphasized, as had Marx, the tendency for productive units to increase in size. Large concentrated firms could exploit economies of scale to their fullest extent, producing large quantities of products at a lower cost. This "comes about more easily the more the products of the firm are standardized " (1928, vol. III, p. 919). This occurred to a greater extent in sectors where standardized goods were mass-produced, while smaller firms could still be found in sectors where goods were less standardized, or demand was lower or more variable.

This brings us to the last aspect of rationalization, consumption. In order to reduce uncertainty and to make the productive process more stable, it was necessary for firms not only to rationalize the use of labor and internal organization, but also to influence consumption, controlling the demand for goods in terms both of quantity and quality, and increasing the production of standardized goods that could be produced in series and which allowed the rationalization of the firm to reach its fullest extent. It is in this context that one may analyze the tendency towards the *homogenization of needs*.

Sombart noted that this was, above all, a consequence of economic development. Communication had increased, the urban population had grown, and the consumption possibilities of the intermediate and lower social strata had improved. These changes in turn led to the breaking down of cultural, traditional and ritual barriers, which had previously led to demand being more segmented according to place and social group. In addition, large centers for unified consumption were established. Some of these were administered by the state (for example, the army, hospitals, asylums, prisons, etc.) and some privately, such as the large commercial centers and the large firms themselves in their consumption of goods provided by other sectors.

However, the tendency towards a standardization of needs was also the result of conscious action taken by firms. Fashion was the main instrument that they used towards this end. Without this, a particular good might have had a longer working life, and there would have been a much wider range of use-goods, as was true in the first period of capitalism. In that phase, it had in effect been impossible for firms to control the preferences of consumers, and they had thus been unable to influence them – as economic analysis had underlined. This was also because firms were smaller, and had limited control of the market. In the period of full capitalism the situation changed. Firms tended to become large in order to exploit economies of scale and they now controlled supply to a greater extent, enabling them to "impose" their choices more easily on consumers. Needs, were, however, also influenced indirectly, through the effects of fashion, particularly in the field of non-lasting consumer goods (typically, the clothing industry).

Initially limited to social groups of the upper class, fashion tended to become more generalized and more rapidly diffused under the new life conditions that went along with urbanization. It became ever more important in the quest to receive affirmation and social recognition from other individuals, in a context where older, community ties had become weaker.[5] This offered industry new opportunities, on the one hand accelerating the pace at which new products were introduced (also using new opportunities offered by technology), and on the other standardizing needs and creating a mass market. This last tendency manifested itself through the production of lower-quality goods which imitated the elite versions that fashion demanded, and which were now requested by a larger public of consumers.

The capitalist rationalization of the economy extended and consolidated with the greater standardization of needs and the growth of a standardized mass market. Large bureaucratized firms dominated the landscape of full capitalism. It was under these conditions that this economic system reached the apex of its development. However, it was, according to Sombart, in the actual process of rationalization itself – through which full capitalism had come to dominate – that the seeds which would lead to its decline were sown. They began to bear fruit after the First World War. This was the period that has become known, mainly through the essay by the German sociologist written for the *Encyclopedia of the Social Sciences*, as "late capitalism" (Sombart 1929).

Sombart did not believe that technological development and the growth of fixed capital would lead to a fall in the rate of profit and growing unemployment, as predicted by Marx. The introduction of new technologies increased productivity, which, if it was not eaten up by an increase in wages, would allow profits to increase and be reinvested, which would, in turn, compensate for and absorb the unemployment created by greater mechanization. Sombart thus believed that unemployment was conjunctural, generated by the continual reorganization of productive processes, and that it would not feed the social forces leading to political revolution. Moreover, economic systems based on *planned economies* would increasingly become established, precisely in order to deal with the social problem created by unemployment, and more generally to better the working conditions of the lower social classes. These implied a return to greater state intervention in the economy, a more important role for the cooperative sector and more extended forms of political regulation of the economy, both directly (through public intervention and legislation) and indirectly (through a more active role for union bargaining over working conditions). This led to a *stabilized and regulated capitalism*. For Sombart, the differences between this type of economic system and a *rationalized socialism* were relatively minor. He also believed, like Simmel, Weber, and Schumpeter, that the most important processes were rationalization and bureaucratization. Socialism could only accentuate these tendencies, not suppress them.

These changes would lessen the cyclical fluctuations of the economy and their social consequences in terms of unemployment. In particular, writing at the beginning of the thirties, Sombart clearly perceived the importance that the new economic policy (which would later be dubbed Keynesianism, after the British economist that proposed it) would have on capitalist development. Sombart's analysis thus concluded with an extraordinarily accurate prediction of the future of capitalism.

Chapter 3
Capitalism and the Western Civilization: Max Weber

While Sombart can be seen as an economic sociologist in the strict sense and as one of the founders of the discipline, Max Weber's aims were wider, more complex and more ambitious, taking him across the boundaries of economic sociology into the more general historical sociology of the West. Even though Sombart clearly understood that the origins of capitalist development could be found in the cultural and institutional features of the West, he did not examine them in any great detail. Instead, he concentrated his attention on how they had shaped entrepreneurship and economic development. Moreover, he attempted to analyze economic change, and was in fact able to do so more successfully than his friend and colleague Max Weber, who died twenty years before him. His area of interest was thus the transformation of capitalism in the nineteenth century, and at the beginning of the new century. Weber, in contrast, preferred to look backward rather than forward, given his profound interest in historical phenomena. He wished to shed light on the complex cultural and institutional conditions that were associated with the birth of Western capitalism. Therefore, in his work he connected capitalism to the Western civilization.

1 Research on German Society

As a young man, Max Weber (1864–1920) carried out important research on German society. He mainly focused on the transformation of agriculture and agricultural labor during the first half of the 1890s (Weber 1924a, 1970, 1979). In this same period, he was also asked to work on a governmental committee investigating the stock exchange, the results of which were published in his essay, *The Stock Exchange*, in 1894. These studies were important primarily because they allowed him to begin to reflect systematically on the origins of capitalism. In other words, they allowed him to make the transition from the micro-sociological level, more centered on the German experience, to the macro-sociological research perspective that characterized his later work on Western capitalism (Bendix 1960).

Studying agriculture in Eastern Germany, Weber was especially struck by the tendency of laborers who worked on the great *Junker* estates to renounce their status as tenant farmers – where they were tied to their land – to become waged workers, or even to emigrate. This tendency could not be explained by looking at their strictly economic motives; tenant farmers, generally speaking, enjoyed better conditions than waged workers, and those who emigrated were not leaving areas where there was an oversupply of labor, and lower salaries. Agricultural workers wished rather to free themselves from their stifling bond of dependency with the *Junkers*, notwithstanding the immediate loss of economic security which this would involve.

The behavior of the operators on the German stock exchange, which Weber discussed in his study on *The Stock Exchange*, was likewise inexplicable in the strict utilitarian terms of economic theory. In this case, it was his comparison of the German and British stock exchanges that led him to draw these conclusions. The operators of both exchanges obviously wanted to make as much money as possible, by playing on the differentials between prices. However, British behavior was institutionalized through a particular system that prevented the degeneration into speculation that the stock market made possible. In Great Britain, as in the United States, stock exchanges were clubs which reserved membership solely for professional traders. The club governed itself, and decided the principles of admission in an autonomous fashion. Membership was handed down from one generation to the next, and if it was bought, the price of the deposit was very high indeed. Thus, the stock exchange was an "aristocracy of money" which required the observance of high ethical standards, and had a high level of control over its members. This did not occur in Germany, where the institutional setting and the values influencing actors were extremely different, leading to a greater risk of incorrect behavior. Paradoxically, it was the restricted access to the status of stock exchange operator that favored the British situation, while the less regulated access in Germany led to a situation in which the stock exchange resembled the free market.

Weber's research during the first half of the 1890s raised important theoretical questions about economic sociology, as well as drawing attention to the crucial role that must be attributed to non-economic cultural and institutional conditions in understanding economic behavior. There is a further element worth mentioning. While studying German society, Weber was struck by the problem of territorial differences in economic development – not only those within Germany, but also the contrast between Germany and other countries, especially the Anglo-Saxon ones. We can hypothesize that it was just in the context of this first body of research that Weber's interest in the macro-sociological problem of the origins of capitalism first matured. Confirmation of this can be found in one of his most interesting but little known texts, a paper given at the Congress of Arts and Sciences held in 1904 at St. Louis. In this paper, Weber dealt extensively with the problem of the differences in development within Germany, which he had noticed when studying its agricultural structure. In South and West Germany, there was a clear trend towards small land-holding peasants with diversified crops. Instead, going eastwards, and particularly towards the north-east, larger land holders predominated with extensive crops of wheat, beetroot, and potatoes.

In order to explain these differences, Weber examined the changes that took place at the beginning of the 1800s. When feudal obligations were formally abolished, two distinct paths were taken. In South and West Germany, land ended up in the hands of the peasants, while in the east it remained in the hands of the land holders, who began to run their farms with paid labor. But if we look carefully, we can see that these different outcomes had their origin in a lengthy previous history that had its origins in the mediaeval era. During this period, conditions in the south-west strengthened the position of peasants, so that lords preferred to become absentee landlords, collecting rent from their newly emancipated serfs and various types of revenue from other local trade. In the east, however, this did not occur, and lords remained directly involved in cultivating the land. The question is, however, why were the eastern peasants unable to stimulate the sorts of changes taking place in the south and the west, and which eventually led to small and medium-sized firms?

In Weber's view, the answer to this may be found in the important role of the city in economic development. Urban development was much less extensive in the east than the south and west, which had significant consequences for the paths of development in the two areas. Moreover, cities became important not only because they stimulated the agricultural market, but also because they influenced one of the key factors in development – entrepreneurship.

Weber's observations on this issue however had a very important theoretical implication. If one wanted to study local and regional development, it was not enough to analyze the natural resources or available capital of different areas to understand their differences in development, treating entrepreneurial attitudes – that is, the capacity of actors to combine resources efficiently – as a constant. Weber proposed a sociological alternative to this perspective, which he saw as being more typical of economics, as well as of Marxism. He suggested that entrepreneurial activity should not be seen as a constant, but as a variable that depended on the institutional context in which actors found themselves. He consequently believed that an appropriate institutional framework was necessary for the sphere of production, as well as for labor and finance. It was only if these settings could support the growth of entrepreneurship that economic development could be generated. Weber's discovery of entrepreneurship in the course of his research on German society pushed him to consider the macro-sociological problems of the origins of capitalism and its territorial development, which would occupy him for many years to come.

2   The Forming of Entrepreneurship

How do cultural orientations favorable to the growth of entrepreneurship come into being? Weber suggested it was the influence of the Protestant religion on the spread of the economic ethic that led to the development of the "capitalist spirit." He discussed this ethic in two famous essays. The first, *The Protestant Ethic and the Spirit of Capitalism* was originally published in 1904–5, and the second, *The Protestant Sects and the Spirit of Capitalism*, written after his trip to the United States, was published in 1906.[1]

Strangely enough, in the *Protestant Ethic*, Weber did not draw any explicit link between Protestantism and the city, although he noted how, together with the influence of Protestantism on the spirit of capitalism, "it would also be necessary to investigate how protestant ascetism was in turn influenced . . . by the totality of social conditions, especially economic" (Weber [1904–5]) 1998, p. 183). We know from his later work, and in particular from his *General Economic History*, that he believed that the role of the Western city and several social groups within it, such as merchants and artisans, was particularly important.[2] Moreover, it is clear that his attention was already focussed on this when he presented his paper in St. Louis.

2.1 The spirit of capitalism

Weber described the spirit of capitalism as an *ideal type*, that is, a conceptual tool based on the analytical accentuation of certain elements of reality (cf. section 5, ch. 1). He underlined that the spirit of capitalism should not be identified with the "acquisitive impulse." Greed for money had always existed and could also be found in precapitalist societies. Indeed, economic behavior was much less scrupulous in these settings, because it was not constrained by ethical norms. This did not, however, lead to the superseding of *economic traditionalism*, but constituted one of its typical components. In order to understand the new elements introduced by the spirit of capitalism, it is thus necessary to define the orientation of economic traditionalism more clearly in ideal typical terms. It appears to be distinct from two main points of view.

First, profit was not seen as fully ethically justified; rather, it was tolerated. For this reason, it was sought primarily through relations with those outside the family or the local community, and in relations with foreigners. Second, acquisitiveness (the orientation to profit-making) revealed itself in trade, war, piracy, and in the predatory capitalism, but did not affect the production sphere, which remained governed by traditional routines. The spirit of capitalism involved profound change in both of these areas.

1   The search for profit was not only seen as ethically justified, but was even encouraged. In other words, whereas profit had hitherto been viewed as falling outside the realms of ethical norms, so that it had at best been tolerated – as the behavior of the medieval church shows – it was now given a place in society's range of values.
2   This orientation was linked to the progressive penetration of the sphere of production by a search for profit that was tied to the rational accounting of capital yields. Previously, when acquisitiveness was not ethically constrained, it had revealed itself in commerce with outsiders and in freebooting capitalism; now, however, it was increasingly found within the rational organization of the productive process. As a result, the static nature of traditional economics was not only broken, but there was a revolution in the sphere of production, which was brought through by private entrepreneurs through the use of their capital.

The "new" entrepreneurs (whom Weber knew directly from his own family background) modified products, production methods, relations with suppliers and the market, in the search to maximize profit. They came from the lower strata of society and did not have much capital, often relying on loans from relatives. However, they had one weapon that was essential for prevailing against the resistance and hostility that their actions met with in traditional economic environments. This was the "ethical qualities of quite a different sort from those adapted to the traditionalism of the past" (Weber [1904–5] 1998, p. 69). These qualities fed the the commitment to his work that was typical of this new economic actor.

For precisely these reasons, Weber concluded by stating that "the question of the motive forces in the expansion of modern capitalism is not in the first instance a question of the origin of the capital sums which were available for capital uses, but, above all, of development of the spirit of capitalism" (Weber [1904–5] 1998, p. 68). How did this spirit come about? What were its origins?

2.2   The economic ethic of Protestantism

According to Weber, the spread of the capitalist spirit can be seen as an unintentional consequence of the economic ethic of Protestantism, in particular the Calvinist denomination[3] Rather than suggesting a strong causal link, the German sociologist aimed to single out the "correlations" between the two phenomena (Weber, [1904–5] 1998, p. 91).

One of the most important features of Calvinism was its adherence to the idea of predestination. The world was created by God for his greater glory. Men cannot, however, understand his divine aims, except for those that he wishes to be known. In particular, it is impossible to know one's individual destiny after death. All that was clear is that some individuals would be saved and some condemned. The elect were predestined to be saved, and were chosen by God at the moment of creation. The destiny of these individuals could not be changed, either by actions or by sacraments. Calvinists denied that the state of grace could be lost or regained through the sacraments of the Church, in particular through confession and communion. Moreover, unlike the Lutherans, they did not even believe that individual repentance could lead to salvation in the afterlife.

Weber believed that this brought to its fullest development the "the great historic process on the development of religions, the elimination of the magic from the world which had become from the old Hebrew prophets and, in conjunction with the Hellenistic scientific thought, hat repudiated all magical means to salvation as superstition and sin" (Weber [1904] 1998, p. 105). However, in taking this process to such an extreme, Calvinism led to deep loneliness on the part of the believer. Nobody could help him gain salvation – neither Church, nor priest, nor sacrament. This clearly led to great psychological anguish for the faithful. One might have predicted that they would develop a tendency towards fatalism and passivity, given the impossibility of changing their individual destiny. This led to a paradox that interested Weber greatly – why did an orientation towards action and innovation develop in the economic field, rather than fatalism?

To answer this, he examined two pieces of advice that were given to the Calvinist believer by ministers. First, they were to think of themselves as being among the elect and to reject any doubts they might have, treating these as temptations.

Second, they were encouraged to view commitment to work as the principal means of reinforcing their faith that they were indeed among the chosen few. In other words, they were encouraged to follow their vocation committing themselves to professional activities because this was the will of God. One can now understand how the creed of Calvinism favored the spirit of capitalism as an unintentional consequence. The idea of predestination generated distress and a psychological need for reassurance. In addition, the believer was obliged to behave as though he was elected and to work hard and rigorously in his chosen profession. Success in one's chosen field was thus interpreted as a sign of election and this led the believer to work even harder in order to maintain and reinforce this condition.

However, the spirit of capitalism did not only involve the search for profit as an ethical duty, but also a commitment to the productive use of capital and a condemnation of luxury goods and pleasures. This second motivational component too could be found in Calvinism, which condemned "the pursuit of riches for their own sake. For wealth in itself was a temptation" ([1904–5] 1998, p. 172). In other words, Calvinism condemned the use of wealth to satisfy material pleasures; discouraged consumption, particularly of luxuries, and attacked material goods more generally. This combination of a driving force towards hard work, and the restriction of consumption was an orientation towards economic activity that encouraged "accumulation of capital through ascetic compulsion to save" ([1904–5] 1998, p. 172).

Having set out this picture of the relations between the Protestant ethic and the capitalist spirit, Weber integrated it with some further observations that can be found in his essay on *The Protestant Sects* ([1906] 1991). While in the United States, Weber had found consistent signs of the influence of the Protestant sects in the wealthy associative networks that characterized American society. However, he underlined the profound difference in individual behavior that derived from being a member of a church as opposed to a sect. In the first case, corresponding to the historical experience of the Catholic Church, one saw an association that administered grace (that is, access to religious goods guaranteeing salvation) where compulsory obligations fell on everybody. The sect was instead a voluntary association that grouped together those individuals whose behavior enabled them to be accepted from the ethical–religious point of view. In other words, while one was born into the church, one was admitted into a sect. In order to be made a member, one had to show that one abided by certain norms, and, once admitted, one's ethical–religious suitability had to be confirmed through successive behavior.

In addition, reflecting on the American situation, Weber noted how exclusion from a sect could involve economic penalties for single actors, because it implied a lack of trustworthiness that could, for example, make it harder to obtain credit. There was also therefore a material interest in maintaining ethically appropriate behavior, and this became increasingly important as the original religious motivations weakened.

It would seem from what has been said above that sects were *organizational forms* that tended to stimulate a more rigorous and coherent style of behavior than could be seen in the Church. This, together with the ethical rationalization of behavior promoted by the Protestant faith (with its ideas of predestination and vocation and commitment to work), means that one must consider the analogous impetus deriving from the particular way that the Protestant sects are organized. "Both aspects were mutually supplementary and operated in the same direction: they helped to deliver the spirit of modern capitalism, its specific *ethos*, the ethos of the modern *bourgeois middle class* " (Weber [1920–1] 1991, p. 321).

Weber thus demonstrated an "elective affinity" between the Protestant ethic and the spirit of capitalism. This choice of words showed that Weber was aware that he had not genuinely demonstrated a causal relationship between the two phenomena. Making this connection would, for example, have required a more thorough attempt to verify the correlation between Protestantism and the spread of capitalism at the territorial level, or to investigate the effective influence of religious belief on the behavior of particular entrepreneurs (Poggi 1983). Weber's thesis of the role of Protestantism in the development of capitalism was, however, the subject of heated debate from its first publication. As it transpired, his critics frequently misinterpreted his position, and, in particular, suggested that his explanation of capitalism was founded exclusively on the influence of Protestantism.[4] In response, in the later editions of *Ethic*, Weber pointed out that research on the origins of the capitalist spirit was not the same as research on its causes, which were much more complex: "we have no intention whatever of maintaining such a foolish and doctrinaire thesis as the spirit of capitalism . . . could only have arisen as the result of certain effects of the Reformation, or even that capitalism as an economic system is a creation of the Reformation" ([1904–5] 1998, p. 91). Indeed, it was precisely his awareness of the need for – and current insufficiency of – an investigation of the capitalist spirit that pushed him into widening the framework of his research, taking account of the other contemporaneous institutional factors that, together with the capitalist spirit, favored the development of the capitalist economic system. It was in this framework that the relations of Protestantism and the city in their mutual influence on capitalist enterprise came to be better clarified.

3   Origins and Features of Modern Capitalism

3.1   The definition of modern capitalism

The first problem that must be addressed, if one wishes to understand the trajectory of Weber's research, is how he characterized "modern capitalism." Since this was his dependent variable, it is clearly important to know how he defined it. He treated this point in several works, but the most precise of his definitions can be found in *Economy and Society* (especially in ch. 2, vol. II) and in *General Economic History* (in particular in chapter 4). By referring to these sources it is possible to reconstruct his concept of modern capitalism as follows. It is, then, *a form of economic organization where needs are satisfied by private firms that produce goods for the market on the basis capital accounting (calculating the profitability of capital), and which make use of formally free waged labor.* This definition contained three important features that enabled Weber to distinguish modern capitalism from both non-capitalist economic organizational forms and other types of capitalism.

The first dimension involved the *satisfaction of needs through the market*. This allowed modern capitalism to be differentiated from the "budgetary management," in which the production or exchange of goods on the part of a budgetary unit – for example, a household or a tribe – was oriented mainly to its own consumption. In addition, the extent to which production was oriented to the market distinguished modern capitalism from other forms of capitalism that had existed historically (as in the West during the Middle Ages, or in Asia), where the satisfaction of needs through the market remained limited.

The other two dimensions allowed modern capitalism to be distinguished from other traditional forms. First of all, accounting was very highly developed thanks to bookkeeping and organizational devices, such as the rational keeping of accounts and the legal separation between the firm and the entrepreneur's family wealth. This *rationalization of capital* accounting was, according to Weber, favored by a third condition that was not to be found in either the household economy or traditional capitalism – the *rational organization of formally free waged labor*.

Weber did not believe that the search for profit was only found in modern capitalism. It had, according to him, always existed, as had the calculation of the profitability of capital. What was distinctive about modern capitalism was that this search not only involved a type of accounting that was more systematic and rational than had previously been possible in forms of traditional capitalism, but – above all – it was concentrated in the sphere of production for the market, employing waged labor. Vice versa, the traditional forms showed themselves in the commerce of goods and credit (particularly with foreigners), when they were oriented by profit opportunities supplied by the market (*economic opportunities*), or when they were concentrated in activities exploiting *political opportunities*.

For Weber, commerce and credit excepted, traditional forms were usually of the political type, that is to say, they were based on the use of force, as in the case of predatory and freebooting capitalism (wars, piracy, etc.), or the use of resources that were politically guaranteed. These usually involved the state (as in tax farming, the acquisition of public offices by private buyers, monopolies of colonial commerce granted by the state, etc.). Corresponding to the distinction between *economic capitalism* and *political capitalism* was the distinction between *economic* and *political entrepreneurship*.

Weber discussed these two concepts in *Economy and Society* (Weber [1922] 1978,

Table 3.1 *Economic and political capitalism*

	Sphere of exchange	Sphere of production
Political resources	War and predatory capitalism. Piracy Colonial and fiscal capitalism	Industrial capitalism with slave labor
Economic resources	Commercial, credit, and financial capitalism. Usury	Industrial capitalism with formally free labor

Source: Schluchter (1980).

vol. I, p. 91 and 164–5) and *General Economic History* (Weber [1958b] 1987, pp. 333–4). He defined entrepreneurial action as "activity which is oriented at least in part to opportunities of profit-making" (Weber [1922] 1978, p. 90). It aimed at increasing the actor's (here the entrepreneur's) power of disposition over certain goods, that is, it had an acquisitive orientation that was realized through the search for profit and capital accounting. However, acquisitiveness could be expressed in two different directions. There was the economic entrepreneurship oriented towards the profit-making opportunities on the market, or the political type, as described above.

In conclusion, Weber had both an extensive concept of capitalism, which included both traditional and modern forms, and a more limited one including the economic, commercial-credit and industrial types. However, the most truly distinctive feature of modern capitalism was *industrial capitalism* (Schluchter 1980, ch. 2). This form exploited the opportunities for profit arising from the market for goods, through activities that were located in the sphere of production, and not only the sphere of circulation (commercial and financial capitalism). Weber was in agreement with Marx in his assertion that modern capitalism could not exist without the working classes. The appropriation of the means of production by capitalists and the formation of waged labor were the preliminary and essential stages of this form of economic organization, and they defined an entire "economic epoch" ([1958b] 1987, p. 276).[5]

This enables us to understand Weber's research problem more clearly: his aim was to elucidate the distinctiveness of Western historical development from development in other parts of the world that had seen freebooting, war or political and commercial capitalism, but not modern capitalism, which was the prerogative of the West. This explains why his research strategy was based on a powerful comparative investigation, which aimed to single out crucial causal factors, isolating those which were present in the Western experience and which were absent elsewhere, or present only in part. He began this project after finishing his studies on Protestantism; it was carried out in a series of essays published between 1915 and 1919 – *Confucianism and Taoism* (1951), *Hinduism and Buddhism* (1958a), and *Ancient Judaism* (1952). These were collected together with his studies on Protestantism and published in 1920–1 as *Gesammelte Aufsätze zur Religionsoziologie* (Sociology of Religion). All this work came to an abrupt end with his early death. His *General Economic History* – based on the lectures he gave in Munich shortly before his death in June 1920 – set out his last comments on the more strictly economic implications of his research. This work was a synthesis, enlivened for didactic reasons by wide-ranging historical examples, which attempted to synthesize his theory on capitalism (Collins 1980). In addition, the theory of capitalist development was treated more briefly (particularly in chapter 4) than in the more analytical and extended form of *Economy and Society*, which is a long, complex, and difficult theoretical treatise.

Before proceeding to the reconstruction of the more mature formulation of Weber's theory, I will first discuss a series of conditions of modern capitalism that are listed at the beginning of chapter 4 in the *General Economic History*.[6] These are a series of conditions that allow the satisfaction of needs by private firms operating on the basis of capital accounting, and producing for the market with fixed capital and a free work force.

1   The first condition was that *the appropriation of the means of production by the entrepreneur*. Private ownership of the means of production, and a lack of constraints on their commercial use were, for Weber, fundamental conditions for capital accounting and decisions about investment on the basis of the opportunities offered by the market.

2   This shows us that the mode through which capitalism satisfies needs presupposes a market. It further requires the *freedom of the market*, which is to say that there should be no cultural or political constraints on the consumption of particular goods. These are the possibility conditions of a market that is large enough that one can base capital accounting and investment on it. Moreover, the freedom of the market was not only necessary for the goods market, but also for the market of factors of production (land, capital, and labor). Capital accounting was possible only when the reallocation of productive factors on the basis of market opportunities was not impeded.

3   The existence of a *free labor force* was thus an essential component of modern capitalism, as opposed to forms of organization based on slaves or servants. This was because it allowed the cost of labor necessary for certain investments to be worked out precisely in advance and thus reduced fixed costs.

4   Another condition was *rational technology*, particularly the availability of mechanical technology that allowed the cost of making goods to be calculated exactly. In addition, it allowed costs to be lowered, and thus the production of mass consumption goods, which was an essential component of modern capitalism.

5   The *commercialization of the economy* was the condition involving the availability of legal tools such as limited liability companies and letters of credit. On the one hand, these facilitated the separation of family wealth from firm wealth (enabling the accounting of the firm to be more rational). On the other, they eased the transferability of capital and made possible a more rational link between savings and investment, this last being helped by the stock exchange.

6   Finally, the satisfaction of needs through capitalism presupposed that economic transactions were guaranteed by a legal order that reduced risks and gave greater predictability to relations between private actors, as well as with the public administration. Thus, it was important for the state to underwrite a *rational legal system*, and render the law calculable.

It needs to be remembered that for Weber these preconditions were ideal types. He was well aware that such conditions were never completely fulfilled, and, precisely because of this, he was able to show the limits of the empirical validity of neoclassical economic theory, for which all of these conditions had to apply fully, if its analytical models were to work. For Weber, they were simply an instrument by which one might gauge the distance between actual economies and the ideal type of capitalist market economy in its initial stages. Thus Weber was able to explain more fully why modern capitalism was a typically Western phenomenon (and also why, within the West, the phenomenon manifested itself to varying degrees).

3.2   The conditions of modern capitalism

Why did the specifics of modern capitalism become established in the West? The conceptual scheme adopted by Weber to explain the origins of modern capitalism highlighted a set of conditions that he considered as being specifically Western, in that they could only be identified in this territorial area (or, at any rate, they were stronger here than in other places). He also discussed some other complementary factors that were not necessarily unique to the West, but that he did not attribute a decisive role to. Four conditions were mentioned in particular ([1958b] 1987, pp. 307–8): wars, colonial conquests and the influx of precious metals, the supply of luxury goods to courts, and favorable geographical conditions. There were two sets of conditions, found in the West, that played a role of primary importance ([1958b] 1987, pp. 313–14). Cultural conditions included the influence of the *economic ethic* on the religious background of the entrepreneur. Institutional conditions involved three main factors: the *Western city*, the *rational state* and *rational science*. It should be noted that both cultural and institutional factors (city, state, and science) were in reality conditioned by some religious factors, in particular by the influence of *ethical prophecy* on Western rationalization. However, the two groups of variables were linked to the Western religious tradition in different ways. Religion influenced modern capitalism both *directly* – through the formation of the economic ethic – and *indirectly* – through its contribution to the emergence of institutional conditions (city, state, and science). These last, however, acquired an independent causal relevance for capitalist development that cannot be reduced to religion.

Let us first examine the cultural conditions, which center around the economic ethic. Weber had first explored this factor when he was studying Protestantism, elucidating the relationships between the Protestant ethic and the spirit of capitalism. His later studies on the sociology of comparative religion integrated these insights and redefined his initial perspective along various lines.[7]

All economic ethics had been characterized for a long period by *traditionalism*, that is, by productive and commercial practices handed down over the ages. Clearly, the sacred character of tradition was usually reinforced by the material interests of those who would have been affected by economic innovation (princes, bureaucrats, landowners, merchants, etc.). However, resistance to change was greatly reinforced by the legitimacy that magic conferred on tradition. Where there was a general belief that the world was dominated by supernatural powers, any innovation might be discouraged by fear of how the spirits might react. This began to change as primitive, fragmented societies were displaced, and the world religions emerged in large bureaucratic empires (such as China and India), or in city-states or small states (as in Greece and Palestine). These changes became especially marked from the fifth century BC on, with Confucianism, Buddhism, Greek ethical philosophy, Judaism, and later on, Catholicism.

One fundamental consequence of this change was an increasing separation between the natural and supernatural worlds. Individual destiny was no longer subject to the whims of the spirits, who had to be appeased with magical rites, but now seemed to depend on people's capacity to conform to the moral obligations imposed by the divinities living in the supernatural world. It is clear that, in this context, salvation in the hereafter – for example, as in the Christian paradise – became extremely important in motivating earthly behavior and rationalizing the conduct of life. How did this change take place? "In all times there has been but one means of breaking down the power of magic and establishing a rational conduct of life: this means is great rational prophecy" (Weber [1958b] 1987, p. 362). The founders of the new religions were prophets – charismatic figures with extraordinary personal qualities, like Zarathustra, Jesus, and Mohammed. They preached the need to obey certain divine commands and put new religious doctrines in place, attracting the consensus of the masses (Weber [1922] 1978, vol. I, p. 440).

The great religions had two important consequences. First, they contributed to reducing the influence of magic (*disenchantment*), thus creating the conditions for a rational explanation of the natural world on the basis of which science and technology could grow. Second, they were more universal than the primitive religions with their magical connotations. These last were restricted to particular social groups, the family, tribe and ethnic group. Each of these had its own divinities. The universal religions tended to monopolize relations with the divinity, claiming their own forms as the only one worthy of veneration; they therefore had a universalistic claim that lead them to cover a wider area of social solidarity than had been found in the fragmented cults that preceded them. This had important economic implications, because it affected the possibility of *overcoming ethical dualism.*

Economic relations within traditionalism were characterized by a twofold morality. This consisted of an *internal ethic*, applying to members of the family, kinship group, and the tribe, that is, to all those who belonged to the same religious group. It excluded the pursuit of profit and was based on reciprocity, fraternal help, and free credit. The *external ethic*, for those who were outside the primary circle of solidarity, where religious sanctions applied, permitted one to seek profit in economic transactions without any ethical constraints. We know that Weber did not believe that modern capitalism could develop without overcoming the ethical dualism typical of traditionalism. In order for this to occur, the search for profit would have to be ethically constrained and the area of relations where it was so constrained would have to expand.

Not all these new religions contributed in the same degree to the reduction of the influence of magic and ethical dualism. This can be seen in the fact that there were two essential types of prophecy: *exemplary* and *ethical*. In the first case the prophet did not present himself as a mediator of God, but showed the way to salvation through examples and did not expect the masses to obey him. A typical example of this was the prophet Buddha in India. He showed through example that whoever wanted to be saved had to leave their worldly affairs and dedicate themselves to the contemplative life. This would, however, be the result of a free choice: not everyone had to go to Nirvana after dying. This meant that only restricted groups of religiously qualified intellectuals followed this path, becoming monks and hermits, while the masses remained under the sway of magic and traditionalism. Ethical prophecy moved along different lines, and was typical of Judaism and Christianity. In this case, the prophet claimed that he had been sent by God to preach the commandments, and he asked that everyone – intellectuals and the masses alike – be obedient as a moral duty. Only by conforming to the prescribed ethic could they gain salvation in the afterlife.

Weber thus made an extremely important distinction between the great universal religions prevailing in India and China, where the ethical prophecy had not taken root, and the Hebrew-Christian tradition, in which environment it had mainly developed. The first group made a more limited contribution to disenchantment and the overcoming of ethical dualism. In India, exemplary prophecy took root, involving the intellectual elites and encouraging them to disengage from active life, leaving the masses subject to magic and the paralyzing effects of the caste system. According to the Hindu system of reincarnation, only scrupulous respect to the obligations of caste, which discouraged economic innovation, allowed individuals to be reborn in a better position. In China, there was no real prophecy. Confucianism was not a religion of redemption that foresaw salvation in the afterlife. It was essentially a set of ethical precepts that prescribed behavior well adapted to respect tradition, leaving intact a set of magical beliefs, all of which discouraged the rationalization of economic behavior. In his discussion of the development of these religions, Weber highlighted how this was also sustained by the interests of particular actors and groups, such as the emperor and his functionaries (the *mandarins*) in China, and princes and priests (*brahamini*) in India, as well as others. However, he underlined that religion could not be reduced to a mere ideology or the reflection of the interests of those social strata that usually supported it. In other words, he believed that religious ideas acquired a specific autonomy that sometimes might influence the behavior of social groups and economic development (Weber 1915–16).

It was in Israel that the ethical prophecy took root. The prophets required obedience in the name of a transcendent God, and they interpreted the good and bad luck of people as dependent on faithfulness to a divinity that was presented as the God of Israel. This meant, according to Weber, that the rationalization of behavior and overcoming of magic, as products of ethical prophecy, went together with ethical dualism. And it was for this reason that he criticized Sombart's thesis on the role of the Jews in the development of modern capitalism ([1958b] 1987, pp. 358–60). After their dispersion to various countries, they became a pariah people, situated beyond the pale of the political community. This effectively pushed them into practicing economic activities, but on a rigidly traditional basis. This commercial and financial activity (credit, lending, etc.) was with private individuals and the state, that is, with outsiders, but it did not involve the developing of the ethically constrained capitalist spirit that stood at the base of modern capitalism, and in particular of industrial capitalism.

For Weber, Judaism's contribution to modern capitalism was important but more indirect, and should be sought in the beginnings of the tradition of ethical prophecy on which Jesus' preaching would subsequently be based. In other words, he was a prophet fighting against the Jewish clergy, which served its own economic and political interests, and he preached universal brotherhood – all men were brothers in the sense that they were the children of God. In this way, the new prophet broke the boundaries restricting the Jewish religious identity, and he laid the foundations of a future universal ethic. The Christian religion was thus able to spread over and unify the Western world.

However, both magic and ethical dualism were limited even further by the Catholic Church. Christ's charisma was institutionalized within this – not as a personal characteristic but on the basis of particular initiation rights that allowed the practice of certain functions, that is, through the work of the clergy. As we have seen, the Church portrayed itself as the administrator of the blessings of salvation. By means of the sacraments, and in particular confession and communion, it allowed the faithful to regain the state of grace that they had lost through sinning. Weber believed that the influence of magical instruments tended to persist in these rituals, weakening individual responsibility and the rationalization of conduct. At the same time, the Church maintained a differentiation between its *ethic of religious virtuosi* and its *ethic of the masses*, and this led to a form, however weakened, of ethical dualism. During the medieval times, the distinction between cloistered religious and the faithful was clear. The former incarnated the ethic of religious virtuosi, and came closest to the religious precepts. This experience was not prescribed for the faithful masses, although it was presented as an ideal of life to which they could aspire. In this sense, then, no break representing the exemplary prophecy took place, although a different intensification of the process of rationalization of behavior did occur. This was most advanced in the monastic communities, where it also led to important developments at the level of economic organization. Such phenomena were, however, limited by the fact that the monastic experience was basically oriented towards an *other-worldly asceticism*, a commitment that went beyond active life and the world. At the same time, the forces pushing the mass of the faithful towards the rationalization of behavior was rather more contained.

In Weber's opinion, it was only with the Reformation that these limits were overcome. The use of magical means to gain grace (sacraments) was overcome, especially in Calvinism. The process of disenchantment reached its climax, with important effects for the rationalization of behavior and the personality. In the same period, the residual distinction between the ethic of religious virtuosi and the masses was left behind. The ideal of external asceticism replaced that of *inner-worldly* asceticism, leading to the active use of the world as an instrument to realize religious precepts. Weber did not, however, restate the idea of predestination as a specific intermediating factor in the formation of the capitalist spirit. In his *General Economic History*, he insisted instead on the idea of vocation as commitment to work and professional activity, and on the role of the sects as a form of religious organization that stimulated the formation of orientations towards production and consumption which were favorable to the capitalist spirit. But the new economic ethic was only one element, albeit an important one, of those contributing to the formation of entrepreneurship. One needed additionally to consider the advent of the urban bourgeoisie as a social strata that provided a favorable basis for the growth of capitalist entrepreneurship.

The Western city

Weber saw the Western city as having a peculiar characteristic that was already present in the Greek *polis*, but which became more pronounced in the communes of medieval Europe. It was only in this context that it began to function as an unitary political community, which is to say that it affirmed a specific right to

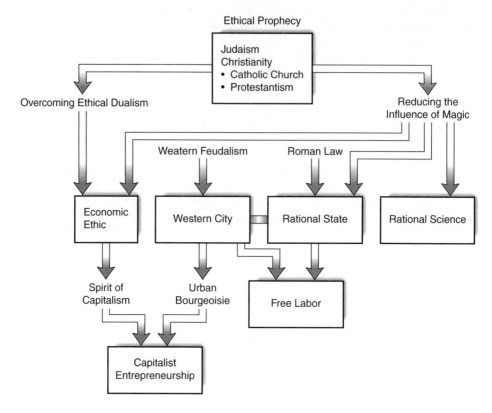

Figure 3.1   *Weber's model of capitalist development*

citizenship, according to which the inhabitants of a city had their own courts and political authorities, and participated as individuals in choosing the officials of these bodies in some fashion ([1958b] 1987, p. 318). This did not happen outside the West, or at least only to a limited extent and in the short term, since cities, although normally seats of commerce and industry, always continued to depend on a landed noble or prince, who held political power. The city's inhabitants had never enjoyed any specific rights as inhabitants.

The reasons for the specificity of the Western city – which had important effects for the development of the rational state as well as for capitalism – lay above all in its political nature. They were linked to the revolutionary character that the formation of the city, as ideal-type, had in its original form. At its base lay the sworn association (*coniuratio*) which sought to capture political power. Thus, in both the Greek city-state and the medieval commune, an armed brotherhood sought to usurp political (although this was a very gradual process in many cases, and was based on concessions and privileges given by princes and landed nobles). There were two main causes for this process, which distinguishes the Western experience. The first was politico-military – even if it was also affected by economic factors – and the second was religious.

Western cities were characterized militarily by a defense association, constituted by all those who were able to use arms and to see to their own training and equipping for the conduct of war. This was not the case in other places, where military organization was instead usually structured vertically. It was, in other words, structured around a prince who provided arms and victuals. In this case, "the development of the city was prevented by the fact, that the army of the prince is older than the city" ([1958b] 1987, p. 320). It was thus the fragility of the larger political units that favored the development of cities as autonomous entities in the West, while the opposite happened in the East. This difference, according to Weber, could also be attributed to economic conditions. For example, in China and in Egypt, the need to manage water for agricultural irrigation led to the early creation of large-scale political-administrative units which were able to address problems through their centralized bureaucracy (further down, we shall see how this same phenomenon discouraged feudalism in the East, with important economic consequences).

The second factor favoring the formation of the Western city was religion. Christianity had led to the end of the ethical dualism characterizing the experiences in other parts of the world. The very possibility of creating an union to found a city, which was born from a specific right of citizenship and allowed non-traditional forms of economic cooperation to develop, necessitated that the barriers to social relations be broken down. Such barriers dominated where the inhabitants of the city belonged to tribes, races, or castes which had their particular cults, while "for its very nature the Christian congregation was a religious association of individual believers, not a ritual association of clans" ([1922] 1978, vol. II, p. 1297). This was why medieval communes had a city Church, a patron saint, and religious festivals.

What consequences did the Western city have in creating the conditions for modern capitalism? In fact, it affected all these conditions, both directly (as through the widening of the market and commercialization, the freeing of the labor force, and the appropriation of the means of production by the entrepreneur) and indirectly (its links with the formation of the rational state, and of science, and thus through the contribution of these factors to rational law and rational technology).

The Western medieval city – as an autonomous political community – had to find its own means of subsistence, as it was unable to count on the redistribution of military or administrative resources found in the non-Western city. In addition, the breaking of ethical dualism and the overcoming of the constraints of race and caste were expressed in the legal status of free citizenship. Weber reminded his readers of the German saying "*Stadtluft macht frei*" (the city air makes free) ([1922] 1978, p. 1239). This also helped encourage the undertaking of economic activities, which were no longer hindered by the traditionalism or the persistence of magic that was still characteristic of non-Western cities. This is why the Western city could to orient itself towards commercial and productive activities preparing the way for a rational capitalism that sought to exploit market opportunities, rather than traditional political and military capitalism ([1958b] 1987, pp. 333–4).

The first important contribution of the city to the conditions of capitalism involved the *widening of the market*. This took place initially through the developing of trade – a process that was typical of the economic life of cities as they became autonomous political communities. In order to increase their ability to sustain themselves, they had to enlarge their traffic and exchanges. However, in order to pursue this aim, medieval cities were soon forced to experiment with new instruments that led to the commercialization of economic life (as Weber illustrated in chapter 3 of his *General Economic History*). For example, the need to reduce the risks of long-term commerce led to the birth of the associative form of the *commenda*, but this also drove a rationalization of accounting techniques and encouraged a separation of family property from the property of the firm. These developments facilitated capital accounting in their turn. In addition, more sophisticated commercial instruments, such as the letter of exchange, helped create forms of credit organization for firms and therefore a type of banking activity that was exclusive to the Western experience, and which would, in fact, be important for modern capitalism.

The urban, commercial and artisanal bourgeoisie that developed in consequence, came into conflict with the original economic organization of the countryside, which was based on land holders with peasants in servitude and a form of production that was predominantly geared to the domestic economy and self-consumption (feudal structures). The conflict was mainly based on the fact that the urban classes "promoted the weakening or dissolution of the manor because it limited their own market opportunities" ([1958b] 1987, p. 94). In addition, it was later in the cities' interests to *free peasants from their feudal obligations* not only to increase the market for their products and guarantee a more secure source of supply of agricultural goods, but also to find a workforce for domestic work entrusted to them by urban merchant-entrepreneurs. Finally, wealthier urban groups had an interest in investing their capital in agricultural land, also for reasons of prestige, and thus in *freeing the land from feudal bonds*, making it saleable on the market.

However, the city also contributed to the liberation of land and labor and to the widening of the market in a more indirect fashion. In an economic context stimulated by activities and trade promoted by the city, landholders were obliged to take any opportunities that presented themselves to rationalize their holdings in a capitalist direction. This led to a process of expropriation of the peasants. The classic example of this took place in Britain, while in Prussia, Eastern Europe, and Russia the peasants were more extensively exploited until feudal services were abolished. Another example was the case of freeholder peasants, as in South-East Germany and other parts of southern Europe, where landholders initially used their property as a source of income.

To understand the different pattern of evolution in other parts of the world, it should be remembered that the existence of large and centralized political units, necessary for the problems of water regulation, discouraged the formation of cities for military reasons, and, as a result, modern capitalism, too. This was all the more reinforced because feudalism, which had only taken root in the West because of the fragility of state structures after the fall of the Roman Empire, was blocked elsewhere. Apart from the West, the only place where a similar system became established was Japan. In the large bureaucratic empires, such as Egypt and Mesopotamia, or China with its Mandarins, a bureaucratic system of functionaries who were dependent on the sovereign prevailed. When the monetary economy developed, the difficulty of collecting taxes sometimes led this civil or military bureaucracy to take on a more feudal character, particularly in the East, where a landed nobility collected tributes in return for a particular territory (as seen in India or

Turkey). This "service feudalism" was almost entirely rooted in fiscal measures that could in principle be revoked by the sovereign, on whom the beneficiary remained dependent. This differed from Western feudalism, which was specifically contractual in nature, with territorial concessions being made in exchange for military services, usually offered by knights who could equip themselves for battle. It thus presupposed the military fragility of the state structure, as well as reciprocal obligations of fealty between the sovereign and the liege-lords.[8]

These differences between prebendal feudalism and patrimonial bureaucracy, on the one hand, and the specifically Western form of contractual feudalism, on the other, had important implications for the political and economic systems. The first have already been discussed. It was on the terrain of contractual feudalism that – in many varied shapes and forms – a landed aristocracy with relatively autonomous powers over its land began to develop. While it was true that feudal services hindered capitalism, Weber noted that the greater stability of the legal system and patrimonial rights favored a slow emergence of bourgeois attitudes ([1922] 1978, vol. II, pp. 1099–100). This occurred through the capitalistic management of lordly holdings, particularly where the city had helped to widen the market and to create new economic opportunities. The opposite was true of patrimonial bureaucracy and fiscal and prebendal feudalism, typical of Eastern cities, which were more favorable to political capitalism. In this case, the aristocracy was more dependent on the power of a king or an emperor and less rooted in the fiefs, therefore it did not break with the traditionalism of forms of agricultural organization based on the village economy. Western feudalism also had important political implications which will be examined below. These were bound up with the inheritance that feudal contractualism left to the Western state, which encouraged the evolution of the constitutional state (*Rechtstaat*) and limited the arbitrary power of the sovereign ([1922] 1978, vol. II, pp. 1036–7).

Up to this point we have discussed the ways in which the city influenced the market and commercialization, and the liberation of the labor force from the land – which in this case went together with the character of the Western landholding aristocracy. We now turn to another important condition for modern capitalism: *the appropriation of the means of production by the entrepreneur*. Weber discussed this in chapter 2 of his *General Economic History*, which he devoted to forms of organization of industrial activity. The starting point of this process can be identified as the progressive weakening of the corporations, on which the economic life of mediaeval cities was based. The corporatist spirit was closely linked to the community spirit typically found when cities came into being, and their members had to struggle – either through revolution or providing compensation – to gain the privileges that were conceded by those who hold power, in order to carry out certain activities. The corporation, or guild, was a regulative organization that "endeavored by every conceivable means to provide equality of opportunity for all guild members" ([1958b] 1987, p. 138). The processes of production, organization of labor, and relations with the market were all regulated in this way.

However, towards the end of the medieval period, processes of differentiation began to appear both within and between the different corporations. In some guilds, individual artisans became merchant-entrepreneurs, giving work to others, while in other cases, some guilds became oriented towards commerce and compelled others into their service. Control over the purchase of raw materials and market relations took on strategic value and affected the process of differentiation. Thus, the figure of the merchant-entrepreneur putting out domestic labor, also to peasants, for example, in weaving (*Verlagssystem*), came into being. In this phenomenon, which manifested itself in different ways across Europe, one may see one of the first signs of the process of appropriation of the means of production by the entrepreneur. However, this was still at an embryonic stage because of the low intensity of fixed capital, even if the merchant-entrepreneur managed to provide home workers (for example, weavers) with the raw materials and the production instruments. In any event, this last stage was seen only in the Western case. The caste system in India and the hereditary system in China impeded the development of home working. In addition, the lack of free labor, and magical thinking and traditionalism were very potent obstacles.

Before moving on to the next stage – the emergence of fixed capital and rational organization of free labor – I shall discuss the other conditions, than the city, that modern capitalism required. Of particular importance was *rational technological knowledge*. This was in turn tied to the development of rational science in the West. The most important factor of the disenchantment characterizing the Jewish–Christian tradition was, for Weber, the planting of the seed of scientific thought, although this did involve some conflict. The institutions in which it developed, such as universities, were initially supported by city policy, and then by national state policy. Furthermore, the more innovative approach of the West to economic activity, already apparent in precapitalist times, was important in stimulating technology, and would later be encouraged by the important legal instrument of the patent.

In this regard, Weber particularly focused his attention on mining activities and the stimulus provided by the need to pump water out of mine-holes, which led to the discovery of the steam engine ([1958b] 1987, pp. 190–1). The full exploitation of fossil fuels made it possible to use iron as a primary input, and the coupling of coal with iron was essential for mechanization. This last phenomenon had two important effects on modern capitalism. First, it encouraged mass production at a lower cost, through that "democratization of luxury" that Weber considered as a "crucial direction of capitalistic production" ([1958b] 1987, p. 309), because it allowed the risks connected to the immobility of fixed capital to be alleviated. Second, mechanization allowed a rationalization of capital accounting with regard to the costs of manufacture.

The state and rational law

The final condition of modern capitalism was *rational law*. According to Weber, this made the law calculable; in other words, it made relations between actors involved in economic activities and the public administration much more predictable. This was extremely important, particularly with regard to the possibility of undertaking activities requiring a strong investment in fixed capital. This condition initially emerged in the West, and was the product of a rational state that had two essential features. The first was that it was based on a legal system that regulated the modalities of access to political power and of its exercise; in other words, a special body of functionaries whose recruitment and activity was regulated by law. In this manner the ideal type of rational state differed from the patrimonial type ([1922] 1978, vol. II, ch. 9), more typical of the East, where political power was a private possession of the lord and functionaries were his personal dependents. These new features of the Western state came into being through a slow process of rationalization, which was particularly clearly described in *Economy and Society*, while it was treated only briefly in *General Economic History*. Three factors were discussed.

The first was religious. Here, the influence of disenchantment allowed the rational intervention of political power to deal with problems faced by society. In India and China, instead, insofar as interventions of this kind, sought to move away from traditional ritualism, they tended to encounter obstacles and strong resistance from religious authorities. In addition, in order for the rational state to affirm itself as a constitutional state, it was particularly important that the right to citizenship be expressed in formal juridical terms. This was possible because of the experience of the Western city, as well, as of contractual feudalism, for the reasons discussed above, with its limiting effects on the exercise of political power.

Together with these wide ranging historical causes, Weber discussed a more specific factor that had allowed the rational organization of the state to come into being: Roman law. Despite the fall of the Roman Empire, its law had been preserved, particularly through the notaries of Italian cities, who adapted it to the problems of the commercialization of economic life, and also through the universities, where a "systematic legal doctrine" came into being. Roman law was not as important for its substantive contents as for its legal formalism, which provided an effective inoculation against a law system oriented towards substantive meaning, and therefore susceptible to being arbitrary. In addition, it was particularly suited to the creation of a specialized bureaucracy – absolutely crucial for a modern state. In the process of creating the absolutist state, sovereigns found a formal legal system based on Roman law to be an important means of promoting politico-administrative centralization through legal unification, and they supported the creation of a body of lawyers who contributed in turn to strengthening this tendency. This was how a calculable law came into being. "The alliance between the state and formal jurisprudence was indirectly favorable to capitalism" ([1958b] 1987, p. 343), because it helped introduce those elements of predictability which capitalism required, and which were never strong enough outside the West.

Naturally, the influence of the state on modern capitalism extended to other factors, and is examined by Weber in many parts of his *History*. Here, we may point to the role played by the state in liberating the labor force, and in the development of credit and a rational monetary system. However, these political determinants of capitalism were not, in Weber's opinion, sufficient to trigger the process of development, even though they were important, and often underestimated (Collins 1980). Neither did he believe that the experience of mercantilism was sufficient. Even if all the factors that had gradually emerged during the pre-capitalist era were present to support industrial capitalism (that is to say, a system based on stable firms producing for a mass market with fixed capital and rational organization of labor), it was still necessary to have a social actor with the right motivations to carry out this task. In this sense, it was necessary for the urban bourgeoisie to develop a favorable economic orientation to modern capitalism. The spread of Protestantism, which found a social base in the cities for its diffusion, made a decisive contribution to this, as well as itself contributing to forming a capitalist bour-geoisie: "In the last resort the factor which produced capitalism is the rational permanent enterprise, rational accounting, rational technology and rational law, but again not these alone. Necessary complementary factors were the rational spirit, the rationalization of the conduct of life in general and a rationalistic economic ethic" ([1958b] 1987, p. 354). Thus the strands of the complex Weberian construction came together, and institutional factors linked to the role of the Western city and state emerged, together with religion, in all their relevance.

4   The Future of Western Capitalism

For Weber, the task of social science theory was not to formulate general laws of development – as has already been made clear in chapter 1. His theory did not deal with economic development in general, but with the construction of the ideal type model of a particular historical development: modern capitalism. His work was influenced by his conception of the basic historicity of human society. He therefore believed that attempts to predict the future on the basis of laws, that would treat society as though it were nature, were a source of error and misunderstanding. This was, in his view, Marx's greatest mistake. For this reason, there was no systematic prediction of the future of capitalism in Weber's more scientific work. The enormous analytic effort that was *Economy and Society* aimed at formulating generalizations about relations between forms of organization of the economy and institutional phenomena, such as different types of community, religion, politics, and the law. This was a rich source of conceptual instruments, an inexhaustible tool box, that ought be applied in concrete terms in his historical–empirical investigation, not to complete analysis but to prepare it. The breadth and flexibility of Weber's analytical categories were criticized because they were viewed as hampering the construction of a theory of society with a high level of generalization (Parsons 1937). However, it was precisely this category of Weber's thought that is the source of his wide influence over contemporary social sciences (Dahrendorf 1987; Boudon 1984).

Despite his methodological caution, Weber did in fact formulate a diagnosis of capitalism. What was important, however, was that he did this in his political interventions, and not in his scientific work (Beetham 1985). The topic was examined in his lecture on *Socialism*, given in Vienna, in July 1918 (Weber 1924b). Weber criticized Marx's idea that the recurrent crises of capitalism led to a collapse of the economic system and a revolution. He believed, instead, in "an evolutionary view which sees the old economy with its masses of competing enterprises gradually growing into a regulated economy, whether this regulation is to be carried out by officials of the state or by cartels with the participation of officials" (Weber [1924b] 1994, p. 294)). In his view, industrial cartels would form with the aim of regulating prices and production, thereby controlling competition, while the banks organized to control credit, using this to limit the risks of overproduction. In addition, state, municipal and cooperative firms would be set up as the expression of a wider commitment by the state to support the standard of living of the population. For Weber, and here he came very close to Tocqueville, "everywhere bureaucratisation foreshadows mass democracy" ([1922] 1978, vol. I, p. 226), insofar as the push towards equality that went along with democratization required a greater level of political intervention.

In other words, the system would change from liberal capitalism to organized and politically regulated capitalism. Weber dealt with several important implications that this would have. The first was the overall increase in bureaucratization. Greater organization meant, above all, that firms grew larger, and having eliminated smaller firms, developed a growing internal bureaucracy of managers and white-collar workers for their functioning and relations with the surroundings. This meant also that state bureaucracy increased, both as a result of its greater responsibilities in the running of the economy, and to oversee the organization of public firms. This gave rise to that paradox of rationalization which Weber saw as characterizing all spheres of activity in modern society. The process of rationalization of the conduct of life tended to increase the control of human beings over the world. On the one hand, bureaucratization in economic, political and military activities, and even in scientific and cultural practices, added enormously to the technical efficiency of such activities. But, on the other hand, this process increasingly threatened the liberty of human beings, who found themselves subject to bureaucratic domination.

For Weber, capitalism was not identified with the market, even if this was one of its most important conditions. It was, rather, based on a series of institutional conditions that were external to it – entrepreneurial and labor motivations, technical knowledge, legal instruments, legitimacy and effectiveness of the state. Not only did capitalism not create these conditions but it also contributes to their erosion through its functioning. This led to what Weber saw as the most crucial problem in the reproduction of modern capitalism. The erosion of the normative basis of religion, the functional problems connected to economic crises and the consequent destabilization of social relations, dependence on "collective goods" such as the willingness to cooperate, technical development, training and so on, all made the regulatory contribution of the state crucial for capitalism. On the other hand, however, an excessive increase in bureaucratization and political regulation could lead to economic and social stagnation (also as a result of the growth in political and financial rents) or, worse still, the end of modern capitalism as it moved either towards political capitalism or state socialism. The problem of the reproduction of capitalism was therefore a problem of balance between state intervention and the autonomy of society and the market.

Chapter 4

The Social Consequences of Capitalism: Durkheim and Veblen

German economic sociology, in particular the work of Sombart and Weber, is a homogenous body of work from the methodological and substantive points of view. It made an essential contribution to establishing economic sociology as an independent approach. However, other seminal work was done outside the German context in this period (the turn of the twentieth century). In particular, one may point to the basic contributions to the discipline made by a Frenchman, Émile Durkheim, and an American of Norwegian descent, Thorstein Veblen.

Unlike the Germans, there was no common point of cultural reference between them; furthermore, neither author influenced the other. However, it is useful to deal with them and their work together for two good reasons. The first is that they both made important contributions to a theory of economic action that was socially conditioned. Although there were certain differences in their views, both provided important critiques of utilitarian individualism as the founding stone of economic theory. Their versions of institutionalism were highly influenced by positivism, and therefore tended to be more theoretical and generalizing than the German sociological approach, which was for its part more historically oriented. Durkheim also viewed institutionalism as a way of providing a scientific basis for sociology, while Veblen saw it as an instrument for reconstructing economics. In fact, there were many points of convergence between the sociological institutionalism of the former and the economic institutionalism of the latter, as we shall see.

From the substantive point of view, the two authors were not greatly concerned with the origins of capitalism or the specific features of the economy and Western society which had been the focus of both Sombart's and Weber's work. They were, instead, interested in investigating the social consequences of market-regulated capitalism, which is to say the liberal capitalism that had come into being in the second half of the nineteenth century as the result of the rapid spread of the Industrial Revolution. In this way, an institutionalist research perspective on the economy contributed to understanding a subject-matter – the destabilizing social effects of market-regulated capitalism – that German sociology had touched upon, but in a less developed and specific fashion. As we have seen, neoclassical economics did not discuss either this topic or the origins of capitalist development. And while Marx and Marxism did focus on certain phenomena of social disorganization like unemployment, cyclical crises, and alienation, that Durkheim and Veblen were also interested in, these subjects were considered in terms of a wider philosophy of history that these latter authors did not share. The social consequences of market capitalism thus became another core-theme around which the discipline of economic sociology developed.

1   The Market and "Abnormal" Forms of the Division of Labor

Together with Max Weber, Émile Durkheim (1858–1917) made the largest contribution to founding the sociological perspective as an independent discipline in its own right. However, unlike Weber, he was very strongly influenced by the positivist approach and held that the study of society should follow the example of the natural sciences, moving towards the search for general laws of social phenomena. While Weber was convinced that sociology could not give a scientific foundation to moral choices, Durkheim's work aimed, from the very start, to lay the foundations of a "science of morals." It was through the rigorous study of "moral facts" and their influence on specific forms of societal organization that he proposed drawing some criteria of orientation for action.

The problem of social order was therefore central to Durkheim's thinking. This led him to disagree, from his earliest work on, with individualistic utilitarianism, since he aimed to throw light on the influence of institutions on individual behavior, even where this was economic. This perspective did, however, bring him closer to German sociology's criticisms of economics. It is significant in this regard that his first work reflected the influence of the German economic historicism that had also influenced Sombart and Weber. His first important contribution therefore criticized economists' theory of action, and formulated an institutional theory. From the substantive point of view, his most important point was that the organization of economic activities in modern societies were socially destabilizing because of "abnormal forms" of the division of labor. After this, however, he widened his intellectual interests to new subjects,[1] with the aim of founding sociology as a general discipline that analyzed different features of behavior through scientific method and empirical investigation. The following discussion will be limited to the aspects of this work that were more closely related to economic sociology.

1.1   Criticism of utilitarianism and the founding of an institutionalist theory

At the beginning of his scientific career, Durkheim leant upon the thinking of various authors of the historical school of German economics, including Wagner and Schmoller. In his first collection of essays on the science of morals in Germany (Durkheim 1887), he agreed with the historicists' criticisms of orthodox political economy. He believed that it was impossible to discuss economic phenomena in the abstract, separating them from the historical setting where they had developed. The actual economic behavior of individuals was influenced by moral norms and rules that altered as society changed. These institutional factors affected economic development and were in turn affected by them.

Durkheim also recognized one of the important contributions of the economists – that of having been the first to see that society, like nature, was influenced by its own laws, and that these needed to be studied through the scientific method. Collective life could no longer be naively explained through the political will of sovereigns or by appealing to the desires of some divinity. In this way, economists also prepared the ground for the development of sociology. However, in the very moment where they presented the economic laws, they fell into a serious error, because they cut themselves off from the real influence of institutions on the economy. Why did they make this mistake? Because of the utilitarian individualism that oriented their analytical perspective, and which was to be found in the work of a sociologist that Durkheim studied with particular interest: Herbert Spencer. In the utilitarian vision, society was constructed by a set of individuals who entered into relations that were chosen voluntarily and directed exclusively by the search for individual interest. Such relations remained stable as long as the interest that had originally stimulated them persisted. Durkheim criticized this view of the problem of social order in two ways. Let us examine each of these separately.

Non-individualistic causes of the division of labor

First, the French sociologist questioned the proposition that society can be understood on the basis of individual behavior: "Collective life did not arise from individual life; on the contrary, it is the latter that emerged from the former. (Durkheim [1893] 1984, pp. 220–1). This could be verified on the level of historical development. Individualism – the idea of a rational individual capable of calculating his own interests and of acting as a result of these – had in reality developed only gradually and recently. In other words, it was a feature of modern society. In primitive and more ancient societies, individual behavior was strongly influenced by social rules, which did not leave much space for individual freedom. Individualism was thus the result of the development of society itself and its changing needs. It should be specifically investigated, which, in fact, Durkheim actually went on to do in his book *The Division of Labor in Society* (1893). In addition, the influence of society was visible not only in the history of the human race as a whole, but also in that of single individuals, as could be seen in the role played by education. It was enough to look at how children were reared – Durkheim noted in *The Rules of Sociological Method* (1895) – to understand that this process was intended "to impose upon the child ways of seeing, thinking and acting which he himself would not have arrived at spontaneously." Education, he continued, "sets out precisely with the object of creating a social being" (Durkheim [1895] 1982, pp. 53–4).

For these reasons, therefore, he believed that one had to go beyond the limits of psychology and biology and study the social causes influencing action to understand individual behavior, even in the economic field. This meant taking account of *institutions*, that is, "all the beliefs and modes of behaviour instituted by the collectivity; sociology can then be defined as the science of institutions – their genesis and their functioning"(Durkheim [1895] 1982, p. 45).

In the first of his main works – *The Division of Labor* – Durkheim developed his criticism of utilitarianism on the topic that seemed most congenial to his opponents, that of the origins and consequences of the growth in the division of labor. First, he wanted to show that the explanations given by orthodox economists and sociologists such as Spencer were inadequate. Second, he wished to show that a society based on a high differentiation of activities and roles could not work without non-contractual institutions or shared moral rules.

Let us begin with the first issue (which Durkheim dealt with at great length in the second volume). According to the traditional explanation, widespread among economists, the division of labor came about as a result of individual actions, because it would increase the advantages enjoyed by individuals – their level of satisfaction – giving rise to greater economic well-being. Durkheim found this argument untenable because single individuals could not easily predict or understand the advantages of greater productivity and well-being (which did, in effect, come into being with a higher division of labor), and would therefore be driven to specialize. In other words, one had to be guard against treating the effects of a certain social phenomenon as though they were the original cause producing them.[2]

The reasons for the division of labor had to be sought in a different, non-individualistic source. Certain variations in the social environment should be examined; in particular, those intervening in the morphology of society, that is, in the distribution of the population, and in the quantity and quality of social relations. These were reflected in forms of solidarity, and were determined by the set of shared moral norms linking people with each other and regulating their relationships. Durkheim's explanation was thus based on the analysis of the mechanisms determining the passage from an ideal type of simple society, characterized by *mechanical solidarity*, to a type of superior society, with a high division of labor in which *organic solidarity* prevailed. Let us analyze in more details this process of social change.

The first ideal type of society was characterized, from the morphological point of view, by its small size (the purest type he envisaged here was the primitive society). These would for the most part be "segmented," having little contact with each other, and being more or less internally homogenous (which was to say that they had a low division of labor). The social order in settings of this type was assured by a form of mechanical solidarity, which was based in turn on particular features of the *collective conscience*, that is, "the totality of beliefs and sentiments common to the average members of a society" (Durkheim [1893] 1984, pp. 38–9). Shared beliefs regulated individual behavior in a precise way, leaving little space for autonomy or choice on the part of single members of society. The problem of order was thus resolved "mechanically," on the basis of an intense emotional attachment to a system of shared values. An empirical indicator of strong social control over individuals could also be seen in the prevalence of penal law based on repressive sanctions. Punishment was, in this view, a passionate reaction – society avenged offense to the shared morality through sanctioning.

Over time, the segmentation and isolation of human settlements became less marked. This occurred as a result of the increase in population, leading to a greater "material density." The growing population became more territorially concentrated, towns grew, and communications improved. Social relations tended to become more frequent because of this process: as people came out of their initial isolation, they moved closer together and therefore increased what Durkheim called their "moral density" or "dynamic density." All this was reflected in a sharper struggle for existence that pushed single individuals to increase their occupational specialization in order to survive in the new conditions. The growth in the division of labor was thus due to society's pressure on individuals.[3]

All this led to the emergence of an ideal-typical "superior society," characterized by growth in size, a higher material and moral density, and a more developed division of labor. As we know, Durkheim emphasized that this type of social structure was not devoid of solidarity (shared moral rules that bonded individuals despite their economic interests). This was now an organic solidarity, triggered by the development of the division of labor that nurtured the sense of reciprocal dependence between different actors (as in the specialized functions of an organism). In this case, the collective conscience regulated a more limited area of individual behavior and did so in a less rigid way, indicating some fundamental values that left more space for individual choice, and were more compatible with the needs of a differentiated society. It was in this setting that the values of individualism spread and individual personality was able to take on its own form, as we have seen in Simmel's work. It was also in this setting that "restitutive law"– of which the civil form was most typical – began to spread. This involved sanctions with restorative aims, that sought reintegration on the basis of the situation that had obtained before the violation of legally protected interests.

Non-contractual conditions of the contract

Durkheim did not limit himself to emphasizing that society should be considered as autonomous and had pre-eminence over individuals, and that institutions were "social facts" endowed with a constrictive force. He made a second criticism of economists in *The Division of Labor*, where he tried to show that even where individualism had affirmed itself as a moral criterion guiding action, social rules were no less important. First, it was true, as Spencer had pointed out, that contractual relations tended to grow in such societies; however, at the same time, "non-contractual relations" regulated by legal or moral institutions persisted or increased. For example, family relations involved a series of rights and duties that were not contractual, and which had to be respected in order to avoid legal sanctions or social disapproval: "Just as the bond of kinship is not the outcome of a binding contractual relationship, it cannot be broken through an undertaking of a similar kind" (Durkheim [1893] 1984, p. 157). More generally, and contrary to Spencer's predictions, in modern societies, the state did not restrict its intervention in social relations to the legal environment or the practice of war. The tasks of looking after the education of the young, protecting health in general, overseeing the functioning of public assistance, and administrating transport and communication began slowly to enter the sphere of action of the "central organs."

Durkheim also emphasized that social action – institutional intervention – made its presence felt in contractual relations themselves, because "in a contract not everything is contractual" (Durkheim [1893] 1984, p. 158).The non-contractual features on which the effectiveness of contracts depended were not limited to legal norms which were crucial to guarantee the contracting parties; they also included traditions and moral norms, such as, for example, those involved in the practice of professions, even though these were often very rigorous and restrictive for the private individual.

In summation, only where there was adequate legal regulation was it possible for contractual relations to develop effectively, satisfying the needs of private actors without damaging the collective interests of society. However, this kind of social order could not be guaranteed by individualistic utilitarianism. This was because the simple convergence of individual interests created bonds that were too weak and superficial to give stability to social relations. Indeed, they tended on the contrary to nourish conflicts and to compromise the ordered development of economic relations: "For where interest alone reigns, as nothing arises to check the egoism confronting one other, each self finds itself in relation to the other on a war footing "(Durkheim [1893] 1984, p. 152).

The origin of institutions

In order for social order to exist it was necessary then to place a brake on individual interests, and to regulate and discipline them. This could happen only where strong institutions existed. In the final analysis, institutions were the result of interaction between individuals that developed in the face of certain problems of collective life. Once established, they took on their own autonomy and constrictive nature that then became imposed on single individuals. Durkheim insisted, however, contrary to the beliefs of the utilitarians, that institutions did not find their roots in contractual negotiations, and were not based on agreements between individuals pursuing their interests and deciding to create rules in order to protect these. On the contrary, their origins were to be found in particular "moments of collective ferment" of the society in which interaction between people became both quantitatively and qualitatively more intense. This led the individual interests and self-centered behavior typical of daily life to melt and disappear into strong collective identities: "It is, in fact, at such moments of collective ferment that are born the great ideals upon which civilizations rest" (Durkheim [1895] 1982, p. 91).

Durkheim's examples of these particular phases of social life were the religious revivals of the Middle Ages and the Protestant Reformation, the French Revolution, and the widespread social movements of the nineteenth century. Although these moments of collective enthusiasm were temporary, the ideals they expressed and developed became the basis for social institutions. In other words, they could be considered as the specification and development of these ideals on the normative level, acting as guiding values that could be adapted to the needs and problems that emerged during more stable phases of social life. In Durkheim's view, then, institutions enabled social relations and economic activities to take place. This was not only because – as we have seen – they regulated conflicts of interest but also, and mainly, because they made it possible for individuals to perceive and define these individual interests themselves, since these always depend on a criterion of evaluation that roots them.

As a result, it is possible to understand why Durkheim, like Weber, increasingly believed that religious experience had a crucial role in creating values and ideals, which were periodically revised in moments of collective mobilization. It should be noted, however, that Durkheim, unlike Weber, attributed less importance to the conflicts that emerged between interest groups in the re-elaboration of these values (Poggi 1972). This led to limits in the capacity of his theory to explain the concrete historical processes involved in the forming of institutions.

1.2   The social consequences of the division of labor

Although Durkheim may have given the impression of being optimistic about the capacity of a society with a high division of labor to generate the solidarity that it required, he did not actually believe that this could be taken for granted. This awareness grew in his subsequent work, starting with *Suicide*. The development of the division of labor was in actuality accompanied by tensions and social conflicts. Durkheim's most stimulating and relevant contribution lies in his examination of just these aspects (Pizzorno 1962).

In his initial work, Durkheim approached the problem of the socially destabilizing effects of the division of labor by labelling as "exceptional" and "abnormal" those situations where the division of labor did not go together with increases in solidarity. He distinguished between two ways in which the division of labor had socially destabilizing effects. In the first, when differentiation grew more rapidly than institutional regulations, a situation of "anomie," or lack of norms, became apparent. In the second, in contrast, the rules that were in place were inadequate for the problems: the division of tasks then became "coercive."[4]

Anomic division

In Durkheim's view, the rapid development of economic activity was the principal source of anomie in modern societies. This was not because it was accompanied by a growth in the division of labor, but because it occurred without adequate institutionalization. Two typical ways in which anomie manifested itself were industrial and commercial crises, and antagonism between capital and labor.

Economic crises, which were now more frequent, occurred as a result of the expansion of the market as a mechanism regulating economic activity. In less developed societies production was directly oriented to the provision of needs; the relationship between the two phenomena was thus delimited in a restricted geographic area. The growth of the division of labor and of production for the market led however to the possibility that there might be a gap between production and consumption – between supply and demand – and this could lead to recurrent crises (of over-production or under-consumption).

Durkheim did not deny that – as the economists maintained – the market tended to re-establish the equilibrium between production and consumption. However, it did so at the cost of continued and prolonged disturbances in social relations, which went along with bankruptcies and unemployment. The division of labor that developed with market capitalism had heavy social costs.

In addition, a similar phenomenon to anomie occurred in relations between capital and labor. This involved both the market and the organization of labor. In the market, Durkheim noted that the diffusion of industrial employment had taken place without an adequate legal regulation of labor relations, implying that the workers were inadequately protected against the vagaries of the market. This was just at the time when a determining element of their life chances involved the sale of their labor force on the market. There was a similar phenomenon in the organization of labor, where the apportioning of tasks, routinization, and a loss of quality of labor reduced the role of the worker to that of an appendix to the machine he worked. He became "no more than a lifeless cog, which an external force sets in motion and impels always in the same direction and in the same fashion."(Durkheim [1893] 1984, pp. 306–7).

This situation, according to Durkheim, who comes close to Marx's analysis of alienation, contrasted with the ideals of individual self-enrichment and perfection that were fundamental to the collective conscience of modern society. It was thus inevitable that this would provoke social conflict, as well as making it difficult to integrate individual actors within the social order.

Coercive division

The social disorder that accompanied the diffusion of modern industrial activities was not only the result of anomie, but also of rules that were not adequate any more. The rules overseeing the distribution of divided labor could be of this type, generating a *coercive* division of labor. This was twofold: first, in the assigning of specialized roles to single individuals; second, in the regulation of remuneration for such roles.

Examining the first aspect, it was clear that a society based on a high division of labor presupposed a weakening of the collective conscience, leaving more room for individual choice. In this setting, ideals took root that attributed a moral value to the perfecting and realization of the individual personality. A "cult of the individual" was established, which prescribed that "everyone is called to fulfil the function he performs best and will receive a just reward for his efforts" (Durkheim [1893] 1984, p. 338)

Although these ideals usually spread among all the members of a society – which one may perhaps attribute to the growth of moral density – they often clashed with preceding rules, thus limiting their full actualization. This led to a first form of the coercive division of labor, resulting from a situation where the assignation of specialized tasks to individuals ended up being compulsory rather than chosen. In other words, the tasks did not correspond to individual vocations, but to the conditioning force of the social class of origin. Examples of rules (both legal and moral) producing effects of this kind can be found in inheritance law, which impacted the competition between individuals over particular roles on the basis of their ability; one may also point to rules limiting access to public roles on the basis of class.

In order to prevent the negative effects of institutional factors of this type, it was necessary for these rules to be modified and new norms created guaranteeing equal opportunities for everybody. This "not only supposes that individuals are not consigned forcibly to performing certain determined functions, but also that no obstacle whatsoever prevents them from occupying within the ranks of society a position commensurate to their abilities"((Durkheim [1893] 1984, p. 313). Only in conditions of this sort could competition between single individuals generate solidarity.

Let us now examine the second form of the coercive division of labor. In this case, it was a question of rewarding divided tasks. In order for a society based on the division of labor to generate solidarity, it was necessary that remuneration for this labor correspond to the effec¡tive utility of the services rendered for that society. Where a high division of labor prevailed, and economic activity was based on market exchange, it was necessary to examine how the exchange value – in particular that of labor services – was established, to see how well it corresponded with the "social value" from which it descended. But how can social value be measured? Durkheim's answer is not at all clear. He did not seem to realize that he was dealing with an issue that was already extremely controversial in economics – that of the theory of value. His answer seemed to allude generically to the neoclassical theory approach to the distribution of income. According to this, the recompense for productive factors, including labor, was determined by their contribution to the value of production under perfect market competition (the theory of marginal productivity). However, it was particularly important for Durkheim to point out that the value assigned in this way to various labor activities, through the market, could be altered by the "influence of abnormal factors." This led to a contrast with the principle that characterized the collective conscience of societies that had a high division of labor and that "finds unfair any exchange where the price of the article bears no relationship to the effort expended and the services it renders" (Durkheim [1893] 1984, p. 317).

In sum, it could be said that Durkheim did not disagree with economics' claim that in principle the market could be an effective instrument to establish a correspondence between the exchange value of a good, or of labor, and social utility. However, he wanted to draw attention to the fact that even when they take the form of freely and willingly signed contracts, market exchanges could hide an imbalance in power between the contractors. This opens a gap between rewards and social utility and prevents market mechanisms from stabilizing an effective equivalence between the two phenomena. The example that Durkheim gave was that of the labor market: "If one class in a society is obliged, in order to live, to secure the acceptance by others of its services, whilst another class can do without them, because of the resources already at its disposal, resources that, however, are not necessarily the result of some social superiority, the latter group can lord it over the former" (Durkheim [1893] 1984, p. 319).

Durkheim believed that this gave rise to a "violence" that ended by threatening the legitimacy of contracts and generating social disorder and conflicts. In this case, as in access to specialized roles, the necessary condition for just contracts was that there was no imbalances of power between the contracting parties. It was thus necessary that remuneration be determined according to "social merit" and not other criteria. Only this could make inequality in a setting with a high division of labor acceptable. Durkheim therefore worried about the "moral conditions of exchange," which were, in his opinion, ignored by economists. This required a regulation of the market that was not limited only to pursuing fraud and enforcing respect for contracts, but also actively addressed those imbalances of resources that could lead to unjust exchanges and thus generate conflicts that jeopardized economic activities. "The task of the most advanced societies may therefore be said to be a mission for justice ... To inject an even greater equity into our social relationships, in order to ensure the free deployment of all those forces that are socially useful" (Durkheim [1893] 1984, p. 321).

1.3   The social construction of the market

Durkheim did not explicitly address the market's role as a mechanism regulating economic activities. However, there is no doubt that, especially in his discussion of abnormal forms of the division of labor, he highlighted the destabilizing effects of the market as a mechanism regulating the division of labor. In his work he did not use the term capitalism, and it is likely that in talking about the division of labor rather than capitalism he wanted to focus on a more profound feature of modern society connected to its morphology (to its "substratum"). His analyses, however, particularly those in *The Division of Labor*, can be viewed as a criticism of liberal capitalism, that is, of the specific form of capitalism in which the market played an important role in the regulation of productive activities and in the distribution of income. It should also be emphasized, however, that this criticism was not based on economic features, such as, for example, the fall of the rate of profit on which Marx and the Marxists insisted in various ways. In his argument, social factors prevailed over strictly economic ones.

According to Durkheim, it was necessary to limit the role of the market in order fully to achieve the integrative potential of the division of labor. However, he was convinced that new institutional rules of an exclusively economic type, for example, some form of planning (as one would say today) to avoid crises and bankruptcies or to control the labor market, would not be sufficient. The stability of economic activities did not depend only on economic compensation, but also on non-economic conditions – on shared criteria of evaluation concerning the relationship between performance and recompense for different specialized tasks. This is why he was interested in the role of corporations.[5] In modern societies, based on the individual, such criteria had necessarily to be inspired by the principles of meritocracy. As a result, the mere replacement of liberal capitalism by a more organized form, or some form of socialism based on state control, would not in itself have been enough to resolve the problems posed by the division of labor. For these problems were primarily social rather than economic in nature, and turned on the extent to which relations of exchange between different specialized roles and, therefore, recompense, were accepted. If these problems were not dealt with effectively, the result might have been to demotivate individuals, or social conflicts which would destabilize economic activities even further.

For these reasons, Durkheim's work helped not only illuminate the processes of transformation of liberal capitalism on the historical level, but it provided important elements of a sociology of the market that would seek to highlight the non-economic conditions of market functioning in a modern society with a high level of division of labor. In these contexts, if the market was be an effective instrument of regulation for specialized economic activities, legal and moral rules that stabilized contracts by allowing them to be respected and by pursuing fraud, were not enough. One also had to address disparities in the resources of actors in their market interaction, so as to reduce imbalances of power. However, even interventions of this type, which were feasible, for example, through anti-trust legislation, legislation on labor or bargaining between interest associations, might not be enough. The market would function better in those contexts in which access to different roles was allocated on the basis of the effective vocation and abilities of the actors, and in which remuneration would be distributed on the basis of "social merit." In these cases a strong social cohesion would develop where on the one hand, individuals would be more greatly committed to their specialized tasks, and, on the other, conflicts would be reduced, to the advantage of economic development. However, all this meant that society should involve non-economic institutions – such as the family, schools, and political institutions – so as to promote a meritocratic distribution of roles and recompense, thus convincing actors that they belonged to a fair society.

2   Waste of Productive Resources and Conspicuous Consumption

Durkheim lived in France during the second half of the nineteenth century, a period of strong social and political tensions, and this experience profoundly influenced his vision of relations between the economy and institutions. While he was certainly interested in highlighting the limits of economic theory and the destabilizing effects on social order of a capitalist economy regulated by the market, his primary preoccupation was to make a contribution to the scientific foundation of sociology.

Thorstein Veblen (1857–1929) lived in the same era, but in a very different context. The United States, emerging from the Civil War, was marked by a series of rapid upheavals and an economic transformation that took it to a role of world leadership in economic and industrial development. From 1860 to 1914 the population tripled, in part due to twenty million immigrants, and employment and production increased enormously. Over the space of a few years, enormous industrial *trusts* formed in the railway, steel and oil sectors, and many others. The grand magnates, such as Rockefeller and Morgan, came to control a considerable share of the national economy. This was also, however, the period of the serious crisis of traditional agriculture in the Midwest, which fell ever more into debt to the banks and capital holders of the East. It was also a period of intense and often violent industrial conflicts involving the emerging working class.

It was in this context that Veblen's reflections on society matured. The son of Norwegian Lutheran immigrants, his family lived in an agricultural community in Minnesota. His intellectual training was primarily in economics, but he soon showed a strong dissatisfaction with traditional economics (classical and neoclassical), which he felt were unable to provide the kind of tools necessary to understand the major economic changes that marked the end of the century. For Veblen, as for Durkheim, the optimistic expectations of economic theory ran into the social upheavals that came as a consequence of market-led capitalism. Further, traditional forms of analysis could not deal effectively with these phenomena. However, while Durkheim's dissatisfaction led him to seek to give sociology a scientific basis as a general theory of society, Veblen tried to redesign economic analysis on an institutional basis, drawing on the evolutionary perspective developed in biology and the natural sciences by Darwin.[6] It is in this sense that his institutional economics is comparable with the model developed by Durkheim, even if it matured in a different social and cultural context, and the authors did not interact in any way. Veblen contributed to a non-individualistic theory of economic action, and he focused on a problem of historical–empirical research that was not dealt with by economics – the social effects of liberal market-based capitalism, and the changes that took place in this model of economic organization prior to the Great Depression of the thirties.

2.1   The criticism of economic theory and institutional economics

Veblen expressed his criticism of classical and neo-classical economics in his first writings, published in the "Quarterly Journal of Economics" in 1898–9, and subsequently collected in the book *The Place of Science in Modern Civilization* (1919a). In one of these essays – *Why is Economics not an Evolutionary Science?* – he presented the essential elements of his critique focussing on three problem-areas. First there was the individualistic conception of human nature embodied in the theory of economic action. Second, was the static nature of traditional economic analysis, that is, its focus on equilibrium rather than change. Finally came the link between the pursuit of individual interest and collective well-being, which he did not believe was automatically guaranteed by the functioning of the market.

Regarding the first aspect, Veblen believed that traditional economic theory held a vision of human nature that was "passive and substantially inert and inevitably given," a vision in which man was seen as a "lighting calculator of pleasures and pains," a mere "globule of desires" (Veblen [1919b] 1990, p. 57). In reality, not only was it inappropriate to talk of human nature in general and ahistorical terms, but human behavior was furthermore not explicable in individualistic terms, and could not be separated from the influence exercised by society through traditions, customs, and habits. By this, he meant stable patterns of behavior, which is to say institutions.

He also believed that if one wanted to examine the bio-psychical factors involved in human behavior, one had to seek them not in any tendency to calculate pain and pleasure, but in the tendency to create and develop new activities. Later, he would speak of an "instinct of workmanship" as the basic human motivation.[7] His vision of man was, in other words, closer to that of *homo faber*, than the maximizing calculator of economic theory (Ferrarotti 1969). In any case, even though his concept of instinct was ambiguous, it was clear that he aimed to move the conception of human action in general, and economic activity in particular, away from a hedonistic and ahistorical conception of its sources. Instead, attention should be focussed on the role of institutions in channeling and shaping behavior, defining how bio-psychic propensities are realized. Institutions were "mental habits," shared and approved models of behavior.

For Veblen too, then, human action was socially conditioned. Human beings were guided by values and norms which they absorbed from the society in which they lived. Historical change depended on transformations both in institutions and individual behavior. Traditional economic theory could not properly grasp this variability in action, since it treated individual preferences and the state of knowledge and technology as givens. Veblen underlined the static and ahistorical nature of neoclassical economics (although he seemed to include the classical approach in this too). For him, the traditional approach was tied to an idea of equilibrium, to a search for mechanisms that stabilized the economy which was influenced by the physical sciences, and in particular by mechanics. All this had resulted in a discipline with an analytical, deductive, and normative bent that distanced it from the investigation of real processes of change (cf. the essays in *The Limitation of Marginal Utility* [Veblen 1919b] and *Economic Theory in the Calculable Future* [Veblen 1934a]). Economics should, instead, be able to take account of the important changes taking place, but in order to do so it had to look towards the biological sciences and their evolutionary stance, and to place the role of the institutions at the center of enquiry.

Herbert Spencer had already sought to develop an evolutionary approach to reconcile the individualism of economic theory with an orientation favorable to *laissez faire*. This skein of thought could also be found in America, for example in the work of Graham Sumner, who greatly influenced Veblen. However, although he was inspired by the theory of evolution, Veblen adopted a non-individualistic orientation that was strongly critical of the social Darwinism then common in American society. Central to this approach was the idea that institutions, not individuals, were important. It was institutions that evolved in order to meet the problems of adapting to the environment, but the selection of institutions did not necessarily lead to the establishment of more efficient ones. It is thus clear that Veblen rejected the idea of a unilinear evolution leading to institutional convergence.

How did institutions come into being and change? Veblen's reply was that they involved collective responses to the problems raised by the environment that human beings must face: "The life of man in society just like the life of other species, is a struggle for existence, and therefore a process of selective adaptation. The evolution of social structure has been a process of natural selection of institutions" (Veblen [1899] 1934, p. 188).

His view of institutions was thus evolutionary: they came into being to regulate relations between people in society and with the natural environment, but – once formed – they helped select certain types of behavior that affected responses to future problems of adaptation. The growth in population, and above all the improvement in knowledge and the development of technology ("the state of industrial arts") led to the emergence of new problems of adaptation.

Science and technology were thus the vehicles of change, but the process, according to Veblen, was by no means linear. They defined the potential for changes in the productive process that had consequences for other institutions (cultural, social, and political), but until new institutions – ways of thinking, customs, and laws – were introduced, it was necessary to overcome the resistance of the old institutions. This did not simply involve the inertia of old habits and ways of thinking. Institutions inherited from the past were very often defended by the social groups enjoying privilege from them, who clearly opposed change, and often managed to influence the lower social classes. Over time, the adaptation of institutions to allow the full exploitation of new knowledge and technologies was possible, but the timing and form of this process were not definable a priori, nor was it possible to identify, as Marx thought, a final stage in the process of change. Evolution was a continual process and society – especially modern society in which technological progress was emphasized – is always facing a lag in institutional adaptation. The result depended on the outcome of a conflict between social groups that were less exposed to knowledge and modern techniques and groups that, precisely because they were more directly committed to the world of production, were driven to adopt a more rational and precise vision of the causes and effects of phenomena, and were therefore more capable of sustaining a process of innovation inspired by these principles (Veblen was thinking in particular of production engineers).

One consequence of Veblen's theory of change was the possible co-existence of societies in which the relation between technology and institutions was different. Veblen did not believe in a process of inevitable institutional convergence, pulled in the wake of technology, which would lead to the establishment of a unique institutional model that could respond more efficiently to the problems of adaptation posed by the economic and social environment. One of his most important works was *Imperial Germany and the Industrial Revolution* (1915), a pioneering investigation in comparative economic sociology. In this study the rapid economic development of Germany in the second half of the nineteenth century was compared to the earlier and more gradual development of Britain. The underlying thesis was that there could be different paths of development, depending on the capacity to graft more modern technologies applicable to the industrial process into an institutional context that was still permeated with traditional values. It was just such a process of grafting that explained the rapidity of German development. Later, Veblen would employ similar reasoning to understan Japan, in his essay *The Opportunity of Japan* (1934b).

The advantage of the combination of modern technologies and traditional institutions was twofold. On the one hand, forms of "group solidarity" and subordination to political authority, formed during the feudal period or in relation to war activities, could be exploited so as to increase the willingness to cooperate by some of the work force. On the other, the grafting of modern technologies might allow one to avoid (at least for a significant period) importing institutions that had developed slowly over time, as in Britain, and that had eventually hampered the exploitation of technology for the general welfare, and, as a consequence, growth in knowledge. In his examination of British development, Veblen noted how it had been anticipated and favored by the country's insularity and relative lack of involvement in the wars on the Continent. However, this led in time to gradual changes in institutions, with effects that hindered development: a loss of entrepreneurial dynamism and the subordination of productive activities in favor of financial profits for owners; a growth in costs due to sales and advertising; an impoverishment of the working class and social conflict; the spread of phenomena like "conspicuous waste," which diverted increasing resources away from collective well-being; resistance to technological change leading to outdated productive apparatus and infrastructures. This was the price that Britain paid for having taken the lead at the beginning of the Industrial Revolution.

It should also be noted that Veblen's analysis made an important and pioneering contribution regarding two important issues. The first involved the variety of possible paths to development, all of which could follow different tracks. There was no one best way. As well as the traditional "development from below," taken by Britain and the United States, there was also the "development from above," adopted by Germany, Japan and Italy, where industrialization was promoted by the state, which tried to safeguard social balance and traditional values.[8] Second, Veblen insisted on the coexistence of different combinations of technology and institutions, which were not necessarily destined to disappear as a result of competition. Combinations which were more efficient and competitive in a particular historical period could later come to lose some of these advantages, without necessarily disappearing. In other words, there were multiple equilibria. This was yet another theme that was extremely important for economic sociology and contemporary institutional economics (Hodgson 1994), as we shall later see in chapters 9 and 10.

2.2   The social costs of capitalism

Veblen employed his theory of change to focus on the problems of adaptation of institutions in modern society, on the basis of his observations of American society at the turn of the century. In his view, there was a delay in the adaptation of institutions to developments in knowledge and technology, all of which led to growing social costs in terms of collective welfare. In the first phase of capitalist development, there was a connection between the pursuit of individual interest and improvements in collective well-being, which was enhanced by the functioning of the market. In the following phase, this connection became looser and economic organization based on market capitalism had led to a loss of collective welfare when one considered the potential advantages offered by techniques and science. Veblen sought to demonstrate this thesis in his work, looking at changes in production and consumption. Let us take the production side first.

In the first phase of the Industrial Revolution, which began in England in the second half of the eighteenth century, the "machine industry" became established. During this period production involved private firms in which the owner-entrepreneurs were both capitalists and organizers of production, bringing economic–financial power together with technical and organizational abilities. Given "the state of industrial arts," that is, the available knowledge and techniques, firms were small and they had no control over the goods market in which they worked. In such a situation, capitalist–entrepreneurs sought profits through improvements in efficiency, under the stimulus of competition from other firms on the market. It was in this setting that one saw the development of interpretive schemas of the economy which held that that the pursuit of individual interest in a context of market competition, unhampered by political institutions, was beneficial to collective welfare. It was true – Veblen recognized – that economic institutions allowed more goods to be produced at a lower cost for the collectivity. In general, the productive potential defined by the development of techniques and science was congruent with the institutions that allowed this potential benefit to society to be used to its full potential (Veblen called this *serviceability*).

In other words, the institutional setting that one may define as liberal capitalism, and on which economic theory was based, worked, but only in a particular historical phase. This period finished at the end of the 1800s, as a result of the latest developments in technology. New techniques allowed economies of scale, and consequently mass production, but they also required large-scale industrial investment. It was at this point that the divorce between economic–financial functions and the management and organization of firms (initially conjoined in the owner-entrepreneur) first came about. Ownership and management were separated. The former was in the hands of a new figure, the "captain of industry," who managed investments and was primarily interested in the financial profit from increases in the value of the capital invested in industrial firms (a capital rendered more mobile by its transformation into shares quoted on the stock exchange). In other words, these were financiers of stock-companies or banker-investors. The actual management of firms was instead handed over to managers who developed the necessary technical and organizational knowledge to apply new productive methods: these were what Veblen called "efficiency engineers."

The division of property and management heralded growing problems, however, for collective well-being. Shareholders' search for profit did not lead to an increase in collective well-being through the greater production of goods at lower prices, as had first occurred in the machine-industry age. The search for greater earnings could lead captains of industry into buying and selling firms merely for purposes of financial speculation, damaging both production and employment, and leading to the unnecessary closure of firms. Given the growing interdependence within the industrial system, crises induced by the search for financial profit became common, generating cyclical depressions and unemployment.

Veblen thus drew attention to how the search for profit in the new setting that technological development had brought about, might not only be to the detriment of greater efficiency, but could block it. This thesis, argued on a more technical level in *The Theory of Business Enterprise* (1904) was further developed in *The Engineers and the Price System* (1921). This book emphasized how the considerable increase in productivity made possible by new technology could lead to a greater amount of available goods at lower prices. This was, however, hindered by capitalist financiers' need to keep profits high. This was what was behind the push to transform the open competitive market into a closed, monopolistic or oligopolistic market through the formation of cartels and trusts, and of formal and informal links intended to limit production, and keep prices high to the detriment of consumers. In other words, what Veblen described as a "conscious suppression of efficiency" began to develop. As well as manifesting itself in the shrinking of production and employment, it showed itself in the growth of the cost of sales (distribution, advertising) that resulted from the competitive struggle, and heavily increased production costs.

Overall then, resources were wasted and collective welfare was lower than it could have been, given the potential allowed by the state of technical development. Veblen's emphasis on the growing gap between technology and economic institutions clearly showed his disagreements with the Marxist framework of the forces and relations of production. Veblen did not see the working class, or the lower classes in general, as being the agent of change. To understand his position better, one needs to examine more closely his work on the theme of consumption, described in his best-known book *The Theory of the Leisure Class* (1899). The book was extremely popular because of its brilliant critique of the customs of American society, and it became a classic point of reference for political and cultural radicalism. It also sharply criticized the individualistic and utilitarian account of how action was motivated, which, as we have seen, constituted a central theme of Veblen's institutionalism.

In Veblen's view, the desire to increase consumption of material goods did not in itself provide a sufficient incentive for people to engage in economic activity. In modern society, in which the economy was organized on the basis of private ownership and the market, the possibility to consume more was sought by individuals because it was a source of prestige and social honor. *Conspicuous consumption* replaced courage and valor in war, which had been signs of social distinction in a previous era. As a consequence, the most profound motive behind actors' economic activities involved their search for prestige in a constant, antagonistic comparison with how other members of society were doing: "The possession of wealth confers honor, it is an invdious distinction." (Veblen [1899], 1934 p. 26).

While it was certainly true that the need to earn a living was a very strong incentive for the poor, the motivations underlying the behavior of these social groups changed as the economy grew in modern societies. As social groups slowly raised themselves above the level of mere subsistence, they became attracted by the utility of consumption as a means of reputation. This mechanism was particularly prevalent among the urban population of the great cities – as Simmel had noted – where the traditional criteria of social recognition were less strong and standards of living were the main markers of social status. As a result, there was an impetus towards the integration of the lower classes and the working class as consumers. Veblen, in contrast to Marx, saw this as the principle reason why the class conflict could not be considered the motor of institutional innovation.

At the center of *The Theory of the Leisure Class* is the notion of *conspicuous waste*, which Veblen saw as leading, on the consumption side to a reduction in the collective welfare of the capitalist economy of his time. Contrary to the predictions of neoclassical economics, consumers did not try to satisfy their preferences and needs in a rational manner, nor had these preferences developed independently of each other. Consumers' behavior was instead influenced by social interdependence, by the continuous attempt to emulate others and to reach a higher social status. This resulted in an unnecessary waste of working energy and the spread of a kind of consumption that Veblen described (often in a moralistic fashion) as superfluous and futile. Veblen may be seen as the first critic of consumerism and the consumer society, a theme which was to assume great importance in later decades, but also as one of the founders of the sociology of consumption (which I return to in chapter 9). He questioned the assumption of the rational consumer, with stable preferences formed independently of the social context, who aimed to optimize according to certain preferences, through a continuous process of adaptation, which was itself governed by the constraints of price and income. Veblen opposed a social emulation model to rational calculation.

In general then, the institutions of market capitalism involved high social costs, and limited opportunities to improve collective well-being through technology, both in production and consumption. The separation of ownership from management, and the search for financial profit by "absentee owners." restricted productive potential, while the diffusion of consumption as a competitive instrument in the quest for social status also led to a loss of well-being.[9] Veblen emphasized this contradiction, which was in his opinion destined to be resolved through adjustment in the institutions inherited from the preceding phase. However, he did not foresee any significant signs of change in his time, and he was very skeptical about the ability of the American working-class movement to affect matters. In his last work, which also reflected the influence of the Russian Revolution, he identified engineers and new techniques of production as possible protagonists of change (Veblen 1921). This social group would be better equipped to evaluate the loss of efficiency involved in capitalist institutions, given its knowledge and role in firms, and could begin to use resources in a planned and rational manner. However, Veblen was vague and uncertain about how this might come about.

3   The Contribution of Positivist Institutionalism

What do Durkheim and Veblen's institutionalism have in common? What are their similarities and differences to German economic sociology? For a start, both authors were more strongly influenced by positivism than Sombart and Weber, who were trained in the markedly anti-positivist cultural climate of German historicism. Durkheim wanted to found a "science of morals" to give a scientific basis to the difficult choices that people faced in modern society. Veblen was openly inspired by the model of the natural sciences, and in particular by the biological sciences, which he used to reconstruct economic analysis on a different basis than traditional theory. Both the French sociologist and the American economist were attracted by the idea of founding the study of society on a basis similar to that of the natural sciences. Their positivist-influenced institutionalism led them away from German economic sociology, which – as we saw in chapter 1 – was formed in open disagreement with the idea of the assimilation between a science of society with that of nature, and was aimed at the construction of theoretical models that were delimited in space and time.

Another very clear difference had to do with their orientation towards economics. Sombart and Weber aimed to develop analytical schema which would interpret specific forms of economic organization. In defending these choices they also recognized the legitimacy of economic theory as an analytical discipline. Their vision of the relations between economics and economic sociology was one of complementarity between the two investigative strands: sociology had to clarify the institutional context within which it was possible to attempt to apply economic schemas, referring both to actors' motivations and regulatory modalities based on the market. Durkheim and Veblen were for their part more skeptical about the ability of economic theory to capture the concrete forms of economic organization. Influenced by their positivistic roots, they were less willing to recognize a discipline that was not founded empirically as being scientific, and they were more open to the idea of a general theory of society. They thus saw economic sociology more as an alternative to economics than as a complement.

However, if one looks at how Durkheim and Veblen put their scientific programs into practice, the differences between their positivist institutionalism and Sombart and Weber's historically-oriented version are noticeably less marked. Despite their language and aims, Durkheim and Veblen practiced a more moderate version of positivism, which differed from the original version of positivist sociology offered by Comte and Spencer, but also from that of Marx. It did not fall into the trap of positing universal and necessary stages of development and evolutionary laws of society, being instead more open to historical–empirical investigation, which recognized the open-endedness and indeterminacy of historical processes. This approach in fact brought to them closer to Sombart and Weber. Thus one may find a convergence between the two approaches in their effort to found the analysis of economic action in socially-oriented action – the perspective that was typical of economic sociology. They all rejected an individualistic vision of economic action, whether it was motivated by utilitarian reasoning or based on biological or psychological givens. Subjects' activity in the sphere of production and distribution of goods was guided by models of behavior provided by institutions (even when they were oriented by individual interest). At the same time, however, institutions were the product of interaction between actors. In particular conditions and moments – which each author sought to clarify in his own way – such interaction led to a change in institutions, but it was impossible to predict in advance how they would evolve historically. Economic sociology took on an empirical–analytical connotation. This approach was mainly used by German economic sociologists to explain the origins and spread of capitalism as a particular form of economic organization, and by Durkheim and Veblen to highlight the social consequences of that development.

Naturally, this distinction was relative. Sombart and Weber too addressed the transformation of capitalism, even if this was not their main theme. Insofar as they deal with this subject, they very accurately predicted a trend towards the increasing organization of the capitalist economy, which would lead to a reduction in the regulatory role that the market had played in the liberal phase, as firms became more bureaucratized, and state intervention was extended. In contrast, Durkheim and Veblen concentrated more on the social problems created by market capitalism once it had become established, problems which demanded new institutional forms of regulation. They focused on the lack or belatedness of such institutions; the old ones were no longer suitable and the new ones had difficulty in establishing themselves. While Weber and Sombart underlined the complex institutional preconditions for the emergence of capitalism for capitalism, Durkheim and Veblen emphasized how developed capitalist economies could not be efficiently regulated by the institutional context in which they had originally formed and this generated increasing social costs. They thus saw the social consequences of capitalism as much more problematic than Sombart and Weber. This perspective was similar to that of Marx, although it differed from it in two important ways. First, it was not pessimistic about the capacity of capitalist economies to continue functioning, providing goods and services. Second, it did not link economic crisis to the emergence of a social actor – the working class – that would take action which would necessarily lead to a socialist economy.

Durkheim and Veblen's respective analytical frameworks thus included both similarities and differences. Neither trusted the capacity of the market to maintain its balance without adequate institutional regulation. The results of this were unemployment, cyclical crises, and social conflicts. These phenomena were, however, the signs of a more general problem – the under-use by market capitalism of the productive potential available for collective welfare. In this sense, the social costs of capitalism were important for both authors. Durkheim formulated this judgment in terms of an incapacity to exploit the advantages of the division of labor to the maximum, because of the deficiencies of institutions, which generated abnormal and pathological forms of the division of competences and levels of reward. This led to problems of coordination and conflicts. Veblen, instead, looked to technology and its capacity to generate production and employment, which were hampered and limited by institutions. On the production side, he pointed to the quest of captains of industry for profit, in a context that was ever more dominated by monopolies. On the consumption side, he looked at the spread of models of conspicuous consumption across all social groups.

These similarities and differences are also apparent in the sorts of solution they suggested. Both Durkheim and Veblen envisaged forms of regulation for the economy that substantially limited the role of the market. Veblen also mentioned, although in a rather vague and ambiguous fashion, a centralized planning process with engineers at the center. This reflected his greater emphasis on cognitive elements, and thus on the development of science and technology in the creation of new institutions. Durkheim concerned himself more systematically with the possible role of corporations. He was convinced that a socialist economic plan was inadequate if the problem of reconstructing moral bonds between individuals with regard to the division of labor was not addressed. In his view, this was the most important objective that corporations could fulfil through their contribution to the regulation of economic activities. His vision tended therefore to reflect his greater emphasis on normative factors – shared moral values – in the processes through which institutions were formed.

Neither Durkheim nor Veblen appeared to be aware, however, of the risks which such a substantial retrenchment of the market would pose for economic development and political democracy. Even though, unlike economic theory, they helped highlight the failures of the market from the perspective of collective well-being, they did not take proper account of possible failures of the state and bureaucratic planning, in part because these had not yet been demonstrated. Their analysis was thus particularly adept in elucidating the social costs of market capitalism, but rather weaker in outlining possible solutions through which institutions could adjust to changes in the economy.

Chapter 5

The Great Depression and the Decline of Liberal Capitalism: Polanyi and Schumpeter

The nineteenth century was the golden age of liberal capitalism. For approximately one hundred years Europe was free of major wars. During this period the market established itself in different forms, and at different points of time, as the main regulating principle of domestic and international economies, thus guaranteeing strong growth in production and exchange. Over time, however, the social and political tensions analyzed in the previous chapter began to emerge. In particular, the working class, which developed at the same rapid pace as industrial activity, began to make new demands for social recognition and political integration. Indeed, by the end of the century the difficulties that liberal capitalism had in maintaining economic growth, social integration and peace in international relations had begun to emerge more clearly. On the economic level, competition became more intense for backward countries, pushing them to seek protection. In reality, however, industrial and agricultural protectionism checked international exchanges and contributed to an intensification of the colonization process. Industrial conflict increased, as did the political tensions between states, leading to the First World War.

After this war, nothing was the same. The conflict had extraordinarily high economic and social costs and accelerated institutional change. Despite attempts to re-establish pre-war systems, economic and social conditions remained very unstable. Following the collapse of the New York stock exchange in 1929, the Great Depression precipitated all the economies of the developed world into a serious and prolonged depression, with a collapse in production, multiple bankruptcies and unprecedented peaks in unemployment.

The Great Depression can be considered as an ideal-typical watershed in economic and social history. This was because the need to deal with this exceptional situation pushed countries into distancing themselves in a consistent fashion (albeit in different ways) from the liberal orthodoxy of domestic and international political economy. Liberal capitalism, which had already been threatened by the Great War and the events following it, was thus progressively replaced – in different ways – by a new institutional setting.

It is these events that form the background to the work of the two authors discussed in this chapter: Karl Polanyi and Joseph Schumpeter. While Durkheim and Veblen helped to elucidate the social consequences of liberal capitalism, Polanyi and Schumpeter focused on the crisis in this form of economic organization. They sought to explain the causes of this decline from the perspective of economic sociology, and they both outlined the processes of change that resulted from the experiments of the 1930s and after. These took the form of a more regulated capitalism, in which the space of the market shrank and the economy – to use an expression that Polanyi liked – was re-embedded into society. Like Durkheim and Veblen, these two scholars came from different backgrounds. They followed independent intellectual trajectories, and they were on opposite sides of the political spectrum – Polanyi was a socialist and Schumpeter was a conservative liberal. However, this makes it all the more interesting that their analyses were markedly similar, and both made basic contributions to the particular research perspective of economic sociology.

1 Market Domination and Society's Self-Defense

1.1 The economy as an institutional process

Karl Polanyi (1886–1964) did work that spanned many disciplines, but both his intellectual trajectory and his interests suggest that he was an institutionalist. His methodological observations were presented in numerous essays, most of which are collected in two posthumous volumes, *Primitive, Archaic and Modern Economies* (1968) and *The Livelihood of Man* (1977). For Polanyi, as for the scholars discussed in previous chapters, institutionalism mainly meant that economic action could not be understood in individualistic terms, but was influenced by social institutions. He also criticized the idea of "economic man," which posited an individual psychological tendency towards barter, exchange and commerce.

Polanyi did not believe that economic behavior was always motivated by the search for profit. He referred, in this regard, to anthropological work on primitive economies, in particular studies by Malinowski on the inhabitants of New Guinea (*Argonauts of the Western Pacific*, 1922) and by Thurnwald (*Economics in Primitive Communities*, 1932). These books showed that "The motive of gain is not 'natural' to man" (Polanyi [1944] 1985, p. 269). In his opinion, it was not possible to understand primitive economies by attributing utilitarian motivations to their protagonists. These economies instead functioned on the basis of complex networks of shared obligations that motivated individual behavior. It was only over the last few centuries, with the growth of the market economy, that the pursuit of profit had become important. This had happened precisely because the economy was increasingly regulated by the market, which is to say by an institution that encouraged, and provided incentives for, the search for profit.

As a result, Polanyi believed that economic investigation could not be separated from historical settings. It was not possible to formulate general economic laws other than on an abstract and analytical level. In historical–empirical reality, different "types of economies" existed, "economic systems" in which the activities of production, distribution, and the exchange of goods – without which society could not survive – took place. These were regulated by specific institutions that changed over time. As we have seen (section 1, chapter 1), Polanyi identified three basic types of regulation for the activities of production, distribution and exchange of goods, which he called "forms of integration" of the economy: *reciprocity, redistribution,* and *market*. Each of these forms differed from the others in how economic activity was organized, and in the relationship between these activities and other spheres of social life (the family, politics, religion, etc.).

When *reciprocity* prevailed, as in primitive societies, goods and services were produced and exchanged on the expectation that other goods or services would be received in ways and over periods of time that were fixed by shared social norms. Such norms of reciprocity were based on specific institutions that supported them and imposed various sanctions on individuals who did not respect them. This especially involved family and kin; indeed, it was mainly through family or kinship groups that the economic relation of reciprocity had developed.

Reciprocity was already linked to *redistribution* in primitive societies, but the latter was more often found in the more evolved societies of antiquity, which spread across a greater territory, and involved larger political units. Indeed, redistribution came to be the prevalent mode of organization in such societies. In this form of integration, goods were produced and allocated on the basis of norms establishing the modalities of labor services and types of resources that should be transferred to a political chief. This was usually some form of tribal chief or a noble with an administrative apparatus, and he would in turn redistribute these resources to members of the society according to specific rules.

The last form of economic integration, *market trade*, was very recent and, in Polanyi's opinion, had reached its culmination in the course of the nineteenth century. To understand this assertion, one must take account of how this form, in organizational terms, did not simply involve the exchange of goods through market-regulated trade, in which prices emerged from the unrestrained interaction of demand and supply. It also required that the production of goods and services, and the distribution of income must depend on a price-regulated market. Thus, one decided to produce on the basis of prices for particular goods, and one paid for labor on the basis of prices that came about through the encounter of demand and supply.

Polanyi wanted particularly to emphasize that one could find forms of trade with prices fixed by the market in non-modern economies. However, in these cases, production and distribution were organized on the basis of reciprocity and redistribution. In settings of this type, commercial forms involving "gift trade" (reciprocity), and "administrated trade," where prices were set in advance by politico-administrative means (redistribution), often went together with exchanges where price was regulated by the encounter between demand and supply on the market. It was only much later that this latter form spread to the sphere of production and to the distribution of incomes. And it was only when this became widespread that one could talk, according to Polanyi, about market exchange as a form of integration of the economy.

The relationship between market exchange as a form of integration of the economy and the institutions supporting it should now be clearer. It required the replacement of family and kin structures supporting norms of reciprocity, and state forms founded on the obligations of fealty and political dependence typical of re-distribution, by markets regulated by price (or "self-regulated markets"). This meant that the institutional prerequisites of self-regulated markets already existed, as had already been mentioned by several other authors, including Marx and Weber. These spoke of the features peculiar to the economic capitalist system: private ownership of the means of production (capital, land, and labor), waged labor, and the full commercialization of all productive factors. It was in this setting – and only this one – according to Polanyi, that it was appropriate to speak of the utilitarian motivations of economic action. Far from being the result of men's natural psychological tendencies, they were instead an effect of the particular institutions that provided the foundations of market exchange, making the motives of gain or of hunger essential components of economic action.

As we shall later see, *The Great Transformation* aimed to explain how the institutional presuppositions underlying market exchange had come into being. Polanyi also, more importantly, described how their progressive transformation in a process that ended with the supercession of liberal capitalism, as modern forms of redistribution tied to the state became more widespread. First, however, let us examine two aspects of Polanyi's methodological argument.

First, there was his idea of *economic system*. This concept, which we know was typical of the tradition of economic sociology, was linked together with that of *form of integration*. The latter involved a stable pattern widespread in a particular economy – thereby defining an economic system – to the extent that it extended to the productive sphere and regulated the use of land and labor. This was also true of reciprocity and redistribution.

The other point that Polanyi emphasized was that forms of integration did not represent "stages of development." There was no particular temporal sequence along which they could be positioned relative to one another, and they usually were combined in different forms in an economic system where one of them prevailed. For example, just as markets were often important, although not prevalent, in antiquity, the other forms sometimes reappeared during the period of market exchange (for instance, during the First World War) and they tended to re-emerge during a crisis of the dominant model. This is why it was necessary to relativize the analytical value of classical and neoclassical economics (see section 1, chapter 1). Economics had developed through the consideration of a particular historical situation, the economic system based on market exchange. However, it tended improperly to generalize its model of analysis in studying the past and future, assuming that utilitarian motivations and the laws of the self-regulated market were universal . This generated what Polanyi called "the economistic fallacy" (1977, p. 6).

1.2 The great transformation

"Nineteenth century civilization has collapsed. This book is concerned with the political and economic origins of this event, as well as of the great transformation which it ushered in" (Polanyi [1944] 1985, p. 3). With these words, Polanyi's most famous work began, taking as its central theme the different forms of the *great transformation* that had overtaken Western society from the 1930s, and which were leading to the replacement of the liberal capitalism that had become established in the nineteenth century. The end of this model involved the resizing of the market's space as a form of integration of the economy, as the state took on a more active role in regulating economy and society. In his analysis, Polanyi sought to answer two questions. First, he inquired into the historical roots of the self-regulated market, and how this form of integration had become established. Second, he was interested in the social consequences of the self-regulated market, and its effects on the functioning of the economy, from the final decades of the previous century to the Great Depression of 1929, when the great transformation had began.

Many factors contributed to establishing the market as a form of integration, but one seems decisive – the invention and manufacture of complex and expensive machines that revolutionized methods of production. These machines, which lowered the cost of production, could be used profitably only if it was possible to sell their maximum output on a predictable basis, and only if one could provide the necessary raw materials and labor. In other words, there not only had to be a wide market, but all the productive factors had to be available, which is to say that they had to be available for purchase in sufficient quantities. If these conditions did not exist, then investment in new machines became too risky. Polanyi's analysis was similar to Weber's in that it emphasized how important it was that all productive factors be fully available in order to allow the economic calculation on which the new form of economy depended.

One may also see similarities with Weber's *General Economic History* in the way that Polanyi singles out the social figures who, by using machines, spurred new forms of production for the market. The capitalist entrepreneur evolved from the old figure of the merchant. Commercial actors initially bought raw materials, making others work them, for example, through weaving work in the home, but at a certain point started to invest their capital in the new machines that had become available, transforming themselves into entrepreneurs and creating the modern factory using waged labor. All of this was possible, however, only if there were both markets on which goods could be sold, and markets on which raw materials and labor could be bought. That is to say, markets had to be created, and those members of society who could make these markets function had to have the right motivations towards economic action: "for the motive of subsistence that of gain must be substituted" (Polanyi [1944] 1985, p. 41). Polanyi thus emphasized that the motivations towards economic action associated with the search for profit were historically contingent, and were not natural as had been claimed by the economists.

The fact that this involved a gradual process did not diminish the importance of this change. One had to pay special attention to its effects on the factors of production (land and labor). As we have seen, it was precisely insofar as market exchange was extended to the sphere of production that one could identify it as a form of integration of the economy. This was not to deny the fact that markets for some goods had existed in antiquity, but they had not regulated production. How did markets for land and for labor come into being?

Polanyi rejected the views of Smith and the classical economists, who believed that they were created through the gradual development of a natural propensity towards barter and exchange. Rather, they emerged as a consequence of political intervention, of administrative measures, and sometimes genuine instances of private violence (for example, in the appropriation of land through enclosures). These interventions took place over a long period of time, running from the fifteenth to the nineteenth centuries, in different forms in different countries. In the case of land, they led to the end of the feudal system and to the secularization of Church property, and ended with full legal recognition that ownership rights could be bought and sold. The growth of cities and the need to support their populations went together with the full commercialization of goods produced by the land. This started with wheat, so that landholders were encouraged to increase production for sale on the market, while legal and traditional limits that had previously restricted the quota of commercial production, and had guaranteed the satisfaction of local consumption needs, were eliminated.

Polanyi's analysis mainly focused on the formation of the labor market, particularly on the English context. In this case too, it was necessary to eliminate social and legal forms of control that had regulated labor relations, as represented in the medieval corporations. In England, which had undergone an earlier development of economic activity in the spheres of land and money, labor remained subject to a wider series of restrictions for many years. Even in 1795, when many of these constraints had been eliminated, a system of subsidies was introduced that limited the extent to which a decent standard of living depended on the sale of labor in the market. This came into being through the *Speenhamland System*, which took its name from an area in Berkshire where the poor were guaranteed a minimum income, regardless of the level of their earnings. If they received a wage beneath a level defined by a standard which took account of family needs, they had the right to a subsidy. However, little by little this system led to a lowering of wages and a consistent increase in subsidies. This situation meant that "a new class of employers was being created, but no corresponding class of employees could constitute itself" (Polanyi [1944] 1985, p. 80). Workers tended to prefer subsidies to work, even if this involved living in degrading conditions. Moreover, public financing decreased as a result of the marked increases in the social area dependent on subsidies. As a result, in 1834, the system was abolished. This marked England's full entry into the system of competitive labor.

Having discussed the processes leading to the creation of the markets for land and labor, and thus to the full establishment of an economic system based on market exchange, Polanyi began to analyze the social consequences of this phenomenon and its effects on the economy, which would lead to the Great Depression at the end of the 1920s. The starting point of Polanyi's main argument in *The Great Transformation* was that labor, land and money were converted into goods, that is, goods that were produced to be bought and sold on the market. However, these goods were not like others, because labor was linked to human life, which was not produced to be sold. In the same way, land was part of nature and was not produced by man, and even money was a symbol of the power to acquire and was not a product. So these were not real goods but "fictitious commodities" (Polanyi [1944] 1985, p. 72, note 1). Treating them as though they were real, as required by an economic system based on self-regulated markets, had destructive consequences for society.

Polanyi underlined that labor's reduction to commodity, the value of which was fixed by demand and supply on the market, had serious consequences for the living conditions of growing numbers of the population. The development of the labor market went together with the progressive destruction of traditional types of protection, including those linked to kinship structures, neighborhoods and trades, as well as those more directly dependent on political power. As a result, individuals and their families were uprooted from the environment and social settings in which they lived and were forced to move in order to find work. Their living conditions thus became dependent on the ups and downs of the market. Especially in the initial stages of the Industrial Revolution, earnings were highly unstable, and pockets of unemployment and new poverty formed on the outskirts of industrial cities, together with degraded conditions of labor and life. In other words, as the labor market came into being so did modern poverty, to an extent that was unheard of in traditional societies, where subsistence had always been guaranteed by the modalities through which social and political institutions incorporated and regulated the economy.

Moreover, markets had equally serious consequences for nature. The full commercialization of land as a factor of production and the abolition of institutional restrictions on trade in agricultural goods – which had aimed to protect forms of household economy and subsistence at the local level, led to growing unrest in the more developed areas of the West, as well as the less developed continents under colonial regimes. The free exchange of products, together with improvements in transport, led to crisis for growing numbers of agricultural producers, especially on the European continent, which was flooded with American wheat. Peasants were forced to leave the countryside to search for work. Which led to the "destruction . . . of rural society" (Polanyi [1944] 1985, p. 182). Nature, too, was endangered, as a result of all the dire consequences that this had on the environment.

Finally, Polanyi observed that the reduction of money to a commodity that was bought and sold on the market had significant social effects. In the system of self-regulated markets during the nineteenth century, money became a means of exchange linked to gold (the "gold standard"). International exchanges came to be encouraged in this system because of the stability of exchange rates, but they increased the risks for domestic economies. For example, if there was a growth in imports, this led to an outflow of gold and thus a reduction in the amount of money circulating in the country. This led to a fall in the sums of money available for domestic payments, and therefore to a drop in sales, which affected productive activities and generated unemployment. Polanyi admitted that the fall of prices led to an adjustment in the domestic economy that benefited exporting firms in time, and thus re-established the balance of external payments. However, in the meantime, deflation had very high costs for economy and society.

In other words, while it was true that markets in labor, land and money were essential for a market economy, society could not bear the costs that this imposed for very long. Precisely for this reason, reactions began to become apparent, involving mechanisms for the "self-defense of society": "Indeed human society would have been annihilated but for protective countermoves which blunted the action of this self-destructive mechanism" (Polanyi [1944] 1985, p. 76). From the last few decades of the nineteenth century, a sort of "double movement" became apparent: "While on the one hand markets all over the face of the globe and the amounts of goods involved, grew to unbelievable proportions, on the other hand a network of measures and policies was integrated into powerful institutions designed to check the action of the market relative to labor, land and money " (Polanyi [1944] 1985, p. 76)

Labor, too, reacted at the social level, through the development of the workers' movement and the growth of union organizations and socialist parties. This was accompanied by new social legislation and labor legislation, in different forms in different countries. This had the objective of limiting the extent to which one's living conditions depended on whether one could sell one's labor on the market (regulation of working time, of children and women's labor, insurance against accidents at work, illness, unemployment, and old age, etc.). The protection of agriculture went together with the protection of labor, especially in Continental Europe. The crisis in the traditional structure of agriculture, challenged by the penetration of the market and increased competition, led to increasing pressure for legislation that would limit its exposure to the market. From 1870 on, protectionist measures and measures supporting agriculture, became widespread. Peasants and landowners united in the face of these threats, often supported by the military or clergy, all seeking to defend traditional society from the threat of the market, for different but converging reasons. Finally, the surge of protectionism also affected the money market. Polanyi drew attention to the role of central banks in different countries, describing how the supply of credit was centralized and controlled. This allowed the eventual negative effects of international transactions to be mitigated. In particular, the deflationary effects of a reduction of money due to international payments could be lessened through an increase in credit.

This new form of protectionism had, however, different effects on society and the market economy. In society it mitigated the costs and tensions associated with the spread of the market, but in the economy it led to growing constraints that hindered the functioning of self-regulated markets in the field of factors of production. Flexibility decreased and the cost of labor increased, while customs tariffs imposed limits on commercial exchange. Moreover, the different forms of protectionism affected each other. For example, the increase in the cost of living resulting from an agricultural protectionism that increased the prices of food goods for national consumers, in turn, fostered the wage demands of workers and thus led industrialists to ask for new duties and protections in their sectors, too. The overall effect was a shrinking in trade and international exchange, which limited sales of goods just when the progress made by technology was increasing the productivity of firms.

Faced with the widening gap between production and consumption, two forms of recourse sought to resolve the crisis of overproduction. The first involved the spread of colonial policies and "economic imperialism," which Polanyi considered as an instrument to obtain both raw materials at low cost and market outlets that were protected from the competition of other countries. Moreover, economic imperialism and the growing closure of economies – together with a virulent political nationalism – eventually was responsible for the political climate that led to the First World War.

The second mechanism curbing economic crises involved the spread of loans and credit at the international level. These managed to prevent an economic crisis, particularly in the years following the First World War, when recourse to credit kept firms afloat and sustained the balance of payments in several countries. However, this mechanism could not work in the long term – loans could not support a real economy that was unable to sell what it produced and which could not lower its costs because of the inflexibility of the new social protectionism. Everything came to a head with the Great Depression of 1929, which, for Polanyi, marked the end of the economic system based on self-regulated markets and led to the end of "liberal capitalism."

In summation, for Polanyi, it was neither the First World War nor the onset of socialism in Russia and fascist regimes in Europe that ended the civilization of the nineteenth century, which had manifested itself in liberal capitalism. Rather, these phenomena aggravated a pre-existing crisis and were symptoms of another and deeper malaise, which could be traced back to the fundamental conflict between the functioning of the market and the requirements of social life.

The crisis had both social and political causes. The new institutional protectionism put in place for the self-defense of society made the functioning of the market less flexible and, eventually, blocked it. This reading of the economic crisis, in which Polanyi distanced himself from Marx, brought him to point out the commonalities between the new forms of economic regulation that were being built upon the ruins of liberal capitalism. Apparently, there were strong differences between the European variants of fascism, the American New Deal and Russian socialism. Indeed, there were clear differences in how power was organized. These differences aside, however, Polanyi believed that these regimes "were similar only in discarding laissez-faire principles " (Polanyi [1944] 1985, p. 244). They were all, that is, experiences born from a common cause – the failure of liberal capitalism – and they moved, albeit in different forms, towards the common objective of reincorporating the economy into society. Thus, they all involved an attempt to reintroduce those forms of social and political regulation that had come to an abrupt end with the advent of an economic system based on self-regulated markets. This economic system, which was historically unprecedented, had brought society to depend on the market.

These experiments with new forms of regulation during the great transformation were thus different solutions to the problem of how to remove labor, land, and money from the markets. But to what extent were these experiments compatible with the persistence of the market and freedom?

With regard to the first question, Polanyi believed that "the end of market society means in no way the absence of markets" ([1944] 1985, p. 252). This meant that competitive markets could continue to function for the production of goods and services, assuring freedom to the consumer and affecting the income of the producers as well as acting as an instrument to calculate how the needs of the population might be satisfied most efficiently. The underlying idea here was that the existence of the market did not necessarily contradict the objectives and instruments of economic planning. In other words, Polanyi's reformist socialism pushed him to embrace the idea of a democratic economic planning.

Just as the market would not necessarily disappear in a society whose economy had been re-embedded into society, and forms of planning would be developed for

economic activity, freedom would not disappear either. Polanyi rejected the argument of many liberal theorists, particularly von Hayek, that the resizing of market
would necessarily menace political democracy (Polanyi 1968). In reality, the collapse of liberal capitalism risked two types of freedom, one involving bad freedoms,
and the other good. Among the first type was the freedom to exploit men, or to
make profits that were not proportional to the collective benefits that derived from
one's own actions. That these freedoms might disappear with the self-regulated
market could not be described as anything other than beneficial. This differed from
those freedoms that had come into being with the market, and which continued to
be extremely valuable: freedom of conscience, speech, meeting, association, and
choice over how one employed one's labor. Such freedoms should be defended,
but it was a mistake to think that they depended only on the existence of self-
regulated markets. This could be well seen in the experience of Britain during the
Second World War, where a wide-ranging economic plan came into operation
without compromising political freedom. Polanyi concluded that the end of liberal
capitalism did not necessarily mean the end of the market or of freedom.

2   The Decline of the Bourgeoisie and Anti-Capitalist Policies

2.1   Economics and economic sociology

Joseph Schumpeter (1883–1950) is usually considered an economist, but very often stepped over the boundary between economics and economic sociology. This
Austrian scholar, who went on to settle in Harvard, had a deep familiarity with the
methodological debate (*Methodenstreit*) that had taken place between the followers
of the historical school of economics and the neo-classical economists, and in particular with Carl Menger's work (see chapter 1). In his book published in 1914,
Economic Doctrine and Method, which was commissioned by Weber, he underlined
that it was mistaken to counter-oppose the historical approach to the economic
one, in the field of economic science. Instead, one ought to distinguish between
"economic theory," "economic history," and "economic sociology." Each of these
perspectives was legitimate and useful in its own way, but it was necessary not to
confuse them or to mix them carelessly. All the same, the theoretical economist
should be informed of the instruments used by other disciplines, and of statistics
too, because it was not possible to move from abstract analytical models to the
investigation of social reality without any knowledge of history or the role of institutions.

Schumpeter never really altered this position, and even restated it in the opening pages of his last book, published posthumously in 1954, the *History of Economic
Analysis*. In his view, "economic theory" involved a set of analytical propositions
from which one could make arguments about validity under determined conditions. As Menger and Weber had already pointed out, the propositions of economic theory did not depend on their immediate empirical validity. According to
Schumpeter "this means that there is a class of economic theorems that are logical
ideals or norms . . . And they evidently differ from another class of economic theorems that are directly based upon observations" (1954, p. 21).

Schumpeter thus used an analytical method, like Menger and Pareto, to defend the validity of neoclassical economics. However, he emphasized that to analyze actual economic activities, one had to take account of their location in the historical process. This was why economic history was important; it allowed one to understand economic and non-economic facts as they combined in real-life experience, and to see how this combination might change over time. In addition, the importance of non-economic factors, that is, institutional factors, in conditioning economic activities and their variation over time and space meant that one also had to take account of the contribution of economic sociology.

2.2   Entrepreneurship and economic development

There is no doubt that – in his wider vision of economics – Schumpeter was more interested in theory than in economic sociology, thus differing from Weber. All the same, it is interesting to see that he was unable to completely separate the two approaches, theoretical economics from sociology. Richard Swedberg (1991) rightly underlines that this was because Schumpeter had moved away from traditional neoclassical economics. It is true that he often spoke of his admiration for the theoretical construction of general economic equilibrium, and in particular for Walras' work. However, it is equally true that he viewed his own theoretical work as an effort to innovate and move beyond the static analyses of neoclassical economics. Let us now see how he viewed the problem of change in his most groundbreaking theoretical work, *The Theory of Economic Development*, which was first published in 1912. Here, we may seek to find out why – despite his stated objective of constructing a purely economic theory of development – Schumpeter in fact made use of social variables.

The starting point of Schumpeter's early analysis was his dissatisfaction with the perspective of traditional economics, which he saw as unable to go beyond a static vision of economic equilibrium. Thus it was unable, for instance, to explain discontinuities in the traditional model of production, and was unable to explain revolutions in production.

Growth should therefore be distinguished from *development*, for which traditional economic instruments – that sought to study the allocation of resources – did not work. The first was a gradual phenomenon, involving continual adjustments, while the second implied discontinuity: "Add successively as many coaches as you please, you will never get a railway thereby, (Schumpeter [1912–26] 1934, p. 64, note1). Development involved "the introduction of new combinations." Innovation might involve any of five dimensions: the creation of products, the introduction of production methods, the opening of markets, the conquest of sources of provision of raw materials or semi-finished products, or finally the reorganization of an industry, for example, through the creation of a monopoly or its destruction.

It is clear from the preceding discussion that Schumpeter was interested in the endogenous sources of development. He recognized how discontinuity differed from the routine of "circular flow" (an economy that carries on without any substantial alteration in the production methods of relations between consumers and producers), and could result from many extra-economic factors, including growth in population or sudden social or political upheavals. His interest was concentrated, however, on how development might be attributed to the role of entrepreneurs. Who were these people? What role did the play in the economic process?

Development, as Schumpeter treated it, was the result of entrepreneurial action. Entrpreneurs introduced new ways of combining the means of production, and innovated products, production methods or markets in one of the ways discussed above. Schumpeter's conception of entrepreneurs differed from that of traditional economic theory. It was not sufficient to differentiate between the capitalist as the owner of the means of production or capital, and the entrepreneur as the manager of a firm that he might not own. One might better distinguish, in the realm of the activity and management of a firm, between those activities that were routine and those that led to innovation, to realizing "new things." It was to this last feature that the specific concept of entrepreneur should be linked.

A series of consequences derived from this position:

(a)   First, the entrepreneur could be the classic independent businessman, as was particularly common in the first phase of capitalism, but he could also be a dependent worker, that is, a manager. This often occurred in the subsequent phase of development, with the creation of large firms and the separation of ownership from management;

(b)   It was not necessary to maintain a stable relationship with one firm only. There were, for example, several actors who played important roles in founding a firm, and then moved on to other activities, while the innovative firm created by them entered into a more routine phase;

(c)   Entrepreneurs did not belong to any specific social class. As a result of their activities, they were able to achieve economic success that transformed them into owners of the means of production, turning them into "capitalists." However, they did not need to be capitalists already when they carried out their innovative activities. Entrepreneurs were able to obtain credit so as to introduce new combinations of the means of production. Indeed, in the most evolved phase of capitalist economy, this was commonplace. The use of accumulated savings for financial investment only took place at a low level. Instead, the necessary funds derived increasingly from the banks, which created additional purchasing power that was relatively autonomous from the amount of savings immediately available from deposits.

Schumpeter thus emphasized the link between credit and innovation. He was, however, well aware that even the multiplication of the power of acquisition of the means of production was not a sufficient condition for innovation if there were not non-economic resources which would allow capital to be used for the purpose of development. These especially involved particular qualities of leadership, which were not evenly spread over a particular society, but were instead rare and concentrated in several particular individuals. Here too, Schumpeter differed from traditional economic theory, which tended to see the entrepreneur as an actor able to allocate resources given market constraints, on the basis of rational calculation. This vision seemed plausible to the Austrian scholar, but only within the setting of a routine economy, where behavior was directed by a perfectly competitive market, in which profits were moderated by competitive mechanisms.

However, if one moved beyond the conditions of "stationary economy," matters changed considerably and one required particular qualities that were not reducible to the traditional rational calculation: "the type of conduct in question not only differs from the others in its object, 'innovation' being peculiar to it, but also in that it presupposes aptitudes differing *in kind* and not only in degree from those of mere rational economic behavior" (Schumpeter [1912–26] 1934, p. 81, note 2).

Things were different then, when one sought to bring innovation about. Innovation required that one deal with a lack of information, and with conditions of greater uncertainty than those found in the context of traditional, well-established behaviors. Furthermore, the actor had to battle and overcome internal resistance, which is to say the well-established mental schemas that might block innovation. Finally, the actor had to overcome the resistance of the surrounding social setting. "Legal or political impediments" could obstruct innovation, for example in the form of social disapproval of practices going beyond traditional channels. These might well be a serious obstacle, particularly in less developed societies. There might be resistance for various reasons, even where the market economy was already consolidated: groups threatened by the innovation, the difficulties of finding the necessary cooperation or of convincing consumers to change products.

These different types of obstacle meant that innovation could not be brought about by all economic actors, but required specific qualities of leadership that were relatively rare. A combination of various characteristics was required: intuition and vision, but also competence and determination. This set of qualities was not, for Schumpeter, reducible to the rational calculation of traditional theory. It is clear then that he introduced psychological factors linked to the individual personality, in order to understand how the innovating entrepreneur emerged. There are similarities between his conception and Weber's theory of charismatic leadership (Swedberg 1991). However, it is equally true that he took account of the social setting in his vision. For example, the force and extent of legal and political obstacles, or social norms that hindered innovative activity helped determine whether entrepreneurs emerged. Schumpeter also mentioned social marginalization as a possible source of enterpreneurialism, after Simmel and Sombart.

To sum up, the basic elements of Schumpeter's theoretical work were already present in his *Theory of Economic Development*. On the more strictly economic level, his attention to the relationship between development and innovation had two important consequences. First, Schumpeter made an original contribution by seeing profit as being earned by the entrepreneur through his or her success in innovation, which made income grow more than expenses. Temporary monopolistic profits were possible until other firms began to imitate the innovation. According to Schumpeter, this allowed one to address one of the unresolved problems of neo-classical economics. This latter model posited a stationary economy in which there was no place for the entrepreneurial function or for profit. There might be a management structure in the firm that received an income as reward for its function ("wage of management"), or even temporary windfall profits, due to market movements that would soon be cancelled out by competition. However, Schumpeter – recalling Walras – underlined that entrepreneurs-managers did not usually make either profits or losses.

In addition, this approach to the process of innovation allowed Schumpeter to give a detailed explanation of economic cycles, particularly in his book *Business Cycles* (1939). The expansionary stage of the cycle was linked to the introduction of the innovation and its early diffusion, which increased the demand for production goods and consumption. Subsequently, however, the old productive units were hit by the competition of the innovative firms and this forced them to imitate them or to exit from the market, with recessive effects on the economy. This was the contractionary phase of the cycle, which would lead to a new temporary equilibrium, to be changed by another cycle of innovation.

Of particular interest here is that Schumpeter's theory was clearly linked to the social and political setting, even though it was presented as an endogenous account – that is, internal to economics – of economic development. While the entrepreneur was certainly characterized by specific personality traits, he did not come into being in an institutional vacuum, but in a context of social stratification and existing institutions, which might change over time. The influence of these social factors on the entrepreneur formed the main theme of *Capitalism, Socialism, and Democracy* (1942), where it was explored in a wider discussion of the transformations in liberal capitalism. Let us now discuss this book in detail.

2.3   Can capitalism survive?

Schumpeter had already begun to question the future of capitalism by the late twenties, and the subsequent period of the Great Depression.[1] However, the main aim of his work was not to predict that capitalism would give way to a socialist form of organization, a prediction which did not come true. Indeed, Schumpeter was aware of the limits of this sort of analysis in the social sciences. Rather, the interest and relevance of this book lie in his account of the transformations of liberal capitalism and the effects of the Great Depression. The perspective he adopted was that of economic sociology, because it emphasized how the functioning of capitalist economies led to a change in culture and institutions that, in turn, obstructed the mechanisms of self-regulation of the markets. This meant that one passed from "non-regulated" capitalism to "regulated" capitalism (Schumpeter 1936), gradually preparing the way for socialism. He was not especially in favor of this outcome, but thought that it was inevitable in the absence of other changes, that did not seem feasible at the time. In this sense, he reached the same conclusion as Marx, but from a different set of assumptions: capitalism would not survive, but because of cultural and social reactions to its working, rather than economic factors.

Why was the decline not caused by economic factors?

Schumpeter initially sought to refute the thesis that the development of capitalism would lead to an increase in unemployment. The growth in unemployment during the thirties was "abnormally high," but it was temporary, linked to a phase of recession of the sort that usually followed a phase of prosperity tied to a period of innovation in the economic cycle. In this case the phenomenon was aggravated by contingent factors (Schumpeter 1931): its coincidence with an agricultural crisis induced by new methods of production that increased productivity; customs restrictions limiting exchanges; the deflationary effects of monetary policy and the re-establishment of the gold standard; war payments; wage levels, which had become more rigid; and increased fiscal pressure. In other words, the crisis of 1929 resulted from a number of causal factors coming together so as to exacerbate the effects of the contractionary phase of the cycle. These factors were rooted in a more general ossification of the mechanisms of market self-regulation, that resulted from what Schumpeter described as "anti-capitalist policies" (Schumpeter [1942] 1961, p. 154) and what Polanyi described as the new "social protectionism" (Polanyi, [1944] 1985, p. 229). These policies helped make the economic situation even more difficult in the decades following the Second World War, particularly because of the increase in fiscal pressures and the expansion of social legislation.

In reality, according to Schumpeter, if the economic system, directed by the market, had been free to function and rebalance itself independently, as in the fifty years prior to 1928, it would have been able to assure a sufficient rate of development to reduce poverty. It would be mistaken to believe that it was possible to eliminate unemployment completely, because this was tied to the mechanism of innovation and the economic cycle that derived from it. However, the necessary resources could be created to lessen the problem of temporary unemployment, and its consequences in terms of poverty. Thus, it was not market capitalism that created less development, but institutional factors such as anti-capitalist policies, that "are no doubt symptoms of an atmosphere in which capitalism will work with decreasing efficiency" (Schumpeter [1942] 1961, p. 70). Before developing this central argument, Schumpeter wanted to remove economic arguments about the decline of capitalism's capacity to create development from the field of play. In particular, he opposed the argument that the transition to a phase in which monopolistic and oligarchic firms prevailed led to less efficiency and dynamism. Second, he wanted to criticize those theories (which also included Keynes's argument) that maintained that there was a "vanishing of investment opportunity."

The costs imposed by monopolies are a traditional concern of economists, who have elucidated how phenomena such as oligopoly and monopoly lead to the control of the market by producers, to the detriment of consumers and the overall efficiency of the system. But we have also seen how such an unorthodox economist as Veblen highlighted the negative effects of monopoly on development. Schumpeter, in contrast held that this criticism of big business was misplaced. First, it did not account for the empirical fact that the rate of increase of production, and the standard of living of the population, had increased during the period when the industrial giants were establishing themselves, which is to say the last decade of the nineteenth century, and the early years of the twentieth. Second, Schumpeter put forward theoretical arguments to suggest that the domination of big business had positive aspects; while he did not reject validity of the assumptions of traditional economic theory, he circumscribed them to the stationary economy, in which production was carried out using the same combination of productive factors.

Schumpeter referred to his own thesis, already developed in *Theory of Economic Development*, to recall that "the problem that has usually been visualized is how capitalism administers existing structures, whereas the relevant problem is how it creates and destroys them" ([1942] 1961, p. 84). If one followed this logic, the *process of creative destruction* became essential in order to revolutionize the productive system through the cycle of innovation. In the course of development the impulse to form new combinations of the factors of production were no longer seen so much in individual entrepreneurs, and instead had tended to become institutionalized within the larger firms that, as Marx had predicted, had replaced the smaller ones. These not only had more financial resources, but also had organizational ones, including those linked to research and control of the market. In the short term, this could effectively lead to high prices and restrictions in production, but in the medium and long term, advantages linked to quality and lower costs prevailed, improving the effectiveness of innovation. Thus, from the dynamic point of view, competition of an oligopolistic or monopolistic type, creating new goods, techniques, sources of supply and methods of organization was "the powerful lever that in the long run expands output and brings down prices" (Schumpeter [1942] 1961, p. 85). The restrictions and entrepreneurial, monopolistic, profits were the necessary but temporary price for innovation and the spread of its beneficial effects throughout the system, so that they finally reached consumers.

Finally, Schumpeter rejected the thesis of the "vanishing of investment opportunity." In his opinion, the ideas of the British economist John Maynard Keynes (cf. chapter 6), adopted and developed in the United States by Alvin Hansen (1941), should be viewed as part of a vision of capitalism that emphasized a fall in expectations of profit, and thus of investments and employment, given available savings. Stagnation was seen as the result of changes which involved a lower level of major innovation, the tendency of innovations to save capital, a reduction in new areas to conquer and colonize, and a fall in birth-rates. Schumpeter, for his part believed that none of these factors were as important as they had been made out to be. In particular, the potential for innovation and thus for the development of capitalism was by no means exhausted. In contrast to the beliefs of the Keynesian school, governmental policies that sought to protect demand and investments from stagnation through fiscal incentives and spending ended by aggravating the ailment that they were intended to cure. Factors such as higher fiscal pressure on firms or labor protection policies had the effect of reining in expectations of profits and investments. For this reason, Schumpeter believed that a different diagnosis of stagnation was needed. In his perspective, stagnation had socio-cultural and political roots rather than economic ones. Over time, the development of capitalism fostered a hostile atmosphere that gave rise to anti-capitalist policies. In reality, "capitalist evolution tends to peter out because the modern state may crash or paralyze its motive forces" (Schumpeter 1954, p. 1173, note 1).

Cultural and social causes for the decline

Let us now move to the second part of Schumpeter's argument: his analysis of the cultural and social reasons for the decline of liberal capitalism. He focused on three main factors: the social and political weakening of the bourgeoisie, the destruction of the social strata that supported the bourgeoisie, and the spread of hostility towards capitalism.

1   The weakening of the bourgeoisie was a complex process with various causes involving the transformation of the economy and its social and political conse-quences.

(a)   First, there was the decline of the entrepreneurial function. The large bureaucratized firm overtook small and medium-sized firms. As Marx predicted, the latter could not long survive competition with the former. This meant that innovation, once the specific task of the entrepreneur, tended to become im-personal and automated. The individual entrepreneur therefore lost his social function, but this had the effect of weakening the bourgeoisie, which in the past had sustained itself through the continual provision of new and successful entrepreneurs. This social class was increasing made up of administrators of inherited wealth, mere *rentiers*.

(b)   Another factor weakening the bourgeoisie involved the "disintegration of the bourgeois family." Attachment to the home and worry over the future of the family "used to be the mainspring of the typically bourgeois kind of profit motive" ([1942] 1961, p. 160). Adapting Weber's arguments, Schumpeter em-phasized how economists had often underestimated the role of these social motivations in stimulating entrepreneurial action: "The capitalist ethic that en-joins working for the future irrespective of whether or not one is going to harvest the crop oneself " (Schumpeter [1942] 1961, p. 160). In its place a utilitarian spirit spread, which showed itself in a tendency to have fewer chil-dren and a narrowing of time horizons. This not only influenced the strictly economic behavior of the middle classes, discouraging savings and long-term investments, but also affected political behavior. The bourgeoisie no longer fought for its life ideals, and ended up no longer believing in them, being influ-enced by the ideas of its adversaries. As a result, it stopped fighting against anti-capitalist policies, especially fiscal policy and social legislation, which weakened private firms.

2   The decline of liberal capitalism was also due to factors involving social stratifi-cation and its relationship with politics.

(a)   First of all was the role of the aristocracy, which had survived the destruc-tion of feudalism in European countries, and had taken on an essential role – well exemplified by the English case – in forming the ruling class. However, over time, this "pre-capitalist framework of society" had been progressively eroded. This led to serious political problems because the exhaustion of the historical role of the aristocracy meant that the bourgeoisie no longer had one of the most important resources that it needed to face domestic and interna-tional political problems, that it could not, given its attitudes and history, ad-dress alone. In Schumpeter's view, it became "politically helpless and unable not only to lead its nation but even to take care of its particular class interest" ([1942] 1961, p. 138).

(b)   Another important social change involved the "destruction of the institu-tional framework of capitalist society." Here, one could refer to the increasing concentration of the structure of production, with the progressive elimination of small agricultural, artisanal, industrial, and commercial firms. This had im-portant political consequences because it deprived the bourgeoisie of its traditional social allies. In addition, the bureaucratization of large firms and the separation of owners and managers led to the creation of new groups of managers and administrators who, lacking a direct interest in the ownership of the firm, did not have the political vigor necessary to defend liberal capitalism from its enemies.

3   This context – a progressive social and political weakening of the bourgeoisie – provided favorable conditions for the growth of the "social atmosphere" hostile to liberal capitalism, that Schumpeter saw as the decisive factor. In reality, the motives for social discontent found in capitalist economies, in particular the cyclical crises and unemployment, would not have been sufficient to lead to open hostility if there had not also been "groups to whose interest it is to work up and organize resentment to muse it, to voice it, and to lead it" ([1942] 1961, p. 145). These groups were made up of intellectuals who fostered criticism of the capitalist institutions and succeeded in gathering a mass following, in part because "the performance of capitalism stands out only if we take the long-run view . . . . In the short run, it is profits and inefficiencies that dominate the picture" ([1942] 1961, p. 145). Two factors in particular fostered this process. On the one hand, there was the increase in levels of education and intellectual unemployment or under-employment, which increased frustration and resentment. On the other, there was the fact that capitalist institutions did not limit freedom of expression or the organization of discontent, and therefore facilitated the spread of the phenomenon.

4   This brings us to the factor that was decisive in weakening liberal capitalism – "anti-capitalist policies." Schumpeter used this term to refer to a set of legislative and administrative measures that became widespread in various countries, through a process that paralleled the weakening of the bourgeoisie and the growth in discontent fostered by the intellectuals. These involved interventions that extended the role of the state or of collective bargaining – policies of deficit spending to support supply and to avoid cyclical crises; redistributive policies, aimed at realizing greater social equality, in particular though a growth of fiscal pressure; regulative instruments such as anti-trust measures to combat monopolistic firms and to control prices through administrative means; the spread of public firms; welfare and labor legislation and the growth of union bargaining on the labor market. All these policies, which spread more rapidly after the Great Depression, marked a growing distance from "*laissez faire* capitalism." They imposed increasing constraints on the functioning of private firms and led to a gradual shift in the governance of the economy from self-regulated markets to various forms of socialist planning. Schumpeter saw the American capitalism of the New Deal and the capitalism that was established in post-war America and Europe as a kind of "laborist capitalism," in which private firms were subjected to growing fiscal and regulatory obligations. Some believed that this more politically regulated form of capitalism would be able to survive in the long term, but Schumpeter was more skeptical. Capitalism was, in his eyes, a specific institutional structure and value scheme: it was a civilization. It was thus difficult for him to believe that a capitalism which had eroded the institutional bases on which it was based could maintain a high level of economic dynamism.

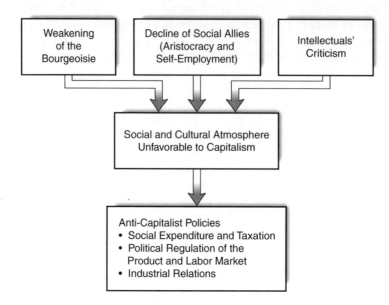

Figure 5.1   *Cultural and institutional causes of the liberal capitalism's decline*

"Can socialism work?" was Schumpeter's final question, in which he made it clear that by socialism he meant a form of societal organization in which the means of production was controlled by the public authority, which was responsible for choices over the production of goods and the distribution of incomes. His treatment of this problem is not directly relevant here; however, he wished to show not only that socialism could be efficient on the economic level, but that it did not necessarily have to be seen as contradictory to the permanency of political democracy. This thesis, even though it was formulated with great caution, would subsequently be disproved through the experiences of the socialist countries. What was very clear to him, and what he personally regretted, was that the old form of liberal capitalism – "the civilization of inequality and of the family fortune" ([1942] 1961, p. 419) – had no future.

3   Analytical Convergence and Political Divergence

Polanyi and Schumpeter, like Durkheim and Veblen, were from different backgrounds and had no contact with each other,[2] even if they were both affected by the atmosphere in Vienna at the turn of the century. The first was a socialist, the latter a conservative liberal. However, despite these differences, it is interesting to note that both contributed analytically by focusing – along convergent lines – on the same problem; the decline of liberal capitalism and the great transformation that began after the crisis of the thirties.

Polanyi was an institutionalist, Schumpeter an economist who overcame the traditional boundaries of the discipline and recognized the importance of institutions in understanding change in the economy: the problem of development was key to his thinking. Polanyi saw drastic limits to the scientific validity of economics, and historicized its analysis. The instruments of the discipline served to understand the functioning of the economy only when it was dominated by self-regulated markets. Its efficacy was thus restricted to the century in which liberal capitalism triumphed – the nineteenth century. Extending its scope in time meant falling prey to the "economistic fallacy." From this point of view, Polanyi was thus closer to Durkheim and, above all, to Veblen. His institutionalism was more an alternative to neoclassical economics than an attempt to integrate it; he wanted to reconstruct an institutionalist economics.

Schumpeter had a completely different view of the role and characteristics of economics, which was closer to that of Menger and Weber. Theoretical economics was an analytical discipline, and as such its scientific status did not depend upon empirical verification of its findings; it therefore did not need to be historicized. However, within the discipline of economics – which he conceived, like Menger and Weber, in wider terms than the neoclassical approach – space should be reserved both for theory – with an analytical edge – and for historical–empirical work. The latter would examine the relationship between economic phenomena and the institutional context, basing itself on the contributions of history and economic sociology. And Schumpeter himself turned to economic sociology when he asked questions about changes in capitalism and its future. From this point of view, he came close to a type of investigation like Polanyi's. Both sought responses to the same problem: why did liberal capitalism decline? And what directions did the process of transformation that began after the Great Depression take?

In addressing the causes of the decline, they converged substantially by emphasizing how the social consequences of the dominance of self-regulated markets in economic organization triggered social and political reactions that, in turn, progressively hampered the functioning of the markets, and their capacity to return to equilibrium. Contrary to Marx, they held that the causes of the decline were social rather than economic, even if they consequently had repercussions for the functioning of the economy. One might even say that they reversed Marx's argument that economic crises accelerated social and political change. Polanyi speaks of the "self-defense of society," a process that expressed itself through the spread of various forms of protectionism (social and labor, agricultural and credit). Schumpeter, instead, referred to "anti-capitalist policies," which became more intense after the Great Depression, but which found fertile terrain in the weakening of the cultural and institutional framework of liberal capitalism and in the growth of social discontent. Polanyi believed that these processes of institutional change had begun at the end of the nineteenth century, and had reached their culmination in the crisis of 1929. Schumpeter explained this last phenomenon as a result of the accumulation of different factors, some linked to the normal dynamics of economic cycles, others more contingent. Unlike Polanyi, he believed that the phenomena of imperialism and colonial wars were influenced by variables that were more political and cultural than economic. Imperialism appeared to him to result from tendencies that were extraneous to the fundamentally pacific spirit of the bourgeoisie and capitalism, involving militarism and outmoded values, which could be found in the ruling classes of aristocratic descent and in the military hierarchy (Schumpeter 1919). More generally, Schumpeter tended to attach more importance to the ossification of self-regulated markets than Polanyi. He considered these phenomena as a consequence of institutional reactions to the depression of 1929 rather than as a factor preparing the ground for the crisis itself. However, this was little more than a difference of emphasis. He also believed that the 1930s were a cusp between unregulated capitalism and regulated capitalism. This prepared the way, in a more long-term and more uncertain perspective, for the onset of socialism.

It was also significant that both scholars came to similar conclusions about the non-economic prerequisites for market functioning. This finding is especially important for historical–empirical analysis, because it implies that it is impossible to understand how actual markets operate without examining their integration in society, which is to say how they interact with an institutional context that provides the resources to motivate economic actors appropriately, and bring them to accept the social consequences of market operations. Markets thus cannot exist without adequate institutional support. Polanyi summed up this belief by underlining the "utopian" character of self-regulated markets: "Such an institution could not exist for any length of time without annihilating the human and natural substance of society" (Polanyi [1944] 1985, p. 3). For his part, Schumpeter held that "No social system can work which is based exclusively upon a network of free contracts" (Schumpeter [1942] 1961, p. 417).

In other words, it was legitimate to study markets on the analytical level, isolating them from their institutional setting. However, when the investigation took place on historical-empirical grounds, it was necessary to take account of the forms and degrees of integration of markets in society. This allowed one to evaluate differences in their economic performance over space (between different societies) and in time (for the same society or for different societies).

Following this perspective, Polanyi and Schumpeter showed how the historical establishment of the market eroded old institutions, generated social and political instability, and led to experimentation with new institutions. The two authors converged significantly in their analysis of the transformation of capitalism, even if they differed in their empirical evaluation of this process. Both suggested that capitalism was moving towards a stage in which the role of the market was more limited, and was more regulated by political and social institutions. This was Polanyi's "great transformation," while Schumpeter talked of a "laborist capitalism" that would probably lead to a socialist form of economic organization. However, Schumpeter was not in favor of the changes in course, and he remained attached to the values of a capitalist civilization that he wanted to defend, even though he believed it was in a state of irreparable decline. Polanyi, instead, believed that the transition to an economy that was better re-embedded into society, and more socially and politically regulated, was not only inevitable but desirable. This was true not only for the future of Western countries but also for the new underdeveloped countries that were now emerging, and that would not necessarily have to bear the social costs of the market.

Part II

Themes and Routes of Contemporary Economic Sociology

Chapter 6

The Legacy of the Classics and the New Boundaries between Economics and Sociology

In the previous chapters, we have sought to reconstruct the developments that took place in economic sociology between 1890 and 1940. This new analytical perspective paid regard to the interdependence between economic and social phenomena, and located the economy in the sphere of society. Of especial importance was the German context, with Sombart, Weber and Schumpeter. These authors' thought took form in a cultural context dominated by the criticism of sociological positivism, and influenced by the methodological debate between historical economists and neo-classical economists (*Methodenstreit*). However, scholars with other intellectual linkages made an essential contribution: Durkheim and Veblen were more influenced by positivism, and Polanyi had his own peculiar trajectory.

All these scholars had some knowledge of economics, but some knew it better than others. Moreover, while most of them were on the borderlines of sociology, Veblen and Schumpeter thought of themselves more as economists, even though they were both critical of the traditional, established approach. We have noted that these scholars did not know each other, nor had they read each other's works, with the exception of Sombart, Weber, and Schumpeter. Their political affiliations were appreciably different too. Some were influenced by socialism, others by more liberal currents of thought. One may take these differences as given; what is more surprising and interesting is the striking convergence in their core methodological and thematic concepts. This has importance because it is precisely this kind of methodological and analytical convergence that can be said to underpin any original and autonomous scientific approach, quite apart from the values and intellectual trajectories which nurture scientific research. In this sense then, it can be said that these authors are the founders of the tradition of economic sociology.

Naturally, any choice of founding fathers is somewhat arbitrary. Other scholars might have been considered.[1] However, these authors' contributions were exemplary in two senses. From the methodological point of view, they share in large part an approach to economic phenomena that is both consistent and different from marginalism. And in substantive terms, they applied this methodological perspective to theoretically and politically important themes: the work of these authors has been especially important and original as compared to other established disciplinary approaches. As we have seen, they are concerned above all with the origins and transformation of capitalism in developed Western societies. We will now endeavor to summarize the essential aspects of this new perspective, since it constitutes the patrimony of the classic models of economic sociology. This focus will enable us to examine how this legacy of the past has been used and how it has been redefined. Therefore, in the second part of the chapter, I shall deal with the question of the boundaries between economics and sociology that emerged after the Second World War, by considering the theoretical and historical factors that influenced relations between the two disciplines and the development of economic sociology.

1   The Methodological Perspective

Economic sociology emerged at the end of the nineteenth century through the convergence of various authors' attempts to fill the empty space left by neoclassical economics. Economics, when it was becoming established as a discipline, did not study economic phenomena in isolation from their social, as one can see in Adam Smith's "grand synthesis." He paid attention to non-economic institutions like the state, and considered it one of the causes contributing to the "wealth of nations," together with the market, private property, and waged labor. However, Smith was also very aware of the importance of shared values and in particular of the moral principles regulating individual interests, for the proper functioning of the market. He did not see the existence and reproduction of these principles as an unchangeable component of nature, as the preceding philosophical tradition had, but as a social product linked to the specific institutions of a country.

As we know, economics, in its later developments progressively lost touch with its cultural and institutional aspects, as it sought to approximate the standards of rigor and generalization of the natural sciences. This trajectory reached its logical conclusion in the "marginalist revolution" of the 1870s. It was at this point that the analysis of economic phenomena began to systematically separate itself from their cultural and institutional context and to concentrate on the study of the "laws" of the market, considered in isolation from the market's social context. A new paradigm of economics was thus created,[2] characterized by a series of clearly delineated elements. Let us look at these briefly to contrast them with the different view of economic sociology.[3]

1   *The conception of economics.* Economic activity was considered as the rational allocation of scarce resources, which could be used for alternative aims. This was done by actors who sought to satisfy their objectives in terms of both labor and consumption, given their available means (labor, income); that is, to maximize their utility. In this sense economic activity is identified with economizing.

2   *Economic action.* Action is thus motivated by the rational pursuit of individual interests, that is, a set of preferences over labor and consumption. In the sphere of production, actors try to maximize their earnings with respect to their availability

to work, and in that of consumption they try to maximize satisfaction given their consumption preferences; these are arranged according to a stable and coherent order of priorities, given the income resources at their disposal. As a result, insofar as it involves the use of resources (which is to say, means with respect to ends), economic action is conditioned on *utilitarian* motivations. Preferences over labor and consumption (that is, the ends pursued by single individuals), are believed to emerge independent of the influence of other actors. In this sense, one can speak of an *atomistic* vision of economic action. In any case, the formation of ends is considered *exogenous* to economic inquiry, and may therefore be ignored, allowing one to concentrate instead on the rational (optimizing) allocation of means.

3   *The rules.* Action is influenced by a limited set of rules that can for the most part be identified with the existence of competitive markets. Specifically, one may assume that there is a large number of buyers and sellers, that there are no restrictions on the exchange and mobility of the production factors (capital and labor), and that the actors who are active have full information about the opportunities offered by the markets, so as to be able to rationally calculate how best to use the resources available. Economists then consider the consequences deriving from economic activity when the rules conform to those of the competitive market, or when they move away from this condition as a result of a distortion; for example, as a result of oligopolistic or monopolistic markets, or where there is a shortage of information (economic research has increasingly focused on these situations). The attention given to the market as an economic institution does not mean that other non-economic institutions are not considered. For example, the role of the state is recognized. The state favors economic activities as far as it does not hamper the market with its political regulations, but guarantees the validity of contracts between private citizens and combats fraud. Even in this case, however, this is treated as an exogenous variable, which is to say exogenous to the subject of research.

4   *The method of inquiry.* Economic action is investigated through a method that is deductive–analytical and normative. In other words, the starting point is the above-mentioned assumption of actors with atomistic and utilitarian motivations, who evaluate consequences given certain rules, which are essentially those of the market. This model also makes use of sophisticated mathematical techniques to analyze outcomes associated with these conditions, culminating in those outcomes – particularly complex – linked to the general equilibrium model. The method is normative in that it also provides guiding criteria for the rational allocation of resources under certain conditions. In any case, neo-classical economists – including, as we have seen, Menger and Pareto – emphasize that the scientific validity of the results is guaranteed by the logical demonstration of the outcomes resulting from particular conditions. In this respect, it is not seen as necessary that such conditions are fully verifiable at the empirical level, whether they involve actors' motivations or the actual rules conditioning their action.

Let us now look briefly at how the classics' approach to economic sociology developed a perspective that was relatively coherent and systematic, and at the same time different from that which then prevailed in economics.

1   *The conception of the economy.* All our scholars criticize the identification of economic activities with the process of the rational allocation of scarce resources. In the nineteenth century, production, income distribution and consumption in developed countries certainly appear to have been affected by such a process. This is a consequence of the spreading of the market as a prevailing principle of economic and social regulation. However, economic sociologists are typically interested in looking at the market economy as though it were a historical phenomenon characterized by a particular institutional context, and as a result they usually prefer to talk of capitalism. Thus, they want to distinguish different types of economy, to understand how liberal capitalism takes shape, why it develops in certain places and not in others (or in some places earlier than in others), and in what ways it might transform itself. In other words, *diversity over space and time* is the focus of interest, and this requires a frame of analysis that does not identify the economy exclusively with market-regulated activity. In fact, it leads to a wider and more general vision of the economy, which is defined by Sombart in almost the same words as Polanyi, as "activity oriented to the search for means of subsistence." This definition, which is substantially shared by the classical authors, allows one to study how the economy is organized in different ways over space and time, and is influenced by economic and non-economic institutions. It also led to the use of concepts underlining historicity and variety, like that of the "economic system" (Sombart, Polanyi), of "forms of integration of the economy" (Polanyi), or, in a more specific outlook, the distinction between a "household economy" and a "profit-making economy" (Sombart, Weber), and the different forms of capitalism (traditional and modern, liberal and organized, market and regulated, etc.) that can be identified in all the classics.

2   *Economic action.* A series of consequences derive from the above assumptions. Action oriented towards the search for means of subsistence does not necessarily involve the rational allocation of scarce resources. This type of instrumental action, based on utilitarian motivations, may have spread as the market expanded, but these authors do not let that blind them either to action oriented towards different goals (non-utilitarian) or the social conditions that underlay instrumental action itself in a market environment. Thus, they did not ignore the margins of variability in economic behavior.

   To cope with these problems, economic sociologists questioned neoclassical economics' atomistic conception of action. In other words, they called into question the idea that the aims of single actors could be formed independently of each other. Economic action should instead be conceived as social action, in the sense that it is always influenced by expectations relative to the behavior of other members of society. Conforming or not to these expectations entails sanctions that may be either positive or negative for the actors. Following Weber, it can be said that such expectations take the form of habits, traditions, legal norms or conflicts of interest, which is to say power relations. It is important to note that all our authors substantially agree about this way of understanding economic action, whether they emphasize the autonomy of the actors over institutional rules (like Sombart, Weber, and Schumpeter) or whether they start with institutions and emphasize more the influence of institutional rules on actors (as Durkheim, Veblen, and Polanyi do).[4]

This means that action cannot be understood without referring to the institutions that systematically condition the formation of goals. Thus, one can identify some kinds of economic action that are historically widespread, and are not particularly oriented by utilitarianism – as in the primitive societies on which Polanyi focused, or in those characterized by a household economy (Sombart, Weber, and Durkheim) before the market came to predominate. Second, this approach allows us to deal with the problem of social conditions that influence instrumental action itself, and thus its variability. Economic sociologists try to explain economic action as social action, avoiding the individualistic atomism of neoclassical economics. This involves understanding better when, where and why institutions legitimize and encourage utilitarian motivations, but also when they limit and channel them. This is why these authors were so interested in the origins of capitalism.

The research interests of the classics do not stop here, however. They also want to improve their understanding of variability of instrumental action, in the sense of clarifying the extent to which the search for profit and utility maximizing on the basis of consumer preferences are concretely influenced by various factors of a non-utilitarian nature. For example, by religious values (Weber), by the degree of social marginalization (Sombart), by different forms of the division of labour and social inequality (Durkheim, Weber, and Polanyi), by the features of the family or different forms of firm organization (Schumpeter). In all these cases, utilitarian motives and non-utilitarian components combine in a concrete mixture to influence entrepreneurial activity, labor choices and consumption. Thus, for example, entrepreneurs' search for profit can be more or less directed towards innovation, investment and the growth of capital in the long term, or towards no innovation and short-term profit maximization. The behavior of workers can be more or less conflictual and their satisfaction with life and working conditions can influence their productivity. The erosion of traditional forms of social integration often leads people to seek a means to recognition and satisfaction in consumption, and this influences consumption choices whatever the income level may be (as Simmel and Veblen in particular emphasize).

In concrete reality, economic action is therefore rooted in a plurality of motivations that can only be reconstructed inductively, through a complex and difficult process of historical–empirical research. Weber points out that the concepts and "laws" developed by pure economic theory "state what course a given type of human action would take if it were strictly rational, unaffected by errors or emotional factors and if, furthermore, it were completely and unequivocally directed to a single end, the maximization of economic advantage. In reality, it takes exactly this course only in unusual cases, as sometimes on the stock exchange; and even there it is usually only an approximation to the ideal type" (Weber [1922] 1978, p. 9). Usually, he continues, the actors in any given situation are subject to "opposing and conflicting impulses." This is why economic sociology finds it necessary to work with ideal types, with generalizations based on historical–empirical inquiry, rather than with a priori assumptions about the rational pursuit of individual interest, as one does in economics.

3   *The rules.* As a consequence, the rules conditioning actors' actions should, be wider and more complex for economic sociology than for economics, where they

are essentially limited to market forms. The classic authors consistently sought to take other institutions into consideration, in order to take proper account of forms of economic organization that are different from market economies, as well as to distinguish between different forms of market economies. They attach different labels to these institutions, but the meaning is basically very similar. For example, they speak of "forms of organization" (Sombart), "forms of integration" (Polanyi), "regulations of the economy" and, more specifically, "regulations of economic activity" (Weber), "institutions" (Durkheim, Veblen, Polanyi, and Schumpeter).

In general, the consideration of institutional phenomena other than the market develops in two directions. On the one hand, one may refer to economic institutions that are based on shared social obligations. The most typical example of this is Polanyi's "reciprocity," but Weber's "traditional exchange" – which concerns the exchange of gifts as opposed to "rational exchange" (market exchange) – is very similar. This illuminates important aspects of economic activity in both primitive and modern societies. These particular forms of regulation are generally produced and sustained by communities based, to use Weber's words, on "the subjective feeling . . . that they belong together" (Weber [1922] 1978, p. 38). Typical examples of this are the family, kinship relations, local, ethnic, and religious communities, as well as – in modern societies – social movements. In all these cases, sanctions upholding the rules are based, as in reciprocity, on some form of social approval or disapproval.

On the other hand there are institutions involving rules that are based on political sanctions, that is, on norms that ultimately rely on the use of force, of both a legitimate type – as in the case of the state – and a *de facto* type – as in the case of criminal organizations. Examples of institutions that involve the political regulation of the economy are Polanyi's "redistribution," Sombart's "planned" or "cooperative economy," and Weber's "regulative" or "administrative organization."[5] Rules of this type are produced and supported by non-economic structures such as those of the state. However, there are examples of other structures – mediaeval corporations, cartels between firms, unions, and various forms of criminality which exercise their power over a certain geographical area, such as the Mafia.

The concrete forms of economic activity over space and time are therefore affected by how these different institutions regulate the activities of production, distribution and consumption, and they condition the actions of actors.

4   *The method of inquiry.* The previous discussion has already illustrated the differences between the classical economic sociologists' method of inquiry into economic action and its consequences, and the method established in the marginalist revolution in economics. While the latter involves an analytical–deductive and normative method, the former is more inductive, based on a historical–empirical approach. The sociological model too seeks to formulate generalizations that allow the consequences of certain economic actions to be explained. However, whereas economics makes certain a priori assumptions with regard to the actors' utilitarian motivations and the presence of the fixed conditions for the functioning of the market, sociologists try to reconstruct the specific conditions affecting economic action through empirical investigation. Further, economic action may result from the expression of non-utilitarian motivations, or from elements of utilitarianism combined with other, different impulses (traditional, emotional, or ideological, to

Table 6. 1 *Methodological aspects of neoclassical economics and economic sociology*

	Neoclassical economics	Economic sociology
Conception of the economy	Rational allocation of scarce resources usable for alternative aims (economizing)	Activity aimed at the search for means of subsistence
Economic action	Atomism and utilitarianism. Rational pursuit of individual interests by individuals acting independently from each other	Economic action as social action Utilitarian and non utilitarian motivations influenced by institutions
Rules	Competitive Market	Market, Social institutions (e.g. reciprocity) Political institutions (e.g. redistribution)
Method of inquiry	Deductive–axiomatic method Abstract models High generalizations	Inductive method Empirically-based models Bounded generalizations

paraphrase Weber). Moreover, the classical authors also seek to understand the rules working in any particular context through a historical–empirical method. Thus, they do not limit themselves to analyzing certain particular conditions in isolation but evaluate the impact of other institutions, together with the market, on action and its actual consequences. It follows that sociological models have more restrictive temporal and spatial limits than economic ones, precisely because they seek to take more account of the historical–empirical variability of institutions and action. However, these models are usually more wide-reaching and "generalizing" than those of history proper. The study of Western capitalism, for example, is at a lower level of generalization than the analysis of the laws of the market as developed in economics, but at a higher level, for example, than the historical investigation of British capitalism. Despite this difference, economic sociology is intimately related to historical analysis, as Weber especially has emphasized. On the one hand, it draws materials useful for comparative analysis from history, which is in fact essential for testing hypotheses, given the unfeasibility of the experimental method in the study of macro-social phenomena. On the other hand, economic sociology contributes to generating new hypotheses that may in turn orient historical investigation.

2   A Reservoir of Hypotheses

Thus far the emphasis has been on the principal features of classic economic sociology from the methodological point of view. It is however important to recall some of the results that have been derived from the application of this perspective. The main focus of research has been the issues surrounding the origins, consequences, and transformations of capitalism. The historically-grounded aspects of the analytical models restrain the temporal and spatial scope of theoretical generalizations. However, it would be a mistake to dismiss a series of convergent and coherent hypotheses that emerge from the work examined above. This is the reason why the legacy inherited from the classics has informed – and continues to inform – subsequent research. It is therefore worthwhile examining this "reservoir of hypotheses" more closely by considering three main themes: the market, development, and consumption.

2.1   The market

In research on the market, it is useful to distinguish analytically between two areas of research, which have been treated with different levels of emphasis and rigor. The first has to do with the process through which the capitalist market was constructed, and the second to do with the conditions for its successful functioning.

With regard to the first problem, there is a basic difference from the position adopted by the economists (although the most rigorous neoclassical economists do not deal with this problem, considering it to be exogenous). In economic thought, it is generally held that market relations spread because of their *efficiency* as compared to other modalities of economic organization, that is, their capacity to satisfy the preferences of single actors at lower costs. Over time, the market's advantages for individuals bring the institutions and motivations that are consistent with the good functioning of the market to fruition, and this adds to the legitimacy of the market itself. This evolutionary – and optimistic – vision of a linear development of the market can be contrasted with that of economic sociology, which is more sensitive to the variability of outcomes over time and space.

At the center of economic sociology's explanation is the notion of *legitimacy*. First of all, in order to establish itself as the main regulatory mechanism of the economy, the market must become socially accepted, but this is a difficult process without any definite outcomes. Much of Sombart and Weber's work is dedicated to precisely this issue, with reference to a particular historical period: the origins of capitalism in the West. They try to show the complex series of cultural and institutional factors that legitimized, encouraged and supported market relations, including religion, the state and the legal system, towns and modern science. This process was more conflictual in other parts of the world, where culture and institutions opposed and resisted the market. Other authors like Durkheim, Veblen, and Polanyi – who were more interested in the consequences of the capitalist market than the conditions that gave rise to it – also share the idea that the successful operation of the market requires, as Durkheim puts it, "some variations in the social environment" to legitimize it. Recalling Marx, Polanyi pointed out that the process was not necessarily a peaceful one and could also involve the use of force (as with enclosures in Britain) and political power.

Once the utilitarian and individualistic motivations consistent with market functioning have been legitimized and established, the advantages in terms of economic well-being and the growth in the scope for individual choice and consumption reinforce the spread of market relations. Efficiency thus goes hand-in-hand with legitimacy. However, the sociological tradition is in general more sensitive to two features of markets. First, the advantages of the market are spread unequally across different social groups: the benefits enjoyed by the entrepreneurial bourgeoisie, who control the means of production, are rather different to those of the workers that are only able to sell their manpower. In other words, economic sociology is more interested in the problems of fairness in real markets, while economics focuses on problems of efficiency, taking it for granted that a fully competitive market will also resolve any problems of equity. In this perspective, everyone would be remunerated according to their contribution – which would be freely chosen – to the value of overall production. Second, for sociologists, the benefits are not confined to greater scope for material access to goods, but also involve increased freedom of choice both in the use of one's own labor and in consumption (this was strongly underlined by both Simmel and Weber, particularly in their early work).

There is little doubt, however, that for both economists and sociologists, the market tends to reduce the space available for other institutions in the sphere of economic activities, once it becomes established as a regulatory mechanism – from the family to kinship relations and the local community, from the corporations to the state. But to what extent can the market be free from social and political regulations without becoming compromised by its own functioning? This leads to the second problem dealt with in depth by the classics.

We know that neoclassical economics presupposes the existence of well informed individuals, morally trustworthy and capable of rationally calculating the optimal way of satisfying their preferences. These agents move in a context of rules that provide for the full negotiability of all goods and productive factors, and the availability of many sellers and buyers. In this picture the role of social rules (for example, of reciprocity) or political ones (such as forms of redistribution linked to the state or to medieval guilds) are seen as a factor potentially distorting the rational allocation of resources, and thus efficiency. For example, family and kinship relations, or state and union interventions, can alter the remuneration of labor with respect to the value defined in terms of marginal productivity, that is, the contribution of the individual worker to the overall value of the product. This would lead to an increase in the costs of the produced goods to the detriment of the consumer. The hypothesis is thus that the market will work better, the greater is the freedom of individuals from social and political conditioning. Thus the market is the place of separation between individuals, who must not be influenced by extra-economic factors. Forms of interaction and cooperation regulated by incentives that are not strictly economic are inevitably viewed with suspicion.

Economic sociology has developed a different framework of analysis. This can better be understood if one notes that its methodology is more closely tied to historical–empirical investigation, and that it problematizes the a priori assumptions of economic theory. Individuals are not normally well-informed or fully capable of rational calculation, and not everyone can be considered equally trustworthy from the moral point of view. The lack of perfect information, together with the risk of moral hazard, makes market exchanges problematic, even where they have been legitimized – that is, where they are socially accepted. In addition, markets are not always fully competitive. This usually means, as for example in the case of the labor market, that those hiring workers can influence the contractual conditions to their advantage, notwithstanding the formal freedom to bargain among contracting parties. This is why Weber, following Marx, talks of "formally free" labor, and underlines the fact that "certain groups with a far-reaching degree of actual control over economic resources have been in a position to take advantage of the formal freedom of the market to establish monopolies" (Weber [1922] 1978, pp. 84–5).

In real societies, therefore, the market works better not insofar as individuals are separated from each other and are impervious to extra-economic influences, but insofar as there are institutions that add to the legitimacy and the social acceptability of market relations by constraining the pursuit of individual interest. Two types can be mentioned here. First, institutions that generate and reproduce *trust* through personal interactions (for example, those tied to families, kinship relations, local communities, etc.) or in an impersonal way, through legal sanctions applied to people who violate contracts (and this is where state institutions are vital). These institutions are important because under conditions of lack of information, where there is the risk of deceit or fraud, many contracts and exchanges of resources that could benefit the contractors – and more generally society (economic development) – will not happen; or they will happen less than otherwise might be possible. Vice versa, if what Durkheim called non-contractual features of the contract take effect, which is to say if extra-economic relations generate trust and if impersonal institutions such as legal ones underpin the credibility of the contracts, the market can be more efficient.

However, as we have already stressed, efficiency does not necessarily mean *fairness*. There is a second type of institutional control to consider: that regarding the balance of power on the market which conditions the freedom of choice of the contractors. If the relations are particularly unbalanced – in particular on the labor market – conflicts may emerge in bargaining relations, which risk endangering productive activities; or alternatively, workers may become less committed to their tasks, lowering productivity. In these cases, the institutions representing the collective interest of workers and introducing political regulation into the labor market, become important. Moreover, state intervention to regulate working conditions (work hours, child labor, health and safety, etc.) may be appropriate. More generally, economic sociologists believe that regulatory interventions by the state should deal with problems of fairness – through redistributive interventions that reduce social inequalities.[6] As Durkheim has emphasized, these can in fact alter the conditions of struggle on the market, which compromise the liberty of choice, and thus delegitimize the market.

We can thus conclude that the sociological tradition is in contrast with neoclassical economics (particularly in its original and more radical version). Since the assumptions adopted by economists are extremely unlikely to obtain in reality, markets should not – in order to work more efficiently – be as isolated as possible from social and political relations, but should on the contrary be *socially well constructed*. What is necessary is therefore a balance – which can be determined only at the empirical level – between the freedom to pursue individual interest and the constraints placed on its concrete exercise by non-economic institutions. Without these constraints, the market's ability to function as an efficient instrument for organizing economic activity will be put at risk. However, it is also true, as Weber and Schumpeter underline among others, that if the constraints exceed a certain threshold – which cannot be defined in abstract terms – the market can be hampered as a form of economic organization. Economic activity, if it is to work in a market context, must be guaranteed a stable scope for profit. If the burden of regulations generates negative expectations in those who control the means of production, the investments necessary for the reproduction of economic activities may be jeopardized.

Therefore, the concern of economists should not be undervalued. The problem cannot, however, be resolved once and for all at the theoretical level. For economic sociology, this is instead an empirical question, because the tolerability of social and political constraints on the market, i.e. the forms of legitimation of the market, can vary over space and time. This means that there are societies in which the prevalent culture and institutions legitimize, or even demand, greater autonomy from the market. These societies accept the social consequences that may derive from market operations in terms of social inequality, and social and territorial mobility, which happen more than in other institutional contexts. This is, for example, the lesson of Weber's investigation into the specificity of Western society with respect to those of the East. As we shall see later, comparative analysis can also make distinctions within the Western context. For example, one can distinguish between Anglo-Saxon societies in which the market has more autonomy (particularly in the United States) and others, such as those of mainland Europe, where there is a greater cultural and institutional need to limit the autonomy of the market so as to legitimize it.

In other words, in evaluating the conditions for the functioning of the market we can draw yet another conclusion from the classic texts: one should avoid searching for an optimal form of economic organization in terms of efficiency. There is no *one best way*; instead, there are several, all of which are conditioned by their social context. Only through comparative empirical investigation can we begin to identify these and to evaluate their respective strengths and weaknesses.

2.2 Economic development

On what does the economic development of a market economy depend? There can be no doubt that it is influenced by legitimacy. Economic sociology as distinct from the neoclassical approach, highlights the dynamic efficiency of the market. It shows how alterations in the allocation of resources may lead to greater future benefits, due to the role played by social and political institutions. For example, a firm that has cooperated with another for some time may decide not to exploit a favorable market situation to demand lower prices, thereby reducing its own prices for the consumer. This loss in efficiency in the short term could, however, be more than compensated by the willingness of the supplying firm to cooperate with higher commitment and trustworthiness on future occasions, thus improving overall productivity over time. This same mechanism can be seen in the labor market. An alteration in the wage level contrary to prevailing market conditions may increase costs for a certain firm in the immediate future and can have negative repercussions for the consumers of the firm's goods. However, it can also create the conditions for workers to really participate in the productive activity, increasing their commitment, involvement, and thus the productivity of labor over time – as Adam Smith had already noted.

The tradition of economic sociology thus suggests that a more solid social acceptance of the market, linked to institutional constraints of a social and political nature, is a condition not only for the stability but also for the growth of a market economy. However, this condition, which relates to the rules influencing actors' behavior, is not sufficient. Economic sociology does not only see the rules as being more complex in real societies, but takes the variability of actors' motivations into account. In contrast, the analytical model of neo-classical economics assumes that actors will behave identically when confronted with external constraints. Agents are well informed, trustworthy and fully capable of rationally allocating scarce resources (capital, technology, labor, etc.), which are assumed as givens. In this perspective, as Schumpeter points out, economic development – understood as the creation of new added resources – is not investigated. In the sociological perspective in contrast, the behavior of actors is variable and resources are not a given. The aim is to explain their growth over time, that is, how economic development occurs. To do this it is not sufficient that the market be legitimized; one needs to evaluate the degree to which economic actors use market exchanges to create new wealth, moving beyond the routine procedures of traditional and consolidated relations. In other words, it is necessary that one joins *innovation* to *legitimacy*.

If the capacity to innovate is to be encouraged, market relations must be highly socially accepted; this eases cooperation and exchanges. However, this is not a sufficient condition. To what extent are these opportunities taken? On what does innovative capacity depend? The classics would respond that it is fundamentally dependent on *entrepreneurship*, that is – as Schumpeter would say – on the capacity to realize new things (new products, new processes and methods of organization of production, and new markets). When one innovates, one creates new relations, and one has to face even more uncertainty about the end results of action, as well as moral hazard. Therefore, Schumpeter emphasizes how the entrepreneur is characterized by particular qualities that allow him to tackle such problems more effectively: determination, capacity for vision, commitment, but also a desire for social success and recognition. This comes close to the combination between the "spirit of enterprise" and the "bourgeois spirit" that Sombart talks about. Viewed in this light, the entrepreneur has a particular set of features, whose aims are different from those of other economic actors, and which cannot be identified as a generic rational pursuit of individual interest. According to Schumpeter, the explanation for these unusual qualities and their spread is not only psychological and individual, rather, it involves social context, that is, the presence of institutions that facilitate or hinder entrepreneurship. Following this perspective, Schumpeter's position is close to that of Sombart and Weber, even if these authors were more oriented towards the problem of the origins of capitalism. As we know, they underlined the importance of factors like religion, or exclusion from citizenship rights, in the emergence of capitalistic enterprise.

In general, economic sociology thus suggests that development depends not only on institutions that legitimize the market by regulating the utilitarian selection of means with respect to the aims, but also on institutions that define the aims of the actors themselves. In other words, one has to look at how actors define and perceive their interests if one wants evaluate whether, and to what extent, entrepreneurship is encouraged. Religion for Weber and Sombart, exclusion from citizenship rights for Simmel and Sombart, and access to technological knowledge for Veblen are all examples of the *constitutive* role played by institutional rules, in contrast with with the *regulatory* role of institutions discussed above in the context of market legitimacy (the regulation of legitimate ways to pursue the goals).[7] In general, the most important constitutive rules are the *normative* ones, which define the ultimate values that guide behavior, a typical example of which are the religious beliefs affecting the origins of market capitalism. However, some scholars, including Veblen, Sombart and Schumpeter, were aware of the growing role that *cognitive* resources – the actors' knowledge, routines and know-how – play in the formation of entrepreneurship and in development in advanced capitalist economies.

This set of hypotheses regarding economic development has been important for the way in which economic sociology has grown, particularly in relation to the study of countries and backward areas which will be discussed in chapter 7. It has also drawn increasing attention over recent years, with the transformation of productive organization along the lines of models based on flexibility and a more important role for small and medium-sized firms, in which personal entrepreneurship is important (see chapter 9). However, it should be remembered that for the classics, the impact of entrepreneurship on the capacity of innovation, and therefore on economic development, must be situated in a historical context. They foresaw that the firm would become increasingly impersonalized and bureaucratized as a consequence of the development of capitalism, while the capacity for innovation would shift from personal entrepreneurship to organizational ability – the "visible hand" of organization as Alfred Chandler (1977) would later call it.

These scholars were concerned about economic dynamism, precisely because of this process. Many of them believed that the bureaucratization of firms and the increasing organization of capitalism – linked to new political rules involving the state and industrial relations – could lead to a loss of innovative capacity. Although on the whole this concern turned out to be exaggerated – as we shall see later – there is no doubt that economic sociology also contributed in this way, highlighting a structural problem of the capitalist economy. In other words, once it has established itself, the market lead to the progressive erosion of the *constitutive* rules that initially supported it: religion, institutions, and traditional ties. This worsens the problems of social acceptance of the consequences of the market over time, as all the classics pointed out, and leads to the growth of new *regulatory* rules (state interventions in the economic and social fields, industrial relations, etc.). At this point the possible contradiction mentioned above arises – the discrepancy between the institutional regulation of the market and economic development. From the dynamic point of view, an excess of regulation can weaken innovative capacity. This hypothesis – which can be drawn from the classics – is particularly fruitful; it allows to set up historical–empirical comparisons dealing with the differences of economic development over space and time.

2.3 Consumption

The problem of consumption is also important for economic sociology. This phenomenon was not the main focus of interest of classical economists, whose real
interest was production. For neoclassical economists, however, it was instead consumers' demand that was the basis for the value of goods through the theory of
marginal utility. Demand was thus analyzed from the starting point of specific
hypotheses about consumer behavior. The assumption is that this behavior aims
to satisfy needs, which are rank-ordered by single actors according to a stable hierarchy of preferences. In this perspective, the formation of preferences is not influenced by extra-individual factors, and is considered as an exogenous factor which
is not investigated by economics. Given the relevant constraints (the prices of goods
and disposable income), consumers tend to distribute their purchasing power in a
way that is exactly proportional to their preferences. Assuming that the satisfaction linked to a certain good diminishes with the consumption of additional units
(marginal utility), it is hypothesized that this good will be consumed until the
added satisfaction equals that of the other goods that he wants to consume. A key
assumption of the neoclassical model is that consumers are attentive, well-informed
about the prices and quality of goods, and are capable of continually calculating
their utility, reacting to the market prices by adjusting their consumption. It is, in
fact, clear that this is how consumers stimulate and condition competition between firms, rewarding the most efficient (which produce the requested goods at
the lowest cost).

Economic sociology also questions the atomism and utilitarianism of the neoclassical theory of action with regard to consumption. It is hard to find consumers
that are independent from the influences of other actors, with stable preferences,
adequate information and a capacity to make precise calculations about their utility in real societies. The interest of sociologists thus concentrates on the concrete
features of consumer behavior in a society where the phenomenon of mass consumption is increasing, in parallel with economic development and a rise in incomes. Given this orientation, attention focuses on the socio-cultural factors
conditioning both preferences and the ways in which they are pursued, influencing utilitarian calculation. Therefore, preferences and individual tastes are not
understood as the result of a subjective evaluation of goods to be consumed, ordered hierarchically on the basis of their use value (the utility that they give to
individual actors), in isolation from other members of society. The goods are instead desired and consumed, to a large extent, because of their symbolic and social
value, that is, the meaning that they take on in social relations with others, functioning as signs of recognition for actors and social groups with whom consumers
want to be identified, and as signs of differentiation from other groups.

Simmel was one of the first scholars to highlight the symbolic function of consumption in the competition to gain higher social status. He noted how the spread
of the monetary economy and market relations went hand in hand with the progressive erosion of traditional institutions (from the local community to guilds,
churches, etc.) which gave identity to individuals and contributed to their integration into a wider society. The individual's place in society becomes less stable, less

linked to established forms of recognition. This means that in growing cities and towns, in which the traditional institutions have even less influence, consumption functions as a means to get one recognized, to gain social status and to mark out an identity. It is in this context that fashion finds fertile terrain, according to Simmel (1911). It serves a double goal: it allows individuals to identify with some social groups and distinguish themselves from others through the goods they consume, which take on a symbolic value that goes well beyond their utility in terms of use value.

For his part, Weber links consumer behavior to the search for status typical of "status groups," groups which have a particular prestige. In modern society, status groups usually have a professional basis (the self-employed, intellectuals, soldiers, etc.) and are distinguished by particular lifestyles to which the quantity and quality of consumption contributes. However, it is above all Veblen, with his analysis of "conspicuous consumption," who linked consumption to the competition for social status. From the privileged observatory of turn-of-the-century America, he was able to capture the growing importance of consumption in a society particularly uncharacterized by traditional ties, extremely mobile, and strongly polarized in terms of social inequalities. In his pioneering study, which became highly successful and influential, Veblen emphasized how growing access to mass consumption is an essential instrument for the integration of disadvantaged social groups. This went together, in his opinion, with a waste of productive resources that, rather than increasing the effective utility of single consumers, would lead them to spend their income on useless goods, chosen for their value as status symbols.

It is clear that the motivations for consumption on which economic sociologists insist – those tied to the symbolic value of goods in status competition – call the elegant neoclassical model into question.[8] In fact, they imply a social rigidity in consumer behavior that leads to reactions that are non-consonant with the rational calculation of utility. This can mean, for example, that a price increase does not lead to less consumption if the good has a high symbolic value; vice versa, if the good loses that value, a lower price may not lead to more consumption.

There is, however, yet another aspect to be taken into consideration, as pointed out by economic sociologists. Flesh-and-blood consumers, even apart from the social pressures discussed above, are not well-informed, and they have few resources to acquire the knowledge necessary to evaluate the quality of the offered goods. This fact tends to be consciously exploited by firms, which try to increase the symbolic value of goods and to control consumption behavior through fashions. Thus, for example, Weber notes that "even though the consumer has to be in a position to buy, his wants are 'awakened' and 'directed' by the entrepreneur" (Weber [1922], 1978 p. 92). Schumpeter adds to this by underlining how consumers do not behave according to the economic textbooks even in the most banal situations: "On the one hand their wants are nothing like as definite and their actions upon those wants nothing like as rational and prompt. On the other hand they are so amenable to the influence of advertising and other methods of persuasion that producers often seem to dictate to them instead of being directed by them" (Schumpeter [1942] 1961, p. 257). By influencing fashion, as well as through advertising, firms can introduce new products more quickly, but also standardizing demand to a greater extent, as Sombart emphasizes. It is thus possible to create a mass market that allows the use of new technologies and the realization of economies of scale. The "standardization of needs" of which Sombart talks is reinforced by the production of lower quality goods that imitate the fashions of more wealthy groups and are offered to consumers at a lower price.

This, in summation, is how economic sociology questions the central assumption of neo-classical economics – the principle of "consumer sovereignty," on which the efficiency of the productive machine depends. If the hypothesis of the well-informed consumer with stable and autonomous preferences, who is capable of continually calculating his utility, does not hold empirically, his power to discipline firms, rewarding those that are more efficient and punishing those that are not, is also weaker. Economic sociology does not deny the potential importance of this mechanism in the market economy but it problematizes it, and suggests that its importance varies. Moving from analytical abstraction to empirical reality, one can appreciate that its positive effect on efficiency will be greater when single actors are not isolated. In any case, these would lack the information and the abilities needed to orient themselves given the prices and quality of the goods offered. On the contrary, one may suggest from this point of view too, that *efficiency is socially constructed*. Only if there are institutions that can improve knowledge by conditioning the behavior of firms and which also educate the consumer by inducing him to organize, can consumers choose better and therefore exercise their positive influence on the efficiency of firms. Once again then, efficiency is linked to the institutional context. It is a variable phenomenon that cannot be determined a priori, and is subject to differences over space and time that should be studied from the historical–empirical point of view and through the comparative method.

3   The Redefinition of the Boundaries between Economics and Sociology

The work of Schumpeter and Polanyi was a turning point in the development of economic sociology. After its publication, there was a decline in the tradition of analysis of the sociology of capitalism that has been described in the previous chapters. This tradition was based on the use of analytical models to interpret the origins and transformations of a specific form of economic organization – Western capitalism – which was historically delimited, through the comparison of different models over space and time. In the post-war period, the legacy of the classics became fragmented and economic sociology moved towards greater thematic and disciplinary specialization. Two main paths emerged in particular.

First, the theme of economic development, which was at the center of the classical tradition, became less important in the study of the more developed Western countries. Macro-economic themes were taken over by the new Keynesian economics. However, economic sociology's original interest in the relation between institutions and economic development did not disappear. Indeed, it continued to flourish mainly in studies of underdeveloped areas and countries. In this field of research, the role of non-economic institutions in conditioning the process of development remained important – and in fact, found new fodder in the process of decolonization and the establishment of new states on the international political and economic scene. From this point of view, it can thus be said that the original perspective of economic sociology was reconstituted first of all in terms of the sociology of development (as we will see in the next chapter). A second direction is that of micro-economic themes, which, in the classical tradition, had usually been dealt with together with the macro-economic ones – for example, the organization of firms and labor, industrial conflict, and labor relations. Studies on these topics now tended to develop autonomously, in part as a result of the growing institutionalization of sociological studies in university teaching and research. Thus, more highly specialized disciplines developed and became independent of the original core of economic sociology: industrial sociology, studies on organizations, labor, and industrial relations sociology.

How can we explain these trends? Clearly, many factors have affected the process of fragmentation and disciplinary specialization, but it is worth drawing attention to two main reasons. The first involves the economic and social transformations that many countries underwent after the Second World War. In different ways, these helped in a redefinition of the boundaries between the state and the market that led to a greater commitment on the part of governments to full employment and the development of the welfare state. This process went together with a period of intense economic growth and social and political stabilization. In other words, many of the worries about the difficult relationship between the economy and society in liberal capitalism – on which the founders of economic sociology had focused their attention – now seemed less important as a consequence of the "great transformation" of capitalism. This occurred particularly in the more developed countries, where Keynesian policies and "Fordist" forms of industrial organization became widespread.

The second reason involves the contemporary redefinition of the boundaries between economics and sociology. On the one hand, economics retrieved its connection with historical–empirical reality, particularly with the "Keynesian revolution," and it proposed new instruments to interpret and guide this new and intense phase of economic growth. On the other, the institutionalization of sociology pushed scholars towards fields that were less studied by economists, and encouraged a more specific fragmentation and disciplinary specialization of economic sociology along the lines described above.

3.1   Economic and social stabilization in the post-war period

The first thing that must be recalled is the historical context in which the new boundaries between economics and sociology were built up. The first three decades following the Second World War, until the seventies, marked a period of extraordinary economic growth. Although the destruction and loss of human life had been much greater than during the First World War, recovery in this period was more rapid, solid, and stable than it had been before.

America's aid policy for Europe played an important role in this process. Most of the European countries were on their knees – the winners as well as the losers. The Old World was on the verge of bankruptcy. The United States wiped out a large amount of the allied countries' debts, but also gave them a large amount of financial aid through the Marshall Plan. This time, they avoided the mistakes made with Germany after the First World War when they demanded a level of compensation that was in practice untenable. While this strategy of aid provision helped reconstruction and recovery, there was another important difference with the post-First World War period. Growth in production benefited enormously from the progressive liberalization of markets, and therefore from a substantial increase in international trade, as well as from the agreements stabilizing exchange rates. This was helped by the close international cooperation which led to the creation of new organizations such as the International Monetary Fund, the European Organization for Economic Cooperation, and later on the institutions of the European Community.

This international institutional picture contrasted starkly with the one that had influenced economic and political events following the First World War. In this new context, demand for goods could grow enormously, boosted first by the requirements of reconstruction and demand for basic commodities, and then, increasingly, by the possibility of satisfying new needs through using modern technology to produce mass consumer goods – from cars to household appliances. In addition, one of the most remarkable founts of development sprang, especially in European countries, from the existence of a large labor supply which came from low productivity sectors and areas, and especially from agriculture. This involved a low-skilled labor force that could be used in the more modern industries, because of the use of new productive technologies and new Taylorist forms of labor organization, which allowed labor tasks to be divided up and simplified. As a result, the wide availability of a low-cost labor force constituted a remarkable competitive advantage, especially in an area like Europe in which the national economies were highly dependent on exports.

However, these economic variables, linked to the growth of demand, availability of low-cost labor, and technological development need to be considered together with the changes that came about in the institutional regulation of the economies of the more developed countries. From this point of view, the "great transformation" that Polanyi had already predicted as a reaction to the crisis of the thirties, continued and consolidated. During the sixties, Andrew Shonfield made a comparative analysis of Western countries and provided one of the most effective syntheses of the changes involved in what he called "modern capitalism," that is, a kind of capitalism that was more regulated at both micro and macro levels and became increasingly different from the liberal capitalism of the nineteenth century. We can use this synthesis (Shonfield, 1965, chapter 4) to throw light on the main differences characterizing the type of capitalism that emerged after the Second World War. "What was it that converted capitalism from the cataclysmic failure which it appeared to be in the 1930s into the great engine of prosperity of the post-war western world?" (ibid, p. 5). This British scholar's question emphasizes four new features of post-war development: first, it was much more regular than in the past, with shorter and weaker recessions; second, growth in production and income had never been so rapid, particularly in Western Europe; third, this new prosperity spread widely among the population – not only did wages rise together with GDP, but, particularly in Europe, the growth in social protection (social services and health care) allowed redistribution towards those social groups that could not count on increases in wages; finally, all this occurred without any ebb in the flow of savings necessary to sustain a high level of investment.

The question of what caused this development, according to Shonfield, cannot be answered solely with reference to the role of international trade, technological development, growing demand or labor supply. What also needs to be considered are the changes in the forms of economic regulation that led to a redefinition of the boundaries between state and market. He thus draws attention to a series of interconnected factors. First, the stronger influence of public authorities in the regulation of the economy and maintenance of full employment. In most countries, this took place to some extent through a substantial growth in public spending, but it also took other forms, including credit control, the role of state firms, and – more generally – market regulation. Governments were influenced by the new Keynesian ideas that were then circulating (Hall 1989). However, state intervention went well beyond Keynes' conception of economic management. Keynes was mostly worried about realizing the full use of given resources – that is to say, he attempted to resolve the problems that had emerged with the Great Depression. In actuality, Western governments went beyond this after the Second World War. Their objective was to increase growth and they did so by adopting various forms of planning, while at the same time promoting redistribution through the welfare system.

"The violence of the market has been tamed," Shonfield noted (1965, p. 66), not only as a result of state action, but also because of changes taking place in firms. The opportunity to exploit new technologies, which made it possible to bring the unit costs of large mass production down, encouraged the creation of large firms which sought to stabilize their long-term profits, so that they would be able to amortize the huge capital investments necessary for production. Planning methods thus also spread into the private sector and were introduced and implemented by managers who replaced the old entrepreneur-owners of the past. As ownership and management became separate, the bureaucratization of corporations increased, and their resemblance to public structures became apparent. All this was encouraged by governments; worried about growth and economic stability, they pushed large firms to collaborate among themselves and with public authorities, in pursuit of long-term objectives.

Certainly, the picture described by Shonfield implied a remarkable amount of optimism about the capacity of these new relations between state and market to guarantee social stability and economic growth. As we shall see, this situation was to change rapidly during the seventies. However, there is no doubt that the tendencies described above do capture the crucial transformations in the relationship between economy and institutions. It was the integration of an interventionist state – later also called the "Keynesian welfare state" – and the large mass-production firms – later called "Fordist" – that gave rise to and ensured post-war development. The first used its fiscal, social and economic policies to regulate demand, sustain employment and stabilize the market for large firms; these were then in turn able to exploit the potential of technology to realize economies of scale in the mass production of consumer goods and to increase production, taking advantage of the liberalization of trade. However, this process was not painless; it entailed a sort of collective learning that took on different forms in different countries, and often took place through sharp social and political conflicts. Peter Gourevitch (1986) has defined this process as a "historical compromise" between business, labor and the state. Business accepted collective bargaining with unions, a growing intervention of the state in the economy and the welfare state in exchange for social peace and the acceptance of the market economy and Taylorist firm organization by labor.

This is the historical context in which we must therefore understand the decline of the sociology of capitalism. It grew weaker because its worries about the intrinsic social and political instability of capitalism found a partial reply in the institutional changes of the post-War period. The historical compromise sought to maintain both economic growth and social stability – and this was an effective form of the social construction of the market.

3.2   The changes in the economy and the "Keynesian revolution"

The second factor that must be examined, if we are to understand the development of economic sociology after the Second World War, involved both its own internal developments and changes in economics. Both of these had a strong influence on the redefinition of the boundaries between the two disciplines.

A first important change concerned economic research. In its early history, sociology measured itself against neoclassical economics, which had left the area of historical–empirical investigation and actual developments of economic systems almost completely vacant. However, particularly from the thirties on, an important change began to take place in economic research. This took several different forms, all of which shared, however, the aim of reducing the gap between analytical models and historical–empirical reality. To describe this process, Daniel Bell (1981) has used the telling image of "bridges towards reality" which are built out from economics. The most important of these was constituted by Keynes's work; before examining this, however, another important change needs to be considered, regarding the micro-economic level.

Traditional neoclassical theory focused its enquiry on two ideal market structures, perfect competition and monopolies. These were unsuitable for describing the concrete reality of markets, however. For this reason, there was growing interest in the thirties in forms of market organization defined as "imperfect competition" (Robinson 1933) and "monopolistic competition" (Chamberlin 1933). Although they adopted different approaches, both these scholars questioned the basic idea that competitive markets involve the exchange of homogenous goods (one should note that it is precisely the homogeneity of the goods that allow fully competitive markets to function). Robinson underlined the fact that, quite apart from problems of information, consumers do not in fact necessarily respond in the same way to differences in the prices of products, because they take various factors into account in their consumption behavior, including the location of sellers and transport costs, as well as guarantees concerning the level of quality and easy payment. Chamberlin focused attention on product differentiation as a resource for firms, allowing them to avoid competition to some extent, which led to a segmentation of the market. With the creation of a trademark, or other devices influencing the reputation and evaluation of the quality of goods (for example, advertising), firms can acquire an almost monopolistic advantage over competitors. This is how the concept of "monopolistic competition" came into being, to describe the market forms that prevailed in real economies.

It is clear that these studies had important implications for both theoretical assumptions them and for the economic policy interventions that were traditionally associated with neoclassical economics. For example, the advantages for consumers are reduced in the competitive conditions delineated by the new studies. Monopolistic competition means that higher prices can be paid than in pure competition, because firms succeed in controlling prices through product differentiation. In addition, it is also difficult for new firms to enter the market. The traditional principles of consumer sovereignty and of the efficiency of the competitive markets were thus called into question, and the ground prepared for the political regulation of the markets to reduce these problems (for example, through antitrust regulation). In other words, without substantially altering the utilitarian and atomistic assumptions of neoclassical theory of action, the new studies allowed economic models to grasp empirical reality. As Daniel Bell underlined (1981), this was particularly true – in the American context – of Chamberlin's contribution, since, by moving attention from the market to the firm, it opened up the way to the empirical study of firms and of forms of industrial organization, which led to remarkable developments. Therefore, economic sociology would later on – during the thirties and post-war period – have to measure itself against the development of a branch of business studies that was more empirically oriented at the micro level and more linked to economic history.

However, the "bridge towards reality" that had the strongest economic theory and state policies in the forty years from the end of the thirties to the early seventies most strongly was clearly the work of the British economist John Maynard Keynes (1883–1946). As Galbraith (1987) has pointed out, one of the most curious aspects of the so-called Keynesian revolution was that it had been anticipated by the actual economic policies of several governments. Indeed, the need to deal with the disruptive effects of the Great Depression of the thirties had led some governments to break with orthodox economics, which, as we know, placed its faith in a self-adjusting market. As a result, experiments to tackle unemployment through state spending on public works, unemployment benefits and new forms of welfare protection, were all tried out in as varied a set of contexts as Roosevelt's New Deal America, Hitler's Nazi Germany, and social-democratic Sweden (Gourevitch 1986). In other words, the state took on a more interventionist role in the economic field, going against traditional economic formulas.

Keynes shared these new ideas and political practices and gave them support. His particular contribution was to give them a solid theoretical foundation using the language and tools of economic science, which were familiar to him because of his training at Cambridge under Marshall. His ideas were laid out in *The General Theory of Employment Interest and Money*, published in 1936. This was a complex and difficult book, with many currents, in which the influential and long-lasting foundations of a new theoretical and practical way of looking at economic phenomena were presented.

In a famous lecture given in 1926, *The End of Laissez Faire*, several of the assumptions that would underpin his later theories could already be discerned. Keynes's rejection of an orthodox and rigid vision of *laissez-faire* was based on the recognition of the fundamental role of uncertainty, and the unpredictability of future events in economic and social life. As he says, "Many of the greatest economic evils of our time are the fruits of risk, uncertainty, and ignorance" (1926, p. 47). These were, in his view, the main reasons for the difficulties that might prevent the full use of productive resources, and were a possible cause of unemployment. Keynes advocated a more active role for the state in regulating economic activities precisely in order to confront the crucial problem of the negative effects of uncertainty. For Keynes, the most basic example of this was the relationship between savings and investments. Precisely because of this uncertainty about the future, private entrepreneurs who wish to make profits do not always transfer savings into investments in a way that is conducive to full employment. If they have unfavorable expectations of market profits, there may well be a lower level of investments than is necessary for the full use of resources and labor.

These views – developed while writing in newspapers and working as an advisor to government bodies – were presented with greater theoretical rigor in his book *The General Theory*, ten years later. In this, Keynes moved the focus of economic inquiry from the micro to the macro level. While neoclassical economics was centered on the formation of the prices of goods and the distribution of incomes, Keynes' attention focussed on the factors influencing the aggregate level of production and employment, given a certain stock of capital resources, labor, and technology. Keynes believed that the remedies proposed by traditional theory to treat depressions – the lowering of wages and interest rates – could in fact give rise to an equilibrium of under-employment This is a kind of trap into which the economic system risked falling if the state is not willing to intervene when entrepreneurial expectations – which are linked to the basic factor of uncertainty – were not sufficient to ensure the full transfer of savings into investments. Therefore, in its capacity as a public actor, the state could make a first crucial contribution to resolving this problem by regulating credit and lowering interest rates, when it was necessary to speed up economic activities and increase consumption. However, to sustain demand and promote full employment, the state should also intervene through an increase in public spending.

Clearly, this approach radically modified the conception of state-market relations inherited from traditional economic theories. While the latter gave a theoretical underpinning to *liberalism* and market self-regulation as a means to economic adjustments, the Keynesian analysis provided a basis for *state intervention* to pursue full employment through demand management. From the point of view of economic policy, certain conclusions could be drawn that on the one hand legitimized the various experiments made by some governments to cope with the problems of the Great Depression and, on the other, acted as a guide for future events, and were subsequently fine-tuned by Keynesian economists. Let us recall some of the features of the new economic policies.

The first is that of *deficit spending*. In the Keynesian perspective, the more government expenditure manages to stimulate additional demand, the more effective it is in reaching full employment. Thus, if expenditure is financed only through taxes, maintaining a balanced budget, it will in fact substitute for other spending by private individuals that would not occur because of taxes. At the same time, it is also clear that the kind of spending that occurs is relatively unimportant. In principle, to take Keynes's famous example, the unemployed could be made to dig holes in the ground. The problem is not one of increasing productive capacity, but of making demand grow through higher incomes. There is also another important aspect which is linked to government action in the post-war period. In the Keynesian perspective, the propensity to consume falls as income grows, and as a result it is lower among wealthier groups. In contrast to traditional theories, this provides a potential justification for redistributive policies by the government (for example, fiscal and social measures) that favor poorer social groups precisely to stimulate demand. In other words, redistribution can be justified not only in relation to problems of fairness, but also to promote the efficiency of the economic system.

Thus, the new Keynesian perspective had all the necessary ingredients to reorient economic investigation, as well as the role of the state in the economy and society. These two aspects are clearly interlinked. It is also worth mentioning that Keynes strengthened the foundations of economics' bridges to empirical reality in another way through his influence on the development of macro-economic models and econometrics. Keynesian economics was based on the short term and considered productive capacity as a given. Very soon, however, economists – influenced by these new ideas – began to explore their implications in dynamic terms and to confront the problem of economic growth. Macro-economic models attempted to estimate the conditions under which the balance between effective demand and increased productive capacity could be maintained, given certain other conditions. These tools were used both to guide governments' choices to achieve the full use of existing resources and to determine their goals over time for economic growth. This happened not only in highly developed countries but also in developing ones. With the spread of development economics, models were created enabling public authorities to work out interventions to achieve increasing growth rates over time. Macro-economic modeling is strictly linked to mathematical analysis and statistical techniques that are fine-tuned by econometrics. This latter enables the establishing of relations of functional interdependence between different economic variables (incomes, consumption, savings, investments, etc.) and the formulation of predictions about their development over time under certain known conditions. This new approach was used widely at both the macro and micro levels, making a significant contribution to empirical investigation in economics.

The "Keynesian revolution," the new studies on market structures, and the spread of econometrics all strongly influenced the redefinition of relations between economics and economic sociology in the post-war period. From this point of view, the most important element was certainly the emergence of Keynesian macro-economics as a tool for interpreting and guiding the development process, particularly in the more advanced countries. Keynesian ideas provided a theoretical base and operational tools for the historical compromise between capital and labor on which the Golden Age of post-war development was based.

3.3   Talcott Parsons and the new boundaries

While Keynes was working on his *General Theory* during the thirties, Talcott Parsons (1902–79) was developing his conception of the role of sociology in a series of articles published in the *Quarterly Journal of Economics*, further developed in *The Structure of Social Action* (1937). This work had enormous influence on sociological studies and on the definition of the boundaries between economics and sociology.

In one of his first written pieces on the relationship between economics and sociology, Parsons discussed the scientific status of economics according to the formulation of an influential neo-classical economist, Lionel Robbins (Parsons 1934). The most important limit, in his view, was the exclusion of the actor's goals. Robbins treated these as given – that is, they were not considered to be an object of inquiry for economics, which instead focused on the relationship between goals and means, presupposing that the actor would concentrate on the rational choice of means to pursue his ends. Parsons was well aware that this direction in economic investigation was linked to the attempt to construct a strong scientific model after that of the natural sciences, particularly the physical sciences. The very task of developing theories with a high level of generalization requires that actors behave homogeneously in terms of the rational pursuit of their ends. However, excluding the investigation of ends leads irrevocably to an atomistic individualism: that is, one presupposes that individuals define their ends independently of their mutual interaction. It is at this point that a serious problem emerges – there is no reason for thinking that "the ultimate ends of individuals should be automatically compatible with each other" (Parsons 1934, p. 518). If there are no factors at work introducing elements of coherence, coordination and integration between the goals of various individuals, society risks becoming "a mere chaos of conflicting individuals." According to Parsons, the solution to the classic Hobbesian problem of social order is not so much one of the capacity of political power to control individual interests, nor of supposing a natural and spontaneous integration of the ends *à la* Locke, but the existence of a set of shared goals – of common values that orient action. This is what forms the objective of sociology.

Given these premises, economics should not be seen as a discipline in a positivist sense, one that is capable of interpreting concrete economic phenomena at the empirical level. Economic laws differ radically from physical ones; they are "an abstraction, a formulation of only part of the forces at work in concrete reality" (Parsons 1934, p. 519). In other words, economic laws are *normative*, indicating the criteria of rational action under certain conditions. Their empirical validity depends, however, on whether actors effectively behave according to these criteria to satisfy their ends. This, according to Parsons, Weber and all economic sociologists, is extremely unlikely in reality.

These arguments already show that Parsons was well aware of the limits of neo-classical economics as a discipline that defines itself in terms of empirical science. He instead opts to defend its scientific validity as an analytical discipline, following the path previously indicated by Menger and Pareto, and accepted by Weber (see chapter 1). This was further clarified in an article where he examined the attempts made to redefine economics to increase its grasp on empirical explanation, that is, to provide complete theoretical explanations of actual economic activities. According to Parsons (1935a), these attempts can be gathered into two types.

The first is the "positivist empiricism" that emerged mainly in the Anglo-Saxon context. This focused on how economic action was conditioned by biological or psychological factors. One example was Bentham's "psychological hedonism," which was the theory of action underlying utilitarianism; there was also Veblen's resort to the theory of instincts as bio-psychic forces conditioning action.[9] More generally, this branch of studies led to behaviorism – an approach tending to de-value the role of ideal factors (values, norms) in the behavior of the actor. The second branch was called "historicist empiricism" (or "romantic empiricism"). In this case attention was drawn to ideal and normative factors; one example is the concept of "spirit of the people" used by German Historicism. However, in the German historical school of economics, this focus on the variety of cultural and institutional factors influencing economic action operates to the detriment of theo-retical accuracy (as Weber had already pointed out, cf. chapter 1).

In sum, Parsons rejected both Veblen's institutionalism and the historical ap-proach. In both cases the attempt to give a complete theoretical explanation of concrete economic actions led to what might be called an encyclopedic social sci-ence, based on empirical generalizations, and not compatible with his idea of sci-ence (Parsons 1935b).

In other words, in their attempt to add other factors to enrich the empirical explanation of economic behavior, both institutionalism and historicism reduce economics to a "branch of applied sociology." In addition, sociology seemed to become an "encyclopedic sociology," a sort of general synthesis of knowledge about society. In this perspective, an economist would be distinguished from other social scientists only because of his greater knowledge of a specific sector of social activi-ties, that of economics. According to Parsons, this was wrong and anti-scientific and it was necessary to work on a different foundation for the two disciplines and their relations, which he called "the analytical factor view" (Parsons 1935b).

The most convincing solution was, in his view, provided by several authors con-sidered crucial to the foundation of sociology: Durkheim, Pareto, and Weber. De-spite their differences, they shared – according to Parsons – a common analytical vision of both economics and sociology. The first must be conceived as the analyti-cal theory of a factor of action based on the rational pursuit of individual interest, a factor that is particularly present in concrete economic activities, although not only in these, and never in isolation. In this sense "orthodox economic theory," that is, neoclassical economics, can maintain its own space undisturbed. It does not concern itself with ultimate ends, but with an intermediate level of the means–ends chain, which is in substance the rational allocation of scarce means useable for alternative aims. For its part, sociology can be conceived as an abstract analyti-cal theory of another factor of action, one linked to "ultimate values." From this point of view, Parsons sees Durkheim's "common consciousness," Pareto's "non-logical actions," and the religious ethics analyzed by Weber, as different ways of formulating both the basis of sociological theory and the study of the influence of normative components (values and norms) on action. Parsons further developed and presented this thesis in *The Structure of Social Action* (1937), in which he formu-lated his "voluntaristic theory of action."

It was at this point that the boundaries he set between economics and sociology became clearer. Both disciplines (but this could be extended, for example, to political science with its the notion of power) examine in detail the basic factors influencing human action "in 'artificial' isolation from the rest" (1935b, p. 647). However, he was very well aware that historical–empirical reality is unitary and that it cannot be compartmentalized: "all important concrete research problems cut across several of the divisions between theoretical science" (1935b, p. 647, note 2). This means that theoretical abstraction is important for defining a scientist's central focus "but the exigencies of concrete research are such that (the scientist) must inevitably venture across the borderlines, probably in several directions" (1935b, p. 660, note 4).

In Parsons' work, there is a clear distinction between the theoretical level at which each discipline analyzes its most fundamental feature in detail, in isolation from others, in terms of abstract analytical models, and the level of research on concrete empirical reality, where it is necessary to go beyond disciplinary boundaries and to examine how different factors work together. In the case of economic activities, for example, this would take the form of analyzing how economic and sociological factors come together. There is no doubt, however, that Parsons' real preoccupation became that of establishing sociology at the theoretical level. He believed that the institutionalist path à la Veblen was dangerous, and he thought that American sociology of the time was generally weak because it was based mainly on a "positivist empiricism." He therefore wanted to do for sociology what had already been done for economics with neoclassical theory – an agenda that was very similar to Pareto's.[10] This would also, in his view, give sociology the advantage of not having to search for academic space at the expense of a stronger and more consolidated discipline such as economics, given that it was still academically weak, even in the United States. This new theoretical reorientation would thus allow sociology "to escape from . . . the irritating pretentiousness of the encyclopaedic view of its scope" (1935b, p. 666).

Parsons followed his goal of moving sociology towards general theory with great determination, and with remarkable results. His influence on American and international sociology grew increasingly strong after the Second World War with the publication of *The Social System* (1951) and other important works. However, an important – and unintended – effect of this was to move the interests of the sociological community away from economic sociology and towards other themes (Gouldner 1970; Granovetter 1990). Previously, in the work of the founding fathers, various important economic and institutional factors were combined to form interpretive models of modern capitalism and its development. Now, attention moved on to the construction of a general theory and towards themes that were more closely linked to the study of institutions in isolation from other factors, for example, those of socialization, social control, deviance and so on. Even when it was more empirically focused, sociology had moved into spheres that were far removed from those of economics, especially at the macro level, where the theme of development was mainly left to the new Keynesian macro-economics. At the micro level, there was a tendency towards disciplinary specialization, with the more autonomous development of fields of study that had been previously part of classical economic sociology. These included, in particular, organizational studies, industrial and labor sociology, and industrial relations.[11] While in the original tradition these aspects were more closely linked to the study of economic systems, in the new situation this link weakened considerably. For this reason, in the following chapters, reference to elements relevant to the organization of firms, or labor and industrial relations, will be made only to the extent that they are strictly related to the sociological investigation of economic phenomena at the macro and micro levels.

It is as well to specify that sociology's tendency to move away from economic themes – and Parson's work was enormously influential in this respect – was not changed by the ambitious attempt he made, together with Neil Smelser, to work out a theoretical model of the relations between economy and society. Even though *Economy and Society* (Parsons and Smelser 1956) seems to have a title linked to the classical tradition of economic sociology, this work is in fact very different. The objective is not to identify an analytical model to interpret a historical phenomenon, that is, the origins and transformations of modern capitalism. On the contrary, its aim is to illustrate, by applying the model to the economy, the general theory of social systems that Parsons had been developing in the mid-phase of his intellectual path, when he distanced himself from the "voluntarism" of previous years.

According to this theory, society is viewed as a system of interdependent parts (structures) that must carry out four fundamental functions to reproduce themselves. The economy represents the sphere of activity connected with the functions of *adaptation*, that is, with the problem of extracting from the environment sufficient resources in terms of goods and services for the reproduction of society. In carrying out these tasks the economy interacts with political structures (which have the function of *goal attainment*), with those that motivate individuals by transmitting and reinforcing values and norms, that is, family, religion, and school (*latency function*), and with those that oversee social stratification, the distribution of rewards and the prevention of conflicts (*integration function*).

Using this framework, Parsons and Smelser attempted to illustrate the complex exchanges that occur between the economy and other structures, highlighting, for example, the importance of the contribution of the latency system to form motivations to work, but also of the economy, by means of income, to the reproduction of motivating structures, and in particular the family. Other important exchanges are to be found in the economic sphere, which provides important resources for the stability of state structures, which in turn, sustain economic growth through specific policies, for example, through the regulation of credit. However, even though the effort to underline the interdependent relations between economy and society is of interest, it remains at a very high level of analytical abstraction and suffers from a complex conceptual framework and a weighty apparatus of classification, with many complications due to the attempt to reproduce the frame of the different functional imperatives within each sub-system (thus also within the economy). Therefore, instead of reviving economic sociology and contributing to a better integration between economic and sociological theory, *Economy and Society* remained an isolated work that neither excited the interest of economists, nor brought sociologists closer to tackling economic issues.

On the other hand, this tendency, although it was maintained by the dominant theoretical paradigm, ended up being accepted because it created new spaces for sociologists in the academic structure (Swedberg 1987; Granovetter 1990). It was easier for a young discipline to expand without coming into conflict with others, such as economics, which were already consolidated and recognized. Paradoxically, while economics – with Keynes and the other tendencies that have been mentioned – attempted to recover its proximity to empirical reality, sociology did not question neoclassical economics and it devoted less attention to the investigation of the economy, with the partial exception – which will be treated in the next chapter – of the development of underdeveloped countries. Therefore, the new definition of the boundaries between economics and sociology that took shape from the thirties to the post-war period reinforced the effects of the socioeconomic changes described above. The result was a decline in the tradition of economic sociology in the study of developed countries, which lasted until the early seventies.

Chapter 7

Modernization and Development of Backward Areas

After the Second World War, the focus of economic sociology on the role of culture and institutional factors in economic development found new applications in the study of backward countries and regions. The socioeconomic stabilization of the West and the redefinition of boundaries between economics and sociology certainly discouraged sociology from the study of more advanced countries, but there were other factors that helped give rise to a new sociology of development. One of the most important of these was the creation of many new states outside the West in the decolonization process, all of which faced the twin problems of creating economic growth and building effective institutions. In addition, the rapid creation of two opposed blocs at the international level, and the climate of the Cold War, made it imperative for the United States and other Western bloc countries to aid the economic development of the new states to prevent them falling under the influence of the Soviet Union. Finally, the new international organizations set up after the war, in which the new countries were also represented, pledged themselves to supporting their development.

Clearly then, there were good practical reasons why the social sciences should move towards the study of development. First came economics, which was strongly influenced at this point by the Keynesian revolution. The theory of "induced development," referred specifically to the problems of backward countries and underlined the importance of state intervention and international aid in triggering and sustaining the process of industrialization. The first work in the area of the sociology of development, therefore, primarily involved the efforts of some American scholars to integrate the views of economists into this approach. It came to emphasize the importance of cultural and institutional factors as elements conditioning the successful outcome of economic policies supporting development and it was in this way that the theory of modernization first began to take shape. Underlying this branch of studies is the idea that Western modernity provides a challenge to less-developed societies, which pushes them ineluctably towards social change. However, there are many different approaches within this broad framework.

The first of these, which was prevalent in the fifties and sixties, represents the *theory of modernization* in the strict sense of the term. Research within this perspective emphasized the importance of sociocultural factors and the endogenous policies of backward countries in conditioning social change. Especially at the beginning, scholars adopted an optimistic view in which the outcome of this change involved backward countries emulating the models provided by developed ones. However, as the gap between these expectations and the actual difficulties faced by the countries of the so-called Third World (Latin America, Africa, and Asia) grew increasingly wide, a more critical approach to modernization began to gain ground. This new approach was called the *theory of dependency*, and it was closely based on the experiences of Latin American countries. Here, the emphasis was placed mainly on the economic influence exercised over backward countries by developed ones. However, as the modernization processes began to take root in the different developing countries, this rather rigid and pessimistic framework was unable to account for the increasing divergences in how Third World countries were modernizing. At this point, another approach emerged. It focused on the Asian countries, which exhibited remarkable economic dynamism. It may be dubbed *comparative political economy*, since it concentrates on the role of political institutions in the process of modernization, also comparing Asian and Latin American countries.

The criticisms leveled against the theory of modernization used in the sixties – including both the dependency approach and, more indirectly, the historical sociology of the modernization of Western societies – have stimulated a reappraisal of their original assumptions. The result has been a new research trajectory emphasizing, unlike previous work, the variety and open-endedness of paths of modernization, which do not ineluctably lead to the outcomes seen in the Western model. As we shall see at the end of this chapter, this perspective is not limited to that of political economy, but also borrows from studies which emphasize the cultural dimension, linking the concept of modernization to that of civilization.

1   The Theory of Modernization

Post-war American sociology and political science were both strongly influenced by the systemic approach to the study of society developed by Talcott Parsons (1951). Although he did not treat the problem of developing countries in any great detail, his complex theoretical framework was the principal source of the different conceptual tools that were to be used later in the theory of modernization. However, the approaches adopted varied substantially.

Some focused mainly on the cultural and structural aspects of traditional societies as opposed to modern ones; others in the field of political science were more interested in the political aspects and problems of modernization; a third group, particularly influenced by social psychology, took as its subject the formation of personality; a final group singled out the different stages of development towards modernity, defined on the basis of the preceding historical experience of Western countries. However, underlying all these different approaches – which we will later examine in greater detail – is one core assumption. This was the belief that backward countries were all shaped by the model of the *traditional society*, a closely interwoven system of cultural and structural features. According to this view, the steadfast resistance of tradition – in terms of culture, structure, and personality – was the primary obstacle for countries to overcome on the path to economic development and in emulating the example provided by modern, developed Western societies. The different theories of modernization approached this kind of change in different ways, and although they always viewed it as desirable and, in the long run, inevitable, they also presented it as difficult and involving strong tensions.

1.1   Approaches influenced by structural-functionalism

It has already been pointed out that the first work on modernization was largely oriented by the structural–functionalist school, albeit only in broad terms. This influence is particularly obvious in some of the attempts to specify cultural and structural features of modern and traditional societies, starting with the "pattern variables" used by Talcott Parsons in his study *The Social System* (1951). Bert Hoselitz (1960) and Marion Levy (1966) were among the first scholars to move along this path. One of the main points of their work is how the economic development of backward countries is affected both by culture and social structure. In particular, they focus on certain cultural orientations that are typical of traditional societies and that are considered as obstacles to economic progress. The most significant of these is the prevalence of norms that make economic relations depend on ascription rather than performance. This means that economic roles – for example, access to certain jobs, or the distribution of goods and services which are produced – are assigned on the criterion of membership of a certain group (through age, gender, family, race, caste, etc.) rather than the ability to perform a certain task. In addition, dominant cultural trends may well not encourage any kind of specialization; this means that roles are not differentiated from a functional perspective and the growth of productivity in economic activities is limited.

Together with these factors, which recall Parsons' variables, Levy deals with the more specifically cognitive dimension of dominant cultural models, contrasting the traditional orientation to the rational one typical of modern societies. In the first case, social action, particularly economic action, is shaped following traditional routines, while in the second it is influenced by scientific and technical developments and is therefore more open to innovation. The predominance of the above-mentioned normative and cognitive orientations, which are typical of traditional societies, leads to a marked lack of structural differentiation in the principal spheres of activity and a limited division of labor both between units of production and within them. Several studies have tried to empirically measure the positions of various societies along the axis between modernity and tradition through the construction of indexes (of economic development, urbanization, literacy, political participation, etc.) (Lerner 1958; Deutsch 1961; Black 1966).

Economic development – emphasizes Hoselitz – requires a significant change in the cultural and social structures of a society. This is because development depends not only on the accumulation of economic capital but on the effective use of this capital; this in turn, as Adam Smith was one of the first to point out, entails a greater division of labor based on specific functional roles. Such specialization will

be stillborn if rational orientations towards economic activity and universal criteria for selecting individuals to carry out highly specialized tasks are not established. This means that the use of criteria based on principles of performance – and
therefore on achievement – rather than on traditional principles of ascription is
required. That is to say, traditional cultural values give rise to patterns of behavior
and social relations which are relatively stable and institutionalized (social structures), and their close interrelation hinders economic development. In order for
development to take off, both cultural and social structures need to be modernized, moving more closely towards the characteristics – also closely interrelated –
of rationality, universalism, performance, and functional specificity, all typical of
modern Western societies. But what is it that triggers modernization?

There are various answers to this question. In general, attention has focused on
the formation of new intellectual, political, and economic elites who introduced
innovation. However, Hoselitz places greater emphasis on the growth of entrepreneurship from below, using Simmel and Sombart's theory of social marginality. In
this, groups with a marginal position in society – for example, foreigners, immigrants or followers of non-mainstream religions – are viewed as being more likely
to innovate in the economic realm and as a result to trigger changes in the dominant social structure. Other scholars have instead focused on the role played by
newly educated elites who play a guiding role in politics. In general, this process is
seen as one of the inevitable consequences of the increased contacts between modern and traditional societies (Lerner 1958; Levy 1966). In this way, there is a diffusion of the aspiration to modernize backward societies and improve the levels of
social and economic well-being after the example of Western societies. It is the
educated elites of these societies who take the lead in this process, and who bring
about political mobilization to change the system.

A more systematic model of social change of modernization was developed by
some authors (Eisenstadt 1964; Smelser 1968), who used Parsons' concept of "structural differentiation" (Parsons and Smelser 1956). In this framework, attention
moves from actors (political and economic elites) to the structural problems that
condition action in the search for greater efficiency, that is, as the capacity of different institutional systems to adapt to and control their environment. In practice
this means that structures which traditionally handled a series of functions become more specialized in the transitional phase. For example, in traditional societies it is difficult to distinguish between economic activities and those carried out
by family or kin. However, once modernization begins, the family loses its economic functions and firms come into being that use waged labor which works for
the market rather than for subsistence and family consumption. This is because
the specialized economic structures, with their more highly structured division of
labor, give rise to more efficient production. But this leads in its own turn to the
detachment of social stratification from ascriptive criteria (i.e. ethnicity, race, or
caste) and its increasing dependence on achievement. The extended family becomes less typical and the nuclear family begins to predominate; this too gives rise
to a change in the traditional types of social control exercised over individual choices.
Economic development increases social mobility and tends over time to under-
mine traditional religious beliefs and to generate new requests for political participation.

However, these changes which weaken traditional cultural models and social structures, by the same token generate situations of tension, resistance and conflict. There is a noticeable difference in the pace and sequence of modernization to that which had happened in Western societies (Germani 1971). The more rapid this process is, the more likely it is that social and political conflicts develop. These usually involve those individuals who have lost their traditional forms of integration without properly being included in new ones, such as, for example, urbanized groups with no stable forms of employment.

Another source of conflict is to be found in the political system – the more difficult is access to the political system for the interests which have been mobilized, the greater is the likelihood of political radicalization and forms of conflict, sometimes verging on the violent. In this situation, theorists of modernization believed that it was inevitable that the state would take a greater part in the development process. However, this was not just because – as development economists maintained – there was a need to promote economic activities and industrialization when there were no entrepreneurial forces from below, but was also to control the conflicts induced by the process of modernization itself. The role that the state takes on in this kind of circumstance should also be more effective if the new political elites are capable of legitimizing themselves through nationalistic ideologies that substitute for the old religious beliefs as a value system shared by the population. Where this option fails as a result of the weakness of the new elite or the resistance of traditional groups to the economic (agrarian reforms) and political (democratization) changes required, the socialist model is a likely alternative.

The more specifically political aspects of the modernization process have attracted the attention of political scientists, who have also been influenced by the structural–functional school. The concept of "political development" has been investigated in this field as a process of differentiation of structures and secularization of the political culture, leading to an increase in the capacity – framed in terms of efficiency and effectiveness – of a political system (Almond and Powell 1966). In analytic terms, the problems of political development are conceptualized as a series of challenges – shaped by the experience of Western countries – which the system must face as it undergoes the process of modernization (Binder et al. 1971; Grew 1978). The number of these challenges can vary, but the following is a fairly representative selection. The first is state-building, that is, the need for political elites to create new structures to regulate social activities and to extract resources so that political institutions can function. The second is nation-building and this has a cultural connotation – the forming of a national identity must be achieved by overcoming local and particularistic orientations. Connected to this second point is that of the legitimization of the new political elites, who must guide the process of modernization. The challenge of participation has to do with the process of the mobilization of the population induced by economic and social development; it involves the responses given to the new demand for political participation through processes of democratization. The last problem is that of distribution; this refers to the capacity of the political system to respond to the demands for greater social equality.

The particular solution found for each successive challenge affects the potential to deal with the next one effectively. What is particularly striking, however, is that while in Western societies the process has extended over long periods of time and with a clear sense of progression from one to the other, the challenges specific to the Third World have tended to overlap with each other. In many cases the challenge of participation, and the crisis relating to it, has therefore had to be faced without a consolidated national identity or strongly legitimated political elite, and with weak state structures. The challenge of distribution, because of cultural opening and the comparisons made with more developed countries, has tended to lead to a growing demand for greater equality and income support, before the state is capable of extracting the necessary resources from the national economy. Consequently, for newly modernizing societies, there is a strong likelihood of political conflict and instability.

1.2   The formation of the modern personality

The theory of modernization was also greatly influenced by a set of socio-psychological studies. Generally speaking, these shared a common framework of ideal types based on the distinction between traditional, modern, and transitional societies. Their particular approach was to investigate the mechanisms by which a modern personality is formed, this being viewed as an essential ingredient triggering the process of change.

Daniel Lerner (1958) was one of the first scholars to adopt this perspective in his work on the Middle East, although he was also close to the sociological approach. Unlike many of the studies previously considered, his book is based on fieldwork, as is most of the psychological research on industrialization. Lerner shared the idea that contact with Western societies stimulated change and pushed the new elites to modernize. This was the same pattern that Western societies had followed, and it could be seen in all the continents, independently of any differences that traditional societies might originally have shown. Several factors were crucial to this process and were measurable through empirical indexes; one of these was urbanization, leading to higher levels of literacy; this gave rise to the spread of mass communication and, finally, a tendency to mobility. It became possible to identify what could be called a "mobile personality," characterized by rationality and empathy, capable of identifying with others and of keeping up with them. Finally, this trend gave rise to a greater economic participation (and thus to higher incomes also) and to the demand for greater political participation.

In Lerner's view, the formation of a modern personality was essentially a process of secondary socialization, in which the roles of education and means of communication as "multipliers of empathy" were viewed as crucial. Other studies, more closely connected to the psychological approach, place more importance on the process of primary socialization, taking place in the first years of life and involving the family to a greater extent. The work of David McClelland (1961) has been very influential in this regard. He tried to show how economic development in any particular society was conditioned by powerful personalities with a strong need for achievement. Influenced by Weber's research on the relationship between Protestantism and the spirit of capitalism, he emphasized the role that Protestantism has played in generating both a widespread motivation towards individual commitment and a commitment to do one's job well. The main beneficiary of this need for achievement – leading one to work for rewards which go beyond the financial – was entrepreneurship and, as a result, economic development. So, in his view, it is not enough to provide economic or even sociological explanations; instead one must look to psychological factors. McClelland sought to test the hypothesis that the need for achievement is connected to features of the process of primary socialization through elaborate research on many developed and backward countries. If parents teach their children to be self-sufficient and to have faith in their own abilities early on, and at the same time show that they have high expectations of them, their children seem to react by developing a high need for achievement.

Everett Hagen (1962) carried out similar research in many countries. Here, in contrast, the focus was on primary socialization in traditional contexts, which tended to discourage the formation of an "innovative personality," instead promoting an "authoritarian personality." This took the form of a mixture of strongly protective and tolerant attitudes when the child was small, followed by a very authoritarian phase, which centered on the role of the father. The child thus perceived the external world as arbitrary, with no possibility of a manageable order, and became habituated to structuring his social relations along the terms of an acritical acceptance of the social hierarchy and of authority in general. This is the complete opposite of what happens in modern contexts; here, the parents' attitude, similar to the situation described by McClelland, stimulates the child into a "creative anxiety": this emotion pushes him to control situations rationally, with extreme intensity. The kind of personality stimulated in this case is one that is open to innovation and entrepreneurship.

The research carried out a few years later by Alex Inkeles and David Smith (1974) was closer in outlook to Lerner's. These scholars had a sociological orientation and set out to challenge psychologists' claim that the fundamental features of the personality were formed in early childhood. Through their research in the Third World they tried to show that the "modern personality" (i.e. open to innovation, with rationalized behavior, viewing education and technical goods favorably, etc.) tended to be closely linked to the influence of education, employment in the industrial sector, exposure to the mass media, and urban life. The authors came to the optimistic conclusion that the ability of developing countries to strengthen these institutions – particularly those which influenced the cultural life of the population – could have significant consequences for the development of the personality, and that this, in turn, would make the passage to modern society much smoother.

1.3 The stages of development and convergence

Walt Rostow's book *The Stages of Economic Growth* (1960) was one of the earliest and most widely cited works on modernization. One of the reasons for its celebrity was its success in moving from its starting point in economic history to synthesize economic, social and political factors. Rostow laid out a more detailed and complex description of the stages of development than was usual in the literature of that time, which was generally limited to a threefold distinction between traditional, transitional, and modern societies. In Rostow's work, five stages were described: traditional society, preconditions for take-off, the take-off, the drive to maturity, and the phase of high mass consumption.

Rostow treated the stage of preparation for industrial take-off in a particularly interesting way. He emphasized how it was necessary for more developed societies to "intrude" into more backward ones if take-off was to succeed: this could take the form of real intrusion, for example through military occupation, or it could be indirect, through increased cultural and economic contacts. This exogenous influence – which we have already seen highlighted in other studies – involved a certain kind of shock for the traditional society. "Reactive nationalism," triggered by the intrusion of a modern society, was in his view the strongest factor influencing the change of traditional societies. The new political elites played an essential role in putting the preconditions for take-off in place through state intervention, which involved a series of measures involving the transformation of agriculture, the creation of a national market, the creation of a fiscal system, and investment in infrastructures and services (particularly education). All of this made it possible to handle the problems inherent to state- and nation-building.

Modernization in the countries of the Third World had advantages and disadvantages when compared to the historical experience of modernization in Europe. Among the former is the greater resources offered by the availability of new technologies; in addition, the new states can rely on loans provided by international organizations for their investment projects, which are given on more favorable conditions now than in the past, when only banks provided them. Among the disadvantages, however, is the fact that the death rate has been lowered as a result of advances made in the field of health. This is particularly important because it means that developing countries are encumbered by an increasing population. As a result, take-off is more difficult because it now requires a greater increase in income than in the early comers. In addition, there is usually a high level of urban unemployment. This is often a source of tension and political conflict because unemployment is more frustrating insofar as the aspirations for consumption are higher now than in the past. In a context of this kind the struggle to reform traditional social structures becomes more difficult which may push the intellectual elites towards solutions of a communist type.

Inherent in Rostow's developmental model was the idea that the route to industrialization necessarily had to pass through a fixed number of economic stages. These can, however, be mediated through different institutional structures, especially in the breakup of traditional societies. There may thus be different paths to industrialization, as exemplified in the alternative between nationalism and communism. In the long term, once industrialization has been consolidated, one could assume a tendency towards the institutional convergence of industrial societies and thus a narrowing of differences between the communist and democratic capitalist models.

The notion of convergence was presented and developed in Clark Kerr et al.'s study, *Industrialism and the Industrial Man* (1960). Kerr believed that there was a "logic of industrialism" which was fundamentally conditioned by technological constraints. In his view, there was a single technology that could assure the most efficient economic outcomes, and this pushed societies into acquiring it, and organizing their institutions in such a way as to be able to exploit it as best as possible. This would trigger a strong push towards institutional convergence, as was already visible on the one hand in the reduction of the market in areas where it had previously played a greater role and on the other in the shrinking of the state functions in those contexts – such as in communist and nationalist states – where it had exercised greater control. Industrialization was viewed as leading to economic and social "pluralism" in which the middle classes increased, conflict decreased and a plurality of economic and social interests developed, influencing the political process and weakening the grand ideologies with their rigid and totalizing effects.

2   Criticisms: the Theory of Dependence and Historical Sociology

The theory of modernization has been criticized on many points since the end of the sixties. These will now be discussed, drawing an analytical distinction between certain principle assumptions on which they are built. However, one should take into account that this is not an easy task because there is no such thing as a single theory of modernization; there is rather a series of different approaches that are not always consistent. There are four points that seem common to them all and are worth discussing: (a) the optimistic conception of development, viewed as inevitable and linear, usually moving through the stages which Western societies have already passed through, up to an institutional convergence with them; (b) the ideal-typical conceptualization of traditional and modern societies as being opposed to each other, each constituted by a closely connected set of elements; (c) the idea that relations between regions and countries and their external environment are always positive for development; (d) the assumption that the stimulus for change is essentially exogenous.

2.1   *The inevitability of development and ethnocentrism*

Optimism about the development prospects of backward countries was widespread and reflected the climate of the decade following the Second World War, which seemed to open up great possibilities for economic growth. New economic concepts – which attributed greater importance to state intervention and international cooperation than to the market – contributed to this optimistic view. In this context, the sociologists, social psychologists and economic historians, who had advanced the theory of modernization, were particularly concerned to emphasize the institutional variables (cultural, social, and political institutions) which might hinder economic development. However, they followed this line of enquiry more in theoretical terms than in empirical ones. The only exceptions were the psychological studies, but these focused on the formation of the personality. No comparative research was carried out on the real processes of development in backward countries. Sociologists influenced by structural–functionalism – but Rostow too when he traced his stages of development – attempted to define the structural characteristics of traditional and modern society and the mechanisms of social change in theoretical terms. In the absence of an adequate body of empirical research, they inevitably ended up making recourse to the historical experiences of Western societies, both to define traditional society by contrast and to uncover the mechanisms of change.

In the light of this empirical weakness, which went together with an inappropriate tendency towards generalizations on the basis of the Western experience, the first wave of criticism is easily anticipated. It focused above all on the optimistic idea that development was inevitable. This was strongly criticized in the light of the real historical experiences of the Third World countries, where initial enthusiasm for political independence soon gave way to economic problems and serious social and political tensions. Therefore development could by no means be viewed as guaranteed and there could be "failures" and "blockages" in modernization (Eisenstadt 1973). However, criticisms were more directly concerned with the presuppositions underlying the theory of modernization, which was seen as founded on an "ethnocentric" vision of society, which held not only that the Western experience was not only inevitable but that it was a positive model for backward countries to emulate so as to better the state of their societies (Bendix 1967; Goldthorpe 1971; Tipps 1973).

2.2   Tradition and modernity as contrasting models

Initial studies on modernization also shared the presupposition that traditional and modern societies were contrasting models based on different sets of interdependent elements. Here too, shallow historical–empirical foundations led scholars to underemphasize the actual diversity of traditional societies. Indeed, the concept of "traditional society" itself was reconstructed on the basis of a deductive logic which defined it in contrast to modern Western societies, and in particular to certain such societies (Anglo-American countries). Critics attacked all the assumptions underlying this view (Bendix 1967; Gusfield 1967; Tipps 1973).

First of all, they emphasized the striking variety of traditional societies from a historical–empirical perspective, and showed how traditional and modern elements could be found to a varying degree not only in non-industrialized countries, but in the developed world too. On the one hand, family and wider kin ties or religious beliefs persist and are important in modern societies. On the other, values oriented towards achievement and entrepreneurship, and bureaucratic structures functioning according to universal criteria, can also be found in traditional societies. Nor is it necessarily the case that traditional values and a reduced structural differentiation in the economic activities of the extended family obstruct the development of modern economies – in fact they can even support them. By the same token, one should not expect to find differentiation in all spheres of a modern context.

As a result, the argument that the constitutive elements of the two models were strictly linked – so that when an element in a traditional society modernized, the others would, as with the sequences experienced by Western societies, automatically follow – was also brought into question. In other words, there could be a "selective modernization" regarding the means of communication, demand for consumption, or military structures, but that this would not necessarily involve the productive sphere or the functioning of political institutions, etc. Processes of modernization of this latter type were common in real societies and they did not necessarily lead to the kind of modernity posited in the model.

2.3 Economic constraints and the dependency approach

A third critique concerned the argument that relations with the external environment were fundamentally positive for the countries which had to modernize, that is, that they functioned as a stimulus to the forces of change, which were seen as fundamentally exogenous. For Lerner and Levy, contact with modern societies acted as a potent solvent on traditional society, in the sense that it stimulated the modernization of cultural orientations and social structures and triggered irreversible mechanisms of change. Rostow, for his part insisted on the advantages that derived from the spread of technology and from international aid for the economy. However, this perspective did not take into account the fact that progressive integration into the international market also gave rise to constraints on economic development. It was now more difficult than before to start the process of industrialization because it was necessary to have higher levels of investment and therefore a more constant accumulation of capital to compete with the industry of more developed countries. In addition, backward countries were generally specialized in the production of raw materials and agricultural goods with unskilled, low-cost labor and were therefore able to export products cheaply. However, these were then exchanged with high-cost industrial products from developed countries so that the capital resources necessary for development were not accumulated, even while competition from the already established industries of other countries created difficulties for the less competitive craft activities of the developing ones.

Entry into the international economy therefore not only produced opportunities, but real problems. These problems were identified in much of the economic literature but they were particularly emphasized in the dependency approach, which re-elaborated the Marxist theory of imperialism. This approach was first stimulated by the failure of efforts to develop in various Latin American countries (Cardoso and Faletto 1967; Frank 1967, 1969), but was widened to encompass a more general vision of the periphery in Immanuel Wallerstein's "world system" theory (1974, 1979). This latter approach holds that an increase of contact with industrialized countries leads to a situation of underdevelopment, instead of favoring economic growth, as the "diffusionist" tendency of modernization studies would suggest. Thus, it would be more correct to talk about "underdevelopment" rather than backwardness, precisely to underline how the difficulties of the peripheries result from their exploitation by the core regions, and are therefore triggered by the integration in the international market rather than by isolation.

Three factors were viewed as determinative for the loss of resources affecting the peripheries. The first was their dependent position in international trade, which led to an "unequal exchange": the prices of the raw materials and agricultural products that were exported were lower than those of the industrialized products imported from the central regions. The second mechanism involved the direct penetration of foreign capital in the sector of raw materials or in agriculture, as well as in the industrial sector, exploiting the advantage of lower labor costs for the production of standardized goods. This led again to a draining of profits to the advantage of the core areas. Finally, the worsening of economic conditions led to increasing dependency on international loans, which thereby brought even more pressure to bear on the resources available for development.

In this framework, which was mainly inspired by the study of Latin America, emphasis was placed on the lack of initiative by the local bourgeoisie, which became "subaltern" to the interests of the core countries, both in the export of raw materials and in industry. Only a sufficient level of state intervention could create favorable conditions "from above," redefining the integration into the international division of labor. Unlike the Keynesian approach to development economics, however, the dependency approach assumed that this would require that a country leave the capitalist framework and move towards a regime based on socialist planning (although in Wallerstein's view this should be an international socialism capable of governing the world system). According to these authors, the Latin American experience showed that not only were the entrepreneurial, commercial and land-owning classes incapable of supporting projects for autonomous development, but they were ready to support authoritarian solutions with the help of the military and core countries (O'Donnel 1979).

This perspective certainly helped to highlight the constraints which the theorists of modernization had overlooked. However, the risks of an approach which simply turned the previous model on its head, making underdevelopment entirely a product of external constraints were just as clear. This way of analysis ignored the influence exerted by the internal institutional context of the periphery countries on the process of modernization. Moreover, it was impossible to evaluate adequately the specific differences that emerged in the paths of the Third World countries, which became ever clearer in successive decades. It is also interesting to note that some dependency theorists – in particular Cardoso and Faletto – perceived these risks, insisting on the necessity of an "integrated analysis" of development linking external constraints and internal institutional factors, and giving more space and autonomy to political actors and their actions.

2.4   Historical sociology of modernization

While the dependency approach's criticisms of modernization studies focused on external economic conditions, another body of work questioned the evolutionary model of change based on structural differentiation. As we have seen, this model was not present to the same extent in all the approaches to the study of modernization, but only in some of them, particularly those influenced by structural–functionalism. The key mechanism – which holds for all societies – is singled out in the process of structural differentiation, the push towards more highly differentiated roles and social structures which results from growing dissatisfaction with the functioning of a particular structure. This leads to a search for greater efficiency, which takes the form of a higher level of functional specialization in the new structures which replace the old ones. Change was therefore seen as a process of adaptation by a society – considered as a system of interdependent elements – to the problems posed by the physical and social environment. It was possible to identify more- or less-evolved structural types on the basis of their level of structural differentiation and thus their capacity to adapt to and control any problems. Modern Western societies were located at the very peak of these stages (Parsons 1966, 1971).

These assumptions were criticized on three fronts. The first set of criticisms, as already mentioned, did not reject the functionalist approach, although it did point out that differentiation did not necessarily lead to the expected growth in efficiency because it could be accompanied by problems of integration giving rise to instability and even to blockages in the modernization process. A second group of criticisms rejected functionalism but can be linked to an evolutionary perspective. These criticisms emphasized the objective difficulty of identifying stages of development based on a greater or lesser ability to adapt (Granovetter 1979). To do this it would be necessary to know what future environmental problems a society was likely to face. Measuring the ability to adapt through the level of structural differentiation is not appropriate since it is by no means certain that the problems that have been resolved successfully by developed societies will be also faced by the backward ones. Past experience is not necessarily a guide because one cannot assume that the societies that have adapted best and have differentiated to a great extent will be able to deal successfully with any new problems and constraints which might subsequently emerge.

All this led to the conclusion that it would be very difficult to establish stages of development on the basis of the structural characteristics of each society. Incidentally, this is also the route taken by modern biology, which does not specify which characteristics allow a particular species to survive better than others but investigates the environmental conditions which favor the adaptation of a particular species to specific structural characteristics. There is thus no one unique path but the possibility of evolution in many directions.

The third group of criticisms discussed whether it was possible to establish evolutionary sequences on the basis of historical experience, given that this assumed that society was a basically closed and consistent system, like an organism whose future state could be predicted on the basis of its structural characteristics at any one moment (Bendix 1967; Nisbet 1969; Goldthorpe 1971). In the opinion of these scholars, change was in fact not only an endogenous process of adaptation, but was conditioned by relations between society and the external environment; in other words, the external environment was presented as continuously changing as history unfolded, which thus involved different opportunities and constraints for individual societies than in the past. The stimuli emanating from the external environment were not viewed as only positive, as the theorists of modernization held, nor were they only negative, as the dependency approach believed. The former did not see that the external environment could have internal ramifications in the course of modernization, that did not necessarily recapitulate the past experience of Western societies, while the latter were particularly interested in the economic constraints which came about from the international division of labor, but tended to overlook the endogenous institutional factors.

Change in real societies is a complex process which involves external economic, political, and cultural forces as well as single contingent events, as is clear from the example of war; but also the internal characteristics of a given society. These not only involve the economy's impetus to greater efficiency, but also the role of the intellectual elite, processes of political mobilization, and state intervention. Within this context it is important to pay greater attention to the subjects who introduce change – to their identity and interests, and their conflicts. In the structural–functional approach this dimension tends to disappear in favor of abstract and impersonal processes, leading to static comparisons of societies rather than to explanations of concrete changes. This critical perspective therefore turns to comparative historical analysis so as to focus on the specific processes of change that cannot be traced through general models.

As it happens, many of these criticisms of modernization were first made by authors in a different field: the comparative study of the historical modernization of Western societies, above all in Europe (Gerschenkron 1962, 1968; Bendix 1964; 1978; Moore 1966). At the center of this perspective is the desire to understand better the different patterns in which industrialization (in the economic field) and democratization (in the political field) have commingled in the experience of Western state and society. Close attention has been paid exactly to the diversity of political paths to industrialization. Why have industrial growth and political democracy proceeded together in some cases, particularly the English and American ones, while in others, such as Germany and Italy, economic development occurred through political regimes of a fascist type or, in others, as in the Russian case, through communism?

The attempt to answer these questions leads these authors beyond the grand theories on modern society set out in the classics. It is Max Weber who has most influenced this perspective, which takes the form of a comparative–historical approach which is applied to the internal workings of societies to understand the similarities, but also the differences, in the paths of development. The result is a greater sensitivity towards the complex and open-ended process of modernization, leading scholars – more or less directly – to question how this was conceptualized in the study of Third World societies. The conclusions can be summed up as follows:

1   There is no one straightforward, linear and ineluctable path to modernization. The point of departure, the path, and the outcomes may be different. This does not deny the possibilities of a sociological approach in favor of a merely historicist approach. It is instead possible, through comparative analysis, to construct ideal types, that permit the formulation of links between theory and research and causal hypotheses to be formulated.

2   The path to modernization is influenced by various exogenous factors and by contingent events such as wars. These factors are not only economic but also political and cultural. In particular, the early comers influence the experiences of late comers, creating favorable conditions for modernization, for example, through "intellectual mobilization" Bendix (1978), but also imposing also constraints linked to economic, political, and military power.

3   The process of modernization is decisively influenced by the kinds of response to external challenges that are possible given endogenous factors. These cannot be understood by reference to a generic conception of traditional societies. Preindustrial

society was characterized by different combinations of the traditional and modern. The influence of these components should be evaluated by identifying concrete social groups, their alliances and their conflicts – namely, by giving attention to the historical subjects of modernization.

3   New Comparative Political Economy

Once the first wave of studies focusing on the countries of the Third World had been exhausted, and after the publication of important works of comparative historical sociology on developed societies in the sixties, the concept of modernization was less often used directly in social theory and research. However, one may show how the problems of change in backward countries were dealt with through an approach influenced by both the criticisms of the first studies, and the results of comparative historical sociology. In other words, a new way of researching the problems of modernization emerged. This did not use the concept explicitly but did interpret the process of change in a more open and differentiated way, one which was more oriented towards a historical–comparative analysis.

In the seventies, and even more so in the eighties, the experiences of Third World countries began to differ more than in the past. Many of these countries experienced continued difficulties; indeed in Africa, matters got worse. In other contexts, however – in Latin America, for example, and above all in East Asia – genuine processes of economic development took place (Gereffi and Wyman 1990). This spurred research in two directions.

First, it led to an increasing awareness of the limits of the initial theory of modernization and of dependency theory. Scholars employing both these generalizing approaches tended to present all the backward countries in a similar way, although the first group formulated optimistic hypotheses about the possibilities of development while the second shared a very pessimistic outlook. Neither of the two thus seemed capable of accounting for the increasing level of differentiation in the process of change. Second, there was increasing acceptance that it was necessary to do more comparative work on a limited number of cases properly to understand the phenomena of dynamism, stagnation or regression. Many scholars therefore compared the countries of the Asian East, while others concentrated on Latin America, and others compared countries from different regions. This approach came to be known as "new comparative political economy" (Evans and Stephens 1988; Evans 1995).

3.1   State and economic development

If modernization studies focused on the cultural dimension, and dependency theory on the economic dimension; political economy concentrated on the role of the state. Naturally this does not mean that the two other approaches failed to recognize the importance of this factor. However, for theorists of modernization and political development and for Rostow, the role of the state was mainly confined to creating the preconditions for the efficient functioning of the market. On the other hand, dependency theory felt it necessary for the state to play a more important role in opposing the processes of exploitation to which periphery societies were subjected, but felt it difficult to achieve this, given the intrinsic weakness of the state institutions *vis-à-vis* internal and international economic interests.

A second characteristic of the perspective of political economy was its approach to relations with the external environment. These were not simply regarded as positive cultural or economic stimuli for development, as in the theory of modernization, nor were they considered only as constraints and instruments of resource expropriation, as in the theory of dependency. External factors – amongst which particular attention was paid to the geopolitical dimension – were considered to be both opportunities and constraints. The capacity to transform constraints into resources was contingent on the role played by the state and on its ability to control and "negotiate" international ties. This was what explained the successful industrial strategies of Asian countries (Deyo 1987) as opposed to Latin America, and also the differences between them (Gereffi and Wyman 1990).

The role of the state in underpinning the success of an industrialization strategy, and in improving market performance, was already highlighted by Gerschenkron in the context of the first phase of industrial growth in Western societies at the end of the nineteenth century. However, emphasis was placed on the need to avoid any implicit functionalism, which would assume the idea that the state would inevitably play an effective role in promoting development (Rueschemeyer and Evans 1985). The behavior of the state has to be seen as variable and historically contingent. In this regard, one may point to the serious problems of the African continent (Bates 1981).

Which factors influenced the effectiveness of state intervention? Two of them seem particularly important. The first was to ensure that effective bureaucratic structures were in place. In other words, to have a good state apparatus, since this was indispensable to negotiate with external interests, to pursue a strategy of industrialization and development, and to keep special interests within bounds. A political leadership which was oriented towards development, and was largely autonomous from economic and social interests, was also crucial. The institutional isolation of the state elite from private interests was especially important. Interest groups tended to be either co-opted into the process of decision-making in a dependent position, as was often the case with business and industrial interests, or to be excluded, as was usually the case with the working class and unions.

On the whole, comparative political economy is a new synthesis, involving a set of elements that distinguish it from previous approaches. It assumes that external conditions – both economic and political – are important, but their consequences vary from one context to another (for example, US influence has assisted development in several Asian countries, for geopolitical reasons related to the confrontation with the USSR, while it has had less benign consequences in Latin America). Moreover, the consequences of exogenous factors are not predetermined but are mediated by the strategic capacity of the state. This is in turn dependent on the formation of coalitions of economic and social interests which create conditions that may be more or less favorable for the autonomy of the political elite; on cultural traditions which may underpin the legitimacy of the leadership; and on institutional traditions influencing the efficiency of the state bureaucracy.

Thus, cultural and institutional factors condition the political process, but it is not possible to predict either outcomes or consequences in advance. The kind of interaction established between social and political actors, on the basis of internal and international conditions, influences the process of development. Therefore, comparative political economy confirms the idea – already developed by historical sociology – of the variety between paths to modernization. In addition, this approach suggests that economic success is usually associated with efficient – but also authoritarian – state structures. These "strong" states operate according to a *dirigiste* logic in the context of an open market economy and pursue interventionist policies. It still remains to be seen if and to what extent this argument will be confirmed in other countries. Moreover, it is not possible at the moment to evaluate if, in the cases of successful industrialization there will be a strengthening of political democracy and the welfare state, or if the authoritarian model will persist together with economic *dirigisme* and a reduced welfare state.

These sorts of question raises issues that were already present in the first theory of modernization. While this perspective allowed for a certain degree of variability in paths of development, there was a strong expectation of a progressive institutional convergence induced by the process of industrialization. Political economy, with its historical–empirical approach, does not directly address this issue, although it does point to variation in the different ongoing processes of development. However, it should be pointed out that several of the recent attempts to treat the question in theoretical terms use Weber's approach as well as his comparative analysis of different cultures.

3.2 Civilization and paths of development

The first of these attempts which is worth mentioning took its impetus from research on "Asian capitalism," i.e. on the newly industrialized countries of this area, and also on Japan (Hamilton 1994). Several typical characteristics of the industrialization process of these countries were identified: not only the role of the state in the economy but also the ways production and labor relations were organized (Dore 1987; Hamilton and Biggart 1988). Production is organized in a distinctive fashion in that it takes the form of networks of firms. In Western capitalism the firm has a strong identity, and a clearly bounded organizational structure which is reinforced by formal law. The Asian experience instead reveals the presence of weak firms in strong networks, with relations formed not only by legal and financial links, but also by personal, family, and community ties (Granovetter 1995). In labor relations, the Western model of impersonal contractual relations gives way to a community-based form of enterprise, with company unions (where these exist).

In his observations on these industrialization experiences and on recent developments in China, Gary Hamilton has pointed that this results from specific features of economic, as well as political, institutions. In his opinion, these specificities give rise to two analytic problems. First, they cannot be adequately explained by the political economy, but also involve the concept of civilization. Second, a closer link between the modernization process and type of civilization in which it occurs suggests that the hypothesis of an institutional convergence dominated by a Western model is mistaken.

With regard to the first point, economic and political institutions, and the relations between them, cannot only be understood by reference to the autonomy and strategic capacity of the state. There are other more general factors, which bring into play models of the legitimization of power, both political and economic. More particularly, there are various cultural features prevalent over a wide area, reflecting visions of the world that find their roots in the influence of the great religions, that is to say, one must refer to the concept of civilization. In particular, the role of Confucianism has been very important. The sphere of influence of an important religion tends to delimit the space of a civilization, understood as a group of societies which share several cultural and institutional features (for example, Chinese civilization is different from the Indian and the Islamic, and also the Western one, which has been shaped by Christianity). It is therefore necessary to turn back to Weber's comparative analysis, focusing on the visions of the world which root the great civilizations. Images of the world – the ultimate values – orient action but do not predetermine outcomes. They establish the "trajectories of development"; they provide frameworks of reference according to which different material and ideal interests can be defined and conflicts take shape in the course of history. In this perspective one could observe – as Weber did – that Confucianism was a civilization that obstructed the development of capitalism but at the same time could offer important cultural resources for its operation once capitalism was established.

Hamilton underlines, in this respect, the obstacles that hinder the full autonomy of the individual, in both the economic and political sphere, and the strong cultural insistence on obligations towards family, kin, and community. Relations with authorities are determined in reference to a harmonious vision of the world in which the position of the individual is defined by the contribution that is expected of him in maintaining this integrated order. It is through this perspective that one may better understand both the forms of political legitimization and the organization of production based on networks and cooperative labor relations. All these "traditional" elements, and the lesser degree of social differentiation associated with them, should, according to the original vision of the theorists of modernization, have obstructed development. Paradoxically, instead, they have become an essential resource for economic dynamism, attracting attention and stimulating attempts to imitate them in the Western world.

But the Asian experience also pushes us to deal with the problem of relations between different civilizations. It leads us to reject the idea that the spread of capitalism outside the West and the ongoing process of economic globalization will lead to a single world civilization. Globalization is not accompanied by a greater institutional uniformity but rather by a differentiation in the processes of modernization. In fact, the framework of different civilizations offer different institutional resources to adjust to the challenge of world economy (see chapter 10).

Shmuel Eisenstadt (1983), one of the first theorists of modernization, also comes to these conclusions in his work, although via a different route. After criticisms of the initial model of modernization, and of the structural–functional approach, Eisenstadt was persuaded that the concept of modernization could be maintained but that it had to be used together with Weber's intuitions and analyses on the internal dynamics of different civilizations. In this perspective he began a research programme which reconstructed the origins of the great variety of symbolic and institutional responses with which societies have reacted to Western modernity. For Eisenstadt too, the future of modernization studies is linked to the comparative investigation of civilizations. At the center of his approach is the idea of intellectual and political elites as institutional entrepreneurs, who struggle to redefine the organization of a particular society on the basis of the cultural frameworks offered by different civilizations. These offer different ways of interpreting social order on the basis of those visions of the world setting out the relationship between human reality and transcendent reality which have been formed by the great religions. As a result, different spaces for "heterodoxies" have been opened: areas where culture is interpreted, redefined, and exploited by elites to form coalitions, nurture processes of mobilization and thus remodel the various institutional spheres and social change in the face of external challenges and internal problems.

Eisenstadt's research, following Weber, focused mainly on the past – on the search for the original frames of reference of the different civilizations. The issue of how to link contemporary modernization processes with the specific features of different civilizations more directly therefore remains open. It is too early to say whether this perspective will be taken up in any significant way in the future, as the work by Hamilton and Eisenstadt would suggest. However, despite the success of comparative political economy – and perhaps precisely as a result of this – the need to link the variety of modernization paths to cultural variables has emerged.

Ronald Dore (1990) has shown how this is particularly important today, but also that this is not simply a job of singling out the similarities between religious ideas and economic behavior. What is needed is a specific historical–empirical approach, which resists the positivist temptations of strong generalizations, in order to focus on aspects such as, for example, the acceptance of authority, impersonal trust, commitment to labor, interest in technology. One should carefully evaluate the extent to which all these factors are shaped by cultural orientations. This would make it easier to understand the success of the Asian countries, going beyond the important results achieved by comparative political economy. The experiences of these countries have called attention to the importance of a climate that is favorable to change, as Gerschenkron (1962) had already pointed out with regard to late industrialization in Europe. This is a climate nourished by a strong desire to overcome backwardness, to catch up with other societies and civilizations, and therefore by a "desire for development" which leads to supporting the elites' efforts. All this encourages a reassessment of civilization. Moreover, other important stimuli in this direction come from the new need to interpret the tortuous changes which the Eastern bloc countries and Russia are currently going through after the fall of the communist regimes (Stark 1992, 1996; Offe 1997). In conclusion, there is a new upsurge of interest in the cultural dimension – which once formed the crux of these studies, and later became less marked because of the criticisms it raised. Now this dimension has attracted a new attention and is considered as necessary, although not sufficient, for a more mature vision, one that is more open and many-sided, of modernization and its outcomes.

Chapter 8

The Keynesian Welfare State and Comparative Political Economy

During the seventies the analytical perspective used by economic sociology began to be widely adopted again in studies of developed countries. The reasons for the post-war fragmentation of the research tradition inherited from the classics and the trend to disciplinary specialization have been described in chapter 6. During the seventies this situation began to change. The tools used in the Keynesian approach seemed to be less effective to adequately explain the new difficulties facing the economies of the more highly industrialized economies. These were simultaneously affected by high levels of unemployment and inflation. Both phenomena had declined during the post-war period but now returned with even greater virulence, stimulating interest in institutional approaches to new problems.

Sociologists, industrial relations scholars and political scientists became more interested in the problems of economic development. They analyzed the crisis of the "Keynesian welfare state," and focused on the striking differences in the adjustments of various countries to the new challenges. Comparison between national cases was particularly useful to discuss how institutional factors influenced the emerging social and economic tensions, and the different responses. Among these factors, special importance was paid to the political dimension and the role played by the state. This led to a reappraisal of economic sociology as "comparative political economy" – an approach similar to that used for backward countries (see chapter 7).

Initially, the most important research problem involved the origins of inflation. The analytical perspective was mainly macro-economic. Subsequently, however, especially during the eighties, research began to focus on the problem of competition among firms and on the dynamism inherent to the different capitalist systems. As a result, macro-oriented analyses began to combine with approaches more oriented to micro levels (firms, regions). What emerged was a sort of cross-fertilization of comparative political economy with a new economic sociology. While the former concentrated on the crisis of the Keynesian welfare state, the latter analyzed the transformations taking place in the other main pillar of post-war development, that of Fordism and the emergence of flexible productive models.

Comparative political economy will be discussed in this chapter, while in the next the focus will be on the new economic sociology. In the final chapter I will discuss recent attempts to combine the two perspectives, especially in the study of different forms of capitalism.

1 The Rise and Decline of the Keynesian Welfare State

It has already been pointed out that the post-war period was characterized by growing economic and social intervention by the state (see section 3, chapter 6). In his brilliant study, Shonfield (1965) rightly underlined that this was not simply the result of the widespread implementation of Keynesian policies to sustain demand. Actually, the British economist had conceived the new policies as ways of helping the economy recover from economic depression. They were therefore seen as short-term remedies to put to full use productive resources that were given. During the post-war period, however, two main changes occurred. The first has to do with the spread of what has been described as "Keynesian growth" (Skidelsky 1996). This was the attempt to use state intervention, and particularly public spending, as an instrument to sustain economic development, and not only to deal with economic recessions. The second was the use of public spending to promote and consolidate political consensus through the widespread implementation of welfare programs, independently of the economic cycle and the state of employment. These are the two basic components of what is known as the "Keynesian welfare state." Their combination led to a kind of state intervention that moved away from Keynes's original frame, and spread to a greater or lesser extent across Western developed countries.

The idea underlying the adaptation of Keynes's theory to the problems of economic growth was that demand policy should not be used only to avoid recessions but also to support the development of productive resources over time. In other words, it was felt that economic development was dependent on the growth of investments, which in turn generated an increase in production and productivity. As a result, demand policy could also be directed towards supporting investments even if there was full employment. This was in turn related, as Shonfield pointed out, to the idea of state planning, for example, through the selection of credit aimed at increasing investments in certain sectors, and also through the direct intervention of public firms. This general tendency took different specific forms and was adopted more widely in countries using planning policies, like France and Japan, or where state enterprises had an important role, such as in Italy.

This differed significantly from more traditional demand policies. For example, a "weak" Keynesian model has been contrasted to a "strong" one (Bordogna and Provasi 1984). In the first case, public intervention through fiscal, monetary and deficit spending policies remains close to Keynesian ideas, attempting to stabilize the economic cycle by sustaining demand in periods of recession and slowing it down when productive factors are being fully used. These measures are also known as *stop and go* policies, with alternation between expansive and deflationary interventions. In addition, social spending tends to be lower. A typical example of this model is considered to be the United States up to the seventies. On the contrary, in the "strong" Keynesian model, there was a greater commitment to full employment and economic growth, as well as higher increases in social spending. Sweden and the other Scandinavian countries are good examples. The two ideal types – between which many European countries can be located up to the seventies – are generally different with regard to several characteristics tied to the system of representation of interests and to the political composition of governments. In general, strong forms of the Keynesian model were associated with stronger and more centralized unions, more highly institutionalized industrial relations, and governments with stable left-wing components committed to the spread of the welfare state as well as to full employment.

In addition to these differences between these strong and weak forms of Keynesian models, many countries also experimented with planning policies in the decades immediately after the Second World War. In this case economic sectors – and in particular industrial ones – were regulated and oriented without any consistent increase in social spending, in contrast with the strong Keynesian model. France and Japan are examples of state planning where the political context of intervention left a large amount of autonomy to the technocratic elites (Salvati 1982; Zysman 1983).

1.1   The expansion of welfare policies

Although there are differences within the Keynesian model, its uniting feature is a commitment to welfare policies. The first interventions in the field of social protection took place around the end of the nineteenth century, while further developments occurred in the period between the two world wars. After the Second World War there was both an extension of the risks covered and an increase in public expenditure. In the early seventies health and old-age insurance covered more than 90 percent of the working population of Western Europe, injury insurance covered an average of four-fifths, and unemployment insurance covered two-thirds (Alber 1982). In 1950 average social spending in Western Europe did not exceed 5 percent of GDP, while it had reached 13 percent in 1974 (Alber 1982, p. 63).

A vast literature tries to explain the tendency of social protection programs to expand. Some general analyses, first appearing in the sixties, highlighted how demands from lower classes led to the gradual recognition of civil, political, and finally social rights (Marshall 1964; Bendix 1964, 1978). Viewed in this light, protection against the risks of illness, injury, old age, and unemployment, and the demand for equal access to educational institutions was increasingly claimed as a basic aspect of "citizenship rights." Bendix, disagreeing with Marx, insisted particularly on the importance of political and social recognition, rather than economic demands, to understand the new demands of the lower classes. Through comparative analysis he showed the importance of the openness of the political system in influencing the outcomes of new demands. Where the political system is more open and favorable to channeling new demands, as was typical of the British case, these can develop gradually, without disruptive crises of democratic institutions. The opposite happens where the institutional tradition and the dominant classes obstruct the recognition of new rights for working classes mobilized by industrialization.

Another very general explanation was offered by the neo-Marxist theory of the state (O'Connor 1973; Habermas 1973; Offe 1972). In this case the emphasis was placed on capitalism's functional needs for reproduction, which push the state to extend its economic and social role. The expansion of social protection programs was explained in terms of the needs of both economic accumulation and maintenance of social consensus. O'Connor, in particular, underlined how, for capitalism to be reproduced, the state had to take on a growing commitment in terms of "social capital expenditures" and the "social expenses of production." The former include "social investment," that is, interventions for the infrastructures and promotion of research, which increase the productivity of capital, and "social consumption," namely, spending on health, education, and housing, which lower the costs of reproduction of labor. The "social costs of production" imply interventions that are more typical of the welfare state, such as those against unemployment and poverty.

Both approaches to the development of welfare – those highlighting the gradual extension of citizens' rights and those emphasizing the role of the state as a stabilizer of capitalism – are weakened by their being too general. They are not able to account for the important differences that exist between different countries in spending on social policies or in specific institutional models. Several comparative studies have attempted to resolve some of these questions, and a clearer picture of the development of social policies has emerged (Flora and Heidenheimer 1981; Alber 1982; Paci 1987; Ferrera 1993). In general, the importance of factors which we can define as "socio-centric," like the mobilization of the lower classes, the needs of the capitalist economy, and the level of economic development (Wilensky 1975), are not disputed. However, the impact of these factors on the pace, extension, and features of social policies is affected by politico-administrative variables. In addition, it is argued that a more detailed analysis of significant differences in the models of organization adopted by various countries requires a careful evaluation of such variables as the culture of the administrative elites and the traditions of public policies inherited from the past (Ferrera 1993).

One crucial factor has been the mobilization of lower classes as a result of capitalist development, since they were increasingly unhitched from the traditional forms of social protection and reciprocity involving kinship and community networks. In his account of this process, Alber (1982) underlined the importance of workers' political organizations. It was following their appearance in the final decades of the nineteenth century that the first compulsory insurance schemes began to emerge. This process took different forms depending on whether the regimes were authoritarian or parliamentary. In the first case – as in Bismarck's Germany, and also in Austria and Italy – the social protection programs were the result of the reaction of the conservative elites, in search of a stronger legitimacy, in the face of the new labor movements. In parliamentary regimes this process took longer, partly because of the resistance of working-class parties, which usually viewed state intervention with suspicion. However, while the initial moves to set up insurance schemes in Western Europe can be seen as a "top down" process, it was mainly in the countries in which the workers' parties were particularly well represented that the most striking advances took place between the two world wars. This pattern was confirmed after the Second World War. Countries in which parties linked to workers' movements were in power spent more on social policies and introduced more extended programs. However, it can be said that there was a more general push towards expansion of social programs, in the form of compulsory national insurance schemes covering the entire population. Therefore, the process was also supported by different political forces, and particularly by the center parties influenced by Catholic culture.

The role of left-wing parties in workers' movements is particularly important if we look at the way in which the social protection system was organized. In general, the literature has supported the idea of three main ideal types of welfare state; these were originally described by Richard Titmuss (1974), and have recently been further developed by Esping-Andersen (1990). The first type – called the "institutional–redistributive" model – covers the principal risks for the entire population on the basis of the recognition of social rights. It involved a major expansion of public programs, providing flat benefits for all citizens on a comprehensive basis; greater importance was given to the provision of services (i.e. health, social and educational services) as opposed to transfer payments. In addition, necessary funds were raised by fiscal measures rather than contributions linked to job status. This model was well established in Northern Europe – Sweden, Norway, and Denmark – where a strong workers' movement and a long-standing presence of left-wing parties in government led to the use of the social protection system as a major weapon in a strategy of reducing social inequality through political redistribution (Korpi 1978; Esping-Andersen 1985, 1990). It should also be pointed out that this model was also originally shaped by the British welfare system set up after the war following the recommendations of the Beveridge Report.

The second ideal type, in contrast, is known as the "residual" welfare model. In this, public social protection is directed towards covering only those social groups in conditions of poverty and need. The programs are very selective and spending is much more restricted. The most typical example of this model is the United States, where welfare programs were expanded in the thirties with the New Deal and subsequently in the sixties; even then they were strongly affected by the strength of liberal ideology, the weakness of the workers' movement, and the absence of socialist parties. Other countries that can be said to share this "liberal" model are Canada, Australia, and the United Kingdom in recent years (though during the fifties it came closer to the "social-democratic" model) (Esping-Andersen 1990).

Finally, there is the third type, which Titmuss calls the "industrial achievement-performance" model, and Esping-Andersen (1990) "conservative–corporatist." In this model, insurance against the principal risks is not based on a citizenship right but on occupational status. Thus, benefits are provided by national insurance schemes which are compulsory, guaranteed, and supported by the state, and vary according to occupational category; financing is based on contributions rather than taxes, and thus the scope for redistribution objectives is inevitably more restricted; in addition, monetary transfers are clearly more important than direct services. This third model is typical of many European countries (Germany, Austria, Belgium, Italy, Spain, Portugal, and to some extent the Netherlands). One striking characteristic of this "continental model" is the particular influence wielded at the political level by Catholic culture. This is reflected in the crucial role of the family

Table 8.1   *Three welfare models*

	Residual	*Industrial achievement performance*	*Institutional–redistributive*
Cover	Marginal	Occupational	Flat
Main recipients	The poor	Workers	Citizens
Institutional	High	High	Low/absent
fragmentation	(localism)	(occupational status)	
Benefits:			
Range	Limited	Medium	Extensive
Requirements	Evidence of	National insurance	Nationality/
	Means	schemes	residence
Financing	Fiscal	Contributory	Fiscal
Expenditure:			
Level	Low	Medium	High
Main	Means-tested		
Component	programs	Transfers	Public consumption

in satisfying social needs, where care-taking functions are mostly assigned to women and paid work carried out by men (Esping-Andersen 1999).

Overall, beyond the differences outlined above, a remarkable increase in state commitment to social protection took place in the two decades following the war in all the more developed countries. Whether this combined with weak Keynesian policies or with more interventionist ones in the economic field, increased social spending made an important contribution to the fast growth of this period. The availability of a work force coming from agriculture, the vast range of needs that could be satisfied through mass production, the liberalization of international commerce guaranteed by new international agreements and the dominant role of the United States, were all factors that favored a "virtuous circle" between social spending, increase in consumption, and economic development in a context of low inflation. The situation began to change at the end of the sixties, however, as a consequence of the success of the Keynesian welfare state itself.

1.2   Social and economic tensions during the seventies

During the seventies a series of factors rapidly and unexpectedly undermined economic growth and social peace in the most developed capitalist countries. Industrial conflict began to rise again after a period of sharp decline; inflation rose to levels that were much higher than those of previous decades; growth rates decreased strikingly; unemployment rose. All this provided new challenges for the theoretical and practical tenets of Keynesianism, which seemed inadequate to deal with the twin features of high levels of inflation and unemployment (the term "stagflation" was coined during this period). In this situation, there was a return to the institutional analysis of the economy.

How can the economic and social tensions of the seventies be explained? One way is through observing how two types of "perverse effects" tend to be generated over time through the institutional regulation of the economy based on the Keynesian welfare state (Regini 1991). The first of these has to do with changes occurring at micro level following reductions in unemployment. The second concerns the macro-economic level and the difficulty of controlling the public spending that goes together with an expansion of social protection systems.

These two perverse effects also illustrate how the political economy that developed after the Second World War diverged increasingly from Keynes's original framework (Skidelsky 1979). In other words, while the British economist had assigned the function of sustaining demand to avoid recession to state intervention, he had not envisaged the use of an active demand policy to promote economic growth. Moreover, his more limited conception of public intervention was based on two institutional assumptions that were revealed by post-war experience to be wrong.

The first concerned the governing of demand policies. Keynes believed that it was natural for this function to be carried out by competent bureaucratic elites devoted to the public interest – a vision which accorded with his experience of the British civil service. In reality, in Western democracies the control of public spending quickly became a crucial instrument by which political elites tried to get support. Policies were influenced by political reasons rather than by strictly technical ones, with a push towards an incremental growth in spending which generated inflationary effects. Secondly, Keynes believed that at the micro-economic level – in the regulation of both production and labor – the market would continue to carry out an essential function. In reality, however, precisely as a result of full employment, market discipline of workers' wage claims became looser. This process was reinforced by social protection policies. These reduced the dependence of individuals' life chances on their position in the market, by offering services and incomes through political redistribution (Offe 1972).

Let us now discuss the effects of the Keynesian welfare state deriving from a situation of full employment. The strong growth of the first two post-war decades exhausted the labor resources coming from agriculture, though in many cases this was countered by an increased use of immigrant labor. In addition, a more stable and stronger working class matured new claims with regard to both wages and social and political recognition (Crouch and Pizzorno 1978). In addition, new forms of Taylorist work organization were developed in the sixties, under the pressure of growing international competition in the manufacturing sector. These tended to exacerbate the social effects of a rigid and hierarchical division of labor in factories. It is in this context that the tendency towards a re-emergence of industrial conflict, and a strengthening of union organizations in a situation of full employment can be understood. The extent of these changes varied, but the general effect was a push towards an increase in wages that stimulated inflation.

On the macro-economic level, it was increasingly difficult for governments to keep social spending under control. Protection from risks involving illnesses, injuries, old age and unemployment had become a crucial resource for the legitimation of modern capitalist democracies (Habermas 1973; Offe 1972). This led to growing pressure by various interests to organize themselves to improve and extend their benefits. It became very difficult for political elites to resist these demands and, even more so, to reduce the programs of social protection once public budgets began to worsen. Therefore, from this side too there was a push towards inflation that resulted from the government's spending policies.

The perverse effects of the Keynesian welfare state began to emerge more clearly at the end of the sixties, although they were reinforced by other factors. Some of these were of a long-run structural type: for example, the saturation of the market for mass-produced goods and the contemporary intensification of competition coming from the newly industrialized countries. Other elements were more contingent, but they played their part in worsening the economic and social situation. Among these were the steep rise in oil prices and the breakdown of the fixed exchange system, linked to the devaluation of the dollar.

We have already noted that in the immediate post-war period the prospects of growth for large mass-production firms were strikingly positive. These could exploit economies of scale in the production of consumer goods – from cars to household appliances. By the second half of the sixties, however, the situation was changing. Signs of the saturation of national markets were increasingly evident (Piore and Sabel 1984). For example, in 1970, in the United States 99.9 percent of families had a television, while only 47 percent had one in 1953; almost every family now had a refrigerator and washing machine; the number of cars in circulation came close to one per every two residents (ibid., p. 184). All this suggested that exports were the solution. And, indeed, international trade developed to a remarkable degree. Between 1960 and 1973, the industrial production of advanced countries increased by 5 percent, exports by 10 percent and imports by 11 percent, while sales to developing countries increased only by 7 percent – obviously due to their lower levels of income.

Summing up, during the sixties the space for mass production narrowed. Increased competition, and the difficulties that firms in more advanced countries had to face, worsened as a result of the emergence of several newly industrializing countries – particularly the Asian ones described in the preceding chapter. By means of some shrewd state-planned policies, the latter promoted a strategy of industrialization and began to grow, especially in the area of low-skilled mass production, using the lower cost of labor as a competitive advantage for their exports to the developed world.

Finally, other contingent factors contributed to complicating and worsening the economic situation. Mass production had profited from the low costs of energy. In 1973, this situation suddenly changed, owing to the decision of the oil-producing countries to organize a cartel to regulate exports. Thus a sharp rise in prices occurred. In the short term this exacerbated the problems of the more developed economies, generating – especially for countries which were more dependent on oil imports – strong inflationary pushes. Moreover, the consequences of the loss of competition on the part of the American economy as compared to Europe and Japan began to be felt at the beginning of the seventies. Afflicted by a growing deficit in its balance of payments, in 1971 the United States was forced to suspend the convertibility of the dollar into gold and to devalue the currency, moving from a system of fixed exchange rates to floating ones. This inevitably led to instability and uncertainty, increasing the difficulties of mass production firms.

1.3   Explanations of inflation and the two political economies

Inflation, the slow-down in growth and unemployment (the phenomena of "stag-flation") would thus seem to be the result of the perverse effects of the Keynesian welfare state, exacerbated by a series of other structural and conjunctural factors. But how should the development of such effects be understood? During the seventies a growing body of literature on the origins of inflation began to be published, focusing particularly on this question, which is obviously both theoretically and practically important. Of particular interest here is that the most innovative branches of this literature attempted to integrate factors of an institutional nature into the explanation, no longer considering them as simply exogenous *vis-à-vis* economic variables. Two branches of neo-institutional study tried to interpret the behavior of governments and of unions and firms in their industrial relations, and to see the effects of this on inflation. Both were called "new political economy." However, while the first branch examined institutional phenomena by applying an economic approach of neo-classical derivation to institutional phenomena, the other is closer to the economic sociology tradition, focusing on the autonomous impact of political and administrative factors and of the system of interest representation on economic phenomena.

The novelty of these two approaches can also be appreciated if they are compared with the "monetarist" interpretation of inflation, which continued to consider institutions as exogenous. Here, inflation is seen as the consequence of the incapacity of governments to control monetary supply in relation to productive trends. The weak capacity of governments to resist "political pressures" against an expansion in spending, and the commitment to support demand and employment, generate inflationary expectations in firms and workers' unions which push them into increasing their income demands. This determines in its turn a strengthening of inflationary tendencies (increase in the cost of labor and prices of goods) in a spiral which is self-sustaining. Substantially then, according to the monetarist interpretation (cf. e.g. Cagan 1979), the main cause of inflation is exogenous with respect to the functioning of the economy.

The two political economy approaches distinguish themselves with respect to this latter interpretation by considering the action taken by governments and industrial relations leaders not as exogenous, but as a central factor needing explanation. They therefore oppose the idea that the problem of inflation can be reduced to a technical error in the management of economic policy. According to this latter view, such error could be corrected by a restrictive policy, and the adoption by governments of market-oriented measures, even at the cost of making unemployment grow in the short term. However, the two political economy approaches differ in the way that they explain the role of governments and industrial relations.

The political economy of neo-utilitarian theories

This approach developed an *economic* analysis of politics and industrial relations to explain inflation during the seventies. Its original points of reference were neo-utilitarian theories of politics, influenced by Schumpeter's *Capitalism, Socialism and*

Democracy and the economic theory of democracy developed by Anthony Downs (1957). However, the closest links were with the theory of public choice, which applies economic analysis to the formulation and implementation of policies (Buchanan and Tullock 1962; Buchanan and Tollison 1972). A first body of work concentrated on the so-called "political-business cycle". This concerns a politically induced expansion of the economy that precedes election as a result of attempts by politicians in office to be re-elected through an increase in public spending and/or a reduction in taxes (Nordhaus 1975; Buchanan and Wagner 1977; Tufte 1978). Particularly interesting in this regard is the work by Samuel Brittan (1978), who provided an interpretation of the longer-term tendencies for growth in inflation.

In Brittan's model, the assumptions regarding the behavior of the actors are similar to those of the theory of public choice and the political business cycle. In this it is assumed that electors will aim to maximize their individual well-being through their votes, while politicians will try to enhance, through their choices, the chances of re-election to office. Using the interactive model outlined by Nordhaus, Brittan produced the following account (1978, p. 168):

1   It is possible to boost production and employment for a certain amount of time by means of monetary or fiscal stimulus, which will give rise to subsequently higher inflation;
2   There is a temporal lag between the expansive effects of the economy and the onset of inflation. This allows expansive policies to be implemented before elections, shifting the costs forwards;
3   Electors' memories are short and thus the incumbents lose less from high unemployment early on in their period of office than from low unemployment immediately before the elections. Moreover, electors are "shortsighted" in the sense that they are not able to evaluate the likely negative consequences of certain policies in the post-electoral phase.

If we stopped at this point, Brittan claims, the negative effects of the political cycle in terms of inflation would be limited. However, workers realize that, with the increase in inflation resulting from expansive policies, they undergo a cut in their real income, and they therefore support the unions' requests for an increase in wages. This leads to a wage rigidity whereby not only are wages not reduced but they tend to rise, to regain their purchasing power. In Brittan's view, then, these are the conditions underlying a continual growth of the inflationary spiral.

Like other public choice theorists, Brittan also underlines a progressive contradiction between market economies and democracies (Brittan 1975), and he looks towards constitutional reforms – for example, the obligation on maintaining a balanced public budget – as a way of controlling the overwhelming effects of such a contradiction. In general, however, this type of diagnosis is accompanied by a preference for a neo-liberal therapy aiming at a drastic reshaping of the role of the state in the economic and social fields and the re-establishment of market discipline. It was this view, also shared by monetarist theorists, that underlay the new political experiments carried out in the United States by Ronald Reagan and in the United Kingdom by Margaret Thatcher.

The political economy of economic sociology

The second political economy approach aims to give an institutional explanation of inflation by looking at the demand rather than the supply side. In other words, it maintains that it is essential to understand what it is that pushes governments to intensify the search for support through a growing supply of money through public spending. This leads to a different focus. Attention is drawn to social changes over the long term which have an effect on the political demand of various social groups (Goldthorpe 1978; Lindberg and Maier 1985). John Goldthorpe (1978) has written a particularly interesting account in which he makes explicit reference to the way in which the market is conceived by economic sociology. In his view, inflation is considered as the monetary expression of a distributive conflict. The growing demands for income by lower classes have been stimulated by two trends working together. First, there has been a delegitimation of existing social inequalities and, second, this has been accompanied by a change in power differentials to the advantage of organized labor (Goldthorpe 1983, p. 53).

With regard to the first aspect, Goldthorpe underlines how traditional forms of legitimation with which the market had initially to deal have tended to erode over time. This is the result of various processes, for example, the growth of urbanization and mobility, and the spread of market relations in a growing sphere of social relations that were previously regulated by forms of reciprocity, namely, by shared obligations. As a result, the "status order" which led lower classes to accept conditions of social inferiority on the basis of shared criteria concerning the relation between rewards and performances, grew weaker. Increasingly, they began to organize themselves and to exploit collective action to improve their position. In addition, social demands and distributive conflicts were strengthened by a balancing in the power relations between the different groups. This was due above all to the effect of the social protection system – which reduced the dependency of individuals on the labor market – and also to the commitment of governments to full employment, which reinforced workers' organizations. According to Goldthorpe, the formation of an extended "second generation" working class, employed in the large Fordist firm and resident in urban areas, also needs to be taken into account. This social group was less involved in traditional forms of status order and authority and more inclined fully to exploit new and more favorable power relations.

This type of analysis highlights how the choices of governments cannot be interpreted in terms of "weak determination" or "technical errors," as traditional monetary theory would have, nor in terms of a simple rational calculation of consensus, as the theory of public choices would suggest. There are in fact social determinants in the demands of the various groups with which governments must increasingly deal. This gives rise to a more complex understanding of relations between the demand coming from social interests and the supply by governments. A good example of this perspective was offered by the comparative study of inflation carried out under the auspices of the Brookings Institution (Lindberg and Maier 1985).

The basic idea is that political demand can vary as a result of cultural factors, since these influence the legitimation of the inequalities produced by the market, and of institutional factors, such as the system of representation (unions, parties), that define and aggregate demands. There can thus be a more intense and short-term demand, or vice versa one that is more moderate and long-term oriented. This depends on the cultural and institutional factors of various countries, and is thus not reducible to a mere tendency towards the maximization of individual well-being on the part of single electors, as in the alternative political economy approach.

Of course, the same thing is also true for the governments' supply. Rather than assume a general tendency to maximize the chances of re-election through inflationary policies, it is necessary to evaluate how the political elites are influenced by institutional factors: political ideology and organizational features of the political system (types of party, electoral rules, etc.). In other words, inflation can be seen as *the consequence of an inability of the representative system to select different demands and to keep distributive conflict between the different groups under control.* In this case weak governments overloaded by demands use inflation as a short-term solution to limit distributive conflict. This, however, brings about a spiral of "stagflation" over time: that is to say, less growth, higher unemployment and higher inflation.

The results of the empirical analysis carried out by the Brookings project support this view of inflation in the seventies, as do other studies that will be described in the following section. They particularly show how the worst performances are to be found in countries where there is a fragmented system of representation, incapable of selecting, filtering and integrating demands, such as the United States, the United Kingdom, and Italy. In contrast, in countries such as Germany, Austria and the Scandinavian nations, more structured representation has limited the inflationary "tug of war" and has allowed a high level of public revenue, moderate inflation and low levels of unemployment to coexist. It was shown that, in the seventies, high inflation, strong deficits and a drop in productivity were not correlated with high levels of public revenue and taxation; often the opposite is true (Cameron 1985). This confirms how the "weak" Keynesian models, with a more limited commitment by the state to support employment and social protection, could stimulate distributive conflicts and could have a worse effect on stagflation *vis-à-vis* the "strong" models. It is among these that the political business cycle was more pronounced as a consequence of a more fragmented representation system (Bordogna and Provasi 1984).

2 Pluralism and Neo-Corporatism

As we have seen above, studies of inflation underlining the influence of the sociopolitical context also highlighted differences between advanced countries. In this sense it can be said that the approach taken by this branch of political economy is different from that based on an economic theory of politics (public choice theory). It is also more comparative. This feature was simultaneously enriched during the seventies by several studies that threw light on one of the aspects also considered as crucial by the studies of inflation: the system of interest representation.

2.1   Interest organizations and policy-making

Why was it that in the early seventies levels of inflation and social conflict were higher in countries like the United States, the United Kingdom and Italy than in the Scandinavian countries, Austria, and Germany? Around these questions, there developed a model of comparative political economy which elaborated the concepts of *neo-corporatism* and *concertation* in contraposition to those of *pluralism* and *pressure-group politics*. Underlying this literature is the idea that better results in terms of control of economic and social tensions, namely, of the perverse effects of the Keynsian welfare state, are associated with a system of interest representation and political decision-making moving away from pluralism. This was the model on which sociology and political science had relied extensively in the two post-war decades to explain the legitimacy and efficiency of democratic political systems in the West (Almond and Powell 1966).

To evaluate this theoretical change it is useful to distinguish two analytically interdependent dimensions. The first refers to two features of the representation system, mainly the degree of concentration (or monopoly of representation) of organizations of functional interests (especially business or workers' organizations), and the degree of centralization of representational power. The second dimension refers to the process of policy-making and considers the relations between interest organizations and governments in the formulation and implementation of public policies. The debate on neo-corporatism was originally started by Philippe Schmitter (1974), who focused on the area of interest organization, while Gerhard Lehmbruch (1977) drew attention to the process of policy-making. The extensive literature which ensued examined relations of interdependence between these two aspects, building theoretical models based on comparative empirical research (Schmitter and Lehmbruch 1979; Lehmbruch and Schmitter 1982; Berger 1981; Goldthorpe 1984).

The first area – dealing with the organization of interests – shows that a pluralistic system can feature a large number of small voluntary associations, which compete between themselves to attract single subjects. They generally express the representation of specific and sectional interests, for example, those of firms or workers of a given sector (metal goods, textiles, etc.). Another aspect is that these types of organizations are also loosely linked, with only a weak capacity to coordinate the interests of a given sector or, even more so, the different sectors. The power of representation is thus not very centralized and peak organizations (for example, national confederations of industrial firms or unions) are lacking or are very weak.

In contrast, neo-corporatist systems feature a small number of large representative associations which gather those belonging to wide economic sectors and professional categories (for example, industry as a whole or agriculture) under their umbrellas. There is thus a kind of representative monopoly or oligopoly. Membership is formally voluntary but in practice there is no alternative; this is partly because only a small number of organizations are in competition between themselves and partly because the monopoly or oligopoly can be reinforced by state recognition through delegation of public functions to interest organizations (Offe 1981).

One example of this is in the field of labor policies. In this way an incentive for potential members to join is created because membership is often the necessary tool to gain access to various public benefits. Moreover, organizations tend to be more centralized in this model: several peak organizations have a strong power of negotiation with other representative and state structures, especially with the central government.

As to the second field – that of the relationship between interest groups and governments in the process of policy-making, there are significant differences between the two models in this case, too. The pluralist system features a high level of competition between the interest organizations influencing political parties, different factions within the political parties, members of parliament and state agencies through lobbying (pressure politics), attempting to influence the decisions that will affect them. In this case the role of parties, political groups, factions and single politicians is more important. These actors compete in their turn in a more open "political market" to gain the support of organized interests. Moreover, they are usually less directly involved in the implementation of policies. In contrast, a neo-corporatist system of representation is usually based on *concertation*. In this case, large encompassing interest organizations – particularly business associations and unions – interact more closely with the government and other public actors in the negotiation of economic and social policies, and they are often involved directly in the implementation stage, especially in the fields of labor policy, training or social policies.

It is useful here to evaluate the reasons why a system of neo-corporatist system of representation and a process of policy-making based on concertation can favor the more effective control of economic and social tensions, and which policies are more likely to be involved in this kind of process. First of all, on the basis of the previous discussion we can define neo-corporatism as *a model political economy in which large interest organizations participate together with the state authorities in a process of concertation of public policies, that is, in deciding and implementing important economic and social policies.* Spreading mainly after the Second World War, apart from the notable exception of Sweden, where it appeared prior to this, the neo-corporatist model is defined in this way to distinguish it from old-fashioned corporatism, typical of authoritarian regimes in power between the wars, and from the experience of Spain, Portugal, and other Latin-American countries where this kind of regime persisted after the war.

These authoritarian regimes took medieval guilds (corporations) as their model to define and redesign a compulsory system of representation imposed by the state. Representation was therefore an instrument by which to impose choices made by government authorities. Vice versa, in the case of neo-corporatism, membership in representative organizations was voluntary and the relationship between these and the public authorities was one of interdependence rather than of dependence, even when the state recognized organizaĩtions and delegated public functions to them. Usually, organization-building came from "below" as the result of the ability of the leadership to find support in the rank and file, even if this process could be more or less reinforced by public recognition and support. For these reasons Schmitter (1974) distinguished between neo-corporatism as "societal corporatism," typical of developed countries with a democratic political system, and "state cor-

Table 8.2 *Pluralism and neo-corporatism*

	Representation system		Policy-making process
	Level of concentration		Level of centralization
Pluralism	Low	Low	Pressure policy Lobbying
Neo-corporatism	High	High	Concertation

poratism," used by authoritarian regimes. Lehmbruch (1977) proposed the category of "liberal corporatism" for the same reasons.

2.2   The logic of political exchange

Why was the neo-corporatist model more successful in controlling stagflation during the seventies (see Fig. 8.1)? From the very start of the debate on neo-corporatism, it has been suggested that its development was tied to the attempt to deal with the perverse effects of the Keynesian model through income policies and wage constraints (Lehmbruch 1979). Essentially, this meant controlling the effects of full employment, favored by Keynesian policies and high post-war development, on wage claims and public spending. But, clearly, in order for this to be accepted, a crucial role had to be played by the workers' organizations. Why should the unions participating in neo-corporatist structures accept wage restraints?

Alessandro Pizzorno (1978) tried to answer this question. He introduced the idea of a "political exchange," namely, a situation in which "an actor (generally the government) which has goods to give is ready to trade them in exchange for social consensus with an actor who can threaten to withdraw that consensus" (1978, p. 279). In the early seventies the unions had very strong market power; they could determine disruptive effects on the economic situation through their claims and through industrial conflict. But under what conditions were they willing to moderate their demands? The offer by governments of a greater amount of political power in terms of institutional recognition and involvement in social and economic policies was not enough. Two other conditions were necessary: a high level of autonomy on the part of the representatives *vis-à-vis* the represented, namely, a centralization of the representative power that would enable a moderation in demands to be imposed on their base; and a state of low competition by rival organizations, which would have exploited the situation to propose themselves as alternative representatives to those sectors of the rank and file which were less willing to accept a strategy of moderation.

As can be seen, the conditions illustrated by Pizzorno are close to the two listed above: the monopoly of representation and the centralization of negotiating power. Let us now suppose that such conditions – without which the unions could not easily accept political exchange – actually exist. What still needs to be clarified is

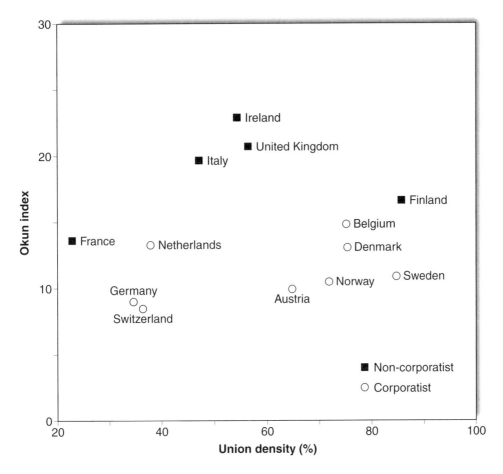

Figure 8.1 *Economic performance and union strength, 1971–1975*
Note: Okun index is based on the sum of the inflation and unemployment rates (percentages).
Source: C. Crouch 1993, p. 257.

what advantages unions would gain from such an exchange. From this point of view it has to be underlined that the advantages were not only those of greater power for the representatives, that is, for the leaders of the organizations. Certainly, institutional recognition, with an eventual delegation of public functions, reinforced the unions as organizations and contributed to stabilizing or increasing the power of the executive. However, "the union's principal benefit is its enhanced ability to deter market outcomes so that they work to labor's advantage" (Regini [1991] 1995, p. 33).

In this sense, workers' organizations can compensate the moderation of wage demands on the economic market with benefits linked to public policies. And it was for this reason that concertation often tended to structure itself around a linked series of interventions (known as "package deals"); that is to say, it was based on complex agreements in which wage moderation was compensated by other benefits in the logic of "neo-corporatist exchange" (Lehmbruch 1979, p. 304). The public policies that were agreed on mainly concerned the economic and labor fields, with the support of governments for full employment and the improvement of working conditions; however, fiscal policy was also often involved, especially social policy, with the extension of welfare provisions.

In addition, it is also important to note that strong and basically monopolistic unions tend to "internalize" the costs to the economy and employment of their short-term claims (Olson 1982). A situation of economic crisis – triggered by high wage increases – would risk compromising the stability of the union organization, by endangering the interests of the rank and file through an increase in unemployment. Therefore, in calculating the consequences of their strategy, organizations of this type tend to avoid wage claims that could have disruptive effects on the economy. This is not the case with small organizations, as Olson underlines, when they have strong power in the labor market. These have fewer incentives to take the overall costs of their action on the economic system into account. Naturally, it should not be forgotten that the unions' calculations are also influenced by the identity of the organizations, their histories, and the values that they share (Lehmbruch 1979). Unions more oriented to the representation of the working class, and not only of some occupational groups, are more inclined to evaluate the overall costs of their action and therefore to pursue a solidarist policy which restrains the market power of the stronger occupational groups to the advantage of weaker ones. That is to say, that there will be a stronger push to reducing pay differentials.

Governments also play an important role in neo-corporatist regulation. When they find themselves facing the demands made by strong unions, they can try to integrate the workers' organizations in the process of policy-making, exchanging political power for consensus and social peace. However, even in this case, the role of political culture should not be underestimated. Left-wing governments, formed by socialist parties, are usually more sensitive to the support of workers and unions. In this case it is more likely that the path of concertation and political benefits increasing the "social wage" will be attempted, although such a choice might well be made or continued by center-right governments also. In addition, pro-labor governments – that is, governments more favorable to workers – usually facilitate neo-corporatist agreements, since unions are more inclined to trust these governments when they have to give up their market power on the market in the short term, in exchange for political benefits that will be delivered later on.

The last question needing to be answered is how the role of employers' associations works within the neo-corporatist model. For business, participation in political bargaining is viewed as "second-best choice" (Schmitter and Streeck 1981). Unlike workers, for whom collective organization is indispensable to increase their bargaining power on the market, employers are in a position of structural advantage, based on their control over the means of production (Offe and Wiesenthal 1980). They enjoy greater contractual power, there being no need for the collective organization of interests either in the labor market – that is, with regard to workers – or in their relations with the state authorities. The latter must take into account the effects of their own actions on the willingness of business to invest, since it is on this factor that production and employment depends in capitalist economies.

Table 8.3   *Strike volume in the post-war period (worker-days lost per 1,000 employees)*

	Denmark	France	Germany	Italy	Netherlands	Sweden	UK	USA
1950–54	3.8	501.0	60.9	300.0	18.0	82.6	81.7	572.0
1955–59	122.0	130.0	34.1	303.0	20.8	15.7	190.0	535.3
1960–64	227.0	150.0	18.6	625.0	29.0	4.9	131.0	277.3
1965–69	31.7	127.0	5.5	812.0	5.0	19.7	155.0	487.6
1970–74	360.0	169.0	47.8	1,049.0	47.7	55.8	578.0	533.4
1975–79	69.8	168.0	42.8	860.0	24.8	26.6	465.5	383.2
1980–84	95.3	73.0	47.1	479.3	17.8	225.0	431.3	185.3
1985–89	211.1	34.1	1.7	143.8	8.0	111.2	155.6	78.6
1990–94	32.7	21.2	18.2	94.2	23.8	49.2	36.3	39.2

Source: Bordogna and Provasi 1998, p. 343

This situation can however change when the unions become stronger, by increasing their control over the labor market, and when the growth of state intervention tends to interfere with the functioning of the market through regulative, fiscal, monetary, and spending policies. When these conditions occur, as happened after the Second World War, employers were also pushed into reinforcing their collective organizations to coordinate their action in the face of union claims and to influence public policies. Especially where the strength of the unions was higher, business representation also tended to take a centralized form to ease the coordination of collective bargaining with unions and concertation with the government. Sometimes, however, the opposite happened, as in the case of several Scandinavian countries (Crouch 1993).

In this way employers managed to gain the benefits of both restraining firm-level claims and controlling industrial conflict. On this latter aspect, the literature on strikes and industrial conflict (Hibbs 1978; Cella 1979; Korpi and Shalev 1980) showed how during the 1970s, levels of conflict were lower in the neo-corporatist countries (see table 8.3). Many workers took part in strikes, but ¡¡these were usually short; that is to say, they were more "political," designed to show the strength of the labor organizations, rather than to hit firms with long strikes, as happened in non-corporatist settings, such as in Italy, France, the United States, and Canada.

Union strength and working-class mobilization cannot alone explain the formation of employers associations with a high monopoly of representation and strong centralization. Different types of productive structure are obviously important. They may be more or less fragmented and diversified, influencing the scope for coordination and collective action. However, the characteristics of the other actors also influence the process. If there is a strongly centralized union and an interventionist government favorable to political exchange, it is likely that the employers associations will be more willing to participate in concertation procedures (Schmitter and Streeck 1981; Martinelli 1994).

In any case, employers' associations usually remain less inclusive and centralized than their union counterparts (Streeck 1992, chapter 3). This can be explained with the greater scope that employers have, *vis-à-vis* workers, to pursue their interest through individual action on the market, as well as with the stronger heterogeneity of business interests: firms can be in competition amongst themselves or they can operate in sectors with different needs. The greatest weakness of employers' organizations *vis-à-vis* their rank and file pose severe constraints on their action, preventing them from taking on direct commitments in terms of investments and employment. This introduces an element of asymmetry into incomes policies – where unions have to make wage choices that are binding on their base. This asymmetry, in turn, can lead to destabilizing tensions in neo-corporate political exchange. In addition, the lower level of autonomy from the rank and file means that business adhesion to concertation is more unstable and dependent on the conditions of the labor market. In other words, the temptation to *exit* is stronger when the constraints that make business accept concertation as a "second-best choice" lessen.

2.3   Variability of neo-corporatist structures and its causes

The above observations suggest that many factors may influence the different forms of neo-corporatist regulation of economies. The early literature, and some neo-Marxist hypotheses on the state, viewed the process as a general transformation of capitalism to deal with its functional problems. However, the idea that neo-corporatism should instead be considered as a specific model of institutional regulation soon gained ground. In other words, it became clear that neo-corporatism did not develop in all capitalist economies and that where it did, it formed with varying degrees of intensity and stability, leading to different outcomes. Some studies underlined this variability, proposing different typologies, and focusing mainly on European countries where the phenomenon was most widespread (Regini 1991; Crouch 1993).

   The first ideal type to be discussed is *neo-corporatism with strong workers' organizations*. This model was widely represented in the Scandinavian countries (Sweden, Norway, and partly Denmark) and Austria. Here, strong unions with a high level of monopoly over the representation and centralization of power can be found together with employers' organizations which are just as strong and centralized, together with socialist parties that had been in power for many years. It is in this context that stable concertation took place. The unions restrained industrial conflicts and kept wage claims under control. In exchange, they obtained the government's commitment to maintain full employment as well as to deliver political benefits through the extension of a welfare state of the "institutional-redistributive" type (cf. section 1.1). In other words, labor was more able to use the neo-corporatist political exchange to its advantage, although without compromising economic development. There was a higher level of control over stagflation, even though with significant differences in the capacity to combine low inflation and unemployment, on the one hand, and the growth of the economy, on the other (Scharpf 1984). Another of the union movement's objectives was that of a solidaristic wage policy, to reduce wage differentials between various occupational categories. To avoid any negative consequences for weaker firms, which were forced to pay high wages despite their lower productivity, "active labor policies" were created – particularly in the Swedish case. These were decided and implemented through concertation and favored the training and mobility of workers towards firms and sectors with higher productivity.

A second type of ideal model can be described as *neo-corporatism with weaker labor organizations*. Typical examples of these are found in the Netherlands, Belgium, and Switzerland, while Germany – where the unions are stronger – can be placed midway between this group and the previous one. More fragmented and weak unions are usually typical of this model. The monopoly of representation was lower, particularly in the Netherlands and Belgium where organizations with different religious and political roots coexisted. However, the unions did develop forms of coordination between themselves, and showed a high level of centralization, as did employers' organizations. Although negotiation had initially been concentrated at the productive sector level, at the end of the sixties interest organizations began to participate more actively in concertation over economic policy. However, the lesser strength of unions meant that centralized political exchange was less favorable to labor. Perhaps the most visible sign of this was the change in the welfare system, which began to take the form of a "industrial achievement-performance" model, featuring closer links between forms of insurance and the occupational status of the workers (cf. section 1.1). In cases where unions were even weaker, as for example in Switzerland (Katzenstein 1984), they were co-opted and incorporated into the process of policy-making for increasing social consensus. In exchange for institutional recognition, which gave them the kind of influence that they could not have on the basis of their organizational strength, unions promoted a moderate wage policy. The lower level of industrial conflict – which also occurred in this second type – reflected a situation of labor weakness.

During the seventies, the need to control industrial conflicts, wage claims and inflationary trends forced governments to work out agreements with the unions, particularly where these were stronger. However, these attempts were not always consolidated and they thus gave rise to what can be called *unstable neo-corporatism*. Examples of this are the United Kingdom and Italy (Regini 1983; Crouch 1977, 1993), although Denmark can also be included, when it diverged from the "Scandinavian model" during the seventies. In terms of union strength, these countries were close to the first ideal type, but they showed a lower degree of union centralization (particularly in the British case). Peak organizations were weaker and in Italy there was also a lower level of monopoly of representation, tied to the presence of various confederations. Moreover, governments were less pro-labor oriented, or they were so in a less stable way, as, for example, in the United Kingdom. Under these conditions, the institutional infrastructure that could stabilize corporatist tendencies was lacking: In the United Kingdom this can be seen in the attempts to draw up a "social contract" between 1974 and 1979, and in Italy between 1977 and 1984 (neo-corporatist agreements were more successful during the nineties, as we shall see below).

These observations show how neo-corporatist tendencies were variable and can help us to summarize the main causes influencing the spread of this phenomenon.

1   The first factor is constituted by the *strength of union organizations*. If these are not strong enough to endanger, with the threat of industrial conflict, the control of employers on the labor market and firms' organization, neo-corporatist trends will be hindered. Employers will prefer decentralized individual or collective bargain-

ing while governments will not be stimulated to intervene because labor relations do not constitute a threat for either the economy or for social order. It is therefore necessary to remember that the strength of the unions is a condition which is necessary but not sufficient since – as we have seen – it can influence neo-corporatism only to the extent that it combines with other organizational features of the system of representation and with other aspects linked to the political composition of governments.

2   As for the organizational aspects, the importance of factors such as the *monopoly of representation* and *union centralization* have already been mentioned. Strong unions that are unable to coordinate and control the claims of their rank-and-file members, or to coordinate between themselves when there are several organizations, do not favor the institutionalization of stable forms of corporatist exchange. Another point that should not be forgotten is the influence of these factors on employers' representation. It is generally true that this last tends to adapt to the model of united and centralized union confederations, but in several cases a concentrated and centralized structure of employers' associations precedes and in its turn stimulates similar trends on the part of the unions.

3   Finally, it is clear that political factors linked to the *presence of left-wing parties in governments* are important. These latter are usually more willing to offer political benefits, mainly in the fields of social and labor policies, to facilitate concertation. In addition, they can also appear more trustworthy to unions, helping them to accept the exchange between immediate wage moderation *vis-à-vis* the future political benefits in terms of welfare provisions. It should not however be forgotten that parties on the center-right, with a strong Catholic influence, can also be interested in concertation, particularly where this is already established and would be costly to break off, as happened, for instance, in Germany. Another important feature has to do with the *efficiency of administrative structures* (Schmitter and Streeck 1985; Regini 1991). State structures must be capable of providing services that guarantee an increase in "social wages" both rapidly and efficiently. The Italian case is a good example of how inefficient administrative structures can make political exchange more difficult.

4   The factors outlined above are often the result of long-lasting historical processes. This element also helps explain differences within non-corporatist models (Maier 1981; Crouch 1993; Trigilia 1982). Looking back, it can be seen how the continuity with pre-industrial corporate structures has been particularly important (Crouch 1993). What does this continuity depend on? One important variable is the *degree of cultural and institutional rooting of liberalism*. From a cultural and institutional point of view, economic liberalism is linked to political liberalism. In this last case, emphasis is placed on parliamentary representation. In other words, in the same way that every type of interest organization on the economic market is viewed with suspicion by economic liberalism, as threatening market inefficiency, so the same applies in the political field. In this case there is the fear that that special interests might distort the pursuit of public interest entrusted to parliament. The stronger and more rooted is the liberal ideology, the greater will be the

diffidence towards the representation of those particular interests, which grew with the process of industrialization, in both the higher and the working classes. This diffidence can be seen in the Anglo-Saxon tradition and in France, particularly following the French Revolution. Vice versa, in Northern Europe, the weakness of liberal elites and the influence of a bureaucratic–centralist tradition have often been accompanied by the persistence of corporatist traditions of interest representation. In Southern Europe instead, weak liberal elites were challenged by the Catholic Church, which strongly opposed the building of a liberal state and dominated pre-industrial corporatist structures. Later on, in its attempt to strengthen control over the political space at the expense of the Church, the state tended to oppose corporatist traditions and bodies. These would be created "from above" by authoritarian regimes, as in the case of Italian fascism; but for precisely this reason they were subsequently delegitimated with the fall of these regimes. This legacy would hinder the institutionalization of neo-corporatist tendencies in the postwar period.[1]

2.4   Recent trends

During the eighties, many scholars of neo-corporatism were convinced that this was path that the different types of capitalism would follow sooner or later, if they had any intention of both respecting fundamental rights to interest organization and meeting the functional imperatives of social peace and expanding accumulation (Schmitter 1989). However, it was in precisely this period that some changes began to be felt. In the United Kingdom and the United States, on the one hand, attempts were being made to overcome the economic and social problems of the seventies – as we shall below – through a neo-liberal experiment of relaunching the market and cutting public intervention. On the other hand, in even those countries that traditionally adopted strong or weak forms of neo-corporatism and concertation, an important change can be perceived. That is to say, a generalized tendency took place towards a decrease in centralized bargaining. Instead, formal and informal kinds of concertation occurred, at a more decentralized level, in firms and sectors and at a local level. To understand this phenomenon it is necessary to consider two groups of factors. The first involves transformations of the organization of production at the micro level. The second has to do with the increasing public spending burden of welfare provisions.

  Regarding the first point, it should be remembered that mass production was affected by dramatic transformations from the seventies on. This will be dealt with in greater detail in the next chapter, and for the moment it is sufficient to recall several of the aspects which have just been mentioned (see section 1.2). First was the saturation of the mass production markets, and in addition the increasing competition on these same markets from newly industrialized countries with lower labor costs. In a context in which uncertainty also increased as a result of the breakdown of fixed exchange rates and of the sudden rise in oil prices, the "Fordist" system based on vertically integrated firms became subject to strong tensions. A deep process of reorganization of productive structures started. Firms tried to become more flexible; low value-added and highly labor intensive production were moved to developing countries. In more developed economies, service industries (research, finance, legal services, marketing, and advertising, etc.) increased instead.

The most striking consequence of this process was the rapid decline of the industrial working class. This social group, which had grown remarkably in the industrializing countries in the post-war period, was the base on which the strength of the unions had grown between the end of the sixties and the beginning of the seventies. Its rapid decline was accompanied by an increase in more highly skilled workers in industry and business services and an increase in the number of jobs requiring lower-level skills in traditional and consumer services. This fragmentation of interests in the world of labor had an important consequence – that of weakening the unions, with an overall decline in unionization rates. In addition, it made collective bargaining more complex and difficult (Crouch 1993).

This gave rise to a basic change in one of the crucial conditions underlying corporatist exchange. Weaker unions, now less able to coordinate bargaining, had less power to condition choices made by employers and governments (Regini 1991). As for employers, it has already been pointed out how the acceptance of centralized bargaining was in some ways a "second-best choice," motivated only by the attempt to restrain conflicts and wage demands at the firm level. These problems were reduced in the new situation. Employers' associations were in turn subjected to increased pressure induced by the need for firms to adapt to different conditions in the use of the workforce and in payment schemes. In this situation employers' associations generally supported a decentralization of bargaining.

As for governments, it was not only the weakened threat of union demands and conflicts that has to be taken into account, but also the increased macro-economic constraints referred to above. From this point of view, one crucial aspect was constituted by the growing burden of welfare provisions on the public budget. We have already seen above how the differences in forms and levels of commitment to social policies were significant in the post-war period. However, increased costs were reported everywhere, linked to three basic and combined factors: the aging of the population, leading to increased pension costs; higher levels of health expenditures, determined by the progress of medical science and the aging of the population; finally, the drop in the years of full-time work typical of the Fordist model which reduced the amount of contributions to finance social provisions. This last aspect, although generalized, particularly affected the welfare systems of continental Europe. Here, more than elsewhere, the growth of employment was discouraged and pressure on the employed to finance the social welfare system was therefore heavier (Esping-Andersen 1990, 1999).

I will return to this below. For the moment it is important to underline the fact that for all governments, but especially those that were previously involved in structures of the corporatist type, it became crucial to limit spending. This was aggravated by another factor which will be dealt with in detail in the next chapter – the growing integration of financial markets, which placed limits on governmental autonomy in the macro-economic field. Governments with high deficits were forced to raise interest rates to avoid capital flows abroad, and to avoid the risk of attacks on the stability of the national currency by financial markets. In this situation governments had fewer political resources to distribute for neo-corporatist political exchange;[2] indeed, they were frequently forced to reduce those which were previously delivered.

Overall, then, a series of factors threatened centralized political bargaining from the eighties onwards: the fragmentation of labor interests and the weakening of unions; the lower vulnerability of both firms and governments with respect to union demands and industrial conflicts; internal tensions in employers' associations, which pushed towards the decentralization of bargaining; finally, the macro-economic constraints placed on government action, which reduced the availability of political benefits. Other factors can also be considered as both causes and effects of change, on a more short-term basis. In many countries, including several Scandinavian ones, the long domination by the left wing was broken, and center-right political forces gained power. New political parties emerged, in particular ecological parties and those supporting the activation (or re-activation) of territorial identities. Political parties regained power in the representative system with respect to the seventies. In other words, the weakening of the complex socioeconomic equilibrium based on Fordism and the Keynesian welfare state led to greater economic and sociocultural differentiation, and left greater space to more pluralistic forms of representation. In addition, in Europe, the building process of community institutions also led to the stimulation of pluralistic forms of representation at the supranational level (Schmitter and Streeck 1991).

Despite all this, however, corporatist models should not be viewed as having lost their power. The data collected by Colin Crouch (1993, chapter 7) show that, although weakened at the central level of bargaining, corporatist structures set up the seventies persisted to a large extent in the following period and influenced forms of economic regulation in much of Europe. Moreover, the countries involved usually continued to get better macro-economic results in terms of lower inflation and unemployment control (figure 8.2). In addition, these same countries – but also others like Italy, in which centralized corporatism had remained unstable – experimented with forms of micro and meso concertation in the eighties, at the level of sectors, local areas and firms (Regini 1991).

To understand this process, it needs to be remembered that an institutional infrastructure favorable to concertation constituted a resource for dealing with the difficult problems posed by the transformation of Fordism. It allowed a restructuring in the direction of organizational models based on flexibility and quality with lower costs for all the actors involved. The restructuring processes of firms raised problems of dismissals, worker mobility, training and re-skilling; but also problems linked to the creation of new services and infrastructures, that is, to the production of collective goods on which firms' competitiveness was more dependent under the new economic conditions. It is in this context that the growing importance of micro and meso forms of concertation should be understood, with cooperation between actors moving from the macro-economic level to a micro level, and from demand management to supply policies. Decentralized agreements did not always have benign effects. In some cases they could, however, lead to increased spending by public institutions. This was clear in Italy, where redundancy payments were widely used to support the joint and consensual restructuring of large firms through micro-concertation (Regini and Sabel 1989).

In any case it should not be forgotten that problems of macro-economic adjust-

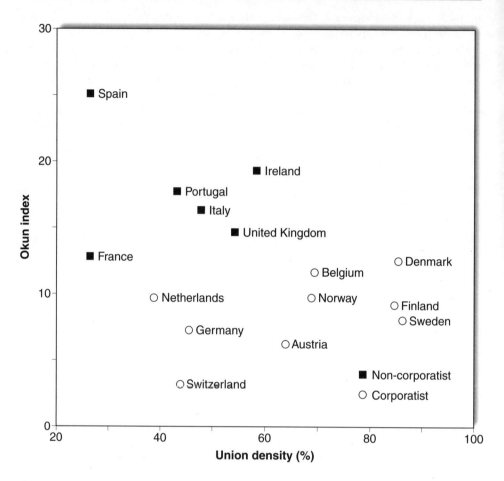

Figure 8.2 *Economic performance and union strength, 1986–1990*
Note: Okun index is based on the sum of the inflation and unemployment rates (percentages).
Source: C. Crouch 1993, p. 281.

ment are difficult to deal with and require forms of co-ordination with organized interests, particularly where unions maintain a high profile and an infrastructure and institutional tradition of a corporatist type persists. As will be seen below, the same macro-constraints brought about by European monetary union have in many cases stimulated a revival of macro-concertation in order to deal with problems of wage moderation, inflation control, unemployment, and the reorganization of the welfare state (Schmitter and Grote 1997).

3   The Variety of Regulation Systems

So far I have dealt with the neo-corporatist model of economic regulation; I have discussed its origins, operation and consequences, contrasting it with the pluralistic model. However, one important aspect emerging from comparative political economy during the seventies has to do with a third type of regulation, that differs from both the corporatist and pluralist models: "government by decree." This model is less widespread in more advanced countries, but it can be helpful in interpreting the political economy of France and Japan. This system of regulation was linked to good economic performances in the seventies and eighties. Its features are similar, to some extent, to forms of regulation typical of the newly industrialized Asian countries. As shown in the previous chapter, however, in those contexts the process of industrialization was also accompanied by serious restrictions on political democracy.

3.1   The market, decree, and agreement

Let us consider, first, the essential features of this ideal-typical model, which Michele Salvati (1982) has called *government by decree*. These can be described as a situation characterized by a higher level of government autonomy from the pluralistic pressure of interests. These last are generally weak, and the structure of public institutions does not facilitate their influence on policy-making. The relative institutional isolation of governments therefore allows a more effective selection of political demands, limiting their inflationary effect. In addition, the very important role that an efficient and motivated bureaucracy plays in the political process is such that the state intervenes in the economy with planning policies through measures of credit, fiscal, regulation, and export support (Zysman 1983).

In this way the behavior of firms – especially the large ones, the so-called "national champions" – is oriented towards increasing economic growth. While weak unions are excluded from policy-making, the relationship developed between the state and industry is crucial, through the work of organizations like the Planning Board in France (Hall 1986) and the MITI (the Ministry of Commerce and Industry) in Japan (Zysman 1983; Dore 1987). In terms of performance, the results feature a relatively low level of inflation and unemployment, and high growth rates (particularly in the seventies and the early eighties). "Government by decree" can be distinguished from neo-corporatism because state intervention did not take on the form of extended welfare and high public spending, but concentrated on regulatory policies in the economic field, more than on redistributive policies in the social field. On the other hand, in contrast to the pluralism typical of the American experience, there was not only more capacity for inflation control but also for state interventions in the economy, which do not form part of the institutional tradition of the United States.

Following Salvati's contribution (1982), it is therefore possible to distinguish three models of regulation: the corporatist model, called *agreement* to underline the role of concertation and joint decision-making in economic and social policies; the pluralist model, defined as *market*, to emphasize the importance that the market takes on not only in the economic system but also in the political context (the main empirical reference being the United States). Table 8.4 shows three dimensions that can help to analyze the different ideal types of regulation. The first, which has already been discussed with regard to neo-corporatism, concerns the strength of the working classes in the market arena (unions) and the state (left-wing parties). In this case, the strength of the working-class movement, which is usually considerable in neo-corporatist settings, is contrasted to the weakness in the decree and the market types. As for the political system, one can distinguish between the neo-corporatist features of the agreement form, the radically pluralist ones of the market type, and the divided polity typical of the decree model, with left-wing parties excluded from access to the government (although this situation changed in France in the eighties).

The ideological dimension also deserves some attention. This concerns the criteria of legitimation for state intervention. In the market model this is related to civil society, and is linked to the strong influence of liberalism – both economic and political – found in these settings. Liberal individualism tends to restrain expectations about state intervention in the economy and society, and is not favorable to the participation of interest groups, viewed as "special interests," in the policy-making process. This cultural legacy is very clear in the British and American cases. Though it is true that the Keynesian welfare state was also adopted in the United States, starting with the New Deal and moving into the post-war period, this trend was limited and there was greater resistance to it than in many European countries. This was also due to the traditional absence or weakness of unions and parties of a socialist orientation. A large and newly formed country, like the United States, with high immigration and varied ethnic makeup, has never been fertile ground for socialist ideas. In Europe, on the other hand, not only was liberalism frequently very weak but it was often opposed by strong socialist movements. All this influenced the criteria of state legitimation, favoring more extended expectations about the responsibility of public institutions in the economic and social fields. Also, under "government by decree," citizens expect the state to play a stronger role and extended interventions in the economic field are seen as legitimate.

A final observation concerns the market model. As we have seen, comparative political economy strongly emphasized the performances of neo-corporatist regulation in controlling stagflation. Salvati (1982) advised more caution. He not only drew attention to the success of the "government by decree" model but also insisted on the success chances of the market model, especially in some settings. Therefore, the recognition of different ways of regulating the economy of more developed countries questions the tendency inherent to several analyses of inflation and neo-corporatism to see this model as a sort of functional prerequisite that capitalism should fulfill everywhere in order to reproduce itself.

The more cautious evaluation of the market model leads to a less pessimistic view of the difficulties of the American economy in the seventies and of its attempt to tackle economic and social tension by means of the neo-liberal experiments, rather than through the European model of neo-corporatism. Some of the literature on inflation during the seventies saw in the neo-liberal project of aiming to reduce state intervention and to strengthen the market the danger of a worsening of the distributive struggle between different social groups with the risk of further economic decline (Goldthorpe 1983). A more careful evaluation of the market model and its viability, allows a better understanding of the neo-liberal response in the Anglo-Saxon countries.

In reality, in countries like the United States, where there are institutional and

Table 8.4 *Market, decree, and agreement*

	Market	Decree	Agreement
Working-class organization	weak	weak	strong
Political institutions	pluralistic polity	divided polity	organized polity
Ideological hegemony	civil society	state	welfare state

Source: Salvati 1982, p.26.

cultural peculiarities of the kind mentioned above, social acceptance of the market is certainly higher than in European countries. This means that attempts to deal with the difficulties of the seventies went in two directions. On the one hand, the scope for market regulation, especially in labor relations, was enlarged. On the other, an attempt was made to reduce state intervention and to thus lessen the pressure of organized interests on public spending. As a result, this path contrasted concertation, for which some basic conditions were lacking (Salisbury 1979; Wilson 1982). It comes as no surprise that an analogous attempt was also carried out in the United Kingdom, the only European country to resemble the United States in the persistent influence of liberalism in relations between market and state. However, the strength of union organizations and the Labour Party tradition made this difficult and complicated to carry out (Crouch 1993). At all events, recent developments have confirmed that a readjustment based on market regulation can lead to significant in terms of economic dynamism and the creation of employment.

These more recent experiences (see chapter 10) contributed to mitigate a fairly unilateral trend in the literature about inflation and neo-corporatism in the seventies. Economic sociology has attempted, in its most recent developments, to take the variety of regulation models more seriously and to analyze the different processes of social construction of the market. In conclusion, it may be useful to deal with another important feature of the political economy of the seventies: certain methodological consequences of this literature for a clarification of the concept of regulation and of its variability.

3.2 Principles and systems of regulation

The "discovery" of neo-corporatism in the seventies led to an attempt to rethink and integrate the traditional forms or principles of regulation of the economy used in economic sociology (see section 1, chapter 6). We know that it is possible to distinguish three forms of regulation: *market exchange* on the basis of prices with self-regulating market institutions; *solidarity* on the basis of shared obligations (Polanyi's reciprocity) sustained by a wide range of institutions (family, kin, local community, and in modern society also social movements); *authority*, which is based on coercion, and backed by state institutions (Polanyi's redistribution), or by

Table 8.5   *Principles and systems of regulations*

	Market	Decree	Agreement
Market Exchange	++	+	+
Solidarity	+	+	–
Authority	+	++	+
Concertation	–	–	++

hierarchical organization at the firm level. To this consolidated typology Schmitter and Streeck (1985), reflecting on the experience of neo-corporatism, proposed adding *concertation* as a form of regulation, and *corporatist association* as institutions supporting it.

In fact, neo-corporatist concertation is close to Polanyi's category of redistribution, precisely because of the important role that political decisions have in the production of goods and distribution of incomes. It comes as no surprise that this process has also been defined in terms of "political exchange" (Pizzorno 1978). However, it is also true that in neo-corporatist regulation the allocation of resources and relations between actors (in particular, workers and firms) does not take place only by means of state commands, but also involves interest organizations as "private governments" to which important public functions are delegated in the decision making of economic and social policies. The "pacts" involving interest organizations and public institutions are thus more important than state commands, typical of traditional forms of redistribution. In this sense Schmitter and Streeck's suggestion can be followed, taking neo-corporatist concertation as a modern variant of redistribution. This helps to clarify some of the regulatory features of advanced capitalist economies (Cella 1997).

There is, however, another important distinction to take into account. Concrete economies will never base themselves on a single form of regulation, as has already been pointed out by Polanyi and other classics of economic sociology. It is therefore useful to distinguish between *principles* or *forms of regulation* and *systems of regulation*.

Principles or forms of regulation concern *rules according to which different resources are combined in the productive process, the income produced is distributed, and potential conflicts between the actors involved in the economic process are controlled* (Lange and Regini 1989). The importance of a certain form of regulation in a concrete economy can thus be tested according to the role exercised by the institutions that support it. Therefore, in primitive economies, the role of the family goes hand in hand with that of reciprocity. In the economies of nineteenth-century developed countries, it is usually the institutions of self-regulating markets that are important. In the post-war period, the diffusion of the Keynesian welfare state signals the role of regulatory forms based on redistribution.

A system of regulation can be defined as a *specific combination and integration between different forms of regulation characterizing a particular economy*. This concept is thus equivalent to that of an *economic system*, understood as an overall modality of the institutional regulation of a particular economy. It favors the development of comparisons in time and space. The classics of economic sociology have generally privileged comparisons over time at a high level of generalization, as in the cases of liberal capitalism and organized capitalism. Comparative political economy, which developed at the beginning of the seventies, has worked at a lower level of abstraction, as in the comparison of national reactions to the crisis of Keynesian institutions.

Salvati's classification (1982) can thus be developed to show that each of the three types or regulatory systems is characterized not only by a main form or principle, but also by a specific combination and integration of the others. Thus, to take some of the examples shown in table 8.5, the minor role of solidarity in the "agreement" model underlines how an extended welfare state tends to reduce the role of institutions such as the family, kin, and voluntary associations, which helped to deal with social risks in traditional societies. Elsewhere, this task is instead left to civil society. The importance attributed to public commands in the "government by decree" model underlines the more important role that economic planning plays in this ideal type *vis-à-vis* the neo-corporatism of the "agreement" type, and the traditional pluralism typical of the "market" model.

A final observation concerns the use of the concept of regulation system at the micro level, to study the specific organization of particular sectors of firms or regional economies. In the area of comparative political economy we can find examples of both. One significant contribution from the sectoral perspective is that of Hollingsworth and Lindberg (1985). These scholars tried to evaluate the different systems of regulation characterizing sectors of the American economy: from the small traditional firms to the large technologically advanced companies. In each of the sectors studied, different and combined forms of regulation have been identified. Thus, together with the market, other principles have also been taken into consideration: *hierarchies*, that is, commands emanating from the state or large firms (*corporations*); the *clan*, which is based on shared expectations and trust (Ouchi 1980), and is important for regulating relations between actors in areas in which complete contracts are difficult to define; *associations* refer mainly to the tendency to form economic associations, for instance, in the case of business organizations in a given industrial sector. A strong variability of regulatory systems is shown by this study of American economy, underlining the usefulness of institutional analysis to interpret the origins, developments, and problems of various sectors.

One example of the use of the regulatory system at the territorial level can be found in Italian research on the development of the small firm in the central and north-eastern regions (Third Italy). I shall return to this topic in the next chapter. Suffice it to note that the regulatory system of Third Italy, in the crucial stage of its development in the seventies and at the beginning of the eighties, was built through a particular combination of market, reciprocity, and neo-localist political exchange involving associations and local government (Bagnasco 1988; Trigilia 1986; 1990). The growth of small firms and industrial districts has been supported by widespread forms of reciprocity supported by families and local communities, which have lowered the costs of labor reproduction and encouraged the supply of flexible labor. In addition, a dense associative network has led to a political exchange in which the unions have moderated their wage demands and favored labor flexibility, in exchange for a local "social wage" and full employment.

To sum up, since the seventies comparative political economy has taken up and adapted the tradition of economic sociology. It originally developed this perspective at the macro level, in studies of inflation and adjustments to the crisis of the Keynesian welfare state. Over time this approach has tended, however, to extend to micro-economic problems (studies on sectors and on local and regional developments). In this way comparative political economy tended to combine with a new economic sociology, which analyzed the crisis of Fordism, industrial restructuring and new flexible models of production. It is from these attempts to better integrate macro and micro aspects that the more recent models of comparative political economy have taken their shape. This will become clear in the discussion of the variety of capitalisms on which the final chapter will focus.

Chapter 9

The Crisis of Fordism and New Economic Sociology

As comparative political economy emerged, economic sociologists once again began to take a serious interest in the macro-level issues raised by the new tensions and transformations of the Keynesian welfare state. At the same time, however, a theoretical and research problem also emerged, traceable to the micro level, and concerning the important changes that the organization of firms and production processes were undergoing. In other words, during the seventies not only were the relations that had been introduced in the post-war boom period between the state and the economy undermined, but new tensions also affected the production model based on large and mass production firms. And, in this case too, the attempt to understand these problems and changes drew attention to institutional factors.

While macro studies focused on the system of interest representation, the composition of governments, and the structure and efficiency of the state, the micro-oriented studies analyzed the institutional factors influencing processes of innovation and adaptation to more uncertain and unstable market conditions. In other words, attention shifted from the regulation of demand to the question of how institutions influence supply – including the innovation of product and productive processes, the growth of entrepreneurship, the professional training of workers, labor relations at the firm and local levels, the availability of services and infrastructure for firms.

A new economic sociology thus began to emerge at the micro level, focusing on these topics. It centered on the origins and developments of a productive organization based on flexibility, i.e. on the rapid readjustment of productive factors to exploit the opportunities offered by technological innovation, and increasingly segmented and unstable markets. However, together with these research-driven studies, another more theory-driven approach should be mentioned. This involved the attempt on the part of both economists and sociologists to provide new conceptual tools to analyze the increasing variety of productive organization. Besides market and hierarchy (i.e., the firm functioning as the bureaucratic organization), an increasing number of hybrid forms were developing, based on a more or less formalized collaboration between firms (joint ventures, alliances, cooperation agreements, controlling relations, etc.). Therefore, the debate revolved around questions concerning the emergence and use of hierarchy, market relations, and other more varied forms of cooperation in economic processes. On the economic side, there were attempts to deal with these questions by developing a type of neo-institutionalism that redefined the theory of action traditionally used by economists, explaining the choice of different institutions in terms of a rational search for efficiency. Meanwhile, a new form of economic sociology began to emerge at the micro level, which linked the emergence and operation of different economic institutions to cultural factors, networks of social relations, and trust.

The last issue to be discussed in this chapter concerns consumer behavior. Given the growing differentiation of consumption, the aim of these studies was to go beyond both the traditional atomistic and utilitarian theories developed by economists, and those focusing on the critique of "consumer society," more frequently developed by sociologists. While the latter underlined the dependence of consumers' choices on pressures exercised by advertising and mass media, new studies analyzed the choices of goods as an active process of identity construction involving lifestyles and different types of consumption, and not only as an expression of the search for status *à la* Veblen.

1   The Crisis and Transformation of the Fordist Model

As already mentioned, it was during the last century that the model of economic organization usually referred to as "Fordist" or "Fordist–Taylorist"[1] spread out all over the world, particularly in the twenty years following the Second World War. It was based on large firms whose principal characteristics can be summarized as follows:

1   Firms were vertically integrated, that is, they included different productive stages which were previously carried out by different firms. This could also extend to forward integration of distribution, for reasons tied to maintenance requirements and customer assistance, which influenced control over the market. However, integration could also extend backwards, to the control of the raw materials and basic components that were necessary to guarantee the stable supply of the inputs necessary for production. In many cases backward integration also included research and development services. The complexity of the productive units and the risks which came about, the problems of organizational coordination, and the high needs of financing led to an overall growth in the size of firms;
2   Firms were committed to mass production, that is, the production of standardized goods through special-purpose machines; this allowed them to lower their costs, exploiting the new technologies for enhancing economies of scale. High levels of production allowed unit costs to decrease;
3   Production was carried out by a relatively semi-skilled labor, which was organized along the lines of the "Taylorist" model, that is, it was highly fragmented. The work itself was sub-divided into simple and repetitive tasks, limiting workers' autonomy. The division between conception and execution was clear-cut and rigid, and the firm functioned like a large bureaucratic organization, based on hierarchi-

cal control. Management played a central role, coordinating, integrating and controlling overall productive activity. There was thus a separation between the ownership of the firm, which could remain within a family or be distributed among various shareholders, and the management, which was entrusted to professional managers.

The use of this new model of productive organization had already been noted in the first studies of economic sociology (in the work of Sombart and Weber, for example). Over the last century, however, it became much more widespread. This can be explained by several factors. First of all, there was the spread of electricity as a source of low-cost, easily distributable energy; together with this, there was a widespread improvement in transport and communication. The former enabled a mass market to be established and supplied, while the revolution in the instruments of communication was essential to coordinate the flux of traded goods (Chandler 1977). However, this does not mean that the model was adopted uniformly in all productive sectors, or that it spread with the same intensity and pace in all industrialized countries.

Concerning the first point, several technological factors, together with the extension and stability of the market, prevented this model from being introduced into all productive sectors. The new technologies were extremely expensive and investment in dedicated machines, that is, tied to the production of specific products, was necessary. Only where there was a stable and wide market could economies of scale be adequately exploited, allowing high returns to finance the substantial investments required. However, for several types of production this was not possible. For example, there was still a substantial demand for non-standardized goods, and, it should be added, even mass production required specialized (non-standard) machines. This kind of demand was thus both limited and non-standardized, and it allowed small to medium-sized firms to cater to the need for machine tools and special machinery. In addition, the demand for high quality consumer goods – which was obviously lower on account of the costs involved – could not be satisfied by the Fordist model. Other kinds of goods, not all of a high quality, fueled a variable demand as a result of varying tastes and fashions. Thus, for example, in textiles, the fashion industry, furniture and other sectors where the market was fragmented and variable, smaller firms, run according to more traditional models, maintained their importance.

A final variant was linked to the presence of smaller firms, which were used by larger ones to cover cyclical variations in demand. A form of decentralization of productive capacity was created through subcontracting relations, the goods produced being marketed by large firms. In other cases, cash savings on labor costs in the productive stages that were simpler and labor-intensive fed the process of decentralization. For all these reasons, Fordism has to be considered as an ideal type that in real economies shared the market with other differently organized sectors – or parts of the same sector – and with a large number of small and medium-sized enterprises (SMEs) run on a traditional basis (personal entrepreneurship, machines used for multiple products, non-Taylorist organization of labor, or more skilled labor) (Berger and Piore 1980; Bagnasco 1988).

Another point also needs to be considered. The rapidity with which the Fordist model spread varied considerably across different countries. These differences were the result of different institutional factors. The size of the market for mass-produced goods was clearly influenced by the size of the state and the level of protection of the national economy, and this was in turn dependent on policy choices. In addition, the same national market could be more or less favorable to mass production, as a result of the differentiation of tastes and lifestyles, and thus of social stratification and national cultures. These features emerged clearly when American, European and also Japanese experiences were compared (Piore and Sabel 1984; Rosenberg 1976).

It is no accident that Fordism first emerged in America and that it took root very quickly in this particular context. In the first place, there was already at the beginning of the century a large national market, unified by early communication infrastructures, in particular railways. Second, the United States was a country of immigrants, so it was not characterized by the social differentiations typical of Europe, and it had a growing population that was much more open to consuming standardized goods. Moreover, unlike the European context, its striking economic development was determined by a strong lack of skilled labor. This meant that firms were particularly favorable to introducing production methods like the Taylorist ones, since these allowed for the rapid use of low-skilled immigrant labor, leading to high savings in costs. Given the absence or lack of these factors Fordism arrived in Europe later and in more limited forms. Here, small firms remained more widespread and they were often integrated at the local level into what Alfred Marshall called "industrial districts" (Marshall 1890, 1919; Becattini 1987, 1990). Organizational forms of this type existed for many years and resisted changes of any sort in many European countries (Sabel and Zeitlin 1985). Another point is that not only did Fordism spread at a pace and to a different extent outside the United States, but its characteristics were affected by different national experiences. Economic historians have studied these differences, showing the influence of several factors such as the ownership and management of firms (corporate governance), the financial institutions (the role of stock exchanges *vis-à-vis* banks), the internal organization of firms and labor, and also factors that have been dealt with in the previous chapter, such as industrial relations, and relations with the state.

Despite these differences, Fordism took on a similar form over different countries, these similarities being reflected not only in the organization of productive processes, following the patterns outlined above, but also in industrial relations and the role played by the state. Particularly after the thirties, the need for economic stabilization led to the extension of collective bargaining and the institutionalization of industrial relations in order to reduce conflict and guarantee the collaboration of a large and homogeneous working class in the factories. In addition, precisely to reduce the gap between production and consumption, various forms of demand management were undertaken by states. In this way, industrial relations and public intervention managed to stabilize the market, creating the favorable conditions for the full development of mass production that characterized the post-war period.

There are therefore very close links between Fordism at the micro level and the Keynesian welfare state at the macro level. It is precisely by taking account of this

integration that the tensions and transformations of the Fordist model at the beginning of the seventies can be understood. For the first point, suffice it to recall
here the crisis factors already discussed in the previous chapter (section 1.2, chapter 8). The saturation of the mass-production market restrained the growth of
Fordism. In addition, stronger competition from newly industrialized countries,
with their lower labor costs for lower quality productions, worsened the situation.
The increase in oil and raw materials prices determined, in turn, a rapid change in
those conditions of low input costs that had also favored the Golden Age of high
growth. Moreover, the breakdown of fixed exchange rates and the greater instability that came about on the international markets did not help the old production model. Finally, the explosion of industrial conflict in the early seventies also
reflected, as mentioned above, a situation of full employment, which strengthened the working classes' claims. In addition, it produced a reaction against intensification of Taylorist work organization, which had been attempted in the late
sixties to deal with the growing competition between firms.

All these factors – some of which were structural, others conjunctural – undermined the Fordist model in industrialized countries by weakening the stability in
labor and product markets that was necessary for its high level of specialized investments. However, as we have seen, these crisis factors acted more or less strongly
depending on the capacity of the institutional setting to reduce industrial conflict
and to sustain demand. In other words, where there was a more highly structured
representation system of the neo-corporatist type, together with concertation practices, the crisis of Fordist firms was less marked. This was certainly the case in some
European countries such as the Scandinavian ones or Germany. Where neo-
corporatist trends were weaker or absent, such as in the United States, the United
Kingdom and Italy, the shock was stronger and the social costs higher.

However, even in neo-corporatist settings, the decline of Fordism could not be
avoided. The whole process was linked to several structural changes that conditioned the strategies of firms at the micro level. In other words, the saturation of
mass goods markets in richer countries was a serious and long-lasting constraint.
An increasingly diversified demand for higher-quality goods emerged in these countries. It was promoted by income growth, but above all by the formation of new
and better-educated social groups developing new lifestyles and consumption patterns. This phenomenon, therefore, cannot be simply related to higher incomes
and to a sort of fixed hierarchy of inferior and superior needs, but involves social
and cultural changes. This point will be discussed in greater detail below; suffice it
here to underline the consequences for mass markets. The demand for mass-
produced goods shrank further and became more substitutive than additional. However, new possibilities opened up for firms in the area of diversified and customized goods of a higher quality. Often it was these same firms which oriented
consumers towards these goods, as a strategy for dealing with the difficulties of
more traditional production (Piore and Sabel 1984).

A second factor favored and promoted the attempt to move towards a more
diversified and better-quality production. This involved the introduction of new
electronic technologies. The possibility of using computers in the productive process had several far-reaching consequences. It was now possible to program machines so as to use them for different tasks and products. In other words, the new

technologies could be reprogrammed through changes in their software. This meant that flexible production costs could be lowered significantly: it was possible to produce non-standard goods of high quality in small series and at a lower cost. Both large mass-producing firms that moved upmarket by increasing quality and smaller artisan firms that extended their quality production were able to take advantage of these new techniques.

These changes in the market and technology allowed firms to react in terms of flexibility, diversification of models, and quality. That is to say, it became more feasible to meet the highly variable demand for high-quality goods produced in small batches, and for which consumers were willing to pay higher prices. In this way, firms could avoid competition with countries with lower labor costs in mass production. Naturally, this did not mean that mass production and the Fordist model were completely abandoned by firms in the more developed countries. Together with the strategies aiming at flexible and quality productions, there were others which tried to reorganize the Fordist model and to occupy the market left to mass production in both developed and undeveloped countries, though this occurred more in the latter. From this point of view, two different trends need to be taken into account: the use of new technologies to reorganize the Fordist model and the push towards the growth of multinational companies.

Concerning the first strategy, a "neo-Fordist" model of adaptation can be detected (Sabel 1988), also defined as "flexible mass production" (Boyer 1988). In this case the objective was to increase the variety of products without abandoning the basic production model, thus maintaining the separation between the conception and execution as well as the rigid organization of work. The development of new products remained centralized, although attempts were made to save time through new technologies. Subcontractors continued to be highly dependent, and the operative units less autonomous from the headquarters. The most important innovation took the form of "programmable automation," with the widespread use of automatic machines like robots in production. This led to a saving in the use of labor, but also to more limited retraining opportunities and lower levels of involvement of the workforce, and therefore was also described as "computerized neo-Taylorism" (Bonazzi 1993). Moreover, in other cases large mass-production firms invested directly abroad, and especially in developing countries, through multinationalization strategies. In this way they attempted to recreate the advantageous conditions which were previously available in the highly developed countries: a growing market with lower labor costs.

In conclusion, we can thus say that, particularly from the seventies on, a clear diversification and pluralization of productive models occurred. The institutional context played a crucial role in filtering the various strategies. To understand these processes, however, it was no longer sufficient to examine the macro-economic level and the role played by the state to see why some countries and regions adapted more rapidly and effectively to the new situation. What was also needed was an analytical perspective on the interaction between firms and the social context in which they are inserted. It was at precisely this micro level that economic sociology began to investigate. In particular, its focus moved to the relations between the institutional context and the new flexible production models.

2 Flexible Production Models and the Institutional Context

It was small firms that initially aroused the most interest. The dynamism of several regions dominated by many SMEs contrasted strikingly with the vision that had consolidated over the preceding years and which viewed large productive structures as being the most vital and innovative component of the economic system. Soon, however, it became clear that new experiments and organizational changes were also beginning to affect larger firms. In both cases, the attempt to understand the most successful processes of adaptation led to the highlighting of institutional factors and their influence on flexible production models.

In their book *The Second Industrial Divide*, published in 1984, Michael Piore and Charles Sabel made a particularly important contribution to this perspective. They outlined the model of *flexible specialization* and contrasted it with the Fordist model of mass production. While in the latter, as we have seen, the production of standardized goods made through specialized machines and semi-skilled labor prevails, the flexible specialization model features the production of non-standardized goods through universal machines that can be used for different models and more skilled labor. The emphasis was specifically placed on the new electronic technology that reduced, as pointed out above, the cost of flexible and diversified production. As a result, a neo-artisanal model could emerge, differing from its traditional predecessors because of its technological dynamism and the wider scope for innovation. Piore and Sabel noted that flexible specialization transformed large firms, especially in countries such as Germany and Japan. They mainly focused, however, on the new possibilities that opened up for small firms.

The ensuing studies, including contributions by Sabel himself (1988), developed three main features. The first was the persistence of mass production through the "neo-Fordist" reorganization mentioned above. The second referred to the extension of flexible specialization to large firms, with their internal transformation and the growth of cooperative relations with sub-contracting firms. The third involved the analysis of institutional factors allowing forms of cooperation to be established between management and workers and those between firms. This cooperation appeared to be necessary for the emergence and functioning of flexible models with a high level of innovative capacity, good labor conditions, and high wages.

In discussing these developments, I shall first concentrate on the phenomenon of small firms and industrial districts, and later on the transformation of large firms. Finally, I will discuss what might be called the other side of flexibility. In other words, I will examine forms of productive organization mainly based on low wages and unfavorable conditions for labor, in the so-called "informal economy." The boundaries between "high" and "low" paths of flexibility are not always easy to trace and the differences between them, as well as the links, require careful analysis.

2.1 Small firms and industrial districts

In several countries, the phenomenon of industrial districts formed of SMEs and concentrated in particular regions, can be seen very clearly. In some cases, these areas were already characterized by productive structures of this type, which, especially during the seventies, began to be characterized by a strong dynamism. In others, concentrations of new firms and productive specializations emerged for the first time. The sectors involved include both "traditional" (textiles, clothing, footwear, furniture, ceramics, etc.) and "modern" products (mechanical engineering, machine tools, electronics and computer industry, etc.). Two combined factors are crucial for the emergence of industrial districts – first, the production process must be divisible into different and technically separable stages, to enable firms to specialize in a certain stage or in the production of a particular part; second, the types of products involved are usually subject to a large quantitative and qualitative variability of demand, requiring flexible forms of organization.

Different examples of districts of small firms have been found by research carried out in different countries over the years (Sabel 1988). Particular attention has been devoted to the Italian situation, given the diffusion of these local productive systems in this country, giving rise to the concept of the industrial district. Local systems of SMEs – although not necessarily industrial districts – have also been signaled in several German regions, in particular in Baden-Württemberg, in Jutland in Denmark, in Småland in Sweden, in several areas in Japan, France, Spain, and also in some regions of the United States, like Silicon Valley in California, Los Angeles, and Boston. Given the importance of the Italian case and the development of the literature on this area, it may be useful to focus on some particular features of this experience.

Industrial districts in Italy

During the seventies, the number of small firms increased sharply overall, although this occurred particularly in the northeast and the center. Indeed, this area came to be known as the Third Italy, to distinguish it from the northwest – the first industrialized area in Italy – and the south – where the process of industrialization was very limited (Bagnasco 1977). Small firms usually show a peculiar feature: they are concentrated in local systems, that is, in small urban areas (usually with no more than 100,000 inhabitants), constituted by one or more neighboring municipalities. These local systems may be identified through integrated labor markets (i.e. in terms of travel-to-work areas) and show a certain level of sectoral specialization in "traditional" but sometimes "modern" products (especially mechanical engineering and machine tools). When sectoral specialization and integration between small firms are high, one can speak of real "industrial districts." This concept was first used by Alfred Marshall (1880, 1919) and subsequently reelaborated to analyze Italian economic development in recent decades (Becattini 1987, 1990; Brusco 1989; Pyke, Becattini, Sengenberger 1990).

A district is formed, then, by many SMEs, each specializing in a particular stage or in the production of a particular component of the productive process. Only a small group of these firms has any direct relation with the final market, however. Their task is to deal with orders, to decide on the quantity and quality of the goods to produce, and to entrust actual production to the "stage firms" (i.e. subcontractors). They act as coordinators of the overall process. In other words, production takes the form of a decentralized process and presupposes a high level of collaboration between specialized subsuppliers and parent firms. In some cases, the parent firms are large and not only coordinate but also carry out some of the stages internally. Sometimes the kinds of collaborative relations they have with their subcontractors are formalized, including agreements or forms of ownership control. This has increased over time to deal with problems of innovation and the improvement of quality.

Two features in particular have emerged from investigation of Italian districts. First, it has been noted that the capacity of individual firms to respond in a flexible way to market changes is based not only on their use of new technologies, but above all on cooperative relations between them. Second, their capacity to innovate and improve the quality of the goods is made possible by the existence of economies that are external to the individual firms but internal to the area in which they are localized. This involves the existence of specialized collaborators, of a labor force that is also specialized and skilled, and of collective services and infrastructure. But it also depends on intangible factors that influence productivity. Marshall was referring to these factors when he spoke of an "industrial atmosphere," characterized by the circulation and rapid diffusion of knowledge and information and by the development of continual incremental innovations.

One important aspect of this phenomenon is the availability of cognitive resources that form over time, leading to "tacit knowledge" or "contextual knowledge" (Becattini and Rullani 1993). In other words, they lead to a widespread know-how and to a shared language that allows "codified knowledge" based on scientific and technical development to be adapted to specific production problems. However, together with the influence of these cognitive components on productivity, there are also others of a normative type that are no less important. In fact, the flexible specialization model requires cooperation within and between firms to be supported by factors of a cultural and institutional nature. Indeed, research has highlighted the role of such factors, in both the origins of districts and their subsequent functioning.

Three factors appear crucial for the development of the small-firm economy and the districts, mainly in the so-called Third Italy (Bagnasco 1988; Trigilia 1986; 1990). First, there was a network of small and medium-sized towns in which widespread traditions of artisan and commercial practices already existed, and which had not been eroded by the first wave of industrialization, mass-production, urbanization, and immigration. It was largely from these traditions – formed over the course of history – that the entrepreneurial resources for small firms derived. In many cases the role played by good local technical schools was also important. A second important institutional factor was the state of agriculture before industrialization, particularly where these were self-employment and large families (share croppers and small peasants). These rural groups supported the initial formation of a flexible and cheap labor force, with the basic skills and motivations adequate for the development of a small firm. A third important factor was the strong rooting of traditions and local political institutions linked to the Catholic, Socialist, and Communist movements. These areas were therefore characterized by political territorial subcultures which strengthened the trust relations that were so important for the development of the small-firm districts; they also influenced industrial relations and the role of local governments. Industrial relations developed on a cooperative and localist model. Local governments in turn provided – directly and indirectly – social services favoring labor flexibility, and often provided services and infrastructure that were crucial for economic development (well-equipped industrial areas, support for professional training and other services for firms).

This cultural and institutional picture is important not only to explain the origins and territorial concentration of the districts and small-firm areas, but also to understand how they operate. First, it is evident that production requires a high level of cooperation between firms, and between entrepreneurs and workers in the productive units. Subcontractors experience a high level of competition within the productive stages in which they are specialized, but this is mitigated by cooperative mechanisms, so that the subcontractor or the parent firm do not try to maximize their short-term utility when they enjoy a more favorable market position. This allows reciprocal advantages in the medium and long term, for example, in terms of delivery dates or in innovation processes that imply risks for both sides. These forms of cooperation, which integrate competitive mechanisms, are based on trust relations supported by the cultural and institutional factors described above.

However, cooperation between firms is often more formal and organized. The small size of firms means that it is difficult to develop internally the services necessary for innovation and growth of productivity. These include professional training, the spread of information on markets and technologies, the promotion of exports and the problem of waste disposal. The success of the districts is thus dependent on their capacity to produce collective goods that individual productive units are unable to do or have no interest in doing on their own, but on which their performance depends. The ability to produce collective goods becomes an important instrument to strengthen the external services crucial for the district. This problem is frequently handled by service centers that are created and managed by local business organizations. In some cases, unions also participate, particularly in the area of professional training. Usually, these initiatives are also supported by local and regional governments.

Finally, additional forms of cooperation have also been set up with regard to the labor market. Production in the districts requires a high level of flexibility in terms of schedules and overtime, as well as the willingness to carry out different tasks and to contribute to the quality of production. Flexible production also leads to a high level of labor mobility between firms in the district because of the high turnover affecting small firms. Acceptance of this type of labor relations is certainly favored by the particular cultural and community framework that was outlined above; over time, however, another specific form of political regulation has also developed, tied to cooperative industrial relations. In other words, both the industrial relations and the actions of the local governments have encouraged the social acceptance of this model of development through forms of redistribution devices of the produced income. Therefore, the role of political redistribution should not be overlooked *vis-à-vis* the mechanisms of reciprocity, linked to family and kin ties. In this sense the social construction of the market is a crucial aspect of the success of districts in flexible specialization.

Districts and institutions

The Italian case is particularly important in the literature on small firms and districts. However, during the seventies, and in the following decade, similar phenomena were also signaled and described in different contexts: in several European countries, the United States, and Japan. A truly systematic comparative study of these cases has never been carried out, probably because of their variety. All the same, several contributions have attempted to highlight some patterns resulting from the studies on various countries (cf. in particular, Sabel 1988; Pyke and Sengenberger 1992; Bagnasco and Sabel 1994; Storper 1997; Cooke and Morgan 1998). Industrial districts oriented towards flexible production are tied to specific cognitive and normative resources. The following features can be underlined in particular:

1   With regard to the cognitive features, two orders of factors influence know-how and entrepreneurship. In many cases, including the Italian one, there were substantial artisan traditions, supported by good technical schools and other training institutions. In others, the cognitive resources mainly derived from the proximity of public and private research institutions (also linked to large firms), and in particular from the presence of important universities developing close exchanges with firms. This factor has been crucial in some of the better known American experiments, as shown by the cases of Silicon Valley, near San Francisco, specializing in the production of semi-conductors, and the area of "route 128" near Boston, specializing in mini-computers (Saxenian 1994). Several other cases, for example, that of Baden-Wurttemberg in Germany, illustrate features typical of both patterns.
2   The variability among these experiences is wider in relation to the normative dimension. However, the capacity for cooperation and the existence of trust relations are vital resources and are usually influenced by distinct local identities that persisted over time. In some cases these have a religious matrix, in others their origin may be either political or ethnic. The embeddedness of the district into the context of a local community (Becattini 1990) appears, however, to be a constant pattern. This kind of territorial rootedness allows for more direct and face-to-face interactions, and favors circulation of information and monitoring of behaviors that support trust. Therefore, those who deviate from shared expectations can be rapidly isolated, through mechanisms of social exclusion. Local identity and community relations, in their turn, are linked to a development that has not been shaped by mass-production, with its sociocultural consequences.
3   Cognitive and normative resources are not only important to explain the origins of districts, but also for understanding how these reproduce over time. As regards specialized knowledge and know-how, one has to consider the role of institutions that favor the continuous adaptation of the local context to the new problems that emerge over time. Some of these aim, for example, at bridging the gap between the local know-how and the constantly evolving scientific and technical knowledge (centers for technology diffusion, for entrepreneurial and labor training, etc.). In addition, there are also institutions for the production of collective goods (information on markets, export promotion, etc.). It would seem in fact

that it is this resource – the provision of "local collective competition goods" (Crouch et al. 2001) – that characterizes industrial districts most strongly, even if the form it takes can vary widely: private centers, promoted by business associations, public bodies usually promoted by local governments, mixed institutions run jointly by private and public actors.

4   The role of normative resources, particularly for the regulation of labor relations, is subject to stronger variability. Flexibility, in fact, requires a high capacity for cooperation and a strong involvement by workers to increase product quality. Traditional cultural identities are also not sufficient to favor labor cooperation, because traditional ties tend to weaken with economic development. Two ideal-typical solutions seem to emerge, with many intermediate possibilities. In the first there is a lack of institutionalized industrial relations. However, less favorable wage and labor conditions are usually compensated by high chances of individual mobility. Contrary to what happened in mass production, many dependent workers may become self-employed and set up small firms. The second involves more institutionalized but cooperative industrial relations. This favors more negotiated and compensated forms of flexibility as, for instance, in the more consolidated Italian districts, or in the German cases. The Italian experience also shows that a gradual movement from the first to the second pattern may occur over time, as local development proceeds.

Summing up, it is worth underlining that the continuous adjustment of cognitive resources and the social acceptance of the economic model are crucial for industrial districts. The success in adjusting to external challenges is by no means achieved once and for all, nor is it simply grounded in previous historical conditions. It is the result of the continuous capacity of local actors to find new solutions and to produce new collective goods on which the well-being of the local society depends.

2.2   The transformation of large firms

After the "discovery" of industrial districts, the investigation extended to large firms, which also began to experiment with models of flexible production, although following diverse patterns. However, some typical features can be identified and described, contrasting them to the traditional model of mass production. The experiences of Germany and Japan are important in this context, because – despite their differences – experimentation with flexible production forms was more widespread and earlier here than elsewhere. In dealing with the variant form of flexible specialization involving large firms, I will use Charles Sabel's summary (1988). For its institutional correlates, the work by Wolfgang Streeck (1992, ch. 1) on the German case and Ronald Dore (1986, 1987) on the Japanese one are of particular interest.

The starting point is the growing instability and fragmentation of markets. Predictability, which was an essential prerequisite of the Fordist model, declined sharply, as did the possibility of large investments in specialized machinery, since these run the risk of not being profitable, given demand variability and the rapid obsolescence of products. As a result, experimental reorganization was undertaken with the aim of offering a wider range of products (since the success of any of these could not be guaranteed in advance), as well as rapidly producing what the market demands.

1   For the large firms that want to compete successfully, it became necessary to reduce the Fordist separation between conception and execution of products, since this means that the introduction of any new products is extremely slow and elaborate, and is subject to rigid procedures. To overcome these problems new forms of decentralized authority were experimented with, to reduce the gap between operating units and the market demands, and to favor more rapid productive adjustment. Thus, headquarters shrank and only dealt with strategic decisions. At the same time, the central research and development laboratories and product design structures were dismantled or cut down, and new facilities of this kind were created in the operating units. In this way it is possible to reduce the gap between conception and execution and to gather and process information from the market more quickly. The operating units took on the form of semi-autonomous firms overseeing distinct productions, while from the financial point of view the large firm, often a multinational, was transformed into a holding controlling the firms now specializing in particular products.

2   Internal organization also changed, especially the organization of labor, and the viability of Taylorist models began to be questioned (Kern and Schumann 1984). The possibility of producing differentiated goods in short series, with continuous adjustments to new demands, required a reduction of redundant resources; this trend had been widely practised by the Japanese with what is called the *just-in-time* organizational principle. This involves the reduction of waste, slack, and buffer stocks, synchronizing production as closely as possible with market demand. However, to achieve these results, a high level of collaboration and involvement on the part of labor is necessary. In addition, the use of less specialized machinery, useable for different productions, requires higher labor skills. Workers must acquire broader skills, they must accustom themselves to group work, which are flexibly formed and reshuffled according to changing productive needs, and they must be ready promptly to intervene to avoid production defects, contributing to quality. In other words, the new organization of the firm and labor requires, unlike the Fordist–Taylorist model, a more active participation and greater amount of involvement by labor.

3   The large firm did not only reorganize internally, but also opened its boundaries, strengthening collaboration with subcontractors who are often localized in areas of product specialization. Since the costs of developing new products increase a great deal, while their life cycle tends to shorten, it becomes less possible, even for multinationals, to do everything on their own. They tended, therefore, to concentrate more on the development of several key technologies, on the design and overall assembly of the final product. The complementary parts were instead increasingly produced in collaboration with a network of subsuppliers, which tend in turn to decentralize the production of simpler components to other second or third tier subcontractors. Moreover, for subsuppliers to be more effective and play a role as partners, rather than as mere dependent units, they were increasingly encouraged not to work for the parent company only. By working for more than one purchaser, and being more exposed to the market stimuli, their capacity to

learn may increase. Moreover, they can compensate for decline in certain products with other orders, enhancing productive flexibility and therefore reducing costs for the purchasing firm. In practice, then, on the one hand, the subsuppliers of the first tier are more closely integrated through formal and informal agreements of collaboration with the parent company; on the other, they are encouraged to compete on the market.

4   Like small firms and the districts, for the large firms that moved towards flexible specialization the role played by cultural and institutional factors was extremely important. Once they started this kind of reorganization, they become more dependent on the external environment – to use one of Polanyi's concepts, they became more embedded – than if they had continued relying on the Fordist model. In other words, it is the institutional context that influences the possibility of adapting rapidly to flexible productive models. As with the districts, the variability of institutional factors is, however, high, and it is thus usually more difficult to move from empirical observations to generalizations. I shall try to do so all the same, using the experiences of Germany and Japan during the eighties, since these provide the most successful examples of large firms using flexible specialization methods. In this case too, a distinction between normative and cognitive factors will be made.

5   The ability to learn through a more intense and efficient cooperation between the various structures and subjects working in the firm environment seems favored in those contexts where the role of hierarchy and the diffusion of low labor skills are considerably less than in the Fordist standard. This, for example, happened in the Japanese case, where the firm was traditionally conceived as a community rather than as a network of contracts, and where commitment to the professional training of the labor force was high. It also occurred in Germany as a result of the procedures known as "co-determination," which features a formalized involvement of the workers in company management, as well as stronger commitment to vocational training than was traditionally the case. These examples also show that the extension of cognitive resources through cooperation is favored by particular normative resources, that is, through institutionalized rules providing incentives for workers to behave cooperatively. The concept of jobs for life, the role of cooperative enterprise unionism, the extension of wage incentives tied to firm performance all supported cooperation in Japan. In Germany, highly institutionalized industrial relations at the firm level, even if unions were more integrated at the sectoral and national level on the national scale, played a similar role. In addition, the existence of constraints and rigidity in the use of labor also constituted an incentive for firms to invest more in the vocationall training of workers, since they could not easily be dismissed. In addition, firms were also supported by external institutions (jointly run by private and public actors) which provided efficient training for workers, thereby lowering the costs of private investment. Without the legal and union constraints on the use of labor, and without these external institutions, firms would in fact be forced to invest less in training and, above all, to invest in training programs more strictly linked to the immediate needs of the firms, thus reducing the overall level of skill which allows for more rapid and effective forms of adaptation to new production. All this helped to create those "redundant resources" in terms of skills which provided a crucial asset for flexible and quality production.

6   Another important factor that affects the availability of cognitive resources for innovation is the diffusion of external collaborations. Large firms searched for contacts with networks of specialized subcontractors, which are usually quite small and localized in areas of productive specialization or in industrial districts, where they benefit from large external economies. Clearly, the possibilities for large firms to experiment with flexible specialization were conditioned by the availability of such subcontractors. This resource is more easily found where cultural and institutional factors have limited the impact of the Fordist model on economic organization. Among these factors one also has to include public policies which have helped SMEs, for example by fiscal measures or the regulation of labor relations. Moreover, public and private initiatives to strengthen cooperation at the local level should also be taken into account. These measures usually favored the innovative capacity of small specialized firms through the production of collective goods (technology, diffusion, market information, training, etc.). From this point of view, the institutional conditions facilitating the large firm variant of flexible specialization tend to coincide with those that were analyzed in reference to districts. The importance of institutional interventions which, for cultural reasons or political consensus, led to the preservation of a socioeconomic environment that was not eroded by Fordism, is confirmed. This is another aspect of that redundancy of resources that was crucial, in the new conditions, for flexible models.

The tendencies examined so far indicate that experimentation with flexible models leads to a certain amount of convergence between the variant based on districts and that centered on large firms (Sabel 1988; Regini and Sabel 1989). Wolfgang Streeck (1992) has also underlined this trend by introducing the concept of *diversified quality production*. This was realized by both large firms using the new flexible technologies to produce large amounts of non-standard quality goods and by smaller and artisan firms which could now enhance their production of non-standard goods at lower prices. In other words, the boundaries between large and small firms blurred. What should be remembered, however, is that the basis of the new flexible model is not only technological but to a large extent organizational. In both cases – for the large and for the small firms – a network model of organization, based on an extended collaboration between firms, develops. It breaks down the vertical and hierarchical integration of the Fordist model. Districts can be seen as *networks of small and medium-sized firms*, while the large firm transforms into a *networked firm*.

The networks function as "learning systems," that is, as sets of formal and informal relations reinforcing the capacity for rapid adjustment to market changes. It is no longer the firm as a hierarchy that decides on its productive objectives and imposes them on the market; instead, it is the market, in a new fragmented and unstable form, which requires more rapid and costly adjustments. Networks allow the speed of adjustment and capacity for learning to be reinforced, as well as the costs of the new products to be reduced, by distributing them over a wider range of subjects and thus lowering the risks. Networks are able to carry out these tasks better because collaboration is based on a series of formal and informal links and does not require a detailed definition of contractual clauses between the involved parties (which would in fact be very complex and inevitably incomplete). But at

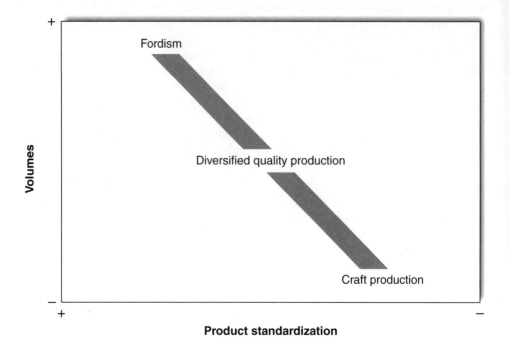

Figure 9.1 *Diversified quality production*

the same time, networks avoid the bureaucratic rigidity and slowness of the hierarchy.

The importance of cooperation for flexible models means that the large and
small firms adopting them become more dependent on the social context in which
they operate. While the Fordist model can be seen as an organizational device that
strengthened the autonomy of the firm from its external environment, in flexible
production this relation tends to be reversed. As we have seen, in contexts where
trust relations facilitate cooperation, and institutions generate and reproduce them,
networks can be constructed more easily and they work better. In Fordism, the
institutional conditions influencing the demand management at the central level
(composition of governments, system of representation, etc.) are most important;
in flexible models, institutional factors influencing the supply side at local and
regional levels become crucial.

2.3   The other side of flexibility: the informal economy

The shortcomings of Fordism and the restructuring of welfare systems also led to
different forms of flexibility in the production of goods and services. These were
tied to reduced economic dynamism, lower capacity for innovation, and less
favorable labor relations. Therefore, interest grew in the *informal economy*, not only
as a device for adapting to the new situation, but also as a widespread tendency in

more backward countries and regions. As a first and rough description, this kind of economy can be considered to be the total production and distribution of goods and services that evade the national accounting system either completely or in part. In other words, the informal economy is identified with the invisible, hidden or underground economy. This general definition includes various phenomena, from direct subsistence production on the part of households, to industrial production through non-registered labor, to the criminal economy in drug trafficking or illegal gambling. It is therefore necessary to distinguish analytically the different relations that each one of these forms has with the formal economy if we want to understand the various patterns of development of the informal economy (Bagnasco 1990; Portes 1994).

A more precise definition of the informal economy can therefore be based on three dimensions: the modalities of production of goods and services, which can be legal or not; the type of goods and services produced, which can also be licit or illicit; and, finally, the destination of production to market or to household subsistence. The formal economy is thus constituted by production destined for the market of lawful goods and services, realized through practices that do not violate the law. In contrast, the informal economy is characterized by the lack of one or more of such requirements. In particular:

1 goods and services that are themselves illegal and produced by illegal means make up the *criminal economy*;
2 goods and services that are themselves legal, but which are produced wholly or partly by illegal means (e.g. with unregistered labor or fiscal evasion) make up the *hidden economy*, or "black" economy, component;
3 goods and services that are themselves legal and produced through legal means, but which are not oriented to a household or a community's direct consumption rather than the market, make up the *domestic* and *communal economy*.

This distinction between a formal economy and the various components of informal economy shows how the boundaries between the two spheres are uncertain and variable. First, for the distinction to hold, it is necessary that a formal economy can rely on well-defined and enforced legal rules for the regulation of economic activities of the market. Where this is not the case, as, for example, in the Third World or other backward regions, it is difficult to distinguish between the formal and informal spheres. In a certain sense all activities tend to be informal

Table 9.1 *Formal and informal economy*

	Methods of production	Products	Market orientation
Formal economy	legal	legal	yes
Informal economy			
Hidden	illegal	legal	yes
Criminal	illegal	illegal	yes
Domestic–communal	illegal	legal	no

(Portes, Castells, and Benton 1989). Second, the type of relations that single components of the informal economy can hold between them and with sectors of the formal economy should be taken into account. Thus, for example, domestic or communal production can provide additional resources for actors working in the hidden economy who produce for the market under illegal conditions. In turn, this production can increase the flexibility of small or large firms in the formal economy, which decentralize the simpler and more labor-intensive components of their production.

From the mid-seventies on, economic sociology focused increasingly on the informal economy, particularly the domestic and communal forms, and the hidden economy. On the one hand, attitudes towards the spread of these activities in the less-developed areas began to change. They were no longer seen as mere forms of economic backwardness and isolation, bound to be overwhelmed by the growth of modern activities (see chapter 7). Instead, they began to be viewed also as possible tools through which these areas could seize new opportunities opening up in the international division of labor. On the other hand, the diffusion of the informal economy in more-developed areas triggered great interest and opened up new research fields.[2] The approach that economic sociology tends to adopt, using empirical investigations and case studies, led to the discovery of the proportions of hidden or domestic economies, which were not revealed by official statistics. Moreover, in all these cases, as for those of the less-developed areas, the role played by some specific cultural and institutional factors is very important for the origin and operation of the informal economy. This is the field where economic sociology has contributed the most, as will be shown below.

In the absence of information and precise measures, it is difficult to establish with any precision if and to what extent the activities of the informal economy have grown over the last few years. The literature dealing with this problem suggests a reversal of the trend that occurred during the seventies. In the early development of liberal capitalism and successively in its more organized and politically regulated forms, the prevailing tendency seems to have been that of a progressive shift of informal activities towards the sphere of the formal economy. In the field of goods production, this has gone together with the growth of large firms, and with the extension of production for the market. In the field of services there has been a decline in traditional forms of provision, which were previously regulated by mechanisms of reciprocity based on the family, kin and community, and were partly substituted by the welfare state. The reversal of both these trends can be linked to the crisis of Fordist production and welfare systems.

With regard to the first aspect, it has been argued that the problems and transformations of mass production nourished the informal economy, in particular in its hidden or black forms. This may occur directly, as a form of adaptation by workers to growing unemployment,[3] and as a reaction by firms in their attempt to make savings in costs by deregulating labor relations and decentralizing production of goods and services to external firms. In addition, the informal economy can be favored indirectly because the higher variability and fragmentation of markets opens up new spaces for flexible production, which can stimulate some components of the hidden economy. Moreover, the improvement of communication technologies and transport facilitates the strategies of decentralization and delocalizing of production by large and small firms of the formal economy, contrasting with the search for lower costs which often involves the hidden economy.

It is also possible to distinguish between direct and mediated influences of the difficulties of welfare states. Among the former there is obviously a trend to increase the self-provision of goods and services by households given the retrenching of welfare systems and growing unemployment. The increase in domestic and communal economies, however, frequently reveals new social demands (for example, for care for the elderly, children, the ill or the disabled) that are difficult to satisfy through traditional and over-bureaucratized public services (Paci 1989). This demand is often covered by family and community networks, based on reciprocity. In some cases, the actors involved are motivated by altruistic attitudes, while in others instrumental orientations prevail and actors are more interested in the exchange of services and goods. It is in this way that research on the informal economy tends to link up with that on the self-provisioning of services, on the so-called "third sector," and on the role of the voluntary associations (Ascoli 1987; Gidron, Kramer, and Salamon 1992).

Some scholars have also drawn attention to other factors that can be included together with unemployment and the restructuring of welfare systems. They have pointed out the high cost of final services offered on the market, in particular in the field of maintenance and repairing of goods, such as, for example, home repair or household appliances, or in the field of personal services (caring). On the other hand, the new technologies now offer instruments that facilitate the self-provision of such services by consumers themselves through direct forms such as "do-it-yourself" and through help exchanges that do not go through the market. This trend has further contributed to the growth of the domestic and community economy (Gershuny 1978, 1985; Pahl and Wallace 1985).

As can be seen, the patterns underpinning informal economies are varied and complex. There is, however, one element that strongly characterizes them all – the use of forms of reciprocity as predominant regulatory principle. In other words, the extension of the informal economy in both backward and advanced contemporary societies signals the existence of a wide component of the economy that is – or becomes – less differentiated from the social relations of a family, kin or community type. This is even more clear in the hidden economy.

In the latter case a series of conditions influences the demand side: the search for greater flexibility in the use and cost of labor by firms in the formal economy; new technologies of communication and the improvement of transport, favoring decentralization and delocalization; the fragmentation and variability of markets which, together with flexible technologies, open up spaces for informal production in small firms, and for self-employed and domestic labor. The supply side of informal work is dependent on the growing unemployment and the reduction in welfare protection. However, it should be considered that these conditions do not lead directly to the spread of a hidden economy. For this to occur a crucial role is also played by the institutional context, since it functions as a sort of intervening variable, like a connecting device between demand and supply.

1   The institutional context involves the role of cognitive resources. Where there is know-how tied to artisan and commercial traditions and to the presence of small

firms and self-employment, or imported through immigration, it is easier to organize autonomous activities. That is to say, a type of entrepreneurship emerges
that is capable of creating and managing informal activities.

2   The institutional context also influences normative resources. From this point
of view, norms obstructing the demand for informal activities can be distinguished
from institutional factors that instead encourage their supply. The level of regulation of economic activities can also be considered. If regulation does not place
excessive constraints on formal activities, for example, through fiscal pressure or
administrative regulations and industrial relations, the demand for informal activities will be more limited. The same goes for the efficiency of state control over
economic activities and the enforcement of regulative norms. If the constraints are
very strong, hindering the productivity and profitability of firms, and if law enforcement is weak, the demand for informal activities will be higher.

3   The increase in unemployment, low income, and the reduced coverage of the
welfare state are not the only factors affecting the supply of entrepreneurship and
labor in the hidden economy. Just as crucial is the role of variables affecting trust
relations and shared values, as well as a commitment to hard work. Social networks are essential because the relations of firms with final buyers, with other
subcontracting firms, and between entrepreneurs and workers, presuppose a high
level of trust. Without this, transactions in the hidden economy could not take
place, since it is not possible to refer to legal contracts, enforceable by the state in
the case of violation. At the same time it is necessary to minimize the risks of these
illegal activities being reported to the authorities. The parties involved must therefore know each other well in order to trust each other. In addition, social networks
are essential not only to procure labor but also to supply the necessary credit for
starting up and carrying out the activities. Clearly, in these cases it is not possible
to refer to the credit structures of the formal economy (banks or stock market).
This problem is resolved through the exchange of help within the family or kinship structures, or at the level of the local community, particularly where there are
strong ethnic identities, for instance, between immigrants from the same countries.

4   The institutional context is thus an essential mediator between the supply of
and demand for goods and services in the hidden economy. Where it is based on a
community fabric that is capable of mobilizing the cognitive and normative resources supporting informal activities, these will be more highly developed. It is no
accident that territorial links are an essential aspect of these forms of economy,
since it is in this type of context that networks of relations can also be fostered,
allowing for the mobilization of resources, the monitoring of the subjects involved,
and sanctions assigned to those who break trust. This explains why different forms
of hidden economies are common within areas of large modern cities, as is clear
from the American case with New York, San Francisco, Miami and many other
cities characterized by ethnic communities and groups of immigrants with strong
internal cohesion (Portes 1994). This is also the case in many backward regions,
both in cities and in minor centers where local traditional communities are rooted,
and where the family plays a crucial economic role, as in Southern Italy, Spain and
other Mediterranean countries (Mingione 1995), or in Latin-American and Asiatic
contexts. The growing importance of immigrant communities in developed coun-

tries has drawn attention not only to trust relations but also to the motivational resources that make immigrants more willing to accept hard and badly paid jobs. These unfavorable conditions are often accepted in the expectation of social mobility through the creation of small family-based firms (Portes 1995). Even traditional communities in backward regions, however, often provide the type of resources that lead those involved to accept very unfavorable labor conditions. For example, in the less-developed regions of the Mediterranean countries, the family receives and redistributes different resources through reciprocity mechanisms (income coming from regular and irregular work of single members, subsidies and other benefits provided by the welfare state, products of the domestic economy often linked to agriculture).

2.4   The high road and the low road

At this point several observations can be made about the flexible productive models analyzed above. There is no doubt that they have increased the variety of economic organization, in comparison to the previous period in which Fordism and mass production prevailed. However, their economic and institutional features need to be examined carefully.

First of all, there is a "high road" to flexibility, capable of dynamism and innovation, with more favorable labor conditions in diversified and quality production. It can be based either on networks of firms (districts) or on networked-firms. This path has attracted particular attention because of its implications for highly developed countries. In fact, these cannot compete only in terms of price factors, and especially labor costs, in simple and standardized productions where the competition of backward countries is stronger. However, the economic sociology approach also shows what a difficult path it is, because it requires a complex institutional infrastructure, influenced by historical legacy, which is not easily constructed or reproduced.

There is also, however, a "low road" to flexibility, which relies on unfavorable work conditions and wages. In this case, competitiveness is more based on price in lower quality productions, which are often partly linked to the hidden economy (evasion of fiscal and labor regulations). This road is certainly easier, particularly in the initial stages, but less than one might expect. In fact, we have seen how important the institutional context is in this case; widespread unemployment, low incomes, or poor welfare provisions are not enough to generate flexible activities in the informal economy. Cognitive and normative resources – especially trust – are required to manage hidden economic activities.

Therefore, research on flexible models suggests that the economy tends to become less autonomous from the social environment than mass production was, but it also suggests careful evaluation of recent trends, which cannot be entirely reduced either to the high or the low road. Actually, both roads seem to be on the increase and the boundaries between them seem to be fluid and uncertain. This is true, not only in the sense that even the high road is supported (at least in part) by price competitiveness – for example, through delocalization and decentralization of more standard and labor-intensive productions – but also in the sense that mobility paths in both directions can occur. Firms or networks that were initially based on the informal economy can upgrade their production and shift to the high paths and more advanced firms or networks can slide downwards into the low road.

From this point of view, as Streeck (1992, ch. 1) has pointed out, institutions should be seen as constraints and opportunities. This means that to encourage the adoption or reproduction of the high road they must restrain economic strategies based on short-term profit maximization, both in inter-firm relations and in labor relations. Constraints can be sociocultural, voluntary and informal, or more dependent on formal rules (industrial relations or public regulation). Without them, however, it is unlikely that actors will renounce their short-term advantages and pursue the strategy of cooperation necessary to follow the high road, as well as to maintain it over time. On the other hand, institutions must also compensate for these constraints by giving greater opportunities for the production of collective goods that increase medium and long-term innovative capacity, thus allowing better labor conditions. This action is successful when "flexible rigidities" are created, as Dore (1987) has called them in his discussion of the Japanese case. Naturally, however, this is a very difficult balance to achieve and maintain. If constraints are too weak, exit from the low path is unlikely; if rigidity prevails, for example in labor relations, with inadequate compensation for productivity and innovation through collective goods, the flexible model is bound to decline rapidly.

The way to adjustment based on the high road is thus difficult to follow, but not impossible. In this regard, it needs to be underlined that the high road is certainly favored by sociocultural conditions which are grounded in history, but it also depends on the political choices of local actors, which may purposefully contribute to creating trust and cooperation by building up appropriate institutions (Sabel 1994). In other words, although strongly influenced by its history, the destiny of a region or a country is more open than is usually believed. In fact, unlike Fordism, flexible models tend to increase the chances for local actors to shape their own destinies through conscious political action, precisely because they emphasize the role of cooperation as an economic resource.

3 Economic and Sociological Neo-Institutionalism

The transformation of the Fordist model has stimulated the development of a new form of economic sociology at the micro level, aimed at analyzing different types of flexible productive organization. While this branch of studies was greatly influenced by empirical research, another approach also developed over the last few decades, more stimulated by theoretical questions. This debate was started by both economists and sociologists interested in developing new instruments for analyzing the growing variety of economic organization. Both groups were fundamentally dissatisfied with the traditional theories prevailing in their respective disciplines. In the economists' view, the explanations of different forms of economic organization based on technological factors were increasingly inadequate. The size of firms, the choice between producing internally or buying goods on the market (make or buy), the recourse to various forms of collaboration seemed to require more complex explanations than those offered by technology, to which economics had usually referred in the past. This led to the attempt to adapt the theoretical tools of the discipline to analyze economic institutions at the micro level (the same attempt with regard to macro-economic institutions was described in the previous chapter, with reference to the political economy).

On the side of sociology, the development of neo-utilitarian (or neo-institutional) economic theories triggered, in turn, new attempts to explain organizational variety. In these studies, the rational choice of the most efficient institutional solutions, typical of the economic approach, was contrasted to explanations that underlined the autonomous role of cultural factors and social networks in influencing economic organization. For sociology too, this orientation is also critical of traditional approaches adopted by the discipline – in particular, that of Talcott Parsons. This has led to an attempt to develop a new theory of economic action. It was in this context that another branch of the new economic sociology emerged, through an approach that is micro-oriented and theory-driven.

3.1 The analysis of transaction costs

From the seventies on, "institutional economics" attracted a growing interest. This approach questioned the idea of the firm as a production function, that is, as a productive unity whose boundaries were substantially defined by technological requisites. Traditional micro-economics was criticized for overlooking the problem of the firm's boundaries and concentrating on the study of the market.

Traditional analyses seem unable to explain why some "transactions" (that is, some exchanges of goods and services) take place in the market and others are internalized in the firm, and why in some cases the firm grows and relies more on hierarchy while in others it stays small. The new approach sees the market, the firm, and the various forms of inter-firm collaboration as economic institutions that can be explained as "networks of contracts" between subjects aiming to maximize their interests. Unlike the standard neo-classical model, the existence of variable "transaction costs" is recognized. They result from conditions of uncertainty and lack of information, which can create favor opportunistic behaviors. As a consequence, a series of contractual devices have emerged aimed at reducing transaction costs in various situations of economic exchange. The variety of economic organization is therefore determined by the attempt at improving the efficiency of transactions rather than by technological constraints.

The contractual nature of institutions is the principal element linking the studies that may be related to economic neo-institutionalism, although specific models are differentiated. Oliver Williamson (1985) includes in this approach the work by Alchian and Demsetz on the capitalist firm as "team production" (1972) and property rights (1973), by Doeringer and Piore (1971) on the internal labor market, and also the studies of "agency theory" (Pratt and Zeckhauser 1985), which explore the relation between principals and agents (buyers and suppliers, shareholders and managers, professional and clients, etc.). However, it is Williamson's "transaction costs economies" (1975, 1985) which particularly interests us here. This theory not only plays a central role in institutional economics but explicitly refers to non-economic variables and calls for a closer collaboration with sociology. And it is precisely the theory of transaction costs that has fueled the most heated debate within new economic sociology.

Williamson relied on several theoretical contributions to build his theory. On the economic side, he made reference to Coase (1937), who first linked the origin of the firm to transaction costs, as well as to the literature on "market failures" (Arrow 1974). However, Williamson thinks that to understand transaction costs it is not enough to refer to "environmental factors" and in particular to market structure, but that it is also necessary to take "human factors" into consideration. In this respect, the postulates of full rationality and optimizing behavior of the actors must be abandoned. Indeed, if these assumptions were fully accepted, transaction costs would disappear, as in fact the traditional approach hypothesizes. Williamson recalls the concept of "bounded rationality," formulated by Herbert Simon (1957), as a crucial tool for a realistic description of economic decisions. This concept underlines the limited capacity of the human mind for resolving complex problems, and implies strong limitations to optimizing behavior.[4] In addition, it is necessary to take into account the role of "opportunism." This refers to the incomplete or distorted disclosure of information, which can lead to the pursuit of one's own interests through deceit.

When conditions of uncertainty-complexity, linked to the difficult prediction of future events, or conditions of dependency in transactions (for example, the impossibility for the buyer of a good to choose among several suppliers in competition between themselves) prevail in the environmental context, the space for human factors such as bounded rationality and opportunism grows. As a result, "transaction costs" emerge, determined by the difficulties of *ex ante* definitions and *ex post* execution of a contract for a specific transaction. In this situation, according to Williamson, actors will seek to increase efficiency by reducing transaction costs. They will do this by coordinating via higher internalizing within the firm. In other words, under given production costs (influenced by technology and economies of scale), the more transaction costs grow the more firms will rely on hierarchy rather than on the market. It should be added that in the initial framework, presented in *Markets and Hierarchies* (1975), Williamson is also aware of the costs of hierarchy. In other words, he recognizes that with the growth of the firm's size there may well be increasing shortcomings in its internal transactions. These result from loss of responsibility and control, and from the emergence of internal conflicts. Thus, the choice of internalization is more complex and entails a comparison between the costs of market and those of bureaucracy.

Williamson followed up this work by further developing his analytical framework in *The Economic Institutions of Capitalism* (1985). Human factors here maintain their important role, but are now considered as given data rather than variables, that is, as biological and psychological characteristics of the actors. As for environmental factors, attention was moved to "asset specificity," that is, to the degree of specialized investments that characterize a particular transaction. For example, if relations between a purchasing firm and a sub-supplier require a high investment on the part of the latter in machinery that cannot be easily used for the supply of goods to other purchasing firms, the transaction has a high degree of asset specificity. The more the resources involved are specialized, the more the transaction is trans-

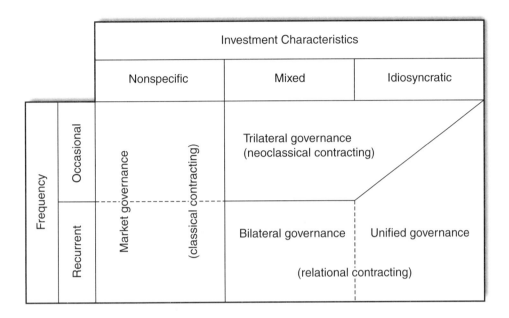

Figure 9.2 *Efficient governance*
Source: Williamson 1985. p. 79

formed into a bilateral relation between the contractors, with mutual risks of opportunistic exploitation. Transaction costs are thereby increased and they require
appropriate governance structures aimed at protecting the interested parties. The
risks grow, moreover, with repetition over time of transactions; frequency is now
therefore given more importance.

Figure 9.1 enables us to see which governance mechanisms tend to be used in
relation to the frequency and specificity of transactions. The following observations can be made:

1   traditional market exchange will tend to prevail for those transactions – either
occasional or recurrent – which necessitate a low specificity of resources (for example, the recurrent purchase of standard material, or the occasional purchase of
standard equipment);
2   for occasional transactions with a higher degree of specificity (for example, the
purchase of customized machines or the construction of a plant), the market can
again be used, but to reduce transaction costs resort will be had to third parties as
arbitrators or mediators (for example, professionals with the task of overseeing the
construction of a house or plant);
3   when the frequency of more highly specific transactions increases (for example, in relations of sub-supplying for high quality components), governance structures seem to become more complex (*relational contracting*). That is to say, a "bilateral
government" mode, using long-term agreements, joint ventures, etc. come into
being. This is the new element in Williamson's framework, which recognizes the
growing scope for intermediate forms of organizations between the market and

hierarchy. Actors hope to use to reduce the transaction costs in a situation in which firms have to rely more on external collaboration, especially in new models of flexible and quality production;

4   finally, with the further growth of asset specificity, and therefore of the idiosyncratic nature of investments which cannot be put to other uses, hierarchy appears to be the most efficient solution to restrain transaction costs.

Summing up, Williamson tries to go beyond conventional models to incorporate into the explanation of economic organization what he calls "human factors." He frequently underlines that these factors allow us to take into account "human nature as we know it." This is an important assumption. In the attempt to introduce non-economic elements into the explanation, Williamson ends up making reference to supposed "natural" psychological tendencies of actors. This position is therefore different from the basic assumptions of economic sociology. From this point of view, both bounded rationality and opportunism refer to actors' wider cognitive and normative orientations that are variable, not given by nature. They are a social construction, a product of the historical process of a certain society. Thus, the sociological concept of entrepreneurship also expresses the variability of bounded rationality in the economic field, and the diffusion of opportunism is also influenced, in real economies, by social and political institutions. Therefore, even highly specific transactions need not be internalized, if the institutional context limits opportunism and strengthens trust relations.

Another questionable aspect of the analytical framework involves the explanation of economic institutions (or governance structures of transactions). Williamson tends to describe their origins in terms of the actors' rational search for more efficient solutions. This perspective raises two problems. First, it overlooks the influence of cultural and political factors, as well as of social networks, in the origins of various forms of economic organization in different contexts; second, it tends to underestimate the persistence of certain organizational structures that may be less economically efficient, but are still able to reproduce themselves precisely as a result of their ties with the institutional context (high social legitimacy or political protection). It is precisely with regard to both these aspects, which are linked to Williamson's consideration of human factors as given psychological tendencies, that the criticisms of economic sociology developed.

3.2   The new economic sociology

Different approaches converge in the new economic sociology. Here, particular attention will be paid to studies focusing on social networks and to those that can be traced to a sociological neo-institutionalism. Before examining these different developments, it is worthwhile underlining the common aspects that both branches share and that distinguish them from the economic neo-institutionalism previously discussed. Two connected features can be mentioned here: the theory of action and the consequences deriving for the explanation of the variety of economic organization.

With regard to the first aspect, the studies in question share a theory of action that is typical of economic sociology – that is, they both view action as socially oriented and criticize the utilitarianism that still shapes institutional economics, despite the qualifications introduced by bounded rationality and opportunism. However, to follow the distinction proposed by Mark Granovetter (1985), it can be said that the criticism affects not only the "under-socialized" conception of the actor typical of economics, but also to the "over-socialized" version of sociology. The latter refers to models in which actors' behavior is strongly conditioned by culture and norms introjected through the socialization process. The main reference is therefore to Parsons' conception of the actor, which appears to be no less unrealistic than the calculating and utilitarian one of the traditional economic model.

New economic sociology tends therefore to develop a theory of action that is more constructivist, having benefited from the criticisms made of Parsons' approach by ethnomethodology and phenomenology (DiMaggio 1994). However, despite sharing this common ground, the two approaches have developed along different lines. The structural approach emphasizes the location of actors in social networks, as a factor conditioning interaction and orientations; neo-institutionalism instead pays more attention to the cognitive and normative features of culture that are reproduced in social interaction. Both positions criticize the explanation of the variety of economic organization offered by institutional economics. This variety does not seem to be reducible to the search for efficient solutions to minimize transaction costs, but is influenced by the social embeddedness of economic action (as Granovetter underlined, recalling Polanyi). For the structuralist, this means that it is not possible to understand economic organization without linking it to the autonomous influence of the networks in which actors are inserted. For neo-institutionalists, it is instead necessary to refer more to the cognitive and normative embeddedness of the action, and therefore to the autonomous role of culture.

The structural approach and social networks

For scholars of the structural approach, action is always socially orientated and cannot be explained only on the basis of individual motivations. Social embeddedness is viewed in structural terms because it is assumed that action is fundamentally influenced by the variable location of single actors in relations of social networks. Stable networks of social relations constitute structures that need to be reconstructed to evaluate the effects on economic behavior. In this respect Mark Granovetter's work (1985, 1990) deserves particular attention, since it has had great influence in clarifying the methodological assumptions and the analytical consequences of this approach.

Granovetter's starting point is his criticism of the theory of action in economics. Williamson and new institutional economics maintain an "under-socialized" vision of the actor. The importance of opportunism is emphasized, but it is believed that this feature can be kept under control by efficient institutions, which minimize transaction costs. Some economists explicitly recognize the importance of trust for the orderly operation of economic activities, but they are more inclined to think that this problem can be resolved by the diffusion of a "generalized morality," that is, by norms of behavior strongly internalized by actors. From this point of view, they end up falling into an over-socialized conception of the actor that is similar to that of Parsonian sociology. Neither of these positions is satisfactory, according to Granovetter. They in fact tend to avoid the principal mechanism through which opportunism is restrained and moral hazard limited: "the embeddedness argument stresses instead the role of concrete personal relations and structures (or "networks") of such relations in generating trust and discouraging malfeasance" (Granovetter 1985, p. 490).

The insertion of actors in stable networks of personal relations enables information to be spread and behavior to be controlled, generating trust and rapidly isolating those who are not trustworthy. As a consequence of this approach, it is not reasonable to explain the various economic organizations as merely efficient responses to the problems of transaction costs by actors who rationally pursue their interests. This conception implies a functionalist explanation of institutions as solutions that emerge mechanically to deal with certain transaction problems. For Granovetter and the other scholars of the structural approach, these institutional arrangements are instead socially constructed, in the sense that they reflect the influence of network relations on the choices of actors.

To better understand the analytical implications of this position, it is useful to see how Williamson's framework is criticized. According to Granovetter (1985), this model tends to overestimate the capacities of hierarchy and the firm to govern complex transactions, and to underestimate those of the market. Actually, empirical evidence shows that complex and potentially risky transactions can also be carried out through the market, if networks of trust relations linking the involved parties exist and thus lower transaction costs.[5] In contrast, simple transactions taking place in competitive markets are often stable and recurrent because they are rooted in networks of personal relations between suppliers and customers. In addition, it cannot be taken for granted that internal hierarchy is always able to reduce transaction costs effectively. This is not the case if the kinds of social relations generating trust and cooperation begin to fail. Recourse to the market, hierarchy or to intermediate forms (relational contracting) will thus be influenced autonomously by the existence and features of social networks: "Other things being equal . . . we should expect pressures toward vertical integration in a market where transacting firms lack a network of personal relations that connect them or where such a network eventuates in conflict, disorder, opportunism, or malfeasance" (Granovetter 1985, p. 503).

This perspective avoids the risks of a functionalist explanation in terms of the efficiency of economic institutions. It cannot, in fact, be claimed that efficient solutions for the problems of transaction costs will emerge automatically. Institutional adaptation will be mediated by social networks, which can be more or less widespread and can take various forms. It should be remembered that social networks can hinder opportunistic or illegal behaviors, but they can also facilitate them, as, for example, in the case of criminal economics or in *insider trading* (namely, the speculative exploitation of inside information by economic operators). In addition, the importance of social networks also allows us to explain the persistence of institutional arrangements that are less efficient, but that can however be reproduced over time precisely because they are supported by consolidated social networks.

The structural approach has been applied in different fields. First, the pioneering study by Granovetter (1974) on the influence of social networks on the labor market should be mentioned. In this research Granovetter not only demonstrates the importance of informal contacts as an instrument for getting jobs, but he also draws attention to the "strength of weak ties" (Granovetter 1973, 1983). His contention is that subjects inserted into networks of weak social relations have a greater possibility of access to a larger and more diversified amount of information *vis-à-vis* those which are obtainable through "strong" ties, that is, through family or kin ties and through close friends. Acquaintances have higher chances of being inserted into social circles that are different from those of the subjects searching for a job, and can therefore put the latter in touch with diverse social and economic environments. This thesis has been widely discussed – as well as criticized – by the ensuing literature, but it has certainly shown the usefulness of the approach based on social networks, also with the aim of complementing economic models (cf. Granovetter 1995).

The contribution of the structural approach to the development of a "sociology of markets" (Swedberg 1994) has been more limited to theoretical debate. The basic idea is that the concrete networks between firms operating in a particular market (market structure) are more useful to understand their behavior than the assumptions of traditional economic models. These usually hypothesize that firms are isolated and independent from each other, merely reacting to consumers' demand. Some network-oriented studies (White 1981, 1992; Leifer and White 1987) refer to the problem of "imperfect competition" or "monopolistic markets" (see section 3.2 of ch. 6) studied by economics in the wake of the initial contributions by Chamberlin. On this view, product differentiation is a strategy adopted by firms to avoid competition by segmenting the market. However, market sociology throws light on a problem that has been largely ignored by economic investigation. This concerns the influence exercised by all firms operating in a given market on the specific strategies of product differentiation, and on the search for a niche, followed by each of these firms. In this sense, markets are seen as *cliques* of producers who keep each other under strict surveillance in order to determine the most advantageous strategy in terms of the quality and price of goods offered. In this view, markets thus respond to a logic of producers' self-reproduction rather than of efficiency in terms of satisfaction of consumer demand at lower costs.[6]

Another important group of studies, particularly developed in the United States, concerns the widespread attempt by firms to avoid competition or to keep it under control by developing networks of relations between them. These involve not only forms of ownership control and shareholdings, but also the cross-participation of representatives on the boards of directors (interlocking directorates). This has already been pointed out by Burt (1983) in his study of American manufacturing firms. Other US research has concerned the banking and finance sectors (Mintz and Schwartz 1985; Eccles and Crane 1988), and relations between political and economic elites through networks that cut through large firms, interest groups and highly prestigious social circles (Useem 1984).

Social capital

The structural approach thus underlines the influence of social networks on various forms of economic organization: the size of firms, relations between them, labor and product markets. The impact of social networks on economic activities is however differentiated. In some cases the information and trust that circulate through personal relations can limit opportunism and facilitate cooperation between actors in the market, but networks can also function as instruments to get round or avoid competition, and can thus reduce efficiency through more or less legal forms of collusion between actors. This opening up of the social networks leading to different economic outcomes is also very well exemplified in the concept of "social capital."

This concept first began to be used in the sixties, mainly in the work of Pierre Bourdieu (1980), but it was above all after the publication of James Coleman's *Foundations of Social Theory* (1990), that it came into wider use and was linked to the problems of development. However, it can be shown that the origin of the concept, even if not the term itself, is to be found even further back in time, during the period of the first developments in economic sociology. For example, an implicit use of the idea of social capital can be found in the essay by Max Weber, *The Protestant Sects and the Spirit of Capitalism* ([1906] 1991). Weber maintained that the Protestant sects had been extremely important in American growth. This influence developed through voluntary associations exercising a strong control over the individuals who were admitted to them. Members of the sects had to show certain ethical qualities which facilitated economic exchange, not only among themselves but also more generally because they provided a social recognition which external actors took into account. In other words, although he did not use the term social capital, Weber did in fact conceive the idea of social networks as an instrument to influence the formation of entrepreneurial activities, thereby facilitating the economic development of a particular area.

However, the consequences of social networks for economic activity are not always positive, as several scholars (Granovetter 1985; Coleman 1990; Portes 1998) have pointed out. They can also be an instrument to avoid or elude competition and can thus reduce efficiency by collusion between the actors. Moreover, networks that are particularly dense can exercise such a strong control over individual behavior as to discourage innovation in economic fields. Therefore it is not possible to provide an a priori definition of the effects of social capital on economic development. Only an extremely detailed and historically oriented analysis can help to clarify how cultural, political and economic variables – interacting among themselves – not only foster or obstruct social capital, but also influence the consequences for local development (Granovetter 1985, 1990). In this perspective, it is thus appropriate to set out a definition of social capital that is sufficiently open *vis-à-vis* its possible consequences on the economy.

Social capital can thus be considered as *a set of social relations on which an individual (for instance, an entrepreneur or a worker) or a collective actor (either private or public) can rely at any given moment*. Through the availability of this relational capital, cognitive resources (e.g. information) or normative resources (e.g. trust) allow actors to realize objectives which would not otherwise be realized, or which could only be obtained at a much higher cost. Moving from the individual to the aggregate level, it may also be said that a particular territorial context is more or less rich with social capital depending on the extent to which individual or collective actors of the same area are involved networks of relations. It is to be stressed that this definition, taken from Coleman (1990, p. 300), places a greater emphasis on social networks as the basis of social capital rather than on shared culture, trust and civicness, as presented in the studies by Robert Putnam (1993) and Francis Fukuyama (1995).

Coleman has underlined how this type of capital – unlike human or financial capital – has the nature of a collective good. Its advantages are not appropriable by individuals, but are enjoyed by all those participating in the network. It is for precisely this reason that individual actors have less incentive to contribute to its production. This characteristic explains, as Coleman pointed out, why "most forms of social capital are created or destroyed as a by-product of other activities" (1990, p. 317). Thus, for example, religious, ethnic, political or other associative relations can serve as a basis for the growth of social capital that can be spent in the economy. This does not exclude, as Coleman noticed, the possibility of explicit and intentional attempts to construct social capital for economic objectives. For example, in institutional economics the concept of "clan" is particularly important as a device by which to regulate the relations between firms informally, especially to deal with complex and recurrent transactions (Ouchi 1980). Nevertheless, from the point of view of local development, it is the aggregate supply of social capital in a particular region which is more important. The overall availability of networks of social relations spread between individual subjects (firms, workers) and collective actors (interest organizations, public institutions) can in fact condition paths of development.

It is precisely this characteristic which also explains why several studies, such as those by Putnam (1993) and Fukuyama (1995), tend to identify social capital with a cooperative culture and to highlight its path-dependent character, its rootedness in the past history of a region. However, the perspective followed by these works leads to two kinds of risks. First is that of slipping into a culturalist explanation which is rather vague with regard to the origins of the phenomenon, and which underestimates the role of political factors (Tarrow 1996; Mutti 1998; Bagnasco 2000). On this view social capital is in fact conceived as a contingent phenomenon, rooted in the historical process; a cultural feature of a region which is reproduced through processes of socialization, in particular through the family, the school, and associations.

This brings us to the second type of risk. As already mentioned, the consequences of social capital for economic development are not always positive, and it is precisely the under-evaluation of politics which makes it more difficult to distinguish under which conditions social capital can have a favorable impact for local development, instead of generating collusion, patronage, political dependence or even corruption and criminal economies. This distinction becomes possible if social capital is not understood generically as a willingness to cooperate based on a shared culture, but as a network of social relations open to diverse economic outcomes. It should be remembered that there is always a particularistic potential in these networks. As Coleman put it, social capital involves "resources which can be used by actors to pursue their interests" (1990, p. 305). These interests can, however, be defined in a variety of ways. Thus, in some cases social capital can generate trust and information which help economic development – and this is particularly true of situations in which, as noted above, greater flexibility is needed in the economy.

However, in other contexts the operation and consequences of the networks can be different or even opposed. These are instruments by which information and trust circulate between the subjects involved, increasing their power with respect to other external actors. As a consequence, there are situations in which the networks function at the expense of consumers or other firms, and avoid competition – a kind of collusion which has worried economists since the times of Adam Smith.

Ethnic economies can be considered as an example of this ambivalence of networks. The concentration of ethnic groups in some areas can favor the growth of economic activities through networks of firms and between local entrepreneurs and workers. On the other hand, these relationships may constitute barriers to the entrance of other subjects, or they can limit local development by placing strong social pressures on individual behavior (Portes and Sensenbrenner 1993; Portes 1998). Those networks which include criminals, but also members of the police, of the bureaucracy or politicians, are also an essential instrument of the criminal economy. The Mafia has its own social capital, which is particularly important given the illegal nature of its activities.

In order to avoid these two types of risks in the use of social capital, it might be more productive to focus on the conditions that may foster positive effects for economic development. To proceed along this path one should not only ask whether networks of social relations tied to family, kinship, ethnic religious communities do exist, but whether politics has favored their transformation into positive resources for local development. It is precisely this question that has remained unanswered in the debate surrounding social capital. The answer would seem to lie in the capacity of politics to modernize itself, that is, to function according to more universal principles that balance and control the particularism that is intrinsic to networks. This means that one should assess whether networks are faced with cultural and institutional barriers blocking their attempts to appropriate political resources (whether regulatory or distributive) in a particularistic way; and whether they are encouraged to work in the economic rather than in the political market. If this does not happen, and if politics is not modernized, the rule of law is not well established and state structure are not effective, there will instead be a trend to form networks developing along the path that Weber called political capitalism, based on a predatory use of political resources. On the other hand, a modern politics, more autonomous from particularistic interests, increases its capacity to provide collective goods that are essential for economic development (e.g. infrastructures, services, security, rule of law, etc.). It is within this framework that the social networks can function as a resource for local development: because they may be used in the economic sphere, they contribute to the widening of the market, and they have a positive impact on its operation through the provision of information and trust.

At this point a second factor which fosters the positive effects of local networks can be introduced: the market. Once local development has been triggered, the pressure from competition continually limits the possible negative consequences of particularism. First of all, it tends to sanction inefficient behavior. If several members of the network, for example relatives, or immigrants of the same ethnic groups, who work in a firm, or as subcontractors, diverge too much from efficient behavior, competition on the market signals this disfunction rapidly and forces them to change. Secondly, the market sends signals that suggest an updating and redefinition of social capital. Certain characteristics of the social network can function well in a given period, but can constitute a constraint in a successive moment and therefore require a change. For example, certain kinship relations initially useful in the first stages of development can act subsequently as a constraint and need to be integrated with different networks, based more on cooperation between collective subjects (e.g. interest organizations, public institutions). Naturally, the market sends signals, but it does not guarantee that new and appropriate solutions will emerge. This depends on the ability of the local actors to interpret the situation and to deal with it, by generating new forms of social capital. If an appropriate reaction does not take place, regressive localism and risks of "lock in" can occur (see Grabher 1993).

These observations suggest that the relation between social capital and local development is complex and may change over time. The positive role of social structures, such as family, kinship, community, or religious, political and ethnic subcultures, as resources for development has been widely discussed in this regard, reversing some assumptions of modernization theory (see chapter 7). However, their relationship with economic development seems more complex and variable. What makes the difference is the combination of these phenomena with a modernized politics and more effective state structures and bureaucracies. This is, for instance, the lesson that can be drawn from recent experiences of regional development in East and South-East Asia in comparison to other backward areas, as the new comparative political economy has shown (Evans 1996, Woolcock 1998).

Sociological neo-institutionalism

In the structural approach, the actor's location in the structure of social relations is crucial to understand his or her actions. This also explains why a strong contrast with the theory of rational choice is not perceived in the work by Granovetter (1985) or in the way in which social capital is conceived by Coleman (1990, 1994). The position of the neo-institutionalists in the new economic sociology is different from that of the structuralists, because they want instead to highlight the autonomous role played by cultural factors in motivating actors. While for structuralists networks determine resources and constraints that condition the rational pursuit of interests by actors, for neo-institutionalists cultural factors contribute to defining the interests themselves and the procedures by which they may be pursued by actors (Friedland and Alford 1991). They draw attention not only to the structural (network-based) embeddedness of action, but also to cognitive, cultural, and political embeddedness (Zukin and DiMaggio 1990).

The theory of action of neo-institutionalism is thus wider than that of the structuralists, and it is multi-dimensional. In this case, criticism of new institutional economics is accompanied by "an interest in institutions as independent variables, a turn toward cognitive and cultural explanations, and an interest in properties of supraindividual units of analysis . . ." (Powell and DiMaggio 1991b, p. 8). It is as well to specify that this position is critical of the "over-socialized" theory of the actor *à la* Parsons. However, unlike structuralism, it does not devalue the role of culture but aims at redefining it under the influence of the turn towards the micro-sociology that was favored by Garfinkel's ethnomethodology (1967), by the phenomenological approach (Berger and Luckmann 1967), as well as by cognitive psychology. This leads to emphasizing the cognitive dimension of institutions as opposed to the normative one (in the terms that have already been described – see section 2.2, chapter 6 – it can be said that more importance is given to "constitutive" rather than "regulative" rules). In other words, the role played by routines – by informal rules of behavior largely taken for granted – is now more carefully investigated; as are shared schemas and frames or rituals helping to define identities and individual interests, as well as the procedures for following them, that is, the "regulatory" rules.

How does the neo-institutionlist approach explain the different forms of economic organization? In this case, criticism of different forms of new institutional economics – that is to say, of considering institutions as efficient responses pursued by rational actors to reduce transaction costs – leads to underlining the legitimacy of organizational choices. Attention is drawn to the appropriateness of action with respect to prevailing frames. In other words, in the face of a lack of information and risks of transactions, it is hard for actors to follow a rigorous rational choice for the most efficient solutions. For this reason, neo-institutionalists are particularly interested in explaining the social processes influencing homogeneity in economic organization. This perspective enables the inertia of organizational structures to be explained even when they lose economic efficiency. Structuralists share this aim. However, in contrast to them attention is not placed so much on the embeddedness of organizational models in social networks as on the persistence of standards of behavior believed to be appropriate (Powell and DiMaggio 1991b; Meyer and Rowan 1991).

A good example of the analytical consequences resulting from the neo-institutionalist approach is the work on "isomorphism" by Powell and DiMaggio (1991c). They attempt to explain the homogeneity of models in certain "organizational fields." These are formed by the set of actors who play a role in a particular field of activity. Concerning the economy, for example, an organizational field covers not only firms competing in a particular sector, but also those providing services, regulative state agencies, union and business organizations, etc. If these actors are analyzed as an interdependent set of units, even though they do not always directly interact among themselves, it is possible to understand how appropriate standards of behavior are formed. Powell and DiMaggio criticize the ecological theory of organizations (Hannan and Freeman 1977, 1989) – inspired by Darwinian orientations – according to which homogeneity in a particular field (for example, in a productive sector) reflects the selection of units that are better adapted to the features of the external environment in which they move. This occurs more frequently in sectors that are open to market competition, where "competitive isomorphism" is stronger, although even in these sectors "institutional isomorphism" is at work (DiMaggio 1994). Of course, the influence of the institutional model is stronger in fields that are further away from the competitive market. The first, and most obvious, form of institutional isomorphism is "coercive." Public regulations (including anti-trust and labor and safety regulations) can lead to compulsory constraints on adopting an organizational model; but industrial relations can also act in this direction. A coercive influence is also exercised by stronger organizations on those that are more dependent on them (for example, purchasing firms *vis-à-vis* their sub-suppliers). "Normative isomorphism" is instead linked to the role of universities and business schools for training managers, or to consulting firms. Managers, both on account of their career mobility and because of their networks of interaction, contribute to spreading professional standards of behavior that take on a high level of legitimacy and are therefore more readily followed by firms. Finally, there is "mimetic isomorphism," especially in sectors where the organizational units are small and have limited resources to evaluate the most efficient solutions. In this case it is likely that to reduce the level of uncertainty models which seem more appropriate, and are thus more legitimated in the organizational field, will be followed. Naturally, the different forms of isomorphism can in reality be combined between each other, reinforcing the pressure to adopt a particular model.[7]

In empirical research, this approach has stimulated numerous contributions in sectors that are not affected by market competition, such as non-profit and cultural organizations (DiMaggio 1987, 1991; Powell and Friedkin 1987; Brint and Karabel 1991), as well as financial institutions and large accounting firms (Montagna 1990). In the industrial field, Fligstein's work (1990), on the productive diversification of large American firms treated as an "organizational field," provided an interesting application of this approach. He showed how the choice of diversifying during last century was initially stimulated by an initial shock (the Great Depression and, following this, the anti-trust action taken by the government). However, organizational innovation first occurred where top management came from marketing or finance departments, and not from previous experiences in productive structures. Once a certain organizational model was adopted by many firms, massive changes tied to isomorphic pressures of the mimetic and normative type were triggered, with the result that new appropriate standards were set.

Another interesting field of application involves the comparison of various forms of economic organization in Japan, South Korea and Taiwan (Orrù, Biggart, and Hamilton 1991). This study shows that the existence of groups of firms with different characteristics in each of these countries cannot be merely explained in terms of efficiency in transaction costs, or in terms of late industrialization. The existence of networks of firms that are strongly isomorphic within each country, but different between countries, can be traced to the influence exercised by specific institutional factors, both cultural and political. Moreover, this work underlines not only that isomorphic trends tied to national institutions are important for organizational units like firms, but also that they must not necessarily be viewed as contrasting with economic efficiency. On the contrary, the success of the countries in question can be explained by their ability to take advantage of their specific institutional resources to promote economic development (see also section 3, ch. 7). This is an extremely important aspect to which I shall return in the discussion on globalization and varieties of capitalism, in the next chapter.

Contrasting models

Summing up, neo-institutionalists criticize institutional economics, underlining the role played by cultural and political factors. Their framework, however, is wider than that of the structuralists, who concentrate mainly on the role of social networks. However, it is also true that in concrete research practices, these differences in the new economic sociology become weaker. In any case, in facing the challenge posed by the new economic theories, there is a common tendency to underline the social and cultural embeddedness of economic action, and the consequences for the variety of organizational models. The shared view is that such variety cannot be explained if "human factors" – to use Williamson's terms – are considered as though they were "natural" bio-psychological features of actors. They are rather to be analyzed as social and historical variables.

The traditional and long-standing divergence between economics and economic sociology is raised once again in these micro level studies. Williamson is aware of the complications to which the consideration of human factors as socially conditioned can lead in the calculation of transaction costs. Indeed, he introduced the concept of "transactional atmosphere" into his original model to emphasize how "transactional attitudes are strongly influenced by the socio-political system in which exchanges take place" (Williamson 1975, 1983, p. 39). However, he later dropped analyzing the implications to which this perspective could give rise. This seems largely due to the problems of operationalizing transaction costs and developing stronger generalizations on the governance of economic activities (Williamson 1985). In other words, his concern – shared widely by economists – is with building analytical models that can be formalized and provide more general parsimonious explanations. However, the advantages of these models face some clear shortcomings when the concrete variety of organizational forms is to be explained. Sheer consideration of the complexity-uncertainty degree of transactions is not sufficient to this end. Under the same condition of "asset specificity," actors could rely on the market, hierarchy or relational contracting, answering in a variable mix and to a different extent. In fact, the choice is influenced by the social quality of the actors – that is, by their cognitive and normative attitudes that vary in relation to the institutional context.

For these reasons, the new economic sociology is more oriented towards comparative analysis and the development of "local models" that can give a better account of the variability of contexts. In this perspective, there are clear similarities between the research-driven approach stimulated by the study of new flexible models and theory-driven studies. In both cases economic sociology points to the social construction processes that may explain the variety of economic organization. As Granovetter underlines (1990, p. 106): "outcomes can vary dramatically even for the *same* economic problems and technologies, if the social structure, institutional history, and collective action are different. . . . Less contingent arguments are cleaner, simpler and more elegant. But they fail to identify causal mechanisms."

Naturally, for this approach there are some possible shortcomings, too. The first, mentioned by Granovetter, is the risk of "sliding along the slimy slope leading to historicism" (ibid. p. 33). To avoid this danger, it seems necessary to strengthen the interaction between theory and research. This can help develop theoretical models more consistent with the high contingency of economic organization. However, there is also a second danger to cope with – that of confusing theoretical arguments with empirical explanations. This, in fact, leads to an underestimation of the specific contribution of economic factors to the emergence and reproduction of organizational models, and therefore to a symmetrical defect with respect to that of economic models. Without any integration between economic and sociocultural factors, it is difficult to provide an effective picture of the concrete variety of economic organization.

4 Culture and Consumption

In both the structuralist and the neo-institutionalist approaches, the new developments of economic sociology at the micro level were mainly concentrated on the production of goods and services. The theme of consumption has not received much attention, despite its importance within the tradition of economic sociology (see section 2.3, ch. 6). This might in part be explained by the fact that many authors close to neo-institutionalism came from the background of organizational studies. In any case, the limited interest in the study of consumers behavior is a serious shortcoming, especially if one takes into account that changes in consumption patterns seem to have played an important role in the emergence of flexible productive organization (Piore and Sabel 1984), and more in general in the difficulties encountered by Keynesian policies.[8] However, some interesting studies have highlighted the influence of cultural factors on consumption behavior over the past few decades. Even though this work is not directly connected to neo-institutionalism, it was largely inspired by the same background. Some of the authors involved come from sociology, but many are anthropologists or social historians.

We have seen how the economic sociology tradition is different from the mainstream neoclassic approach. Attention is given to the influence of sociocultural factors in the formation of preferences and in the choice of means by which the actors attempt to satisfy them. The symbolic value of goods is therefore underlined: they are chosen and consumed largely for the meaning they acquire in social relations. Consumption is viewed as an essential component of the processes of identification with other social groups, with which a certain lifestyle is shared, and at the same time of differentiation with other groups. With respect to this tradition, more recent developments are characterized by a twofold tendency. On the one hand, more recent studies seem less influenced by the Veblenian model that closely linked consumption to competition for social status. On the other, they are also critical of those models that stress the passive subordination of consumers to the choices imposed by firms and supported by advertising and mass media. It may be useful, therefore, to distinguish between an approach which emphasizes the search for social differentiation and another that is more interested in the role of culture in shaping consumers' behavior.

With regard to the first approach, the work of Jean Baudrillard (1968, 1970) should be mentioned. Following Veblen, he underlines the role of competition for status in consumers' behavior patterns. In contemporary society, the logic underlying social differentiation is, however, further exacerbated by the weakening of traditional forms of identification (based on family, local community, or status groups). In addition, the consumer models by which actors tend to differentiate themselves are increasingly mediated by mass media. In this situation single individuals identify themselves socially by consumer objects and are constantly involved in the manipulation of such objects as signs, that is, as the carriers of a symbolic value in terms of adhesion to certain cultural models through which to distinguish themselves. Consumers have the illusion of freely choosing between these models, but in reality they are strongly conditioned by the media system that imposes them. In this sense, they are social robots that adapt passively to stimuli coming from the external environment.

Pierre Bourdieu's approach (1979) is slightly different. For him too, consumer behavior responds to a logic of competition for status, pushing individuals to identify with the particular life styles and tastes of certain groups in order to differentiate themselves from others. However, in this case attention does not focus on the media, but on the influence exercised on individuals as a result of their position in the social stratification system. This differs from the Veblenian model in the more complex and multidimensional explanation given to "social distinction." This is linked to the attempt to reconstruct social stratification in a more complex and sophisticated way by introducing – together with the economic capital possessed by each individual – cultural capital (inherited from the family and bought through education) and social capital (linked to networks of relations). From the combination of these different dimensions a very detailed picture of social groups emerges. These are distinguished from each other by highly specific lifestyles, which involve consumer patterns: clothes, home furnishings, food, sport as well as aesthetic and artistic taste or cultural activities. It is thus through belonging to the same social group – defined by the combination of different types of capital possessed – that the formation of a particular *habitus* is favored. This results from a set of dispositions and orientations that shape lifestyles and consumption patterns, and becomes an important instrument in social differentiation. Single actors still do not, however, seem to have any margins of autonomy in the consumer sphere, although for reasons that are partly different from those highlighted by Baudrillard. For the latter, it is the media that defines the standards in the competition for status; for Bourdieu, it is the social groups sharing the same *habitus* that do so (or as Weber would have said, the status groups).

In contrast to the approach insisting on differentiation, the other sort of studies, which is closer to neo-institutionalism, focuses on the role of cultural factors in shaping consumption more than on competition for status, and underlines the active role of actors. In this perspective, consumption is by necessity seen as "eminently social, relational and active rather than private, atomistic or passive" (Appadurai 1986, p. 31). A particularly important contribution has been made in this direction in the work by Mary Douglas and Baron Isherwood (1979). The focal point in this is the symbolic value of goods, *vis-à-vis* their functional utility in consumer choices. In this case, however, emphasis is placed on the role that objects play in the relationship between actors and the cultural values prevailing in a given context, as signs of identification, or detachment, or even of opposition. For example, this can be seen in the formation of subcultures (youth, ethnic, political, religious, etc.). In other words, the objects that are chosen serve to construct people's identities, to give a sense to their experience and to communicate with others, not necessarily to compete with them. An interesting example of this perspective can be found in the work of Sahlins (1976) on food consumption and clothes in the American case.

Consumption is thus also a fundamental field where the battle is fought to define values, to give form to the basic frames of reference for social organization: "Instead of supposing that goods are necessary essentially for subsistence or competitive exhibition, let us hypothesize that they are necessary to make cultural categories visible and stable" (Douglas and Isherwood 1979, p. 59). It is in this context that Douglas highlights the greater autonomy of the consumer from the influence of the market and fashion. This feature has also been underlined by Daniel Miller (1987), who drew attention to the possibility of active "strategies" of consumers, and to experiences that allow them to resist the cultural influence of mass consumption and to contrast the commodification of social relations.

Viviana Zelizer (1988) is also particularly sensitive to the theme of market influence. In her view, the new sociology of consumption tries to distinguish itself from the conception of a " boundless market" (that is, from the idea of a progressive diffusion of utilitarian and individualistic values. She criticizes the view that the market exercises a standardized and homogenizing effect on actors' behavior. The market is not only not conditioned by social networks (a view typical of the structural approach), but is strongly influenced by cultural factors. This is particularly apparent in consumer behavior. For example, Zelizer has shown how in some markets for goods considered to be "sacred" – linked to life and death – cultural factors play an important autonomous role in orienting consumers' behavior and the value of the goods. She used this approach in her pioneer study of the life insurance market, in which consumption is influenced by the prevailing conceptions of the value of human life (Zelizer 1983), and in the study of the "child market" (adoptions, insurance, "sales," etc.), which is also affected by the variable value attached to children's lives over space and time (Zelizer 1987). According to Zelizer, moreover, cultural factors can be seen not only in particular markets, like those mentioned above, but also in the use of money as a standardized means of exchange, utilized in different contexts according to different and specific rules. Rules reflect particular cultural frames, for example, according to whether money is used for gifts, for domestic use, or for charity (Zelizer 1994).

In conclusion, then, we can say that new approaches have emerged also in the sphere of consumption, which can be linked to the new economic sociology. Some of them underline the structural embeddedness of choices (again the work by Bourdieu); others, coming from various backgrounds, emphasize more the autonomous role played by cultural factors. These studies also tend to limit the importance that the model of competition for status, inherited from the tradition of the classics, has had on the sociology of consumption in the past. While the attention devoted to cultural factors tends indirectly to link this approach to sociological neo-institutionalism, it should however be noted that the relationship between consumer behavior trends and the variety of economic organization is still substantially unexplored. Recent tendencies in the sociology of consumption attribute a more active role to consumers in defining their choices and in contrasting the influence of firms, advertising, and media. This emphasis seems to be largely in line with those processes of qualitative and quantitative differentiation of demand that have been underlined by scholars studying the emergence of new models of flexible organization. However, a research strategy aimed at linking these trends in consumption and production has been lacking so far in the new economic sociology. Therefore, this problem has been mainly analyzed by marketing studies.

Chapter 10

Globalization and the Diversity of Capitalisms

In the last chapter the development of economic sociology over the last thirty years was described, and the differences between comparative political economy at the macro level and the new branches of study at the micro level were examined. In this conclusive chapter I will look at several of the more recent trends that have attempted to integrate the two approaches. The objective of this literature is to define different models of national capitalism, characterized by a particular institutional context. Attention is thus focused on economic policies, in particular studies of neo-corporatism, and on models of productive organization, and therefore on the results of research on flexibility. As we shall see, these studies tended initially to highlight the advantages of "coordinated market economies," that is, a model of capitalism that is more organized, as in the Japanese or German types, *vis-à-vis* the "non-coordinated market economies," prevailing in Anglo-Saxon settings.

However, particularly since the end of the eighties, these advantages have been questioned. This is because there have been signs of recovery and dynamism in the British and American economies, and, more generally, because of a need to account for the phenomenon of globalization. The growing interdependence and integration of economies at the global level seems to threaten the more organized models of the economy, where markets are restrained by other forms of regulation. Anglo-Saxon capitalism – which is more dependent on the market – instead shows signs of superior adaptation to this new situation, at least in the short term. A new debate has opened on the possible impact of globalization on the different regulatory systems of economic activities, that is, on the national varieties of capitalism. In this discussion economic sociology warns against accepting uncritically any hypothesis about a progressive institutional convergence induced by globalization. In the arguments presented to support this view, the specificity of its approach and the importance it gives to the autonomous role of institutions, and thus to society, in orienting economic activities, can be seen.

1 Two Types of Capitalism

During the seventies the principal problem with which the economies of the developed countries had to grapple was that of inflation. In chapter 8 we saw that the neo-corporatist model attempted to show that arrangements between governments and large organized interests could resolve these issues, with both inflation and unemployment remaining relatively low. However, the "government by decree" model, based on greater autonomy of the state from organized interests, also managed to achieve good results in terms of control over these variables. In the case of pluralist systems – especially in the United States and the United Kingdom – it was more difficult to control inflation and this led to higher levels of unemployment, particularly in the early eighties. However, once the inflation issue had been resolved, attention moved towards another feature that seemed to have an increasingly strong influence over economic development: firms' ability to innovate. Given these developments, comparative political economy tended to converge with studies on the transformation of Fordism and new flexible models.

At the beginning of the eighties, the ability of firms in a particular country to compete on the international market became even more important for economic development and employment.[1] The boundaries of different national economies began to open up, and these began to feel the influence of other countries more strongly. A growing share of production was oriented towards international markets, and the income of a country became more dependent on the ability of its firms to compete with imports in domestic markets and to export to foreign ones. At the beginning of the nineties, a series of studies focused on the reactions of different types of national capitalism to the new challenges posed by this situation (Soskice 1990, 1993; Dore 1987; Streeck 1992; Hollingsworth, Schmitter, and Streeck 1994; Hollingsworth and Boyer 1997a).

In one of the first analyses of the ability of national economies to adapt to international integration, David Soskice (1990) pointed to the limits of the neo-corporatist model in the new situation. The crucial problem was no longer the control of inflation but the balance of payments, that is, the capacity of national firms to innovate and increase exports in relation to imports, in the context of a slower overall growth of the world economy and greater competition between producers. In doing this, it was not enough to focus on the institutions that regulated wages, that is, on industrial relations at the central level, as in the neo-corporatist model. Wage moderation and inflation control, achieved through centralized agreements between governments and encompassing interest organizations, were not sufficient to maintain employment. This last was now more dependent on the capacity of firms to innovate, maintain, and increase their market shares on the international market. This, in turn, required a particular institutional context favoring adjustment towards flexible and quality production, both of which were aimed at reducing price competition coming from developing countries with low labor costs.

Given this perspective, the macro and micro approaches discussed in the two previous chapters began to integrate more closely. The dependent variable – the problem at the center of the investigation – ceased to be the control of inflation or unemployment, as it had been for the first models of comparative political economy. The emphasis instead moved to firms' innovation capacity, on which depended the penetration of the domestic and international market, and therefore the income and unemployment of the country. As a result, the set of causal factors also changed – the independent variables – and extended from the institutions influencing macro-economic policies and the control of aggregate labor costs (in particular, industrial relations at the macro level) to those conditioning innovation by firms at the micro level: finance, corporate governance, the role of management, the regulation of labor relations, the training of workers, and the availability of services for firms. It is precisely the diversity of the institutional environment that leads to different models of national capitalism with respect to their capacity to adapt to the international market. To illustrate the adjustment I will proceed by focusing on the conditions facilitating firms' innovation, and will then move to the influence of different institutional contexts on the outcomes.

Firms' innovation capacity

Soskice (1990) indicated five conditions on which the capacity of firms in the more developed countries depends if they are to move towards flexible quality production, in order to avoid price competition tied to the cost of labor.

1   First is a *long-term managerial strategy*. Innovation is a risky process requiring time and investments with a deferred return. Managers with a long-term horizon, and evaluated on this basis, can better promote innovation.
2   The improvement in the quality of goods is linked to innovation of the process and product requiring high *levels of professional competence*, on the part of both management and also labor. The training of human resources needs to be continually updated.
3   Together with competencies, the *capacity for cooperation between management and workers* is equally important. Innovation now requires a stronger involvement of workers in the pursuit of the firm's objectives, overcoming the rigid hierarchies of the Fordist system.
4   Finally, to achieve flexible production of quality goods a high *capacity of cooperation with customers and sub-suppliers* is also crucial. This allows information to be exchanged and favors innovation through trust relations, in a context in which the costs of the development of new products are high and their yield on the market brief.
5   Together with these factors, which influence non-price competitiveness, the role played by *wage containment* is also important. If wage increases exceed productivity growth, overall efforts to innovate are clearly compromised.

The next step is that of showing that these conditions are not determined simply by the voluntary choices of firms' managers, but are favored or hindered by the institutional context, that is, by a series of institutions that act at the macro and micro levels, and that are closely interrelated between each other. The literature on the varieties of capitalism underlined two aspects of this phenomenon. First, the non-contractual origins of institutions are highlighted. These slowly developed through history and are not reducible to the rational choice of efficient solutions by actors. As a result, there is a certain amount of integration and coherence between them – an "institutional logic" – also reflecting a common cultural matrix formed over a long period of time (Hollingsworth and Boyer 1997b). Studies of varieties of capitalism share, in this respect, the position of sociological neo-institutionalism and its criticism of new institutional economics, as discussed in the previous chapter. This leads to a vision of institutional change in which capacity to change in the face of new challenges is structured by the preceding historical path (path dependency) (Zysman 1994).[2] The institutional legacy inherited from the past is not very flexible (this point will be taken up again below, to discuss the impact of globalization on institutions).

The second aspect, the national dimension, is emphasized by the literature on varieties of capitalism. The historical path is seen as having shaped the institutional legacy, and this leads to a recognition of the continuing role played by each nation-state in forging an institutional complex that is both specific and integrated (Zysman 1994, 1995). For example, research on the regulation mechanisms of economic sectors in various countries highlighted how these are organized in different ways. Different sectors within the same country show some organizational similarities, clearly influenced by the national institutional context (Hollingsworth, Schmitter, and Streeck 1994).[3]

In other words, the organization of sectors is affected by a sort of contextual or "societal effect" which cuts across technological or market specificities (Maurice, Sellier, and Silvestre 1984). Naturally, this does not mean that the sub-national dimension (in particular, the regional dimension) cannot also be important. As we saw in the preceding chapter, it tends to become even more important with models of flexible organization; the development of industrial districts is a particularly clear example of this. However, in this case too, the national dimension of institutions needs to be examined in order to understand the phenomenon (Trigilia 1997).

The institutional conditions of competitiveness

How do different institutional contexts influence the innovation process? According to studies of varieties of capitalism, the situation of developed countries can be traced to two ideal types. Soskice (1990), for example, distinguishes between "co-ordinated market economies" and "non-coordinated market economies." The first type features a regulation system in which the market role is more limited *vis-à-vis* the state or associations. Although there are differences between them, Central and Northern European countries can be singled out as forming part of this group: Germany, Austria, Switzerland, The Netherlands, and the Scandinavian countries. Japan is also considered close to this model. Non-coordinated economies, in which the role played by market regulation is more extensive, include the Anglo-Saxon countries, the United States and the United Kingdom, as well as Canada, Australia, and New Zealand.

The differentiation between these two types, and the other countries that are similar, has been taken up by other studies. In particular, the essay by Michel Albert, *Capitalism against Capitalism* ([1991] 1993), has been remarkably influential, with the distinction he makes between the "Anglo-Saxon" model and the

"German–Japanese model" (this last is also known as the "Rhine model"). The labels used by Albert highlight how ideal types can be especially useful for comparison between the market capitalism of Anglo-Saxon countries and the more organized kind typical of Germany and Japan, that is, the countries which were most successful during the eighties (the classification of other countries is more residual and uncertain[4]). In reality, studies on the varieties of capitalism aim to show that coordinated economies, or capitalisms of the Rhine–Japanese kind, have given rise to institutional contexts that were more favorable to firm innovation. They mainly attempted to clarify the institutional bases of the economic success of Germany and Japan during the eighties.

In what way do coordinated market economies favor innovation? To answer this question, several institutional dimensions need to be analyzed.

1   First comes *the financial system and corporate governance of firms.* This has a particularly strong influence on innovation. In non-coordinated economies, firms were usually financed through the stock market. They were more frequently quoted on the stock exchange, particularly the larger firms, and ownership of the capital was shared between different actors: investment funds, private investors, or also members of the families that originally owned the firm. At all events, these actors were not usually tied to firms by long-term traditions. As a result, the decision to keep or sell shares was more influenced by evaluations of their return in the short term. This tended to discourage managerial strategies oriented towards the long term, and therefore might obstruct the kind of innovation requiring investments with a riskier and delayed return. The high risk of hostile takeovers put pressure on top management and favored the search for short-term profitability, also through the development of financial activities. In fact, a change in ownership might entail replacement of the management.

In the coordinated market economies, and in particular in Germany and Japan, the stock market was considerably less developed than the Anglo-Saxon countries. The long-term financing requirements of firms were mainly satisfied by the banks. In addition, firms, particularly large ones, were owned by a small group of share holders, in which banks and other financial institutions played an important role (in Japan the large groups – *keiretsu* – all have a bank in their internal structures). These actors tended to have a long-standing relation with the firms, and were able to monitor the prospects of profitability in the long term, and had an interest in doing so. In addition, especially in Europe, the active role of banks in many firms increased their capacity to influence managerial strategies. In this situation the management was less threatened by the risks of hostile takeovers, since these were made more difficult by the institutional rules prevailing in the legal system. As a result, top managers were instead more encouraged to undertake investments and projects in the longer term, on whose yield they were then evaluated by the shareholders.

Of course, the institutional structure of Rhine–Japanese capitalism does lead to some shortcomings too. "Patient" capital can constitute a weak stimulus for management, while the "impatience" of the stock market exercises a stricter control over the efficiency of industrial management. I shall return to this discussion below. For the moment it is enough to underline how studies of varieties of capitalism highlight an important difference in the functioning of the economy. In one case institutional regulations give more influence to the shareholders. These actors have a determining power over the firm's strategies and tend to consider it as a "network of contracts" aimed at maximizing short-term profit. The other model is very different. The influence of the stakeholders – the management and workers – is much greater. Indeed, the whole conception of firms, as Albert points out ([1991] 1933), is different. In the German case it is a true "community of interests," and even if its origins and cultural connotations are different, the idea of the firm as a community is even more marked in the Japanese case. I shall come back to this because it is tied to the regulation of labor relations in the firm.

2   Another important institutional dimension that differentiates the two forms of capitalism has to do with the regulation of *occupational training*. This aspect influences both the competition of workers and the scope for acquiring the various kinds of skills that will allow them to carry out different tasks and to participate more actively in production, contributing to both flexibility and quality. In non-coordinated market economies, specific components of this training were more dependent on firms linked to the particular type of production in which workers were used. More general skills were bought by individual workers on the market. However, financial institutions were usually unwilling to make loans to individuals without guarantees for an activity like training, whose future value is difficult to evaluate in advance. All this leads to a more limited supply of occupational training with respect to the needs of innovation. Firms will not invest in it, beyond their specific and immediate requirements, for fear that workers can then leave them for other firms which did not contribute to their training. The more the management is oriented towards short-term profitability, the more this is the dominant trend. In addition, given the uncertainty, individuals will be less encouraged to improve their basic skill.

Occupational training poses a problem typical of collective good production. Individual firms and workers have no interest in contributing beyond a limited extent to the production of this good on which depends both the capacity of innovation of firms and the well-being of the workers themselves. In coordinated market economies the problem is resolved not only with a greater commitment by the state to training, which is offered as a public service (as, for instance, in the German, Swedish, and Japanese cases), but above all through forms of cooperation with firms and their organizations. To prevent basic training from becoming remote from firms' concrete needs, it is necessary for them to be involved in training programs, for example through incentives to include workers in practical experience, as happens in the case of apprenticeships in Germany. In Japan, the initial training does not lead to skills which are useable on the market at the level of industrial sector, as it is in Germany, since these are much more closely linked to the technical and organizational requirements of the specific firm to which the worker is tied by a long-term relationship. Also, regulatory systems which tend to stabilize labor relations – either through the formal industrial relations system as in Germany and the Nordic (Scandinavian) countries, or the use of lifelong jobs as in the large Japanese firms – constitute a greater incentive for firms to invest in the occupational training of their employees, who cannot be dismissed as easily as in Anglo-Saxon capitalism.

3   This last feature is closely tied to another institutional dimension, that of *industrial relations at the firm level*, which influences cooperation between management and workers. We have seen that in non-coordinated market economies the financial mechanisms and the corporate governance provide incentives for a more short-term orientation by management. This trend was strengthened by a system of industrial relations characterized by weak unions and weak legal regulation of dismissal. Both factors encouraged firms to be extremely flexible in terms of hiring and firing. In other words, the workforce was increased or reduced according to the needs of short-term profitability. However, this also entailed greater difficulty in developing a relationship of stable cooperation and of active involvement on the part of labor and middle management. In other words, it was increasingly difficult to improve "functional flexibility" (adaptability to different tasks). Consequently, one of the crucial resources for innovation in the area of flexible and quality production tended to be scarce.[5]

How was this problem dealt with in the coordinated economies? Mainly through the system regulating labor relations, partly dependent on bargaining between unions and employers' associations in the area of industrial relations, and partly dependent on labor law and legal rules. This system was generally more rigid in comparison to the other model, in the sense that it imposed more constraints on "numerical flexibility" (freedom to employ and dismiss workers) and recognized a more active role for union representatives in the running of firms (in Europe this took place through the representation of highly centralized national unions at a plant level, while in Japan enterprise unions prevailed). The regulation of labor relations discouraged workers' mobility, although it did favor functional flexibility within firms, unlike the other model. Not only were firms given incentives to invest more in training to take full advantage of human resources of which they cannot free themselves easily in downturns, but the greater stability of employment encouraged the involvement of workers and the development of flexible forms of work organization. This was also because of stronger institutional guarantees that commitment and involvement would be remunerated. In the Japanese case too, the role played by institutional rules (in particular, life employment, the internal labor market, pay systems tied to the firm's performance) were no less important than traditional cultural orientations in assuring the cooperation of the work force.

4   In dealing with flexible production models we have already seen how important cooperative relations with customers and suppliers are for these forms of productive organization. In this regard, Soskice underlined that non-coordinated market economies were usually less rich in *informal and formal social networks tied to business associations*. These last are important for the production and circulation of information and trust necessary for innovation, especially in an economic context in which speed and costs of introducing new products or models were growing, while their yield over time in the market was decreasing. Therefore, the economic value of cooperation rose. Since Anglo-Saxon capitalism tended to rely more on both the market and hierarchy as regulatory mechanisms, this limited their capacity for innovation through cooperation. The opposite happened for coordinated market economies. In this case, networks of cooperation based on informal rela-

tions and the diffusion of business associations were more widespread. Just as in the case of professional training, this institutional dimension enabled another collective good that is important for economic performance to be supplied, even if in different ways. In Northern Europe, business associations and informal networks promoted forms of cooperation above all at the industrial sector level (for example, for training, transfer of technology or industrial relations); in the Japanese case, instead, cooperation mainly occurred at the level of large industrial groups – *keiretsu* (Soskice 1993,1999).

5 The final institutional dimension concerns the problem of wage containment. The coordinated market economies usually used forms of wage control based on centralized bargaining between strong unions, employers organizations and governments. However, Soskice also highlighted, making reference to the Japanese case, how similar results in terms of effective containment are also possible through decentralized industrial relations and company unions that share the firms' objectives and are institutionally integrated in their internal structure. But, in non-coordinated economies, however, where unions are weak, wage control depended to a greater extent on the diffusion of unemployment as a regulatory mechanism of workers' wage claims. This may have shortcomings to the extent that the needs for firms to rely on highly skilled workers increases. In this situation it is more costly to dismiss workers who possess firm-specific skills and to replace them with unemployed people who do not. This is particularly true in non-coordinated economies because they usually provide, as we have seen, lower levels of marketable skills among workers. As the "insider–outsider approach" (Lindbeck and Snower 1988) shows, the power of employed workers is thus stronger even where there are high levels of unemployment. In the non-coordinated systems, which allow the job market to determine wage levels, firms can thus find themselves in a difficult dilemma. They can invest in professional skills to deal with the requirements of innovation, but this would raise the cost of labor, since workers would be more inclined to exploit their market power because of the lower job stability. The other choice is not to invest, taking advantage of lower wages through the easier substitution of the employed workforce, but at the cost of depressing the resources for innovation.[6]

On the whole, the set of phenomena considered above shows us two ideal types of economic system with different institutional frames. In addition, as Albert has underlined ([1991] 1993, ch. 7), the institutional differences also involved state intervention in the social field and the impact of regulatory systems of labor relations on social inequalities. It is true that in among coordinated economies, i.e. Rhine–Japanese capitalism, there are several important differences (see section 1.1, chapter 8). In the Rhine component public welfare and redistribution through fiscal measures were more extended than in the Japanese one, where fiscal pressure was lower and company welfare more important. However, in all coordinated economies social inequalities were lower than in the Anglo-Saxon cases: differences of income and welfare between various social groups were more contained. This diversity seems to reflect, in the final analysis, a cultural legacy which was more highly influenced by liberalism and individualism in the Anglo-Saxon type, while the more organized forms of capitalism were all influenced by cultural legacies that emphasize collective responsibility in shaping individual life chances.

The joint consideration of the economic and social features of Rhine–Japanese capitalism has led scholars working on the varieties of capitalism to underline the competitive advantage of this model *vis-à-vis* the Anglo-Saxon one. This latter was more based on the market as a system of economic and social regulation – particularly after the neo-liberal turn triggered during the eighties by President Reagan in the United States and Mrs Thatcher in the United Kingdom. In addition, at a more theoretical level, it was pointed out that the market tends to lead to considerable shortcomings not only in terms of social equity, but also of economic efficiency, if its action is not subjected to institutional constraints by other regulatory principles (state, associations, informal networks) (Streeck 1994; Hollingsworth and Boyer 1997b).

2   The New Dynamism of Anglo-Saxon Capitalism

The picture described in the literature on varieties of capitalism at the end of the eighties has been questioned, mainly as a result of two phenomena. First, the economic success of Germany and Japan has declined, while Anglo-Saxon economies – particularly the USA – have shown new signs of dynamism. Second, the growth of globalization, and the process of European unification, have raised important questions as to the stability and reproduction of the institutional framework of the coordinated economies. The new challenges posed by globalization not only affect the regulative role of national states in social and economic fields, but also other institutional dimensions, such as the financial system and corporate governance as well as industrial relations.

Together with the declining performance of the most typical examples of coordinated market economies – Germany and Japan – the growth of the American and British economies during the nineties has undoubtedly contributed to altering the image of Rhine–Japanese capitalism as the most successful form of social and economic organization. In one sense this questioning of the preceding assumptions is useful. In fact, it may help to limit several of the risks in the literature on varieties of capitalism, in particular, that of underestimating the possibility of an economic revival of market systems of regulation. As we have seen, these risks were already present in the literature on neo-corporatism. However, it should also be pointed out that given the current state of knowledge, it is not possible to establish to what extent the growth of Anglo-Saxon capitalism and the difficulty of the other model are due to factors of a conjunctural nature or, instead, to fundamental changes that are more structural and over the long run.[7]

The highest number of jobs in the last ten years has now been created in the United States, above all in the services, leading to the lowest levels of unemployment for years. British performance has been less brilliant, even though there has been a significant decrease in the unemployment rate and new jobs have been created especially in the private service sector. In manufacturing industry the trends are more ambiguous. In the United Kingdom there are no substantial signs of a change and the innovative capacities of industry remain low. The situation is different in the United States, where, during the nineties, there has been significant industrial restructuring. Productivity has increased at consistent rates and employment has stayed stable, with mobility towards new sectors that have compensated for those in decline.

All the same, the improvement in American industry is difficult to interpret, since different factors seem to contribute to it. Many medium to large firms, under pressure for short-term profits, have followed the "low road" of adjustment in traditional sectors, based on a reduction in the work force and the decentralization of stages or components of production, often abroad, to reduce costs. Other firms have instead followed an innovative path introducing new technologies and developing new products. They have adopted a "high road," often experimenting with new institutional arrangements, especially in labor relations, similar to those of more organized types of capitalism (commitment to training, internal flexibility, cooperative relations, company welfare, etc.) (cf. for example, Lester 1998). However, together with the reduction of labor ("low road") and the improvement in competition ("high road"), an important factor in the growth of productivity was provided in the early nineties by the devaluation of the dollar *vis-à-vis* the German mark (equal to 60% between 1985 and 1995) and the Japanese yen (equal to 100%) (ibid. p. 46–7).

American industry shows, however, several strong points in the field of high technology and these seem to have been further consolidated in the last few years (aerospace industry, computer and communication industry, biotechnology, etc.). This specialization is linked to several specific factors in the institutional context that were underestimated in the first studies of varieties of capitalism (and which can also be found in the United Kingdom, even if high technology sectors are less strong than in the United States) (Soskice 1993,1999). The importance of the American military–industrial complex should be considered first here, since this stimulated substantial spending flows for research and innovation in high-technology sectors. High-level university structures and high-level research centers, closely connected with the world of firms through research contracts and frequent personnel exchanges, also contributed to the development and local concentration of high-tech firms (Saxenian 1996). Finally, the role played by another institutional factor was extremely important – the presence of venture capital, namely, of institutions that are equipped and competent to provide risk capital for the financing of innovative projects and start-ups, often carried out by small firms with Schumpeterian entrepreneurship. Following Soskice (1993,1999), this explains why American capital, and to a lesser extent British, provided an institutional context that was more suitable for "radical innovation." This same context, however, for the reasons mentioned above, was less able to sustain adaptation and utilization of radical innovation in large-scale manufacturing production, i.e. the development of flexible and high-quality productions. This implies incremental adaptations and innovations requiring the long-term involvement of researchers, skilled labor, collaborative relations between management and the workers, and between the parent company and suppliers. In other words, an institutional context more typical of coordinated market economies is necessary.[8]

As can be seen, the emerging picture of Anglo-Saxon capitalism, especially in the USA, is more balanced than that offered by the analyses of the eighties. The economic system showed several important innovative features for industry, as well as for business and financial services; the economy was capable of creating new employment in these new sectors, but especially in the low value-added private services for the consumer. The growth of workers in this low productivity sector was favored by the deregulation of labor relations, which enabled low labor costs.[9] This was an advantage *vis-à-vis* the more organized forms of capitalism, particularly the European type, where the existence of centrally coordinated industrial relations did not allow for the reduction of labor costs and the degree of flexibility in hiring and dismissals that would be necessary to increase employment in low-productivity private services, as was the case in the Anglo-Saxon models. As Esping-Andersen (1990, 1999) has shown, this problem was avoided in Scandinavia, by creating new employment, especially female employment, in the public welfare services. In European countries with a welfare system based on monetary transfers to the employed and their families, rather than on services (cf. section 1.1, chapter 8), there were growing difficulties for the unemployed, especially the young and women. Both these European strategies, however, contributed to an increase in public spending and fiscal pressure, and therefore hindered investment and the creation of new employment. On the other hand, the picture of dynamism of Anglo-Saxon capitalism has to be balanced by considering the fall in real wages, the growing inequality of incomes, and thus the increase in social polarization between wealthier and better-educated groups and poorer and less-skilled workers (Lester 1998, ch. 2).

Summing up, Anglo-Saxon capitalism does not seem to exhibit either a clear economic superiority (taking into account the competitiveness of industry and not only employment) or a capacity to reduce social inequalities. It can be said, however, that its signs of dynamism lead to a correction of a rather unilateral vision promoted by the institutionalist literature, which went as far as to claim that an economy can be competitive only with the support of a benevolent policy and a cohesive society (Crouch and Streeck 1997). The American case, in particular, shows how economic competitiveness can be compatible with high levels of social inequality. Rather than pointing to the superiority of one model over another, it is more useful to think of multiple equilibria with different strong and weak points. Moreover, this vision is rooted in the tradition of economic sociology because it is consistent with the idea of different degrees of legitimacy of the market, which condition its functioning (cf. chapter 6). A society that is strongly characterized by liberal individualism, historically marked by the central role played by immigration and by the search for success through individual mobilization, can accept levels of inequality that are higher in comparison to those tolerated in societies with a different cultural tradition or institutional legacy, like those in Europe or Japan.

3   Convergence or Diversity?

There is, however, a final and more subtle argument questioning the idea of varieties of capitalism. Here, it is not a case of pointing to the current competitive advantages of Anglo-Saxon capitalism, but rather of underlining that this model could adjust better to the constraints imposed by globalization in the long run. In addition, however, the new conditions of competition prevailing at the international level could determine a progressive erosion in the regulative institutions of coordinated economies. The final result would be a progressive convergence towards the institutional model of Anglo-Saxon capitalism. As can be seen, in this view the concept of globalization does not only refer to the growing openness and interdependence of national economies, but also assumes that globalization implies an extension of regulatory models based on the market. To what extent is this hypothesis well grounded?

To answer this question, several trends that encourage globalization will first be considered at the empirical level. Following this, the consequences for the future of various forms of capitalism will be evaluated.

The components of globalization

First, it should be remembered that the period of low growth rates for the developed countries, which started in the early seventies, also continued in the following years: from 1975 to 1995 the average rate of growth of GDP was about half the amount relative to the period between 1955 and 1975. This low growth went together with a strong increase in international commerce. International trade grew nearly twentyfold between 1967 and 1994, going from 292 billion dollars to 6,490. In the same period world GNP increased by a factor of 10, going from 2,290 to 25,570 billion dollars (Lafay 1996). In the OECD countries the ratio of exports to GDP roughly doubled between 1960 and 1990, going from 9.5 percent to 20.5 percent (Wade 1996, p. 62). This means that the cake to be divided tended to grow slowly, while competition between countries for bigger slices increased sharply. The geography of world production also changed, with a decrease in the proportional importance of the United States and Europe and growth concentrated especially in Japan and the other Asian countries (figure 10.1).

Together with international commerce, a second indicator of the growing international integration of the economy is provided by foreign direct investments. These too are on the increase, pulled by the search on the part of firms for more favorable locations, in terms of both market outlets and lower labor costs (see figure 10.2). According to several estimates, the share of manufacturing production under foreign control would reach around 25 percent of world manufacturing output around the year 2000 (Lafay 1996). During the eighties, foreign direct investments quadrupled, growing three times faster than trade flows and almost four times faster than output (Wade 1996, p. 63).

The third feature marking the growing interdependence of different economies concerns the integration of financial markets. Commercial and industrial internationalization stimulated the capital flows that were necessary for financing trade and investments, insuring against currency risks, moving profits made abroad, etc. The breakdown of the international monetary system based on fixed exchange rates, which occurred at the beginning of the seventies, in turn accelerated this process, favoring the growth of the market for financial products such as futures and options. There was also an autonomous innovation, tied to the growth of new types of financial products ("derivatives") which met the demand for investments, coming in particular from the oil-producing countries. In addition, the improve-

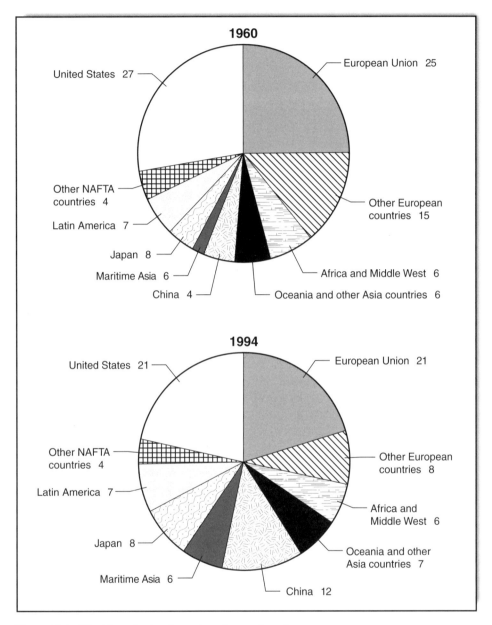

Figure 10.1 *World production by regions (percentages)*
Source: Lafay 1996.

ment in communications favored by the computer technologies lowered transaction costs, and enabled integration in real time between the main financial centers. Naturally, this process of integration was able to develop because the pressures on national governments to liberalize capital flows also increased (this will be dealt with in more detail below). Thus enormous amounts of capital, in the form of

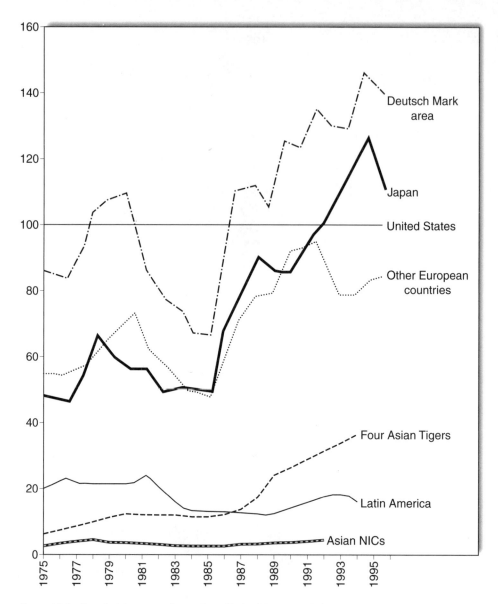

Figure 10.2   Hourly labour cost by regions (United States = 100)
Source: Lafay 1996.

bonds and shares, futures and other financial products, were transferred every day on the financial markets. It has been estimated that at the end of the eighties on the foreign exchange market alone around 900 billion dollars were transferred each day, compared to the overall monetary reserves of all the central banks of about 700 billion (Albert [1991] 1993). The stock of international bank lending loans (cross-border lending and domestic lending denominated in foreign currency) went from 4 percent of OECD GDP in 1980 to 44 percent in 1990. It has also been estimated that international currency flows were more than thirty times higher than trade flows (Wade 1996, p. 66).

Taking all these three indicators into account – international trade, foreign direct investments and capital flows, economic globalization can be understood as growing openness of individual economies as well as interdependence among them. What were the consequences of this process for the different models of capitalism? Is it possible that a further intensification of globalization would favor Anglo-Saxon capitalism, to the detriment of the more organized forms? And how well-grounded is the idea of an institutional convergence towards more highly regulated market models?

The future of different forms of capitalism

Suzanne Berger and Ronald Dore (1996) have collected various contributions with the twofold objective of evaluating the extent of globalization processes and discussing the institutional implications of the regulation of capitalist economies. On the first point, much of the work argue that the effects of globalization should not be overestimated, as some popular books tend to do (a typical example of this is *The Borderless World* by Ohmae 1991). Although international trade and foreign investments are on the increase, as we have seen above, in the larger developed countries about 90 percent of production is for the domestic market, and 90 percent of consumption is produced at home (Wade 1996, p. 66; cf. also Hirst and Thompson 1996). In addition, Robert Boyer (1996) underlined the fact that there was no significant convergence between macro-economic indicators, other than for the eight most developed countries, and even this was very limited and had only been noticeable over the last few years. Persistent differences in growth rates and employment, profit and interest rates can be traced to the influence exercised by the institutional context.

Finally, it is undeniable that the much lower labor costs in developing countries constitutes a major threat, especially for coordinated economies, which aim at flexible and quality production with high wages for workers. Given that technological and communication developments allow more complex productions to be decentralized towards these areas, this threat is rising (Crouch and Streeck 1997). However, it is also true that more organized economies can rely on rich external economies and on institutional settings that allow them to keep the lead in processes of innovation and to develop the productive stages with a higher value added. On the whole, then, more caution is necessary when interpreting the phenomenon of globalization.

However, the supporters of the institutional convergence thesis could object that what really counts is the overall trend over time, apart from the slowness of its pace. Can we thus assume that convergence will be realized in future? Suzanne Berger (1996) has summarized three main arguments used by those who believe that this is so:

1   The first argument concerns market pressure and growing competition at the international level. This increases the economic costs of social protection exercised

by states, both directly through redistributive interventions that raise taxes, and indirectly through regulation of the labor market and legal support for industrial relations and collective bargaining. More generous forms of redistribution and the extensive regulation of labor relations can induce firms to move elsewhere. The autonomy of states in establishing an economic policy at both macro and micro levels is inevitably restrained, and this gives an advantage to systems that are already more deregulated and based on the market.

2   A second argument refers instead to the imitation of those institutional rules, which give good results in terms of economic performance, at both the macro and micro level – for example, with regard to the financing system and corporate governance. This might trigger forms of hybridization between different institutional forms, giving rise to convergence.

3   Finally, a third feature deals with the negotiated introduction, through international agreements, of similar forms of regulation. There are numerous international agreements of this kind, aimed at abolishing protective barriers and introducing common standards. A particularly interesting example of this is the economic integration processes of the European Union.

Suzanne Berger contrasts these points with others which question the extent of institutional convergence:

1   One deals with the ambiguity of the pressures brought to bear by the market. In other words, increased competition signals the need for adjustment, for example, in economic policy and industrial relations, but is incapable of establishing a standard institutional response to these challenges. It is more likely that a solution will emerge through the influence on actors' choices of the institutional legacy inherited from the past and through the conflicts of interest between upholders of the old rules and supporters of change. The choices will thus be *path-dependent* (as already pointed out in section 1 of this chapter).

2   One can in fact formulate the preceding argument in terms of "functional equivalents." Different institutional responses can emerge in response to competitive problems in different productive sectors (for example, the German firm, the Japanese firm, or Italian industrial districts). These institutional arrangements might, however, lead to equivalent competitive capacity, either in the same product markets or in particular niches within those markets. A good empirical example of this position can be found in the research on the regulation of different industrial sectors by Hollingsworth, Schmitter, and Streeck (1994).

3   Finally, a third argument picks up on the idea of "institutional logic," which was already discussed in the analysis of varieties of capitalism. Here reference is made to specific forms of interdependence between the various institutions characterizing a particular national setting; these are tied to a common cultural matrix that has evolved over time (Hollingsworth and Boyer, 1997b). In this case emphasis is placed on the difficulty of *institutional shopping*, namely, to introduce variations into particular aspects of regulation mechanisms without changing the overall setting; Ronald Dore (1987) has, for example, drawn attention to the numerous attempts made to imitate the organization of Japanese firms and to their shortcomings.

As can be seen, the arguments put forward by both sides are serious and do not allow simple answers to questions of the institutional consequences of globalization, also because such questions cannot be immediately resolved through empirical research. We are dealing here with possible future trends. However, as things currently stand, a balanced view would seem to be to recognize that globalization will have – and in fact is already having – a series of destabilizing consequences, especially for organized economies, which are more dependent on non-market institutions and therefore place stronger constraints on the holders of an increasingly mobile capital. It does not, however, seem likely that such changes will bring about a real convergence. On the contrary, a readjustment of coordinated market economies can be hypothesized, which will be accompanied by persisting multiple equilibria, that is to say, by institutional systems characterized by differentiated strong and weak points. To demonstrate this it may be useful to analyze in greater detail the consequences of globalization for economic and social policies.

There is no doubt that the liberalization of capital flows and the growing integration of financial markets place serious constraints on the autonomy of national states in the formulation and implementation of their economic policies (cf. for example, Strange 1996). The pursuit of traditional macro-economic policies of the Keynesian type is increasingly difficult for a single country in isolation from others. Expansionary policies, leading to an increase in the public deficit and national debt rapidly generate negative expectations and unfavorable pressures on the exchange rate of national currencies. That is, an increase in the sales of such currency can be determined, leading to currency crises and devaluation. However, restrictive policies, based on raising national interest rates, can also fail to achieve the desired effect, because firms can increasingly rely on credit from abroad on better terms than at home. These constraints on the autonomy of macro-economic policies are also reinforced by trade integration and foreign investment. Thus, an expansionary policy combined with pressure from the financial markets could lead to a growth in imports, if the national production system is not very competitive because of high fiscal pressure or labor costs. In addition, high interest rates, or a heavy fiscal burden, can also be seen as a stimulus for foreign direct investments. As for the European countries involved in the process of monetary and economic integration, it is clear that the conditions posed by globalization are reinforced by those deriving from the European agreements made by the states (for example, the Maastricht Treaty), since these place specific constraints on public spending.

While most scholars agree on this analysis, they differ in their evaluations of the consequences. Crouch and Streeck (1997), for example, believe that the loss of autonomy in macro-economic policies will weaken national states and extend to other policy fields: welfare provisions and the institutional mechanisms supporting the role of associations and concertation in the more organized forms of capitalism, particularly the European ones. In other words, macro-economic constraints and trends towards deregulation would come together, penalizing to a greater extent coordinated economies. In fact, the latter are more dependent on state support for cooperation between organized interests (thus German capitalism would be more strongly hit than Italian industrial districts or Japanese firms, which are more dependent on regulative mechanisms that are less closely linked to the state as such). Consequently, a weakening of more organized capitalism would in effect come about, and this would go together with an overall convergence towards the Anglo-Saxon model, even if with a loss of competitiveness of the developed economies and greater social inequality. In other words, according to the hypothesis formulated by Albert ([1991] 1993), even if Rhine–Japanese capitalism is both economically and socially more efficient, it would inevitably lose ground in the end and would end up by converging on the Anglo-Saxon version.

An important component of this process concerns the pressure of financial capital on corporate governance, that is, on the ownership structure and management of firms. In reality, the higher mobility of financial capital and the greater scope for short-term profit in the international market tend to destabilize the long-standing network of relations between banks and firms that was typical of Rhine–Japanese capitalism (cf. for example, Albert 1991; Rhodes and van Apeldoorn 1997). On the one hand, the banks located in organized capitalism countries are increasingly moving towards foreign financial markets and are willing to seize opportunities to invest in the Anglo-Saxon capitalism countries. On the other, American and British financial capital penetrates into the firms' equity in more organized types of capitalism. Using Powell and DiMaggio's neo-institutional categories (1991c), it could be claimed that a sort of "normative isomorphism" has developed, also favored by the large consulting firms. This consists of a set of regulatory practices that reinforce the role of the shareholders in orienting the management strategies of firms, at the expense – especially in Europe and Japan – of the traditionally important role played by the stakeholders, that is, management and workers. In other words, shareholders become less "patient," and more oriented to the pursuit of short-term profits and influence management and the organization of firms so as to achieve this aim. There are several advantages to this. One is that the firm's management is obliged to take on greater responsibility, but – as we know – there can also be a weakening in the long-term innovation processes that constituted the strong point of organized capitalisms, more based on diversified quality production. It should also be remembered that in Europe the new forms of corporate governance have also been greatly reinforced by the regulatory intervention of community institutions (Rhodes and van Apeldoorn 1997).

Despite the soundness of these arguments, other scholars share a more complex and doubtful vision of the outcomes in terms of convergence through deregulation (Zysman 1994, 1995; Berger 1996; Dore 2000). These authors underline that macroeconomic constraints – which are undeniable – do not necessarily reduce the autonomy of the regulatory or redistributive policies of states, or for supply-side public interventions at the micro-economic level. For example, different options can be followed to increase competitiveness and thus also compensate the macro constraints: occupational training, research and development, regulation of sectors and labor relations. Interventions by states in these fields do not necessarily have to take the form of deregulation or privatization, relying exclusively on market mechanisms. In addition, if it is true that macro constraints on public spending bring about the need for restructuring and retrenching the welfare state, and for making the labor market more flexible, there are several directions that the readjustment can take, adapting to the legacy and institutional logics of each country. These are not in any case easily digested. Around this legacy a conflict emerges between those (including unions) defending the old institutions, which are more favorable to their interests, and those wanting to modify them. The outcomes of this conflict are open, however, and are not strictly predetermined by efficiency constraints.

Evaluation of the impact of globalization on processes of concertation also calls for caution. As we saw in chapter 8, while there has certainly been a weakening of the old forms of centralized concertation aimed at controlling inflation, globalization – as well as the process of European integration – could create spaces for new forms of concertation. These aim at favoring a reorganization of the welfare state and fine-tuning of micro-economic interventions to support productivity and the growth of competitiveness, precisely as effective instruments to deal with the new challenges posed by globalization (Schmitter and Grote 1997; and for the interesting Dutch experience, Hemerijck and Visser 1997). There is no doubt either that the more new forms of regulation are worked out at the international level, the greater will be the scope for a significant persistence of institutional specificities at the national level. In fact, this trend will enable the gap between markets – which are globalizing – and institutions – which are still anchored at the state-nation level – to be reduced. This process is particularly clear in Europe, where economic and monetary integration has widened the space of markets to the detriment of the regulatory capacities of the national states, while the political institutions of the European Union remain weak and scarcely legitimized (Scharpf 1997).

In conclusion, there are many good reasons for assuming that globalizing trends will go together with significant institutional changes and a redefinition of the boundaries between the different forms of economic and social regulation. However, the institutional differences and their consequences for the economy and society are not found to disappear. This hypothesis is linked to the idea of multiple equilibria, rather than to a single equilibrium gaining ground gradually and inexorably. The globalization of markets will create pressures and constraints that will continue to be filtered by specific institutional settings inherited from history. There can, thus, be particular advantages and disadvantages in the various countries and regions in dealing with economic competition. And there will continue to be variable combinations of economic efficiency and social equity (Block 1990,1994). Some societies will choose to develop less in economic terms and to maintain a more cohesive social structure. Others will opt for an opposite equilibrium. The problem that each of these will have to face is not that of leveling out the logic of deregulation, but of creating an intelligent and reflexive regulation. There will be a need for actions that attempt to use the institutional legacy inherited from the past in the best possible way.

It is unrealistic to think that this outcome can be achieved by opposing globalization and obstructing the markets with protectionist closure policies, be these economic or not, since they can only be unsuccessful. A more effective response to these challenges is instead more likely to emerge where the long-standing legacy of each civilization is taken adequately into account. In this perspective, economic sociology will still have a job to do. Coherent with its roots, planted over a century ago, it will contribute to clarifying the social construction of the market. In a constant dialogue with economics, it will contrast different institutional models in space and time, singling out their strong and weak points and their economic and social outcomes. It is in this way that it will continue to contribute to a reflexive construction of society.

Notes

1 From Classical Economics to Economic Sociology

1   It should be pointed out that Weber defined the concept of institution in a more restricted and specific sense than that used in the text (see Introduction). For him, an institution (*Anstalt*) was a compulsory organization, a social group with a system of formal rules determining the action of individuals, for example, a state or church (Weber [1922] 1978, vol. I, p. 52).

2   Weber used the term "social-economic" (*Sozialökonomik*) in his essay on *"Objectivity" in Social Science and Social Policy* (1904). Later, in his essay on *The Meaning of Ethical Neutrality in Sociology and Economics* (1917), he uses the expression "sociology of economics" (*Soziologie der Wirtschaft*). In *Economy and Society*, he also uses the term "economic sociology" (*Wirtschaftssoziologie*). Sombart also uses the expression "economic sociology" (*Wirtschaftssoziologie*) in *Modern Capitalism*, particularly in the Preface to the 1916 edition. On the use of the term economic sociology, cf. Swedberg (1987, p. 135, n. 1).

2 The origins and Developments of Capitalism: Simmel and Sombart

1   The difference between the definition of the economy prevailing in the institutional perspective of economic sociology and that of the neoclassical economists would subsequently be emphasized by Polanyi (1977, ch. 2). He distinguished between substantial and formal definitions of the economy (see Introduction, section 1 and chapter 5).

2   Sombart was criticized on this point by those who argued that the search for greater gain might also guide behavior in precapitalist societies. He replied that he did not wish to deny the existence of greed for money but was interested in whether it prevailed within the sphere of production. In such societies, the search for gain did not orient the economy but unfolded outside it, for example, in the search for precious metals, conquest, adventures, or usury (Sombart [1916] 1922, pp. 34–5). As we shall see further on, Weber also too insisted on the difference between political capitalism and economic capitalism.

3   Sombart referred explicitly to the introduction of the assembly line and organization of work in the pioneering example of Henry Ford's American motor industry (cf. in par-

ticular, Sombart 1928, Vol. III, pp. 917–18; this topic is also discussed in chapter 9).

4 Sombart here referred to to the work by F.W. Taylor (1856–1915), an American engineer and pioneer of studies on the scientific organization of work. This has often been called "Taylorism" (see chapter 9).

5 Simmel's essay on this topic is of considerable interest (1911).

3 Capitalism and the Western Civilization: Max Weber

1 Weber revised both these essays and later republished them together with other work on religion (Weber 1920–1).

2 Bendix (1960) has played an important role in putting forward this interpretation of Weber's thesis, which highlights the links between the Protestant religion and the Western city. See also Poggi's interesting interpretation (1983).

3 Weber talks about "ascetic Protestantism," including four main streams in this category: Calvinism, Methodism, Pietism, and the Seven Baptist Church.

4 While Weber's supporters have often underlined the deeper complexity of his interpretation of capitalism, they have underplayed the lack of direct empirical evidence, which continues to have important consequences for the perceived role of Protestantism (Marshall 1982).

5 Weber used the concept put forward by Sombart in his *Modern Capitalism*.

6 I do not discuss these in the order that Weber presented them in his book. A slightly more detailed treatment of the various preconditions is given in *Economy and Society* ([1922] 1978, vol. I, pp. 161–2).

7 As well as in his essays in *Sociology of Religion*, Weber dealt with this topic in *Economy and Society* (see in particular, chapter 5 of vol. II).

8 In his *General Economic History* ([1958b] 1987, pp. 56–64), Weber distinguished between the Eastern feudal system and Western feudalism. He discussed the features of the latter in great detail in *Economy and Society*.

4 The Social Consequences of Capitalism: Durkheim and Veblen

1 However, the theme of *sociologie économique* continued to be cultivated in the journal founded by Durkheim, *L'Année sociologique*. Several of his students and collaborators, such as F. Simiand, M. Halwachs, and M. Mauss, published important theoretical and empirical articles on this topic.

2 This hypothesis was furthermore contradicted by empirical evidence, according to Durkheim. While it was true that the division of labor could satisfy a greater number of needs, it did not automatically lead to an increase in individual happiness, since this was linked to the balancing of needs and the means for satisfying them. The division of labor led to new problems, needs and reasons for being unhappy, as the high levels of suicide in modern society illustrated. Durkheim developed this theme in his famous study of *Suicide*, published in 1897.

3 Durkheim's work on the origins of the division of labor, described above, was widely criticized. Talcott Parsons (1937), for example, viewed it as a sort of "biologism," where demographic pressure determined the division of labor on its own. Durkheim's arguments do seem to reflect a certain unilinear conception of social evolution, in which the growth of the division of labor was the inevitable outcome of the struggle for life. Durkheim was sensitive to this kind of criticism, which surrounded his work from the

first moment that it was published. Later on, in *The Rules of Sociological Method*, he attempted to explain that it was not simply an increase in the density of the population that determined the division of labor, but that there also had to be an intensification in social relations (moral density) which did not necessarily derive from the former. In other words, a specific social factor had to intervene in order for this to occur.

4 Durkheim also mentioned a third "abnormal" division of labor that occurred in modern economic firms characterized by a high specialization of individual tasks. In these cases, there was a lack of coordination between specialized functions, generating waste, and a lack of solidarity. This type was close to anomic division.

5 These institutions should adapt the medieval model of guilds to new requirements, and should be constituted by representatives of employers and workers from all sectors. Durkheim also discussed the idea of "labor courts" to resolve economic and labor disputes, set up with the same mixed representation of the different interests. It should be noted, however, that he did not conceive corporations as voluntary associations, but as "public institutions" with compulsory membership, organized hierarchically over the territory (from the center to the periphery). Together with their specific economic functions, they were to carry out collateral tasks of social assistance, professional and technical training, and to organize cultural and recreational activities. Durkheim believed that these functions were particularly important because, in his view, corporations should stimulate the forming of moral ties between actors involved in particular activities – a task that could not be carried out by the state.

6 Veblen's work formed part of a wider set of studies that developed in the United States with an institutionalist orientation. This approach included other authors such as W. Mitchell and J. Commons.

7 Following the language and developments of the psychology of the period, Veblen also dealt with other instincts: the "parental bent" or instinct of solidarity and the instinct of "idle curiosity," which stimulated scientific research and technical development.

8 This perspective was supported and developed in the work of famous scholars such as Gerschenkron (1962) and the historical sociologist Barrington Moore (1966).

9 It is clear, then, that Veblen challenged the individualistic assumptions of neoclassical economics with his institutionalist theory. In his view, it was possible to make an "objective" evaluation of collective well-being that should not be reduced to the sum of individual utilitiy of single consumers (Hodgson 1994, p. 63).

5 The Great Depression and the Decline of Liberal Capitalism: Polanyi and Schumpeter

1 Schumpeter wrote about this in his essay, *The Instability of Capitalism* (1928), and in his lecture *Can Capitalism Survive?* (1936). This question was also central to his book *Capitalism, Socialism, and Democracy*.

2 Polanyi read Schumpeter's work and, in particular, referred to his *History of Economic Analysis*. However, the Austrian economist made no reference to Polanyi's work.

6 The Legacy of the Classics and the New Boundaries between Economics and Sociology

1 For example, in their interesting study on the origins of economic sociology, Jean-Jacques Gislain and Philippe Steiner (1995) include Durkheim, Schumpeter, Veblen

and Weber in their analysis, as well as Pareto and Simiand, although they exclude Sombart and Polanyi. The absence of these last is certainly questionable. Moreover, if one uses the twofold criteria of methodological and substantive importance, it is difficult to attribute a crucial role to Pareto, since he is mainly interested in developing a general sociological theory and only peripherally considers questions of economic sociology.

2 According to the historian of science Thomas Kuhn (1962), a paradigm is constituted by a set of theories and methods giving rise to particular traditions of scientific research that are consolidated and coherent, that is, to a "normal science."

3 For similar comparisons, cf. Swedberg, Himmelstrand, and Brulin (1987); Hirsch, Michaels, and Friedman (1987); see also Block (1990) and Smelser and Swedberg (1994). However, one should note that these authors (and indeed this chapter) only examine the more traditional positions held by neoclassical economics confronted by the founders of economic sociology. As a result, more recent attempts to innovate within the neoclassical paradigm, such as the development of game theory or new institutional economics are overlooked (see chapter 9). In addition, no account is taken of the more unorthodox views in economic thought, which have also questioned the underlying assumptions of the theory of action of the neoclassical paradigm, leading to closer contact with economic sociology. In this context, one must refer in particular to Albert Hirschman, who, starting from the need to complicate the traditional theory of action, has developed a series of innovative analyses of important issues such as economic development, the organization of production, and consumption (Hirschman 1958, 1970, 1982, 1986). The positions of other, well-known heterodox economists (including Thomas Schelling and George Akerlof as well as Hirschman) are presented in a collection of interviews on the relations between economics and sociology edited by Swedberg (1990).

4 This implies that from our point of view the difference between "methodological individualism" (Sombart, Weber, and Schumpeter) and "methodological institutionalism" (Durkheim, Veblen, and Polanyi) should not be over-emphasized (also see the introduction and section 3 of chapter 4). Both these positions recognize the need to take actors and their motivations into account in the explanation of social phenomena and they recognize that institutions are created through interaction between actors. Once formed, however, they condition actors. In this sense the differences between methodological individualism and methodological institutionalism are less important than they might seem (cf. Boudon 1984). From this point of view at least, neither of these positions diverge from economics, which is also based on an individualistic methodology. The difference between economic sociology and mainstream economics has more to do with the atomism and utilitarianism of economic models of action. Where there is a truly radical difference is with approaches which deny any role to actors in the explanation of social phenomena, in particular in systems theory and functionalist theories. These last fall fully into the category of "collectivism," or, more precisely, "methodological holism." There is no denying, however, that methodological institutionalism sometimes run a greater risk of falling into holism, more particularly – as we have seen (section 3, chapter 4) – in the formulation of its research program and methodological perspectives than in its practical application.

5 The "regulative organization" regulates production and consumption, putting constraints on the autonomous economic action of actors, as in the case of the corporations, cartels between firms, and modern unions. The "administrative organization" instead administers production, redistribution and consumption systematically and directly, as is the case in an economy that is entirely controlled by the state (Weber 1922).

6 This does not mean that there is no interest in the problem of equity in economics.

Over the last few decades the branch of economics dealing with welfare and social choice has dealt extensively with the problem of distributive justice (cf. for example, the work of Kenneth Arrow and Amartya Sen). However, this approach mainly aims to give a *normative* basis to public intervention, or to forms of voluntary regulation (associative) to deal with the problems of equity that the market does not resolve, and which can compromise the freedom of individuals. In economic sociology, questions of equity are analyzed from the *empirical* and *comparative* points of view, to evaluate how inequalities influence economic development in various contexts (see for example, the discussion of different types of capitalism in chapter 10).

7   The distinction between constitutive and regulatory rules was first made by the philosopher John Rawls (1967); for its implications in the field of economic sociology see, for example, DiMaggio (1994).

8   Veblen's intuitions have been confirmed by some famous empirical investigations, such as those by Halbwachs (1933) on working-class consumption, and Warner and Lunt (1941) on Yankee City. The interdependence of individual choices, resulting from social conditioning, also underpins the important work of the economist Duesenberry (1949).

9   This interpretation of Veblen's work seems rather reductive. As we have already seen (chapter 5), Veblen actually attributed great importance to institutions – viewed in their normative and cognitive (technological) components – in orienting behavior. In this way he introduced an element that is close to Parson's ultimate ends as shared values and norms. In fact, the crucial difference lay in Parson's rejection of institutionalism as a theory aimed at explaining concrete economic activities. This also went together with a clear antipathy towards Veblen's political radicalism.

10   In *Sociological Elements in Economic Thought* (II) (1935b), Parsons also associates Durkheim and Weber with this program, but this makes the convergence he sets up between these scholars and Pareto very strained on several points (the problem will come up again in *The Structure of Social Action*). While Durkheim's interest in founding a sociological theory is clear (see chapter 4), this is carried out in a positivist framework where there is little space for an "analytical" vision of economics and sociology *à la* Pareto. In addition, it is true that Weber defends the scientific foundations of economics as an analytical discipline, distancing himself from historicism. But we have seen (chapter 1) how he rejects the path of a general theory for sociology of either an analytical type, as Parsons would like, or following a positivist model. For him, economic sociology should develop a perspective different from that followed by economics: producing historically founded analytical models (the ideal types) that combine economic and institutional factors and are always directed towards the interpretation of historical phenomena.

11   Disciplinary specialization had already begun before the Second World War, and in some areas it became more established between the forties and fifties. One example of this was the branch of studies on organization initiated in the United States by Taylor in the early years of the century; important research was also done on labor performance and integration by Elton Mayo, during the thirties, and by the school of human relations; the British tradition of studies on industrial relations, beginning with work by the Webbs, is another important example, as is the research on the sociology of work and carried out in France during the forties and fifties (George Friedman, Alaine Touraine, and Michel Crozier).

8   The Keynesian Welfare State and Comparative Political Economy

1   However, the Spanish "social pacts" formed with interest organizations at the end of the seventies played a very important role in the country's transition to democracy

(Perez Diaz 1986).

2 Here I am referring to traditional forms of political exchange. However, as will be seen below, new types of agreement can be stimulated by the specific need to reorganize the welfare state and to improve flexibility and quality in production.

9 The Crisis of Fordism and New Economic Sociology

1 The term Fordism recalls the pioneering role played at the beginning of the century by the American automobile industrialist Henry Ford in the experimentation with the new organizational model of the firm, in particular with the introduction of the assembly line. The term Taylorism instead refers to the influence that the ideas and studies on the "scientific organization of work" by Frederick Taylor (1911) had in the development of the model.

2 The study of informal activities in the transformations of the socialist economies, both in Eastern Europe and the Soviet Union before the fall of the communist regimes, was particularly fertile (cf. for example, Szelenyi 1988; Stark 1989; Grancelli 1991).

3 There is also the tendency to offer work in the hidden economy (usually in the service sector) outside wage and legal standards. This trend usually involves workers who already have a job but want to increase their incomes.

4 In practice, it is impossible to know all the alternatives and all their possible consequences when one has to take a decision. Rationality is thus always limited and aims to obtain *satisfactory* rather than optimal results, basing itself on the selection of a restricted amount of information.

5 This view is also confirmed by the industrial districts studies discussed in the preceding section (Dei Ottati 1987), and by the operation of small-firm systems in Japan, as described by Dore (1986), who also used this evidence to criticize Williamson (Dore 1983). Granovetter (1985) explicitly claims that the persistence of sets of small firms can in some cases be explained by the existence of a "dense network of social relations" which reduces pressure on vertical integration.

6 One of these studies, by Baker (1984), deals with the market of shareholding options on the stock market. Baker shows that in this context the traditional assumption that markets will become more competitive and prices more stable the higher is the number of operators does not hold. This outcome is due to the social structure of the market. By increasing the number of stockbrokers, personal social networks break down. This reduces the homogeneity of actors' behavior, increasing the volatility of prices.

7 It should be noted that this approach shows some similarities with respect to the interesting developments of evolutionary theory in economics, in particular the work done by Nelson and Winter (1982). These authors also criticize the new institutional economy. They view the behavior of firms as governed by routines that form over time, constituting a sort of equivalent to genes in biology. Using their specific routines, single firms attempt to adapt to market stimuli, which constitute the principal selection device of choices. In this way the firms managing to adapt best are rewarded (although the less efficient ones do not necessarily disappear). The basic differences with sociological neo-institutionalism concern the role of these routines conditioning behavior. These are seen by sociologists in less atomistic and more relational terms – that is, they are more strongly influenced by a particular institutional context. Second, the selection mechanism conditioning evolution is not necessarily dependent on the market, but is also influenced by the state and prevailing professional standards. Mechanisms other than the market are important above all for the organizations that are less exposed to competition. In this sense neo-institutionalism is more interested in populations of firms

(or other organizations) and in their homogeneity of behavior, while the evolutionary approach is more interested in the individual differences between productive units, and the consequences that derive for innovation and economic development.

8   Hirsch (1977) has underlined this point, drawing attention to "positional goods," that is, to goods that do not grow with the increase of demand, because they are available only in limited quantities (for example, works of art) or because enjoyment deteriorates where consumption increases (for example, a house in a quiet tourist spot). With the increase in income, the demand for these goods – given their clear symbolic component – grows, but this generates a growing frustration, which in Hirsch's view influenced the tensions of the seventies and the inflationary pushes. Similar to this argument is the hypothesis developed by Hirschman (1982). He suggests that the disappointment of consumers might have been connected to the rapid expansion of durable consumer goods and services in the post-war period. The drop in the quality of services, as well as the decrease in satisfaction deriving from durable consumer goods (for example, household appliances and cars), nourished collective mobilization and protest movements in the seventies.

10   Globalization and the Diversity of Capitalisms

1   As Krugman (1994) pointed out, the competitiveness of a firm should not be confused with that of a country. First, a state cannot go bankrupt and is thus not sensitive to market sanctions in the same way as firms. Second, the influence of globalization is more important the smaller the country and its domestic market (this is, for instance, not the case of the United States).

2   This neo-institutionalist position is also very close to that of the economic historian Douglas North (1990), who, after having initially attempted to use the tools of institutional economics – in particular the analysis of transaction costs – in historical investigation, developed an approach to institutional change based on an evolutionary and incremental logic. Path dependency plays a decisive role in this new perspective.

3   The influence of the national institutional context on the sectoral specialization and the "technological trajectory" of a particular country also emerges from the evolutionist approach in economics, which analyzed the "national system of innovation" (Nelson 1993). The focus is placed on the institutions influencing the development of scientific and technological research, but these are, in their turn, connected with the widest national institutional context (Zysman 1994).

4   More specific typologies for the European countries have been developed by De Jong (1995) and Moerland (1995). In these cases a "market-oriented" model of capitalism, similar to those of the United Kingdom and Ireland, is contrasted to a "network-oriented" type. This last is in its turn subdivided into two groups: that of the "social market economy" (Germany, Benelux, Holland and Denmark) and the "Latin" type (Italy, Greece, Portugal, and Spain). The Latin countries are distinguished, in particular, by the greater number of family controlled firms, by cross-shareholdings among the most important companies, and by the extensive role of state-owned companies. The position of France is more unclear in this kind of model, as it is also in Albert's typology (1991).

5   It was no accident that attempts to restructure by successful American manufacturing firms tried to deal with precisely these aspects, creating the institutional conditions for more stable relations and greater involvement of workers and staff (cf. for example, Lester 1998).

6   Soskice's evaluation of the scope for the wage containment in non-coordinated market

economies requires some qualifications especially for non-industrial sectors. Wage containment may be achieved through market regulation. In fact, real wages have grown less in non-coordinated market economies (Lester 1998, pp. 36-7), and this was accompanied by good employment performance, above all in private services for consumers, where market regulation of wages has enabled lower labor costs to compensate for the low productivity of such services.

7   Regarding conjunctural factors, some of the obvious areas to be taken into consideration have to do with the over-evaluation of the German mark and the Japanese yen *vis-à-vis* the dollar, extending over most of the nineties. For Germany there was also the heavy burden of unification with East Germany, and, for Japan, the serious crisis of the banking system. On the decline of Rhine–Japanese *vis-à-vis* Anglo-Saxon capitalism, see the balanced account by Dore (2000).

8   In this respect, Soskice's work is close to the main tenets of evolutionary economics (Dosi, Pavitt, and Soete 1990; Nelson 1993), though he uses a wider institutional explanation.

9   The possibility that decentralized wage regulation systems could have positive effects on economic performance, and in particular on employment, had been underlined in an important contribution by Calmfors and Driffil (1988) at the end of the eighties. These authors bring empirical evidence to show empirically how good employment performances can come about through both centralized regulation systems, like neo-corporatist ones, and decentralized systems, with weak unions and greater market space (they included the United States, Canada, and Japan here). The worst results came from intermediate systems. A similar hypothesis had been formulated by Olson (1982). He pointed out that strong unions at the sectoral level, but not well coordinated at the central level, would be less interested in and less capable of taking into account the consequences of their demands for the functioning of the economy. This happens in neo-corporatist systems, while in those that are more decentralized and deregulated, weak unions are not able to alter the effects of wage moderation exercised by the labor market. Ensuing research has not, however, confirmed this hypothesis fully, showing that employment cannot be explained simply by the system of wage regulation (Calmfors 1993).

References

Alber, J. 1982. *Vom Armenhaus zum Wohlfahrtsstaat*. Frankfurt/Main: Campus Verlag.

Albert, M. [1991] 1993. *Capitalism against Capitalism*. London: Whurr.

Alchian, A. and Demsetz, H. 1972. "Production, Information Costs and Economic Organization. *American Economic Review* 62: 777–95.

—— 1973. "The Property Rights Paradigm." *Journal of Economic History* 33: 16–27.

Almond, G. and Powell, G. 1966. *Comparative Politics. A Developmental Approach*. Boston: Little Brown & Company.

Appadurai, A. 1986. "Introduction: commodities and the politics of value." Pp. 3–63 in *The Social Life of Things: Commodities in Cultural Perspective*, edited by A. Appadurai. Cambridge: Cambridge University Press.

Arrow, K. 1974. *The Limits of Organization*. New York: W. W. Norton.

Ascoli, U. 1987. *Azione volontaria e Welfare State*. Bologna: Il Mulino.

Bagnasco, A. 1977. *Tre Italie*. Bologna: Il Mulino.

—— 1988. *La costruzione sociale del mercato*. Bologna: Il Mulino.

—— 1990. "The Informal Economy." Pp. 157–74 in *Economy and Societies: Overviews in Economic Sociology*, edited by A. Martinelli and N. Smelser. London: Sage.

—— 2000. "Trust and Social Capital." Pp. 230–9 in *The Blackwell Companion to Political Sociology*, edited by K. Nash and A. Scott. Oxford and Cambridge, MA: Blackwell Publishers.

Bagnasco, A. and Sabel, C. 1994. *PME et développement économique en Europe*. Paris: La Découverte.

Baker, W. 1984. "The Social Structure of a National Securities Market." *American Journal of Sociology* 89: 775–811.

Bates, R. 1981. *Markets and States in Tropical Africa*. Berkeley: University of California Press.

Baudrillard, J. [1968]. 1996. *The System of Objects*. Translated by James Benedict. London, New York: Verso.

—— [1970] 1998. *The Consumer Society: Myths and Structures*. London: Sage.

Becattini, G. 1987. *Mercato e forze locali: il distretto industriale*. Bologna: Il Mulino.

—— 1990. "The Marshallian Industrial District As a Socio-Economic Notion." Pp. 37–51 in *Industrial Districts and Inter-Firm Co-operation in Italy*, edited by F. Pyke, G. Becattini and W. Sengenberger. Genève: ILO.

Becattini, G. and Rullani, E. 1993. "Sistema locale e mercato globale." *Economia e politica industriale* 80: 25–48.

Beetham, D. 1985. *Max Weber and the Theory of Modern Politics*. Cambridge: Cambridge Polity Press.

Bell, D. 1981. "Models and Reality in Economic Discourse." Pp. 46–80 in *The Crisis in Economic Theory*, edited by D. Bell and I. Kristol. New York: Basic Books.

Bendix, R. 1960. *Max Weber. An Intellectual Portrait*. London: Heinemann.

—— 1964. *Nation-Building and Citizenship*. New York: Wiley & Sons.

—— 1967. "Tradition and Modernity Reconsidered." *Comparative Studies in Society and History* 9: 292–346.

—— 1978. *Kings or People*. Berkeley: University of California Press.

Berger, S. 1981. *Organizing Interests in Western Europe*. Cambridge: Cambridge University Press

—— 1996. "Introduction." Pp. 1–25 in *National Diversity and Global Capitalism*, edited by S. Berger and R. Dore. Ithaca, NY: Cornell University Press.

Berger, S. and Dore, R. 1996. *National Diversity and Global Capitalism*. Ithaca, NY: Cornell University Press.

Berger, S. and Piore, M. 1980. *Dualism and Discontinuity in Industrial Societies*. Cambridge: Cambridge University Press.

Berger, P. and Luckmann, T. 1967. *The Social Construction of Reality*. New York: Doubleday.

Binder, L., Coleman, J., LaPalombara, J., Pye, L. W., Verba, S. and Weiner, M. 1971. *Crises and Sequences in Political Development*. Princeton: Princeton University Press.

Black, C. 1966. *The Dynamics of Modernization*. New York: Harper & Row.

Blaug, M. 1968. *Economic Theory in Retrospect*. 4th edn. Cambridge: Cambridge University Press.

Block, F. 1990. *Postindustrial Possibilities: A Critique of Economic Discourse*. Berkeley: University of California Press.

—— 1994. "The Roles of the State in the Economy." Pp. 691–710 in *The Handbook of Economic Sociology*, edited by N. Smelser and R. Swedberg. Princeton: Princeton University Press.

Bonazzi, G. 1993. *Il tubo di cristallo*. Bologna: Il Mulino.

Bordogna, L. and Provasi, G. 1984. *Politica, economia e rappresentanza degli interessi*. Bologna: Il Mulino.

—— 1998. "La Conflittualità." Pp. 331–60 in *Le nuove relazioni industriali*, edited by G. P. Cella and T. Treu. Bologna: Il Mulino.

Boudon, R. [1984] 1991 *Theories of Social Change: A Critical Appraisal*. Translated by J. C. Whitehouse. Cambridge: Polity Press.

Bourdieu, P. [1979] 1984. *Distinction: A Social Critique of the Judgement of Taste*. Translated by Richard Nice. Cambridge: Harvard University Press.

Boyer, R. 1988. "Alla ricerca di alternative al fordismo: gli anni Ottanta." *Stato e Mercato* 24: 387–423.

—— 1996. "The Convergence Hypothesis Revisited: Globalization but Still the Century of Nations?" Pp. 29–59 in *National Diversity and Global Capitalism*, edited by S. Berger and R. Dore. Ithaca, NY: Cornell University Press.

Brint, S. and Karabel, J. 1991."Institutional Origins and Transformations: The Case of American Community Colleges." Pp. 337–60 in *The New Institutionalism in Organizational Analysis*, edited by W. Powell and P. DiMaggio. Chicago: University of Chicago Press.

Brittan, S. 1975. "The Economic Contradictions of Democracy." *British Journal of Political Science* 5: 129–59.

—— 1978. "Inflation and Democracy." Pp. 161–85 in *The Political Economy of Inflation*, edited by F. Hirsch and J. Goldthorpe. London: Martin Robertson.

Brusco, S. 1989. *Piccole imprese e distretti industriali*. Torino: Rosenberg & Sellier.

Buchanan, J. and Tollison, R. 1972. *Theory of Public Choice*. Ann Arbor: University of Michigan Press.

Buchanan, J. and Tullock, G. 1962. *The Calculus of Consent*. Ann Arbor: University of Michigan Press.

Buchanan, J. and Wagner, R. 1977. *Democracy in Deficit*. New York: Academic Press.

Burt, R. 1983. *Corporate Profits and Cooptation*. New York: Academic Press.

Cagan, Ph. 1979. *Persistent Inflation*. New York: Columbia University Press.

Calmfors, L. 1993. "Centralisation of Wage Bargaining and Macroeconomic Performance. A Survey." *OECD Economic Studies* 2: 159–88.

Calmfors L. and Driffil, J. 1988. "Bargaining Structure, Corporatism and Macroeconomic Performance." *Economic Policy* 6: 14–61.

Cameron, D. 1985. "Does Government Cause Inflation? Taxes, Spending and Deficits." Pp. 224–79 in *The Politics of Inflation and Economic Stagnation*, edited by L. Lindberg and C. Maier. Washington D.C.: The Brookings Institution.

Cardoso, F. and Faletto, E. [1967] 1979. *Dependency and Development in Latin America*. Translated by Marjory Mattingly Urquidi. Berkeley: University of California Press.

Cella, G. P., ed. 1979. *Il movimento degli scioperi nel XX secolo*. Bologna: Il Mulino.

—— 1997. *Le tre forme dello scambio*. Bologna: Il Mulino.

Chamberlin, E. [1933] 1962. *The Theory of Monopolistic Competition*. 8th edn. Cambridge, MA: Harvard University Press.

Chandler, A. 1977. *The Visible Hand. The Managerial Revolution in American Business*. Cambridge, MA: The Belknap Press of Harvard University Press.

Coase, R. 1937. "The Nature of the Firm." *Economica* 4: 386–405.

Coleman, J. 1990. *Foundations of Social Theory*. Cambridge, MA: Harvard University Press.

—— 1994. "A Rational Choice. Perspective on Economic Sociology." Pp. 166–80 in *The Handbook of Economic Sociology*, edited by N. Smelser and R. Swedberg. Princeton: Princeton University Press.

Collins, R. 1980. "Weber's Last Theory of Capitalism: A Systematization." *American Sociological Review* 45 (December): 925–42.

Cooke, Ph. and Morgan, K. 1998. *The Associational Economy*. Oxford: Oxford University Press.

Crouch, C. 1977. *Class Conflict and the Industrial Relations*. London: Heinemann.

—— 1985. "Conditions for Trade Union Wage Restraint." Pp. 105–39 in *The Politics of Inflation and Economic Stagnation*, edited by L. Lindberg and C. S. Maier. Washington D.C.: The Brookings Institution.

—— 1993. *Industrial Relations and European State Traditions*. Oxford: Clarendon Press.

Crouch, C. and Pizzorno, A., eds.1978. *The Resurgence of Class Conflict in Western Europe since 1968*. London: MacMillan.

Crouch, C. and Streeck, W. 1997. "Introduction: The Future of Capitalist Diversity." Pp. 1–18 in *Political Economy of Modern Capitalism*. London: Sage.

Crouch, C., Le Galès, P., Trigilia, C., and Voelzkow, H. 2001. *Local Production Systems in Europe. Rise or Demise?* Oxford: Oxford University Press.

Dahrendorf, R. 1987. "Max Weber and Modern Social Science." Pp. 575–80 in *Max Weber and His Contemporaries*, edited by W. J. Mommsen and J. Osterhammel. London: Allen & Unwin.

De Jong, H. 1995."European Capitalism: Between Freedom and Social Justice." *Review of Industrial Organization* 10: 399–419.

Dei Ottati, G. 1987. "Il mercato comunitario." Pp. 117–41 in *Mercato e forze locali: il distretto industriale*, edited by G. Becattini. Bologna: Il Mulino.

Deutsch, K. 1961."Social Mobilization and Political Development." *American Political Science Review* 40: 493–514.

Deyo, F. 1987. *The Political Economy of the New Asian Industrialism*. Ithaca, NY: Cornell University Press.

DiMaggio, P. 1987. "Nonprofit Organizations in the Production and Distribution of Culture." Pp. 195–220 in *The Non-Profit Sector: A Research Handbook*, edited by W. Powell. New

Haven: Yale University Press.

—— 1991. "Constructing an Organizational Field As a Professional Project: U.S. Art Museums, 1920–1940." Pp. 267–92 in *The New Institutionalism in Organizational Analysis,* edited by W. Powell and P. DiMaggio. Chicago: University of Chicago Press.

—— 1994. "Culture and the Economy." Pp. 27–57 in *The Handbook of Economic Sociology,* edited by N. Smelser and R. Swedberg. Princeton: Princeton University Press.

Doeringer, P. and Piore, M. 1971. *Internal Labor Markets and Manpower Analysis.* Boston: Heth & Company.

Dore, R. 1983. "Goodwill and the Spirit of Market Capitalism." *British Journal of Sociology* 34: 459–82.

—— 1986. *Flexible Rigidities.* Stanford: Stanford University Press.

—— 1987. *Taking Japan Seriously.* London: The Athlone Press.

—— 1990. "Reflections on Culture and Social Change." Pp. 353–67 in *Manufacturing Miracles. Paths of Industrialization in Latin America and East Asia,* edited by G. Gereffi and D. Wyman. Princeton: Princeton University Press.

—— 2000. *Stock Market Capitalism: Welfare Capitalism. Japan and Germany versus the Anglo-Saxons.* Oxford: Oxford University Press.

Dosi, G., Pavitt, K. and Soete, L. 1990. *The Economics of Technological Change and International Trade.* New York: Harvester Wheatsheaf.

Douglas, M. and Isherwood, B. 1979. *The World of Goods.* New York: Basic Books.

Downs, A. 1957. *An Economic Theory of Democracy.* New York: Harper and Row.

Duesenberry, J. 1949. *Income, Saving and the Theory of Consumer Behavior.* Cambridge, MA: Harvard University Press.

Durkheim, E. 1887."La science positive de la morale en l'Allemagne" in *Revue Philosophique.* 24: 33–48, 113–42, 275–84.

—— [1893] 1984. *The Division of Labor in Society.* Translated by W. D. Halls. New York: The Free Press.

—— [1895] 1982. *The Rules of Sociological Method and Selected Texts on Sociology and its Method.* Translated by W. D. Halls. London: The Macmillan Press.

—— [1897] 1989. *Suicide. A Study in Sociology,* edited by G. Simpson and translated by G. Simpson and J. Spaulding. London: Routledge & Kegan.

Eccles, R. and Crane, B. 1988. *Doing Deals: Investments Banks at Work.* Boston: Harvard Business School.

Eisenstadt, S. 1964. "Social Change, Differentiation and Evolution" *American Sociological Review* 29: 235–47.

—— 1973. *Tradition, Change and Modernity.* New York: Wiley.

—— 1983. "Development, Modernization and the Dynamics of Civilizations." *Cultures et Developpement* 15 (4): 217–52.

Esping-Andersen, G. 1985. *Politics against Markets.* Princeton: Princeton University Press.

—— 1990. *The Three Worlds of Welfare Capitalism.* New York: Polity Press.

—— 1999. *Social Foundations of Postindustrial Economies.* Oxford: Oxford University Press.

Evans, P. 1995. *Embedded Autonomy. States and Industrial Transformation.* Princeton: Princeton University Press.

—— 1996. "Government Action, Social Capital and Development: Reviewing the Evidence on Synergy." *World Development* 24 (6): 1033–7.

Evans, P. and Stephens, J. 1988. "Development and the World Economy." Pp.739–73 in *Handbook of Sociology,* edited by N. Smelser. Newbury Park: Sage.

Ferrarotti, F. 1969. "Introduzione."Pp. 7–32 in T. Veblen, *Opere.* Torino: Utet.

Ferrera, M. 1993. *Modelli di solidarietà.* Bologna: Il Mulino.

Fligstein, N. 1990. *The Transformation of Corporate Control.* Cambridge, MA: Harvard University Press.

Flora, P. and Heidenheimer, A. J. 1981. *The Development of Welfare States in Europe and America*. New Brunswick: Transaction Books.

Frank, A. G. 1969. *Capitalism and Underdevelopment in Latin America. Historical Studies in Chile and Brazil,* New York: Monthly Review Press.

Friedland, R. and Alford, R. 1991. "Bringing Society Back In: Symbols, Practices and Institutional Contradictions." Pp. 232–63 in *The New Institutionalism in Organizational Analysis*, edited by W. Powell and P. DiMaggio. Chicago: University of Chicago Press.

Fukuyama, F. 1995. *Trust*. New York: The Free Press.

Galbraith, J. 1987. *Economics in Perspective*. New York: Houghton Mifflin.

Garfinkel, H. 1967. *Studies in Ethnomethodology*. Englewood Cliffs NJ: Prentice-Hall.

Gereffi, G. and Wyman, D. 1990. *Manufacturing Miracles. Paths of Industrialization in Latin America and East Asia.* Princeton: Princeton University Press.

Germani, G. [1971] 1981. *The Sociology of Modernization*. New Brunswick, NY: Transaction Books.

Gerschenkron, A. 1962. *Economic Backwardness in Historical Perspective*. Cambridge, MA: The Belknap Press.

—— 1968. *Continuity in History and Other Essays*. Cambridge, MA: Harvard University Press.

Gershuny, J. 1978. *After Industrial Society: The Emerging Self-Service Economy*. London: Macmillan.

—— 1985. "Economic Development and Change in the Mode of Provision of Services." Pp. 128–64 in *Beyond Employment. Household, Gender and Subsistence*, edited by N. Redclift and E. Mingione. Oxford: Basil Blackwell.

Gidron, B., Kramer, R. and Salamon, L. 1992. *Government and the Third Sector*. San Francisco: Jossey-Bass.

Gislain, J. and Steiner, P. H. 1995. *La Sociologie Economique 1890–1920*. Paris: Presses Universitaires de France.

Goldthorpe, J. 1971. "Theories of Industrial Society: Reflections on the Recrudescence of Historicism and the Future of Futurology." *Archives Européennes de Sociologie* 12: 263–88.

—— 1978. "The Current Inflation: Towards a Sociological Account." Pp. 186–214 in *The Political Economy of Inflation*, edited by F. Hirsh and J. Goldthorpe. London: Martin Robertson.

—— 1983. "I problemi dell'economia politica alla fine del periodo postbellico." *Stato e Mercato* 7: 47–87.

—— 1984. *Order and Conflict in Contemporary Capitalism*. Oxford: Clarendon Press.

Gouldner, A. 1970. *The Coming Crisis of Western Sociology*. London: Heinemann.

Gourevitch, P. 1986. *Politics in Hard Times. Comparative Responses to International Economic Crises*. Ithaca, NY: Cornell University Press.

Grabher, G. 1993. *The Embedded Firm*. London: Routledge & Kegan.

Grancelli, B. 1991. "La formazione dell'imprenditorialità in URSS e in Ungheria." *Stato e Mercato* 32: 289–315.

Granovetter, M. 1973. "The Strength of Weak Ties." *American Journal of Sociology* 78: 1360–80

—— 1974. *Getting a Job, A Study of Contacts and Careers*. Cambridge: Harvard University Press.

—— 1979. "The Idea of 'Advancement' in Theories of Social Evolution and Development." *American Journal of Sociology* 85: 489–515.

—— 1983. "The Strength of Weak Ties. A Network Theory Revisited." *Sociological Theory* 1: 201–33.

—— 1985. "Economic Action and Social Structure: The Problem of Embeddedness." *American Journal of Sociology* 91: 481–510.

—— 1990. "The Old and the New Economic Sociology: A History and an Agenda." Pp. 89–112 in *Beyond the Marketplace. Rethinking Economy and Society*, edited by R. Friedland and A. F. Robertson. New York: Aldine de Gruyter.

—— 1995. *Afterword 1994. Reconsiderations and a New Agenda* in *Getting a Job: A Study of Contacts and Careers*. Chicago: University of Chicago Press. Pp. 139–82.

Grew, R. 1978. *Crises of Political Development in Europe and the United States*. Princeton: Princeton University Press.

Gusfield, J. 1967. "Tradition and Modernity: Misplaced Polarities in the Study of Social Change." *American Journal of Sociology* 72: 351–62.

Habermas, J. [1973] 1975. *Legitimation Crisis*. Translated by Thomas McCarthy. Boston: Beacon Press.

Hagen, E. 1962. *On the Theory of Social Change*. Homewood, IL: The Dorsey Press.

Halbwachs, M. 1933. *L'evolution des besoins dans la classe ouvrière*. Paris: Alcan.

Hall, P. ed. 1986. *Governing the Economy: The Politics of State Intervention in Britain and France*. Oxford: Polity Press.

—— 1989. *The Political Power of Economic Ideas: Keynesianism across Nations*. Princeton: Princeton University Press.

Hamilton, G. 1994. "Civilizations and the Organization of the Economy." Pp. 183–205 in *The Handbook of Economic Sociology*, edited by N. Smelser and R. Swedberg. Princeton: Princeton University Press.

Hamilton, G. and Biggart, N. 1988. "Market, Culture and Authority: A Comparative Analysis of Management and Organization in the Far East." *American Journal of Sociology* 94: 52–93.

Hannan, M. and Freeman, J. 1977. "The Population Ecology of Organizations." *American Journal of Sociology* 82: 929–64.

—— 1989. *Organizational Ecology*. Cambridge, MA: Harvard University Press.

Hansen, A. 1941. *Fiscal Policy and Business Cycles*. New York: W. W. Norton.

Hemerijck, A. and Visser, J. 1997. *A Dutch Miracle: Job Growth, Welfare Reform and Corporatism in the Netherlands*. Amsterdam: Amsterdam University Press.

Hibbs, D. 1978. "On the Political Economy of Long-Run Trends in Strike Activity." *British Journal of Political Science* 2: 153–75.

Hirsch, F. 1977. *Social Limits to Growth*. London: Routledge & Kegan.

Hirsh, F. and Goldthorpe, J., eds. 1978. *The Political Economy of Inflation*. London: Martin Robertson.

Hirsch, P. and Michaels, S., Friedman, R. 1987. "'Dirty Hands' versus 'Clean Models'. Is Sociology in Danger of Being Seduced by Economics?" *Theory and Society* 16:317–36.

Hirschman, A. 1958. *The Strategy of Economic Development*. New Haven: Yale University Press.

—— 1970. *Exit, Voice and Loyalty*. Cambridge, MA: Harvard University Press.

—— 1982. *Shifting Involvements. Private Interest and Public Action*. Princeton: Princeton University Press.

—— 1986. *Rival Views of Market Society and Other Recent Essays*. New York: Viking.

Hirst, P. and Thompson, G. 1996. *Globalization in Question*. Cambridge: Polity Press.

Hodgson, G. 1994. "The Return of Institutional Economics." Pp. 58–76 in *The Handbook of Economic Sociology*, edited by N. Smelser and Swedberg, R. Princeton: Princeton University Press.

Hollingsworth, R. and Boyer, R. 1997a. *Contemporary Capitalism. The Embeddedness of Institutions*. Cambridge: Cambridge University Press.

—— 1997b. "Coordination of Economic Actors and Social Systems of Production." Pp. 1–47 in *Contemporary Capitalism. The Embeddedness of Institutions*, edited by R. Hollingsworth and R. Boyer. Cambridge: Cambridge University Press.

Hollingsworth, R. and Lindberg, L. 1985. "The Governance of the American Economy. The Role of Markets, Clans, Hierarchies and Associative Behaviour." Pp. 221–54 in *Private Interest Governments – Beyond Markets and State*, edited by W. Streeck and Ph. Schmitter. London: Sage.

Hollingsworth, R., Schmitter, W. and Streeck, W. 1994. *Governing Capitalist Economies*. Oxford: Oxford University Press.

Hoselitz, B. 1960. *Sociological Aspects of Economic Growth*. Glencoe IL: Free Press.

Inkeles, A. and Smith, D. H. 1974. *Becoming Modern*. London: Heinemann.

Jevons, S. [1871] 1965. *The Theory of Political Economy*. 5th edn. New York: Kelley.

Katzenstein, P. 1984. *Corporatism and Change. Austria, Switzerland and the Politics of Industry*. Ithaca, NY: Cornell University Press.

Kern, H. and Schumann, M. 1984. *Des Ende der Arbeitsteilung? Rationalisierung in der industriellen Produktion*. Munchen: Verlag Bech'sche.

Kerr, K., Dunlop, J., Harbison, F. and Myers, C. 1960. *Industrialism and the Industrial Man*. Cambridge, MA: Harvard University Press.

Keynes, J. M. 1926. *The End of Laissez-Faire*. Dubuque: Brown Reprint Library.

—— [1936] 1974. *The General Theory of Employment, Interest and Money*. London: Macmillan.

Korpi, W. 1978. *The Working Class in Welfare Capitalism*. London: Routledge & Kegan.

Korpi, W. and Shalev, M. 1980. "Strikes, Power and Politics in the Western Nations, 1900–1976." *Political Power and Social Theory* 1: 301–34.

Krugman, P. 1994. "Competitiveness: A Dangerous Obsession." *Foreign Affairs* 2: 28–44.

Kuhn, T. [1962] 1970. *The Structure of Scientific Revolutions*. Chicago: Chicago University Press.

Lafay, G. 1996. *Comprendre la mondialisation*. Paris: Economica.

Lange, P. and Regini, M. 1989. "Introduction." Pp. 1–25 in *State, Market and Social Regulation. New Perspectives on Italy*, edited by P. Lange and M. Regini. Cambridge: Cambridge University Press.

Lehmbruch, G. 1977. "Liberal Corporatism and Party Government." *Comparative Political Studies* 10: 127–52.

—— 1979. "Concluding Remarks." Pp. 299–309 in *Trends Toward Corporatist Intermediation*, edited by. Ph. Schmitter and G. Lehmbruch. Beverly Hills: Sage.

Lehmbruch, G. and Schmitter, Ph. 1982. *Patterns of Corporatist Policy-Making*. London: Sage.

Leifer, E. and White, H. 1987. "A Structural Approach to Markets." Pp. 85–108 in *Intercorporate Relations: The Structural Analysis of Business*, edited by M. Mizruchi and M. Schwartz. Cambridge: Cambridge University Press.

Lerner, D. 1958. *The Passing of Traditional Society*. Glencoe, IL: The Free Press.

Lester, R. 1998. *The Productive Edge*. New York: Norton.

Levy, M. 1966. *Modernization and the Structure of Societies*. Princeton: Princeton University Press.

Lindbeck, A. and Snower, D. J. 1988. *The Insider–Outsider Theory of Employment and Unemployment*. Cambridge: MIT Press.

Lindberg, L. and Maier, C., eds. 1985. *The Politics of Inflation and Economic Stagnation*. Washington: The Brookings Institution.

Maier, C. 1981. 'Fictitious Bonds . . . of Wealth and Law': On the Theory and Practice of Interest Representation." Pp. 27–61 in *Organizing Interests in Western Europe*, edited by S. Berger. Cambridge: Cambridge University Press.

Malinowski, B. 1922. *Argonauts of the Western Pacific*. London: Routledge & Kegan.

Malthus, T. [1798] 1989. *An Essay on the Principles of Population*. 2 vols. Edited by P. James. Cambridge: Cambridge University Press.

—— [1820] 1986. *Principles of Political Economy*. Clifton: Kelley.

Mandeville, B. [1714] 1988 *The Fable of the Bees or Private Vices, Public Benefits*. 2 vols. Edited by F. B. Kaye. Indiana Polis: Liberty Classics.

Marshall, A. [1890] 1920. *Principles of Economics*. 8th edn. London: MacMillan.

—— 1919. *Industry and Trade*. London: Macmillan.

Marshall, G. 1982. *In Search of the Spirit of Capitalism*. London: Hutchinson.

Marshall, T. H. 1964. *Class, Citizenship and Social Development*. Garden City: Doubleday &

Company.

Martinelli. A. 1994. "Entrepreneurship and Management." Pp. 476–503 in *The Handbook of Economic Sociology*, edited by N. Smelser and R. Swedberg. Princeton: Princeton University Press.

Marx, K. [1850] 1978. "The Class Struggles in France, 1848 to 1850." Pp. 45–145 in Karl Marx and Frederick Engels, *Collected Works*, vol.10. London: Lawrence & Wishart.

—— [1852] 1978. "The XVIII Brumaire of Louis Napoleon." Pp. 99–197 in K. Marx and F. Engels, *Collected Works*, Vol. 11. London: Lawrence & Wishart.

—— [1867–94] 1996–8. "Capital." In K. Marx and F. Engels, *Collected Works*, Vol. 35–37. London: Lawrence & Wishart.

Marx, K. and Engels, F. [1846] 1976. "The German Ideology." Pp. 19–539 in K. Marx and F. Engels, *Collected Works*. Vol. 5. London: Lawrence & Wishart.

—— [1848] 1976. "Manifesto of the Communist Party." Pp. 477–519 in K. Marx and F. Engels, *Collected Works*. Vol. 6. London: Lawrence & Wishart.

Maurice, M., Sellier, F.and Silvestre, J. J. 1984. "Rules, Contexts and Actors: Observations Based on a Comparison Between France and West Germany." *British Journal of Industrial Relations* 22: 346–53.

McClelland, D. 1961. *The Achieving Society*. Princeton: Van Nostrand.

Menger, C. [1871] 1981. *Principles of economics*. Translated by J. Dingwall and B. F. Hoselitz. New York: New York University Press.

—— [1882] 1985. *Investigations into the method of the social sciences, with special reference to economics*, edited by L. Schneider and translated by Francis J. Nock. New York and London: New York University Press.

Meyer, J. and Rowan, B. 1991. "Institutionalized Organizations: Formal Structure as Myth and Ceremony." Pp. 41–62 in *The New Institutionalism in Organizational Analysis*, edited W. Powell and P. DiMaggio. Chicago: University of Chicago Press.

Miller, D. 1987. *Material Culture and Mass Consumption*. New York: Basil Blackwell.

Mingione, E. 1995. "Labour Market Segmentation and Informal Work in Southern Italy" *European Urban and Regional Studies* 2: 121–43.

Mintz, B. and Schwartz, M. 1985. *The Power Structure of American Business*. Chicago: University of Chicago Press.

Moerland, P. 1995. "Corporate Ownership and Control Structures : An International Comparison." *Review of Industrial Organization* 10: 443–64.

Montagna, P. 1990. "Accounting Rationality and Financial Legitimation." Pp. 227–60 in *Structures of Capital*, edited by S. Zukin and P. DiMaggio. Cambridge, MA: Cambridge University Press.

Moore, B., Jr. 1966. *Social Origins of Dictatorship and Democracy*. Boston: Beacon Press.

Mutti, A. 1998. *Capitale sociale e sviluppo*. Bologna: Il Mulino.

Nelson, R. 1993. *National Innovation Systems: A Comparative Analysis*. New York: Oxford University Press.

Nelson, R. and Winter, S. 1982. *An Evolutionary Theory of Economic Change*. Cambridge: Harvard University Press.

Nisbet, R. 1969. *Social Change and History*. London: Oxford University Press.

Nordhaus, W. 1975. "The Political Business Cycle." *Review of Economic Studies* 42: 169–90.

North, D. 1990. *Institutions, Institutional Change and Economic Performance*. Cambridge: Cambridge University Press.

O'Connor, J. 1973. *The Fiscal Crisis of the State*. New York: St. Martin's Press.

O'Donnel, G. 1979. *Modernization and Bureaucratic-Authoritarianism. Studies in South American Politics*. Berkeley: University of California Press.

Offe, C. 1972. *Strukturprobleme des kapitalistischen Staates*. Frankfurt/Main: Suhrkamp.

—— 1981. "The Attribution of Public Status to Interest Group: Observations on the West

German Case." Pp. 123–58 in *Organizing Interests in Western Europe,* edited by S. Berger. Cambridge: Cambridge University Press.

—— 1997. *Varieties of Transition: The East European and East German Experience*. Cambridge, MA: MIT Press.

Offe, C. and Wiesenthal, H. 1980."Two Logics of Collective Action: Theoretical Notes on Social Classes and Organizational Form." *Political Power and Social Theory* 1: 67–115.

Ohmae, K. 1991. *The Borderless World*. New York: HarperCollins.

Olson, M. 1982. *The Rise and Decline of Nations*. New Haven: Yale University Press.

Orrù, M., Biggart, N. and Hamilton, G. 1991. "Organizational Isomorphism in East Asia." Pp. 361–89 in *The New Institutionalism in Organizational Analysis,* edited by W. Powell and P. DiMaggio. Chicago: University of Chicago Press.

Ouchi ,W. 1980. "Markets, Bureaucracies and Clans." *Administrative Science Quarterly* 25: 129–41.

Paci, M. 1987. "Long Waves in the Development of Welfare Systems." Pp. 179–99 in *Changing Boundaries of the Political,* edited by C. S. Maier. Cambridge: Cambridge University Press.

—— 1989. *Pubblico e privato nei sistemi di Welfare*. Napoli: Liguori.

Pahl, R. and Wallace, C. 1985. "Household Work Strategies in Economic Recession." Pp.189–227 in *Beyond Employment. Household, Gender and Subsistence,* edited by N. Redclift and E. Mingione. Oxford: Basil Blackwell.

Pareto, V. [1916] 1963. *A Treatise on General Sociology*. Translated by Andrew Bongiorno and Arthur Livingston. 2 vols. New York: Dover Publications.

Parsons, T. 1934. "Some Reflections on the Nature and Significance of Economics." *Quarterly Journal of Economics* 48: 511–45.

—— 1935a. "Sociological Aspects in Economic Thought I." *Quarterly Journal of Economics* 49: 411–53.

—— 1935b. "Sociological Aspects in Economic Thought II." *Quarterly Journal of Economics* 49: 646–67.

—— [1937] 1968. *The Structure of Social Action*. 2 vols. New York: Free Press.

—— 1951. *The Social System*. London: Routledge & Kegan.

—— 1966. *Societies. Evolutionary and Comparative Perspectives*. Englewood Cliffs, NJ: Prentice-Hall.

—— 1971. *The System of Modern Societies*. Englewood Cliffs, NJ: Prentice-Hall.

Parsons, T. and Smelser, N. 1956. *Economy and Society: A Study in the Integration of Economic and Social Theory*. Glencoe, IL: The Free Press.

Perez Diaz, V. 1986. "Politica economica e patti sociali in Spagna durante la transizione." *Stato e Mercato* 16: 57–91.

Piore, M. and Sabel, C. 1984. *The Second Industrial Divide*. New York: Basic Books.

Pizzorno, A. 1962. "Introduzione." Pp. xvi–xxxiv in E. Durkheim, *La divisione del lavoro sociale*. Milano: Comunità.

—— 1978. "Political Exchange and Collective Identity in Industrial Conflict," Vol. 2, Pp. 277–98 in *The Resurgence of Class Conflict in Western Europe since 1968,* edited by C. Crouch and A. Pizzorno. London: Macmillan.

Poggi, G. 1972. *Images of Society. Essays on the Sociological Theories of Tocqueville, Marx and Durkheim*. Stanford: Stanford University Press.

—— 1983. *Calvinism and the Capitalist Spirit*. London: Macmillan.

Polanyi, K. [1944] 1985. *The Great Transformation*. Boston: Beacon Press.

—— 1968. *Primitive, Archaic and Modern Economies*. New York: Doubleday.

—— 1977. *The Livelihood of Man,* edited by Harry W. Pearson. New York: Academic Press.

Portes, A. 1994. "The Informal Economy and Its Paradoxes." Pp. 426–49 in *The Handbook of Economic Sociology,* edited by N. Smelser and R. Swedberg. Princeton: Princeton University Press.

—— 1995. *The Economic Sociology of Immigration*. New York: Russel Sage Foundation.

—— 1998. "Social Capital: Its Origins and Applications in Modern Sociology." *Annual Review of Sociology* 24: 1–24.

Portes, A., Castells, M. and Benton, L. 1989. *The Informal Economy: Studies in Advanced and Less Developed Countries*. Baltimore: The Johns Hopkins University Press.

Portes, A. and Sensenbrenner, J. 1993. "Embeddedness and Immigration: Notes on the Social Determinants of Economic Action." *American Journal of Sociology* 98: 1320–50.

Powell, W. and DiMaggio, P. 1991a. *The New Institutionalism in Organizational Analysis*. Chicago: University of Chicago Press.

—— 1991b. "Introduction." Pp. 1–38 in *The New Institutionalism in Organizational Analysis*, edited by W. Powell and P. DiMaggio. Chicago: University of Chicago Press.

—— 1991c. "The Iron Cage Revisited: Institutional Isomorphism and Collective Rationality." Pp. 63–82 in *The New Institutionalism in Organizational Analysis*, edited by W. Powell and P. DiMaggio. Chicago: University of Chicago Press.

Powell, W. and Friedkin, R. 1987. "Organizational Change in Nonprofit Organizations." Pp. 180–92 in *The Nonprofit Sector: A Research Handbook*, edited by W. Powell. New Haven: Yale University Press.

Pratt, J. and Zeckhauser, R. 1985. *Principals and Agents: The Structure of Business*. Boston: Harvard Business School Press.

Putnam, R. 1993. *Making Democracy Work*. Princeton: Princeton University Press.

Pyke, F., Becattini, G. and Sengenberger, W. 1990. *Industrial Districts and Inter-Firm Co-Operation in Italy*. Geneva: ILO.

Pyke, F. and Sengenberger, W. 1992. *Industrial Districts and Local Economic Development*. Geneva: ILO.

Quesnay, F. [1758] 1968. *François Quesnay: the economical table (Tableau économique)*. New York: Bergman.

Rawls, J. 1967. "Two Concepts of Rules." Pp. 144–70 in *Theories of Ethics*, edited by Ph. Foot. Oxford: Oxford University Press.

Redclift, N. and Mingione, E. 1985. *Beyond Employment. Household, Gender and Subsistence*. Oxford: Basil Blackwell.

Regini, M. 1983. "Le condizioni dello scambio politico. Nascita e declino della concertazione in Italia e Gran Bretagna." *Stato e Mercato* 9: 353–84.

—— [1991] 1995. *Uncertain Boundaries: The Social and Political Construction of European Economies*. Cambridge: Cambridge University Press.

Regini, M. and Sabel, C. 1989. *Strategie di riaggiustamento industriale*. Bologna: Il Mulino.

Ricardo, D. [1817] 1975. "On the Principles of Political Economy and Taxation." Pp. 1–443, vol. 1, in *The Works and Correspondence of David Ricardo*. 11 vols., edited by P. Sraffa with the collaboration of M. Dobb. Cambridge: Cambridge University Press.

Robbins, L. [1932] 1984. *An Essay on the Nature and Significance of Economic Science*. London: Macmillan.

Robinson, J. [1933], *Economics of Imperfect Competition*. London: Macmillan.

Rhodes, M. and Apeldoorn, B. van. 1997. *The Transformation of West European Capitalism?* Florence: European University Institute Working Papers RSC. 97/60.

Rosenberg, N. 1960. "Some Institutional Aspects of the Wealth of Nations." *The Journal of Political Economy* 6: 556–70.

—— 1975. "Adam Smith on Profits. Paradox Lost and Regained." Pp. 377–89 in *Essays on Adam Smith*, edited by A. S. Skinner and T. Wilson. Oxford: Clarendon Press.

—— 1976. *Perspectives on Technology*. Cambridge: Cambridge University Press.

Rostow, W. 1960. *The Stages of Economic Growth*. Cambridge: Cambridge University Press.

Rueschemeyer, D. and Evans, P. 1985. "The State and Economic Transformation: Toward an Analysis of the Conditions Underlying Effective Intervention." Pp. 44–77 in *Bringing the State Back in*, edited by P. Evans, D. Rueschemeyer and T. Skocpol. Cambridge: Cambridge University Press.

Sabel, C. 1988. "Flexible Specialisation and the Re-emergence of Regional Economies." Pp. 17–70 in *Reversing Industrial Decline*, edited by P. Hirst and J. Zeitlin. Oxford: Berg.

—— 1994. "Learning by Monitoring: The Institutions of Economic Development." Pp. 137–65 in *The Handbook of Economic Sociology*, edited by N. Smelser and R. Swedberg. Princeton: Princeton University Press.

Sabel, C. and Zeitlin, J. 1985. "Historical Alternatives to Mass Production: Politics, Markets and Technology in Nineteenth Century Industrialization." *Past and Present* 108: 133–76.

Sahlins, M. 1976. *Culture and Practical Reason*. Chicago: University of Chicago Press.

Salisbury, R. 1979. "Why No Corporatism in America?" Pp. 213–30 in *Trends Toward Corporatist Intermediation*, edited by Ph. Schmitter and G. Lehmbruch. Beverly Hills: Sage.

Salvati, M. 1982. "Strutture politiche e esiti economici." *Stato e Mercato*. 4:3–43.

Saxenian, A. 1994. *Regional Advantage: Culture and Competition in Silicon Valley and Route 128*. Cambridge, MA: Harvard University Press.

Scharpf, F. 1984. "Economic and Institutional Constraints of Full-Employment: Sweden, Austria, and West Germany, 1973–1982." Pp. 257–90 in *Order and Conflict in Contemporary Capitalism*, edited by J. Goldthorpe. Oxford: Clarendon Press.

—— 1997. *The Problem Solving Capacity of Multi-Level Governance*. Florence: Robert Schuman Centre, European University Institute.

Schmitter, Ph. 1974. "Still the Century of Corporatism?" *The Review of Politics* 36: 85–131.

—— 1989. "I settori nel capitalismo moderno: modi di regolazione e variazioni di rendimento." *Stato e Mercato* 26: 173–208.

Schmitter, Ph. and Lehmbruch, G. eds. 1979. *Trends Toward Corporatist Intermediation*. Beverly Hills: Sage.

Schmitter, Ph. and Streeck, W. 1981. *The Organization of Business Interest*. Discussion Paper IIM/LMP 81–13. Berlin: Wissenschaftszentrum.

—— 1985. "Community, Market, State and Associations? The Prospective Contribution of Interest Governance to Social Order." *European Sociological Review* 1(2): 119–38.

—— 1991. "From National Corporatism to Transnational Pluralism." *Politics and Society* 2: 133–64.

Schmitter, Ph. and Grote, J. 1997. "Sisifo corporatista: passato, presente e futuro" *Stato e Mercato* 50: 183–215.

Schluchter, W. 1980. *Rationalismus der Weltbeherrschung*. Suhrkamp Verlag: Frankfurt Am Main.

Schumpeter, J. [1912–26] 1934. *The Theory of Economic Development*. Translated by Redvers Opie, 2nd edn., Cambridge, MA: Harvard University Press.

—— [1914] 1954. *Economic Doctrine and Methods*. London: George Allen & Unwin.

—— [1919] 1991. "The Sociology of Imperialisms." Pp. 141–219 in Schumpeter, *The Economics and Sociology of Capitalism*, edited by R. Swedberg. Princeton: Princeton University Press.

—— 1928. "The Instability of Capitalism." *Economic Journal* 38: 361–68.

—— 1931. "The Present World Depression: A Tentative Diagnosis." *American Economic Review Supplement* 1931: 179–82.

—— [1936] 1991. "Can Capitalism Survive?" Pp. 298–315 in J. Schumpeter, *The Economics and Sociology of Capitalism*, edited by R. Swedberg. Princeton: Princeton University Press.

—— [1939] 1980. *Business Cycles: A Theoretical, Historical and Statistical Analysis of the Capitalist Process*. New York and London: McGraw-Hill.

—— [1942] 1961. *Capitalism, Socialism, and Democracy*. New York: Harper and Row.

—— 1951. *Ten Great Economists from Marx to Keynes*. New York: Oxford University Press

—— 1954. *History of Economic Analysis*. New York: Oxford University Press.

Shonfield, A. 1965. *Modern Capitalism*. Oxford: Oxford University Press.

Skidelsky, R. 1979. "The Decline of Keynesian Politics." Pp. 55–87 in *State and Economy in Contemporary Capitalism,* edited by C. Crouch. London: Croom Helm.

—— 1996. *Keynes.* Oxford: Oxford University Press.

Simmel, G. [1900–7] 1978. *The Philosophy of Money.* 2nd edn. Translated by T. Bottomore and D. Frisby. Boston: Routledge & Kegan.

—— [1903] 1950. "The Metropolis and Mental Life." Pp. 409–24 in *The Sociology of Georg Simmel.* Translated and edited by K. H. Wolff. New York: Free Press.

—— [1908] 1950. *The Sociology of Georg Simmel.* Translated and edited by K. H. Wolff. New York: Free Press.

—— [1911] 1971. "Fashion." Pp. 294–323 in *On individuality and social forms. Selected writings.* Edited and with an Introduction by Donald N. Levine. Chicago: University of Chicago Press.

Simon, H. 1957. *Administrative Behavior.* New York: Macmillan.

Smelser, N. 1968. *Essays in Sociological Explanation.* Englewood Cliffs: Prentice-Hall.

Smelser, N. and Swedberg, R. 1994. "The Sociological Perspective on the Economy." Pp. 3–26 in *The Handbook of Economic Sociology,* edited by N. Smelser and R. Swedeberg. Princeton: Princeton University Press.

Smith, A. [1759] 1976. *The Theory of Moral Sentiments,* edited by D. D. Raphael and A. L. Macfie. Oxford: Clarendon Press.

—— [1776] 1976. *An Inquiry into the Nature and Causes of the Wealth of Nations,* edited by R. H. Campbell, A. S. Skinner and W. B. Todd. 2 vols. Oxford: Clarendon Press.

Sombart, W. [1916] 1922. *Der moderne Kapitalismus.* 2 vols. Berlin: Dunker & Humblot.

—— 1928. *Der moderne Kapitalismus,* vol. 3 (*Das Wirtschaftsleben im Zeitalter des Hochkapitalismus*). Berlin: Dunker & Humblot.

—— 1929. "Capitalism" in *Encyclopedia of the Social Sciences.* New York: Macmillan.

Soskice, D. 1990. "Reinterpreting Corporatism and Explaining Unemployment: Coordinated and Non-Coordinated Market Economies." Pp. 170–211 in *Markets, Institutions and Corporations: Labour Relations and Economic Performance,* edited by R. Brunetta and C. Dell'Aringa. New York: New York University Press.

—— 1993. *Product Market and Innovation Strategies of Companies and Their Implications for Enterprise Tenure: A Comparative Institutional Approach to Cross-Country Differences.* Berlin: Wissenschaftszentrum.

—— 1999. "Divergent Production Regimes: Coordinated and Uncoordinated Market Economies in the 1980s and 1990s." Pp. 101–34 in *Continuity and Change in Contemporary Capitalism,* edited by H. Kitschelt, P. Lange, G. Marks, and J. D. Stephans. Cambridge: Cambridge University Press.

Stark, D. 1989. "Bending the Bars of the Iron Cage: Bureaucratization and Informalization in Capitalism and Socialism." *Sociological Forum.* 4: 637–64.

—— 1992. " 'The Great Transformation'? Social Change in Eastern Europe." *Contemporary Sociology.* 21 (3): 299–304.

—— 1996. "Recombinant Property in East European Capitalism." *American Journal of Sociology* 101: 993–1027.

Storper, M. 1997. *The Regional World. Territorial Development in a Global Economy.* New York: The Guilford Press.

Strange, S. 1996. *The Retreat from the State: The Diffusion of Power in the World Economy.* Cambridge: Cambridge University Press.

Streeck, W. 1992. *Social Institutions and Economic Performance.* London: Sage.

—— 1994. "Vincoli benefici: sui limiti economici dell'attore razionale." *Stato e Mercato* 41: 185–213.

Swedberg, R. 1987. "Economic Sociology: Past and Present." *Current Sociology* 35 (1): 1–221.

—— 1990. *Economics and Sociology. Redefining Their Boundaries: Conversations with Economists and Sociologists.* Princeton NJ: Princeton University Press.

—— 1991. "Introduction." Pp. 3–98 in J. Schumpeter, *The Economics and Sociology of Capitalism,* edited by R. Swedberg. Princeton, NJ: Princeton University Press.

—— 1994. "Markets as Social Structures." Pp. 255–82 in *The Handbook of Economic Sociology,* edited by N. Smelser and R. Swedberg. Princeton: Princeton University Press.

Swedberg, R., Himmelstrand, U. and Brulin, G. 1987. "The Paradigm of Economic Sociology." *Theory and Society* 16: 169–213.

Szelenyi, I. 1988. *Socialist Entrepreneurs.* Madison: University of Wisconsin Press.

Tarrow, S. 1996. 'Making Social Science Work Across Space and Time: A Critical Reflection on Robert Putnam's 'Making Democracy Work'." *American Political Science Review* 2: 389–97.

Taylor, F. W. 1911. *Principles of Scientific Management.* New York: Norton.

Thurnwald, R. 1932. *Economics in Primitive Communities.* Oxford: Oxford University Press.

Tipps, D. 1973. "Modernization Theory and the Comparative Study of Societies: a Critical Perspective" *Comparative Studies in Society and History* 15: 199–226.

Titmuss, R. 1974. *Social Policy.* London: Allen & Unwin.

Trigilia, C. 1982. "Modernizzazione, accentramento e decentramento politico." *Stato e Mercato* 4: 45–92.

—— 1986. *Grandi partiti e piccole imprese.* Bologna: Il Mulino.

—— 1990. "Work and Politics in the Third Italy's Industrial Districts." Pp. 160–84 in *Industrial Districts and Inter-Firm Co-operation in Italy.* edited by F. Pyke, G. Becattini, and W. Sengenberger. Geneva: ILO.

—— 1997. Italy: "The Political Economy of a Regionalized Capitalism." *South European Society and Politics* 2(3): 52–79.

Tufte, E. 1978. *Political Control of the Economy.* Princeton: Princeton University Press.

Useem, M. 1984. *The Inner Circle.* Oxford: Oxford University Press.

Veblen, T. [1899] 1934. *The Theory of the Leisure Class: An Economic Study of the Evolution of Institutions.* New York: Modern Library.

—— [1904] 1978. *The Theory of Business Enterprise.* New Brunswick: Transaction Books.

—— [1915] 1966. *Imperial Germany and the Industrial Revolution.* Ann Arbor: University of Michigan Press.

—— [1919a] 1990. "Why is the Economics not an Evolutionary Science?" Pp. 56–81 in *The Place of Science in Modern Civilization,* edited by T. Veblen. New Brunswick and London: Transaction.

—— [1919b] 1990. "The Limitations of Marginal Utility." Pp. 1–31 in *The Place of Science in Modern Civilization,* edited by T. Veblen. New Brunswick and London: Transaction.

—— 1921. *The Engineers and the Price System.* New York: Huebsch.

—— [1934a] 1964. "Economic Theory in the Calculable Future." Pp. 3–15 in *Essays in Our Changing Order,* edited by L. Ardzrooni. New York: Kelley.

—— [1934b] 1964. "The Opportunity of Japan." Pp. 248–66 in *Essays in Our Changing Order,* edited by L. Ardzrooni. New York: Kelley.

Wade, R. 1996. "Globalization and Its Limits: Reports of the Death of the National Economy are Greatly Exaggerated." Pp. 60–88 in *National Diversity and Global Capitalism,* edited by S. Berger and R. Dore. Ithaca, NY: Cornell University Press.

Wallerstein, I. 1974. *The Modern World-System: Capitalist Agriculture and the Origins of the European World-Economy in the Sixteenth Century.* New York: Academic Press.

—— 1979. *The Capitalist World-Economy.* Cambridge: Cambridge University Press.

Walras, L. [1874]1954. *Elements of Pure Economics.* Translated by W. Jaffée. 4th edn. Homewood IL: Richard Irwin.

Warner, W. and Lunt, P. 1941. *The Social Life of a Modern Community.* New Haven: Yale

University Press.

Weber, M. [1894] 1978. "The Stock Exchange". Pp. 374–7 in *Max Weber Selections in Translation*, edited by W. G. Runciman and translated by E. Mattews. Cambridge: Cambridge University Press.

—— [1903–6] 1975. *Roscher and Knies: The Logical Problems of Historical Economics.* Translated and with an introduction by Guy Oakes. New York: New York University Press.

—— [1904] 1949. " 'Objectivity' in Social Sciences and Social Policy." Pp. 49–112 in *The Methodology of Social Sciences*, translated by E. A. Shils and H. A. Finch. New York: Free Press.

—— [1904–5] 1998. *The Protestant Ethic and the Spirit of Capitalism*, translated by T. Parsons and with an introduction by R. Collins. Los Angeles: Roxbury.

—— [1906] 1991 "The Protestant Sects and the Spirit of Capitalism." Pp. 302–22 in *From Max Weber: Essays in sociology*, edited by H. H. Gerth and C. Wright Mills. London: Routledge & Kegan.

—— [1915–16] 1991. "The Social Psycology of the World Religions." Pp. 267–301 in *From Max Weber: Essays in sociology*, edited by H. H. Gerth and C. Wright Mills. London: Routledge & Kegan

—— [1917] 1949. "The Meaning of Ethical Neutrality in Sociology and Economics." Pp. 1–47 in *The Methodology of Social Sciences*, translated by E. A. Shils and H. A. Finch. New York: Free Press.

—— [1919] 1991. "Science as Vocation" in *From Max Weber: Essays in Sociology*, translated and edited by H. H. Gerth and C. Wright Mills. London: Routledge & Kegan.

—— [1920–1] 1991. *Gesammelte Aufsätze zur Religionsoziologie.* Tübingen: Mohr.

—— [1922] 1978. *Economy and Society: An Outline of Interpretive Sociology*, edited by G. Roth and C. Wittich and translated by E. Fischoff. 2 vols. Berkeley: University of California Press.

—— 1924a. *Gesammelte Aufsaetze zur Sozial- und Wirtschaftsgeschichte.* Tuebingen: Mohr.

—— [1924b] 1994. "Socialism" in *Political Writings*, edited by P. Lassman and R. Speirs Cambridge: Cambridge University Press.

—— 1951. *The Religion of China. Confucianism and Taoism*, translated by H. H. Gerth. Glencoe: The Free Press.

—— 1952. *Ancient Judaism*, translated by H. H. Gerth and D. Martindale. New York, London: The Free Press.

—— 1958a. *The Religion of India: the Sociology of Hinduism and Buddhism*, translated by H. H. Gerth and D. Martindale. Glencoe: The Free Press.

—— [1958b] 1987. *General Economic History.* New York: Greenberg.

—— [1970] 1991 "Capitalism and Rural Society in Germany." Pp. 363–85 in *From Max Weber: Essays in Sociology*, edited by H. H. Gerth and C. Wright Mills. London: Routledge & Kegan.

—— 1979. "Developmental Tendencies in the Situation of East Elbian Rural Labourers." *Economy and Society* 8 (2): 177–205.

White, H. 1981. "Where Do Markets Come From?" *American Journal of Sociology* 87: 517–47.

—— 1992. *Identity and Control.* Princeton: Princeton University Press.

Wilensky, H. 1975. *The Welfare State and Equality.* Berkeley: University of California Press.

Williamson, O. 1975. *Markets and Hierarchies: Analysis and Antitrust Implications.* New York: The Free Press.

—— 1985. *The Economic Institutions of Capitalism.* New York: The Free Press.

Wilson, G. 1982. "Why Is There No Corporatism in the United States?" Pp. 219–36 in *Patterns of Corporatist Policy-Making*, edited by G. Lehmbruch and Ph. Schmitter. London: Sage.

Woolcock, M. 1998."Social Capital and Economic Development: Toward a Theoretical

Sinthesis and Policy Framework." *Theory and Society* 27: 151–208.

Zelizer, V. 1983. *Morals and Markets: The Development of Life Insurance in the United States.* New Brunswick NJ: Transaction Books.

—— 1987. *Pricing the Priceless Child: The Changing Value of Children.* New York: Basic Books.

—— 1988. "Beyond the Polemics on the Market: Establishing a Theoretical and Empirical Agenda." *Sociological Forum* 5: 614–34.

—— 1994. *The Social Meaning of Money.* New York: Basic Books.

Zukin, S. and DiMaggio, P. 1990. "Introduction." Pp. 1–36 in *Structures of Capital*, edited by S. Zukin and P. DiMaggio. Cambridge: Cambridge University Press.

Zysman, J. 1983. *Governments, Markets, and Growth.* Ithaca, N.Y: Cornell University Press.

—— 1994. "How Institutions Create Historically Rooted Trajectories of Growth." *Industrial and Corporate Change* 3: 243–83.

—— 1995. "National Roots of a 'Global' Economy." *Revue d'economie industrielle* 71: 107–21.

Index